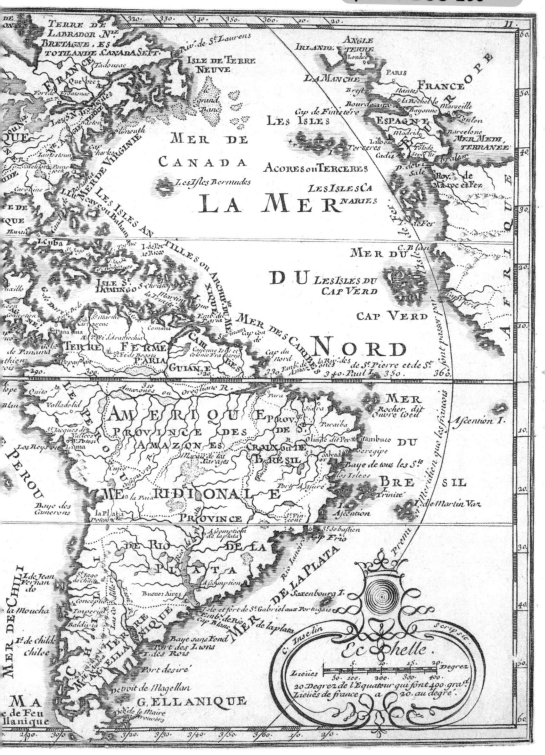

ADAM COLLINGS

CALIFORNIA

WEST OF THE WEST ™

Edited By
Diego Garcia

ADAM COLLINGS
CALIFORNIA/WEST OF THE WEST

FIRST EDITION

CALIFORNIA/WEST OF THE WEST™
ADAM R. COLLINGS

LIBRARY OF CONGRESS
CATALOGING-IN-PUBLICATION DATA:

ADAM COLLINGS
CALIFORNIA/WEST OF THE WEST
INCLUDES BIBLIOGRAPHY AND INDEX
ISBN O-9725835-O-5
1.CALIFORNIA 2.SPANISH AMERICA 3.HISTORY
2003090487

BOOK DESIGN BY ADAM R. COLLINGS
TYPESETTING PREPARED BY ASHLYN PENTONEY/
PAUL HAVEN DESIGN

INSIDE FRONT AND BACK COVER ART,
"L'AMERIQUE MERIDIONALE ET SEPTENTRINAL,"
DATED 1703 AND DEPICTING CALIFORNIA AS AN ISLAND.
REPRODUCED COURTESY OF THE SOUTHWEST MUSEUM,
LOS ANGELES, CALIFORNIA.

ETCHINGS THROUGHOUT THIS VOLUME
DESIGNED OR CREATED BY CASH DONOVAN

PRINTED IN CHINA

PUBLISHED BY ADAM COLLINGS ENTERPRISES, INC.
ORANGE COUNTY, CALIFORNIA

To my Mother and Father

There exists
an invisible California,
as yet undiscovered by the
multitudes;
peopled with gods,
and with mythic heroes,
and made wonderful
by their grand adventures.

BOOK ONE

NEW SPAIN

THE GOLDEN AGE

SIEMPRE ADELANTE NUNCA ATRAS.

ALWAYS FORWARD NEVER BACK.

Fr. Junipero Serra

brother junipero serra

California a prioribus Geographis semper
habita suit quædam pars Continentis, at capta per
Hollandos ab Hispanis tabula quædam Geographica
compertum est insulam esse et continere ubi latissima
est 500 leucas. A Cap. Mendocino uero usq. ad C.S.Lucæ
repertum est testibus tabula prædicta et Francisco
Gauls extendi in longitudinem 1700 leucarum

A **M**

S

C. Blanco

C. de S. Sebastian

C. Mendocino

Pº Sir Francisco
Draco

Punta de los Reyes

Pº de monte Rey

Pº de Carmba

Punta de la
Conception

Canal de S.
Barbara

Punta de la
Conception

I. S. Cathalina

Pº de S. Diego

S. Clemente

I. S. Martin

Baia de Todos
Santos

I. de Parnasos

B. de S. Quintin
B. de las
Paginas

C. de Engaño

R. de Fran-
cisco

I. S. Marco

B. de S. Simon

Punta de S.
Bartolome

Sierra Pintado

I. de Ceutas

Pº de Rosju

I. de la Carro

B. de las
arenas

R. de S.
Cristoual

Punta de S.
Apolinat

R. de S.
Martin

Pº Madre
dalena

P. de la Mar
yuz

P. de Cenot

P. de S.

I N S U L A   C A L I F O R N I A.

M A R E N O V E R Z I A.

Rey Coromedo

Lago de
ora

R. de S. Anacolli

R. del Tison

R. de Coral

S. Miguel

Las Playas

Pº de S. Clara

Pueblos de
Moqui

Real de Nueva
Mexico

Rio del Norte

S. Francisco

Petarlan

Coliacan

Pº de Simalos

Aslaban

N U E V A   B I S C

Eudebe

Topia

S. In

S. Bar

N

G R

Costa del Pedro

M I O.

R. de Nazias

R. de Pascua

P. I. Muchos

S. Moraba

I. Pasilla

S. Schastian

Nombre de Dios

puruguas

Tunas

Elcorena

Zacatecas

C. de S. Luce

Las tres Ma-
rias

Mas de
castas

Pº del S. Santo

Pr del Singui
quipili

I. de S. Andreos

Sierra de Xalisso

C. de Corrientes

Xalisco

Compostella

I. del Pilots

Acatlan

Zacatecas

I. Xores del
fronteras

Nª Sª de los Lag

N U E S

Nueva

Galicia

Colima

Mechoacan

E

Zacatule

Acapu

I. Lanublada

Roca Partida

Yllao

BOOK ONE

TABLE OF CONTENTS

I: DISCOVERY

II: The Mission

III: California Pastoral

BOOK TWO
EL DORADO

BOOK THREE
AMERICAN EMPIRE

BOOK FOUR
NATION STATE

A Note From The Author

Armed with Michael (Junipero) Serra, Mickey Mouse (Walt Disney) and Dr. Robert H. Schuller as role models for launching a self-styled career, it comes as no surprise to anyone that my own personal outlook on the world at large has remained ever hopeful and, shall we say, "sunny."

An arguably overblown optimism subsequently tempered through sobering years of missionary work in South America followed by several enigmatically successful business failures here at home in California.

Gratefully, and despite life's vicissitudes, that inner wellspring from which I continually draw courage has never failed me. Nor have family and friends. So it is that I remain, like any soul worth its salt, "sunny" notwithstanding.

If a brutally honest connectivity with humanity can be construed as defining literati then I'll confess to having ever been a writer. Said "misguided industry" underscored by my own deep and abiding passion for California.

This small, all but inaudible whisper of a lover never ceasing to speak up if only as rhetorical counterpoint against the booming voices of compromise that perennially threaten both my own and California's soul.

Audacious hyperbole arriving most often festooned with important sounding titles and impressive diplomas. Dispensed by those who discard true- life experience and common sense in favor of methodologies hearkening back to the dawning of academic pursuit.

When void of any genuine familiarity with the given subject in question it would first be killed and thereafter interpreted through dissection.

An impossible proposition to be sure. As rendering the same a cadaver void both of life force and motivation leads even the most perspicacious to but egregiously faulted conclusions.

Those endorsing such analysis taking endless delight in thereby sublimating something otherwise grand with the cynicism that results from being in possession of a ton of knowledge while armed with but an ounce of understanding.

Focused upon impressing the student rendering themselves deaf and blind to any reality yet standing alive and breathing around them.

Only by witnessing and listening even to disciples perceived as "less educated" can a true scholar capture that essential essence of the how and why behind any question mark.

For it cannot be garnered from analysis of the written record alone.

As without understanding motivation, all academic pursuit is rendered bankrupt of its own otherwise inherent humanity.

I am nothing more (nor less) than a writer. I tell stories solidly anchored in the facts, to the extent that such "facts" can be established. And while my tales are fashioned with the intent of accurately recounting events as they have transpired, my purpose remains rather one of intellectually stimulating and drawing each reader into that Great Conversation which leads us all towards understanding.

Correspondingly popularly held notions and foregone conclusions mean little to me. The fact that everyone says such and such despite the academics behind said conclusions does not make it so.

Removing these bones and dissected bodies from out of the library and archive to flood that written record through open discussion with the brilliance of California's sunshine brings me tremendous personal satisfaction.

Only by so doing can we See, Hear and begin to UNDERSTAND history. And thereby responsibly call into question our own oftimes false perceptions.

So it is that I teach unconventionally and without conventional credentials.

For which I make no apologies. Having soundly anchored my own qualifications through a life spent both in the libraries and archives as well as out in the field actively pursuing every aspect and possibility surrounding this California that I so love.

Such an education, albeit haphazard, is nonetheless valid. And capable of fueling insight otherwise unattainable to one traveling a more well ordered course. I call to my defense Abraham Lincoln. A brilliant and yet entirely self-schooled intellectual. And perhaps the greatest president my country has ever had.

When challenged concerning conclusions suggested I remain patient. With an open mind and heart intent not upon safeguarding some affectation of myself as academician but rather desirous of arriving at the truth of the matter.

I will listen. And consider. That is how we all learn.

For this is the enduring process by means of which one gains precious and otherwise unattainable insight into any given situation.

Through such considerations comes the enlightenment that enables us to approach with some degree of certainty that ever-elusive commodity we so anxiously refer to cavalierly as "the truth."

Concerning my own acquired knowledge and "enlightenment" if you will when it comes to California's story, I owe many teachers, some intellectuals others not, a tremendous debt of gratitude.

Beginning with men like the conquistador Herrera and Franciscan Torquemada who excelled in historiography and were present when this Idyll began.

Hubert Howe Bancroft and Zephyrin Engelhart for spending their entire lives collecting and assembling the historical record in question.

Charles Fletcher Lummis and Charles E. Chapman, most importantly perhaps because each stood up against a revisionism that ultimately regardless swept both men together with their works away.

A concise list of individuals who have aided me together with my complete roster both of primary and secondary sources consulted can be found in this tome's bibliography.

Aside from which I must defer, as did California's first historian Francisco Palou Amengal, to the importance not of this inept and unworthy writer but of the story itself (and I paraphrase from his Spanish text):

As the soul of this story is the simple truth,
you, the reader, have my assurances that everything
I present herein has been carefully reviewed and
thoughtfully researched.

Ultimately, be mindful that even Homer among
the great Poets, Demostenes of the great Orators
and Aristotle and Solomon
(among the most wise of both the great
Orators and Poets)
were nonetheless men
and therefore capable of error.

It's grand the mystery of our existence;
and while the men and women of whom
I write about herein
never cease to be but mere mortal men and women,
they are 'mere mortal men and women'
of whom we do well to take note.

Remember your own frailties,
and have compassion for mine.
The story is the thing
and IT'S value to us
far outweighs my inability to adequately retell it.

It is my sincere hope that by condescending to travel with me from the far side of ignorance, you the reader will experience in that which follows both authentic pleasure together with the euphoric thrill of discovery.

Adam R. Collings
August 1, 2003
San Clemente, California

BELIEVE

Eighteen years of blood, sweat, tears and triumph crucified by an acronym spoken obliquely from the other end of my telephone receiver. A receptionist whose face I'd never see and name I'd never know, answering,

"RTC."

Prompting my spontaneous, "Excuse me?"

To which she responded flatly,

"Resolution Trust Corporation, Sir. May I help you?"

I had dialed my client, a large Savings and Loan for whom we were presently producing as a premium item yet another of the lavish portfolio style books upon which I'd built a successful publishing house.

And thinking to have perhaps input the wrong number suggested,

"I'm sorry, I was trying to reach,"

whereupon I recited the name of the institution and number desired.

"Sir, the entity you are calling has been seized by the Resolution Trust Corporation. Which is an agency of the Federal Treasury set up to administer shutting down this financial institution and others like it. May I help you with something?"

I would soon discover yet another of my projects being swallowed up by this same leviathan government bureaucracy.

Were either of these works produced and delivered there would be no remuneration.

Paradoxically not to produce and deliver both publications was to jeopardize my standing with the RTC.

And so it began.

Awakening startled from out of a sound sleep by the shrill beeping noise emitted from a tow truck dispatched to repossess my vehicles.

The foreclosure sign planted in front of my beautiful Lake Arrowhead estate.

That sting of unconscionable betrayal at my Garden Grove office.

And subsequent struggle to somehow make ends meet. Only to meet in the end with Bankruptcy and the embarrassment and indignities analogous to said status.

Those years ensuing remaining hazy to me now.

All that I am certain of is one particularly sunny and never to be forgotten afternoon when sitting beside a dumpster sorting through what little remained of my life packed away as it was in boxes I came across this manuscript:

California/West Of The West.

Sensing even while lifting it from the box a certain quality of otherworldliness.

Here was something extraordinary.

Where had it come from?

How did it get here?

Then in slipping the book from its gold stamped leather casing finding myself staring with wondering awe at the likes of something I had never before seen.

This was no ordinary tome. And in a moment I would discover the tale it contained to be no ordinary story.

Stamped across its worn frontispiece was but a single word:

BELIEVE

PROLOGUE

CALIFORNIA. Mere sentience in elocution of the word, as it trips off a tongue to resound in the ear, evoking an enthusiastic if disparate litany between fact and fantasy. While simultaneously sounding humanities eternal propensity for optimism.

Spanish terminology, contrived in legend and spread throughout a medieval world poised on the edge of great discovery and enlightenment, CALIFORNIA as fiction carrying the romance of knights in shining armor into yet one more dispensation of time, before cynicism striking its near fatal blow both to chivalry and belief in things neither seen nor touched but rather felt with the heart.

Contemporaneous tales speaking of golden treasures, fantasy kingdoms and beautiful Amazonian women all ultimately realized by the passage of time.

Whilst those first in arriving upon the scene searching after riches, political conquests and forays into sensuality leaving incredibly disillusioned.

Rendering misunderstood and dismissed a most mysterious and exotic of realms to forthwith yield fortunes in romance, adventure and gold. Launching its own inauguration as a self-made nation/state that today holds fast the world's rapt attention with far more appeal than all past and false illusions.

Wielding previously inconceivable and titanic economic and political power. It's Hollywood dream factories alone conjuring imagery in art and storytelling enough to set even esthetic Medieval Spain reeling in complete disbelief.

Gilding with personal per capita income ranked amongst the highest on earth a gross agricultural, manufacturing and service-oriented industrial output second only to that of the entire United States combined. Placing itself more properly on par with other industrialized nations of the world.

In sheer landmass third largest of America's states (following successively after Alaska and Texas), its vast landscape not surprisingly embracing stunning physical contrasts. A magnificent Sierra Nevada exceeding in height to rival for beauty that of the Rocky Mountains. Great forests of primeval redwood found nowhere else on earth. Breathtaking twelve hundred-mile Pacific littoral punctuated with world-famous and legendary Carmel, Big Sur, San Diego and San Francisco.

Correspondingly most populous and urbane of America's extensive confederation, the State of California sitting underscored by nothing less politically transcendent than a constitutionally framed government modeled after that of the United States.

And in possession of a lavish artistic identity perennially fostered and nurtured by an equally extraordinary system both of public and private education.

As the world's foremost exporter of high and popular culture, its uniquely indigenous schools of thought, art, music and literature becoming readily identifiable globally.

Leaving even Californians themselves to grapple with the astounding phenomenon that is their own living reality.

Beyond ethereal legend and corrupted historiography that which follows attempting to establish and set forth an accurate and comprehensible account concerning the discovery, conquest and development of this unprecedented "country." As, per the maxim, truth in and of itself constituting a far more tantalizing and edifying tale than either the mystic poetry of medieval minstrels or romantic musings of modern playwrights.

And in this case formulating a story that however distant today from the place of its origin, remains inseparably interwoven with the fabric of Spain. Contributing an exuberance of color and design to the ever- expanding tapestry of Hispania.

PART ONE

DISCOVERY

THE MOTHER COUNTRY

C hivalry blossomed late on the Iberian Peninsula. Knighthood's recalcitrance catching even astute Charlemagne unawares. Who in seeking to reunite all Christendom found himself undone by a haphazard conglomeration of fiercely independent and renegade Spanish kingdoms.

Unexpected disaster striking him high in the Pyrenees, when thought to be amongst fellow Servants of Christ (Knights) made to witness in horror the unanticipated ambush and slaughter of his own unsuspecting army.

A surprise bloodbath immortalized foreverafter in the somber Chanson de Roldan (Song of Roland):

Taillefer who was famed for song,
mounted on a charger strong,

rode on before the Duke, and sang
of Roland and of Charlemagne,

Oliver and the vassals all
who fell in fight at Roncesvalles.

Count Roland in anguish and in pain,
bright drops of blood springing from his mouth,

veins in his forehead cracking with the strain,
threw himself beneath the pine
whilst turning his face away from Spain.

Of many things calling the memory back,
of many lands that he, the brave, had conquered.

Of Charlemagne his lord, who yet knew not
of the attack.

But soon with whom he wept and sighed…

Arguably most famous of all Medieval canticles, Roland's Song of triumph and tragedy preserving for mankind the lamentation of Western civilization's most famous Christian king. While simultaneously introducing into the evolutionary laboratory of language previously unrecorded orthography.

As distraught Charles the Great (Charlemagne) grieves:

Now the Saxons shall rise up against me,
and the Bulgars and the Huns-
Apulians, Romans, Sicilians,
and the men of Africa and of Califerne.

The lattermost geographic contrivance being fashioned to identify those lands of the caliphates (Islamic rulers) or in other words Asia Minor.

In annihilating Catholic brothers as potential assailants the confusion and anarchy of Medieval Spain stood exposed. And while elsewhere a Frankish King would succeed with forging his Holy Roman Empire, never again did he attempt setting foot on the Iberian Peninsula.

Long coveted and strategic stepping stone between Africa and Europe, the Hispania of Charlemagne's day standing compromised as the very crossroads of two great developing world religions.

Correspondingly remarkable physical beauty of Spain's exquisitely distilled, if yet politically unexceptional population holding fast a key that could unlock either to Christianity or Islam virtually all of Mediterranea.

It's story accordingly a seemingly endless procession of those who courted and conquered her in countless bold attempts to effectively bridge both worlds.

Yet Iberia's true narrative actually beginning much earlier. When sculpted clay figurines, engravings on bone, antler and ivory and extraordinary paintings first appeared in and around what is today Spanish Altamira. Suggesting a human presence dating back more than 30,000 years.

By 1600 B.C., benign Celtiberian herdsmen presumably submitting willfully to Phoenician occupation. Around 550 B.C. a still obscure populace surrendering again, this time before the sons of Zeus.

Greek aggressions squelched by Africa's Carthaginians, who in turn faced expulsion at the hands of a Germanic tribal collective remembered to history as the Visigoths.

Aryan Visigothic domination itself subsequently suspended following the advance of Imperial Rome.

Who established a far-flung and diverse economy fueled by gold. In which the Iberian Peninsula abounded.

Western Civilization's first great republic casting covetous eyes upon mineral- laden Spanish Asturias.

Placers and foothills of the Pyrenees yielding fortunes in precious metals extracted by an expeditiously conquered and subjugated Hispanic work force.

Leaving Spain forever after wed to the illusory allure of gold and allied as vassals of Rome with Catholicism.

Which overtime many "Spaniards" embraced. Whilst others not surprisingly adopted Islamic traditions and the prophet Mohammed.

Predictably isolated factions consistently resisting religious or political alignment with either.

Nomadic pagan Visigoths in particular rather renewing efforts to dominate territories confiscated by Muslims and Christians. And remarkably succeeding ultimately with overwhelming that which had ever seemed unassailable.

When Rome fell, in 711 A.D., Hispania standing submerged in Moorish hordes. As wave after wave mounted upon Arabian steeds and wielding gleaming steel scepters swept in from out of Africa across the Straits of Gibraltar to occupy a sudden vacuum created by the unexpected disappearance of Roman law and order.

The Moor (meaning black or dark) represented an accomplished and exotic race of mixed Arab and Berber descent. And brought with him an unsurpassed legacy of science and academics inherited from Greece by way of the Arab world.

Spanish clans clamoring for autonomy nonetheless perceiving these newest invaders as rather barbarians.

With Germanic barbarians accusing Islamic Moors of barbarism, even Spanish Muslims rising up in open rebellion against otherwise brothers in faith.

Their universally shared contempt manifesting itself amongst all the many factions of Spain. Ersatz even today at the first sign of troubles a Spaniard being apt to quip,

Beware, there be Moors along the Coast.

Yet despite this common "enemy" unification of Iberian Christians, Muslims and Pagans proving evasive.

As so factioned all became caught up in the devastating and chaotic scenario of guerrilla warfare into which an unsuspecting Emperor Charlemagne had unwittingly marched.

In 1095 Moor-like Saracens seized control of Christianity's birthplace at Jerusalem before setting sights upon conquering Christian Byzantium.

Beyond Iberia chivalrous Charlemagne's Holy Roman Empire rallying to defend both Constantinople, the last great bastion of Christendom, as well as a Holy Land in fact claimed by Christian and Muslim alike.

Thus beginning three centuries of Crusades.

Leaving troublesome Hispania to "rescue" itself.

With Iberian "salvation" from Moorish domination arriving in the breathtaking form of an extraordinary native son. Whose name, Rodrigo Diaz de Vivar, would resound through the ages as protagonist of a Homeric poem entitled The Song of El Cid.

Rodrigo forthwith set out upon the road,
And took with him twenty knights.

And as he went he did great good,
and gave alms, feeding the poor and needy.

And upon the way they found a leper,
struggling in a quagmire,
who cried out to them with a loud voice,
'Amar a Dios,' which is to say,
'help me, because you love God;

And when Rodrigo heard this
he alighted from his beast
and helped him,

And placed him upon the beast before him,
and carried him with him in this manner
to the inn where he took up his lodging that night.

At this were his knights little pleased.

And when supper was ready he bade his knights take
their seats,
and he took the leper by the hand,
and seated him next to himself,
and ate with him out of the same dish.

The knights were greatly offended at this foul sight,
insomuch that they rose up and left the chamber.

Whereupon Rodrigo ordered a bed to be made ready
for himself and for the leper,
and they twain slept together.

When it was midnight and Rodrigo was fast asleep,
the leper breathed against him
between his shoulders,
a breath so strong that it
passed through him,
even through his breast.

And he awoke,
being astounded,
and felt for the leper by him,
and found him not;

And he began to call him.
But there was no reply.

Then he arose in fear.
And called for light.
And it was brought him.

And he looked for the leper and could see nothing;

So he returned into the bed,
leaving the light burning.

And he began to think within himself
what had happened,
and of that breath which had passed through him,
and how the leper was not there.

After awhile, as he was thus musing,
there appeared before him one in white garments,
who said unto him,

'Sleepest thou or wakest thou, Rodrigo?'
And he answered and said,

'I do not sleep:
but who art thou that bringest with thee such
brightness
and so sweet an odour?'

Then said he,

'I am Saint Lazarus,
and know that I was the leper to whom
thou didst so much good
and so great honour for the love of God;

'And because thou didst this for His sake
hath God now granted thee a great gift;

'for whensoever that breath which thou hast felt
shall come upon thee,
whatever thing thou desirest to do,
and shalt then begin,
that shalt thou accomplish to thy heart's desire,
whether it be in battle or aught else,

'so that thy honour shall go on increasing
from day to day.

'And thou shalt be feared both by Moors and
Christians alike.

'And thy enemies shall never prevail against thee.

'And thou shalt die an honourable
death in thine own house,
and in thy renown
for God hath blessed thee—

Therefore go thou on
and evermore persevere in doing good.'

And with that Lazarus disappeared.

And Rodrigo arose and prayed to our lady and
intercessor Mary,
Queen of Heaven,
that she might beseech her blessed son Jesus
to watch over his body and soul
in all undertakings.

And he continued to pray thusly till the day broke.

Then proceeded on his way,
doing much good
because he loved God.

According to Medieval chronicler Per Abbat of
Castile the syllogism of Spanish 'El" or 'The' and
Arabic 'Cide,' or seigniorial lord alone seemed
sufficiently unique and appropriately grandeloquent
enough for summing up an individual as honorable
and virtuous as Vivar.

Who born and raised in the shadow of both cathedral
and mosque emerged a consummate diplomat.
Schooled in Catholicism yet respectfully honoring

Muslim neighbors. Ultimately out of innate goodness abandoning stifling traditions of upholding dogmatic family alliances above otherwise "community" concerns.

Astride his steed Balieca, wielding the sword El Segundo as backup, claiming allegiance but to God alone.

Thereafter confronting the invading Moor in particular as rather a "common" threat to every Spaniard.

His bold gesture appealing to Christian, Muslim and pagan alike. And over time precipitating miracles.

So it was that Iberia's fractured kingdoms rose up united,

> because of their love for God
> which is the glory of Spain.

The Cause championed by El Cid consuming more than two centuries. Rendering Iberians preoccupied in fighting this crusade of their own out of step with the remainder of an otherwise distracted continent.

So that by the time King Ferdinand and Catholic Queen Isabella expelled from his stronghold at Granada the last Moorish caliphate, crusaders of a Holy Roman Empire running counterpoint sat resigned to their loss of Jerusalem and Constantinople both.

Having exhausted all manpower and resources, Europe beyond the Pyrenees languishing in the political, economic and social backwater of its own Dark Age.

Curiously then at precisely this moment, when the glorious Days of Chivalry seemed extinguished elsewhere, knighthood sprang to life in glorious resurrection amongst of all people the Spanish themselves.

As a Golden Age dawned upon the long dismissed, war-weary Iberian Peninsula. The fulfillment of one man's dream propelled by a commitment of generations, Spain emerging at last from political turmoil to inherit its shared destiny and common purpose.

Together Hispania having not only successfully vanquished its own "infidel" but now miraculously standing in by default as standard bearer for Charlemagne's equally resilient Holy Roman Catholic Empire.

A previously unremarkable rag-tag collection of kingdoms and principalities endlessly plagued with infighting and continuously bordering upon (and presumably destined to succumb to) anarchy, forged at the dawning of 16th century Europe into a consolidated power destined for world greatness.

Providentially armed with an inherent humanitarian idealism honed through centuries of subjugation and contradictorial religious crusades.

To bestow upon the continent arguably its most vivid cultural identity. Knighthood flowering anew. Teutonic imagery of gallant heroes in shining armor astride white horses summarily dismounted however by the very Latin incarnation of a Spanish Conquistador.

As against the strikingly beautiful landscapes of Granada, Valencia and Seville, a pageant unrivaled in the annals of Western civilization began to unfold.

Universities were founded. Artists were funded. Spanish caravels, sails unfurled, careened through uncharted seas towards worlds as yet unknown.

Conquistadors, each the certain reflection of El Cid himself, sallying forth astride Arabian chargers in a naïve-become distorted crusade focused upon expanding the boundaries of Christendom through warfare and exploitation.

On March 15, 1493, amidst thundering cannon and cacophonic bell ringing, Cristobol Colon (Christopher Columbus) sailing into the Spanish port of Palos. Announcing that courtesy of his generous Iberian patrons he had made contact with what everyone presumed to be the East Indies. Surely Cipango (Japan) and Cathay (China), together with all the riches of the Orient now lying within Europe's grasp.

Spain proclaiming their newest champion,

Admiral of all the Ocean Seas.

Continental broadcast of his success re-animating previously jaded Europeans.

Present amongst whose celebratory throngs standing an outwardly common and otherwise insignificant eight-year-old boy by the name of Hernan Fernando Cortes. Who as awestruck witness to Colon's parade of exotic parrots, copper-skinned "Indians" and trinkets of gold through the streets of Barcelona set his own sights then and there upon becoming the world's greatest conquistador.

THE MYTH

As reward for extraordinary courage and valor displayed during the taking of Granada's Alhambra Garci Rodrigo Ordonez de Montalvo found himself being knighted by Queen Isabella of Aragon.

Not unlike most Spanish hidalgos (hijo de algo or as translated literally 'son of something,' something inferring 'someone' of importance, 'someone' ultimately being interpreted rather as a nobleman), Montalvo having since the days of his privileged youth served Spain well with sword and shield.

Years of crusading against the Moor effectively transforming Iberian aristocracy into impassioned warlords; conquest and plunder becoming virtually the only trade men such as Montalvo had ever known.

And so following the Rubicon of Granada that was Spain's successful expulsion of its last Moorish caliphate, crisis loomed large over a finely honed and abruptly unemployed fighting machine.

Their soldiering services no longer necessary, many a proud hidalgo caught scratching his head, wondering how best to survive in a realm suddenly at peace with itself.

Fortuitous indeed being the arrival of that little caravel commandeered by Cristobol Colon scudding into port as it did bearing news concerning the planting of

Spanish colors on a Far Eastern shore!

Instantly providing new worlds to conquer:

> for the glory of God and His most holy Catholic
> monarchs, Queen Isabella of Aragon
> and King Ferdinand of Castille and Leon.

Not since Byzantium's plea for the liberation of Constantinople had such a grand and noble cause ignited Europe. The clamor to join Spain in its new Conquista (Conquest) echoing throughout the courts of every castle across the continent.

An era of Discovery and Conquest had dawned. To be orchestrated by newly empowered Spanish nobility and yet promising a great rebirth for all.

Metaphoric spring bursting forth at last to banish an interminably long European winter of intellectual and technological stagnation.

Teased by the possibilities inherent with Colon's grand discoveries, an Old World faced with suddenly antiquated and correspondingly devalued known quantities glancing back over its collective shoulder to stamp some vestige of continental glories past upon the otherwise disconcerting question mark that was about to become its future.

Employing references to medieval crusaders while inserting popular heroes as comfortable leaven for conversations otherwise peppered with inexplicable New World anomalies.

And by so projecting certain history upon an uncertain future becoming engaged in discussing a New Age of Chivalry. Setting traditional sights upon sallying forth to inaugurate an anything but traditional Crusade.

At fifty-five Sir Garci Rodrigo Ordonez de Montalvo considered "sallying forth" to anywhere, let alone a New World, as beyond the scope of his advanced years.

As with many of his contemporaries long-since already resigned himself to indulgences in acquired plunder. Wherein he discovered reassuring solace reveling in memories of those presently bandied about glories past.

Unlike colleagues who simply disappeared behind the doors of a monastery cloister or castle keep, however, Montalvo's self-imposed sequestering having an uncalculated effect of catapulting him into the European limelight. His personal introspections subsequently scribbled and broadcast precipitating a timely boon for both commoner and hidalgo alike.

As ever the knight, chivalrous Garci in characteristic largesse had recognized by so doing but another opportunity for once again making a difference. This time from the heady arena of literature wherein he wielded that proverbial pen which is mightier than the sword.

Dedicating himself to the cause of keeping chivalry,

Which is the glory of Europe,

alive. Launching an initially lonely Crusade by translating northern European tales of knighthood into Ibero-Spanish language. Single handedly introducing Spain to the likes of Beowulf, Amadis and Arthur of the Britons.

And in effect providing role models for a new generation of would-be knights about to embark upon a great quest of their own.

Montalvo's translations being shared in public forum and talked about wherever people gathered; to achieve in modern vernacular full stature as bestsellers.

Meanwhile reports filtering back concerning the New World exploits of Cristobol Colon intriguing Spain's prolific translator. Whose own self- acquired lambent knowledge concerning lands of legend, coupled with actual news extolling tropical islands and exotic peoples, inspired a sagacious chronicler to embark upon composing an anthology of his own creation.

In his the consummate boy's adventure novel, Garci's ingenious spin on an otherwise familiar tale wherein,

> monsters and marvels are hurled at nearly invulnerable knights,

finding our hero Esplandian (in English Splendoor) intent upon rescuing the Christian capitol of Constantinople from invading Turkish infidels.

And providing formidable adversaries for his champion by conjuring a land and people so exotic that they have fascinated and tantalized the World's imagination from that day to this.

It had been the great adventurer Marco Polo who circulated rumors suggesting existence of an island populated by female warriors. Polo referring to these women as Amazons. Shocking Europe when describing how they amputated their right breast in order to facilitate use of the bow and javelin. Having been told such fascinating tales while in the courts of the Great Khan of China.

Was not Cristobol Colon at the very gates of China now, making his way through a maze of exotic islands, encountering strange and mysterious, previously unknown peoples whilst searching for that Far Eastern shore?

Aroused by such possibilities, a master storyteller conjuring Calafia, queen of an Amazon nation. The Islamic derivation of her name borrowed from caliph, or ruler.

Her Island kingdom christened California after caliphate, or kingdom of the caliph. All terminology hearkening back to the Song of Roland with its Califerne, land of the caliphates, or Asia Minor.

Not only were such names exotic, but they invoked the familiar language of Moorish "infidels" so recently routed from Spain. And through further mixing fact with fiction, created a "history" that rang true to Montalvo's 16th century audience.

Building upon the heroic attributes of Colon himself, Montalvo penning a didactic Las Sergas del Muy Esforzado Caballero Esplandian (Deeds of the Very Brave Knight Splendoor), as postscript to his four volume Amadis of Gaul which he'd translated previously from Norman and Saxon texts.

Not surprisingly then during an age of myth most hearing tell of the Knight Splendoor's great deeds accepting them as factual. Unable as they were to discern (what with a virtual flood of accounts concerning remarkable adventures bombarding them) the difference between fairytales and news reports.

So it was that in short order fictional Esplandian became perceived by a mostly nescient population as being not merely real but an authentic hero.

Montalvo had sparked the imagination of a generation, and in so doing coined terminology that would come to grace not only the pages of his fictional chronicles but the actual atlas of an ever-expanding "known" world.

Garci's story commencing with the same "Once upon a time..." endearment of a Grimm Brother's Fairy Tale; from which point it rapidly plunged into a nightmare of vulgarity and gore that could but have excited even more a rising generation of conquistadors about to besiege the American continent:

> Has no one ever told you
> that on the right hand of the Indies
> nearest the earthly paradise
> spoken of in Genesis of the Holy Bible
> there is an island called California?

It is a mysterious place of uncommon beauty
and unparalleled wealth.

All about its shores are steep mountains
and rugged cliffs.

Perched atop its promontories and palisades
one can see many griffins;
a wild and savage beast
that is said to be half eagle and half lion
and is found nowhere else in all the world.

The rivers emptying into the sea from California's
interior are full of gold.

Indeed, there is no other metal in all the Island,
except gold.

Yet, even more wonderful than its great wealth
and extraordinary fauna
is the mysterious and beautiful woman
for whom the land is named.
And the peculiar circumstance of her nation.

She of whom I speak is Calafia,
an ebony queen of African descent,
known far and wide for her great strength
and unsurpassed beauty.

Amongst all the kingdoms of the world
the mere mention of her name
invoking an image of divine womanhood.

Calafia's subjects are all women;
without a single man amongst them.

And live after the manner of the Amazons
in magnificently ornate structures
built into the chambers of natural caves.

Robust of body,
strong and passionate in heart,
possessed of great valor,
they adorn themselves with pearls
and all manner of precious stones.

Harness wild beasts to ride upon,
and employ weaponry made of pure gold.

In the season when griffins give birth to their young,
Calafia's people shield themselves with thick hides
and carefully snare the animals' offspring,
which they take to their caves.

Where they raise and train the beasts
to do their bidding.

Now, here is where you put the little ones to bed, as
suddenly the bucolic fairytale takes a twisted plunge
into a nightmare of sex and carnage.

Montalvo continues:

And being quite a match for these monsters,
the women feed them men
whom they have taken captive as breeding partners
and any manchild to whom they have given birth
as a result of their liasons.

All of which is done with such skill
that the griffins become

thoroughly accustomed to women
and do them no harm.

While contrary wise any man
who should come, unwittingly, upon this Island
is quickly killed and eaten by these monsters.

According to Montalvo, Calafia, the quintessential
woman, who, like the quest she would inspire many
a young man to embark upon, remained forever out
of reach, impossible to attain, let alone conquer:
aspired to execute nobler actions
than had previously been performed
by any other ruler.

Reasoning that remaining on the Island
doing nothing other than that which
her ancestors had done
would be tantamount to being buried alive.
And unwilling to so live out the rest of her days
like the living dead
without fame and glory
as if but a dumb animal,
searched the world over
for a challenge worthy of her noble birthright.

Calafia finding that cause
when from far away came spurious rumors
concerning a wicked people
referred to as Christians
who were attacking the Islamic world of Asia Minor.

She was told that the great
Muslim city of Constantinople
lay under siege.

Unaware of the true nature of Christianity,
yet desirous of participating in a crusade,
Queen Calafia resolving
that she and her people must needs take action
against such blatant effrontery.

And vowing to lead her loyal subjects
in a war
against the Christian infidel.

Arguing that both great honor and great profit
would belong to California
should they support her in this siege

insisting further that regardless the great fame
they could achieve
throughout the world
by virtue of undertaking such a glorious crusade
would in and of itself be reward enough.

So it was that together with a thousand
female warriors,
courageous sister, Liota
and five hundred trained griffins
Calafia set sail for the beleaguered
capitol of Byzantium.

Where upon her arrival,
she discovered, from sultan Radiaro,
that the Muslim cause was going badly.

And anxious to demonstrate both California's
military superiority
as well as that of her own,
insisted she be permitted to attack the city

with army effete alone;
promising in return
Constantinople's delivery into Radiaro's hands.

Out of desperation an otherwise orthodox sultan
agreeing to Calafia's scheme.

Men present that day witnessing
the strangest invasion ever seen
and certainly never before dreamed of.

As Californians marched upon Constantinople,
releasing their griffins;
whereupon a scene of unparalleled
bloodshed ensued.

Many Christian soldiers
being seized and eaten by the monsters.
Others carried off into the air
and then allowed to fall;
dashed to pieces upon the rocks below.

Neither arrows nor swords
(not even lances),
could pierce through the thick-feathered,
tough-bodies of these previously unknown creatures.

Then as coup-d-etat
Calafia summoning Radiaro and his exultant Turks
to themselves charge the city.

When without warning all present
witnessed in horror
as man-eating griffins turned upon the sultan's men
with a ferocity equal

to that exhibited towards any male,
Christian or otherwise.

Before she could restrain them
Calafia's flying beasts decimating Turkish ranks;
turning stunning victory into fantastic defeat.

That she might salvage her 'misguided' crusade,
a shamed Queen dispatching sister Liota as emissary
into the fortified city,
there to propose, as means of resolving
their mutual dilemma,
a double duel to the death.

Remaining anxious with regard to demonstrating
her superior battle skills,
Calafia proposing that she,
together with the sultan Radiaro,
do battle against Amadis of Gaula,
King of the Britons,
and his son (and our hero) Esplandian;
leaders of the Christian camp.

Suggesting that the outcome of said double duel
be used to ascertain
whether Christianity or Islam
should prevail over Asia Minor.

Admittedly humored at this prospect
of doing battle with a woman,
Amadis agreeing to the unusual proposition.

But when Liota returned to her people,
she carried with her more than the message of a
British acceptance to their Queen's challenge.

Revealing that the Christian leaders
were very beautiful to look upon.

The noble knight Esplandian, in particular,
being the most extraordinary example of manhood
she had ever seen.

Overcome by curiosity
Calafia determining to see and speak with this
Esplandian herself.

And abandoning military garb,
dressing provocatively, in exotic fabrics.
The beauty of her ample breasts revealed
and adorned with gold and precious stones.

Astride a splendid black beast,
riding off boldly unescorted
into the city fortress.

That day the beguiling Calafia herself falling victim
to the charms of handsome Esplandian.

Yet angered by his dismissal of her sexual advances,
but arranging terms for the combat
before departing in rage.

At the appointed hour a duel taking place.

Esplandian managing to overcome Radiaro
while Calafia fired with indignation
continued raining blows down upon Amadis.

Unwilling to draw his sword against a 'lady,'
Amadis carefully catching each stroke with his shield.

Then subduing the embittered Queen,
when Calafia's blade shattered,
with but a portion of her own weapon.

Christianity prevailing.
All Californians being compelled to
confess their 'sins'
before a Catholic priest.

Calafia admitting she knew nothing
of the Christian way.
While confiding to having fallen hopelessly in lust
with Esplandian.

Amadis explaining the Christian tenets of chastity
which had prevented his boy
from acquiescing earlier to her sexual posturing.

In the male dominated world of 16th century Spain
(remember, this is a boy's book):

chivalrous Esplandian, responded with a
magnanimous gesture of extreme benevolence,
by arranging for Calafia's introduction
to his somewhat less pious cousin, Talanque,
whom it was said looked so much like
the King's son
as to have often been mistaken for him.

Talanque, by assuming the missionary's position,
successfully converting California's Queen
to Christianity.

In gratitude for which
Calafia presented her Island

67

> with all of it's rich treasures of gold,
> pearls and precious stones
> to the Church;
>
> Whereupon
> following full confession
> an African queen and Saxon prince
> were wed in proper Christian form.

Needless to say, Garci's tale read like a dream come true for every would-be conquistador. Adding fuel to passion's fire, its storyline serving as motivation (and indeed road map) for many a hopeful Esplandian anxiously setting out in search of gold, lustful adventure and, of course, to defend the Cross.

As but another of History's many fateful twists, the name of Italian cartographer Amerigo Vespucci, who followed after and drew and sold maps illustrating the voyages of Colon discovered his own name inadvertently ascribed to identify the Western Hemisphere.

For his part Colon remaining convinced he had, in fact, discovered rather Eden.

This concept of an earthly paradise to which humanity might trace it's origins persisting throughout mankind's communal myth; appearing consistently in the literature and folklore of nearly every culture upon the face of the earth.

The existence of what was referred to in the Judeo-Christian tradition as a Garden of Eden remaining uncontested amongst the scholars of Montalvo's day.

Belief in such a place fostering hope for "since fallen" humanity. As to its specific whereabouts, however, no one seemed certain.

According to writers in the Middle Ages, a handful of travel-weary sailors and religious exiles had serendipitously happened upon it's shores. Most resigning themselves to remain (and who wouldn't). With but a reluctant few returning to share stories yet dying with the Garden's secret location locked safe in their hearts, unwilling to divulge Eden's whereabouts to a world gone mad with greed and treachery.

It would even be voiced abroad that one such prodigal had revealed to Colon the actual compass headings that ultimately conducted a correspondingly emboldened explorer safely through to paradise.

True it was that an ancient mariner had found refuge in the Colon household prior to Cristobol's voyage of discovery. An aging captain being selflessly cared for until his demise. Any notion that such generosity on the part of Colon had been reciprocated with gifts of secret charts, however, remaining so highly improbable as to render most all disbelievers. Yet, the story of "Cristobol's anonymous pilot" persisted.

The fact stands that Old World scholars believed in the tangible, geographical existence of Eden. Colon being certain he had discovered its whereabouts. Montalvo in placing the mythical Island of California at its right hand not only successfully dignifying but adding stature to his creation, while instigating still further confusion even amongst the educated contemporaries of Amerigo Vespucci; who in responding generated charts reflecting geographies far more fantastical than factual.

Simultaneously Garci's mighty and heroic Amadis and Esplandian attaining status as household gods. With contemporary chroniclers cautioning that anyone considering disparaging said notions might risk invoking the wrath of disciples anxious to avenge the honor of their heroes.

So it was that as Deeds of the Very Brave Knight Splendoor grew in popularity, a popular notion concerning the existence of an Island called California,

nearest to the earthly paradise

became widespread.

Gifted as he was, Garci had unwittingly conjured a land reflective of another, which indeed did exist. There was a "California," with palisades soaring out of the sea, giant beasts and gold- laden rivers. In fact, a land so strikingly similar to that of the novelist's own as to suggest some unlikely pretense of plagiarism were such an act possible.

Beyond Colon's tropical island paradise in the blue-green Caribbean- beyond the soon to be discovered, extravagantly wealthy Mescheca empire of the Aztecs- beyond the sea of burning sands in what is today recognized as Northern Mexico and the American Southwest- at the very edge of the world- there was such a place.

THE LAND

Rising stupendous from out of the sea, at the edge of an as yet obscure continent, stood a land of such beauty and abundance as to have eluded even the eloquence of a poetic minstrel in his failed attempt at extolling if obliquely upon its many virtues.

Expansive white sand beaches graced by remnant populations of prehistoric fan palms delineating southern parameters of a coastal paradise. Rugged mountains to the north cloaked in primeval forests of redwood and perennially shrouded by fog dropping abruptly into the surf at near perpendicular angles.

Out of the oceans of time having emerged what were, in fact, three separate islands, subsequently fused through geologic contrivance to form collectively a province as diverse and self-contained geographically as it would one day prove itself to be socially, economically and politically.

That a region's cultural history be influenced if not shaped by geography is understood. Yet rarely would such dichotomy merge more powerfully than here upon this Island of CALIFORNIA.

Has no one ever told you that three hundred twenty million years ago volcanic activity mid-Pacific referred to by geologists as sea-floor spreading launched two distinct islands on a headlong collision course with the great North American continent.

Overriding said landmass one hundred twenty five million years ago to become effectively beached astride it.

Such bold geographic assertions occasioning formation of a new and breathtaking coastline. Itself rippling eastward like a great wave into the interior of terra firma.

Rising first as an undulating twenty to forty mile wide swell of Coastal Mountains. Dropping off into the calm trough between sets that is California's great Central Valley. Before cresting to cloud-break in a tremendous eighty-mile surge of breathtaking granite peaks.

Debris tossed up when overriding islands tapped to simultaneously release violent volcanic activity producing both majestic Shasta and beautiful Trinity Alps.

Whilst lacing a rising Sierra Nevada with nothing less extraordinary than molten gold.

Even as a third great island, drifting in from points south atop tectonic plates, careened into the continent.

Sending yet another geologic wave of equally dramatic stone ripples crashing upon the shore. Rendering Southern California fractured with its Transverse and Peninsular Ranges. Both whirling in opposition to Northern California's granite shore break, forming a great coastal eddy as it were by assuming a contrary south to north configuration.

So it was that plowed under by overriding islands a new and splendid Xanadu, thrown up from the depths of the sea, came to define North America's West Coast. And yet as a grafted subcontinent remained by geographical definition an island still. Imposed upon but unique and apart from the continental landmass.

And not unlike fictional Pellucidar, effectively walled in. Breached only by the gap of a great bay. It's southernmost boundaries lying open and exposed but to the sea alone.

A new, still distinct and islandic creation sitting precariously perched atop North America, to remain perpetually on shaky ground as geography ever in flux.

Forty-five million years ago conditions replicating California's genesis sending the true subcontinent of India slamming into Asia's southern coast. Correspondingly thrusting a mighty Himalaya five miles high into the sky.

Many climatologists and geologists suggesting such dramatically altered geography occasioning new global weather patterns when consequently stripping carbon dioxide from out of earth's atmosphere. Prognosticating reverse greenhouse conditions that indeed did ensue.

As timing of such theorized events is consistent with the sudden appearance of polar ice caps.

Whether or not triggered by India's rising Himalaya the fact remaining that a sudden chill struck planet

Earth. Setting into motion episodic freezing referred to cumulatively as the Ice Age.

With expanding sheets of ice systematically annihilating ecosystems which had previously remained unchanged throughout millions of years.

Sea levels dropping in direct correlation with congelation at earth's extremities.

Nature correspondingly drawing back her Pacific cloak to render even what are today California's own islands above water, as a prehistoric littoral skirted temporarily west of its contemporary configuration.

Whilst, mimicking polar ice caps, massive glaciers formed atop not only the Himalaya but uplands elsewhere including those of North America's own West Coast subcontinent.

Distance from encroaching icefields and the marvelous geologic contrivance of California preserving within its now glaciated walls primeval climatic conditions that over time came to contrast markedly with otherwise dramatically altered landscapes and weather extremes subsequently established beyond an insulated province.

Prehistoric redwood giants continuing to flourish even as elsewhere Ice eradicated their kind globally. Refugee boreal forests of pine and fir crowding in amongst oak, cedar, aliso and palm conjuring one of the most unique and diversified woodlands on earth.

Endless varieties of suddenly marginalized plant species gathering under the protective blanket of a once globally ubiquitous now sublimated fog belt. Still nurturing in California this final vestige of worlds otherwise extinct.

Lending an esthetic of mysticism to landscapes already rendered sublime in shades of pastel and muted earthtones.

Riotous seasonal displays of prehistoric wildflowers yet carpeting mile after mile of undulating geography in dazzling color and heady fragrance set adrift upon a carpet awash in every conceivable shade of green.

Beyond the great walls sheltering California's Pleistocene garden paradise stretching vast open savannas punctuated by primordial stands of Joshua trees.

Forming as dramatic counterpoint a contrary outland destined to remain analogous as acolyte to the great West Coast subcontinent it bordered.

And upon which now congregated hundreds of thousands of wandering beasts seeking refuge from the ravages of a thirty thousand year long winter.

Great herds of lumbering elephants, bison and giant elk pressing in to avail themselves of the unparalleled luxuriance discovered adjacent in an Eden preserved.

LIONS AND TIGERS AND BEARS

Perhaps earth remains even yet locked in the grips of its Ice Age. With temperate conditions of the present suggesting but a brief respite between freezes.

Regardless an era marked by globally frigid conditions yielded if tentatively about ten thousand years ago. When correspondingly glaciers shrouding California's high mountain walls began to melt away.

Unleashing rushing torrents of icy floodwaters sent careening down slopes of today's Cascade, Sierra Nevada and Transverse and Peninsular ranges. Leaving in their spate the breathtaking U-shaped valleys of Hetch Hetchy and Yosemite together with an extraordinary network of artesian waterworks by means of which to irrigate a remnant Pleistocene landscape.

Which when viewed through modern eyes, particularly in the south, where vast stony streambeds funnel little more than seasonal runoff to the sea, reveal great channels carved in the aftermath of glacial meltdown.

So it was that as elsewhere civilizations began to appear along Egypt's Nile and the Tigris and Euphrates of Mesopotamia, California's own great river systems commenced draining a vastly diverse and luxurious primeval wilderness.

Depositing rich alluvial soils and unrivaled beaches while nurturing abundant timberlands.

It's mountain walls continuing to harvest as snowpack now but seasonal moisture blown in from off the Pacific. Precipitating annual replication of glacial runoff. And laden with gold.

California's often breathtaking coastline, forever torqued and eroded by machinations both of the sea and an underlying North American landmass, rendered even more dramatic by that pervasive and formidable fogbank. Where having prevailed continued nourishing these ecosystems of an otherwise lost world.

Prowling more than a thousand feet deep over the ocean.

Summoned on shore most often at sunset. Bathing coastal valleys and canyons in a great tumultuous sea of ephemeral moisture.

Surrendering at daybreak but to begin anew a cycle set in motion when updrafts of air warmed by the sun conjure a vacuum into which an atmospheric ocean distilling offshore tumbles.

Daily elevation of temperatures elsewhere across California's great valleys and basins invoking from gigantic marshlands this same primeval phenomena of evanescent moisture. And thus extending equally nurturing conditions into the very heart of a charmed province.

Providing an insulating blanket of intense temperate humidity held in place by stupendous mountain walls.

This gigantic marine layer with its daily routine being solely responsible for setting up what climatologist herald today as arguably the most affable climate on earth.

Halcyon days prevailing in the aftermath of global winter.

Yet subtle climactic changes remained afoot. And would encroach even upon an Eden, as weather patterns dictated elsewhere continued transforming landscapes around the world.

With now but seasonal shifting squalls prognosticating further permutations.

The same Sierra escarpment producing, through theft of moisture, a steel blue sky but exacerbating advent of desertification. Aggravating the effects of increasingly diminished precipitation already being experienced most acutely east of those granite mountain ramparts in what was rapidly becoming a land of little rain.

Rendering as desert a vast Mojave savanna stretching ever out of sight, yet tangibly sensed and seemingly omniscient on the other side of California's great walls.

The presence of this sea of sage and creosote held at bay as it were by those self same moisture harvesting bulwarks now watering Eden at the expense of all else. Locking a coastal treasure chest away behind an effective disguise of austerity.

Signaling the westward migration of creatures both great and small. All of whom now jostled for space in an increasingly limited habitat.

Placing mounting stress upon livestock suddenly crowded and effectively corralled along the coast. Occasioning reduction in their own reproductive activity.

Bringing about a decline in the number of mammoth and mastodon, which correspondingly precipitated demise of predatory lions and tigers and bears.

Yet peripheral effects of desertification were not the only elements suddenly working against California's fantastic population of megafauna.

At the height of an arguably banished Ice Age many herding animals migrating across a then frozen Bering Strait bridging Asia with North America.

And not marching alone.

As shadowing the beasts traipsed culturally dependent human populations.

Sculpted cutting tools discovered on the Mojave (near Barstow) suggesting these predominantly Shoshone migrants encountering already ensconced descendents of Paleolithic cultures gathered previously.

So that with the dawning of civilizations elsewhere California found itself populated by a varied, curiously cosmopolitan assemblage of ancient peoples. Numbering somewhere between one hundred fifty and three hundred thousand and representing the highest concentration of humanity settled anywhere in North America outside of what is today Central Mexico.

With opportunistic Shoshone arriving upon the scene availing themselves of a bounty discovered contained here on an Island in time. As super-predator prospering amidst a plenitude of readily harvestable game.

Where climatic conditions thinned the herd, ever-burgeoning throngs continued hunting without restraint. Why ration or store supplies ever available and in such great abundance?

So it seems that populations of big game diminishing naturally from crowding through a constriction of habitat and food supply, were suddenly driven into extinction courtesy of sustained slaughter.

With all California pachyderms, aside from isolated populations suddenly estranged on what in the advent of a rising sea level became "offshore" islands, eradicated by 3,500 B.C.

Ever threatening cave bear, lion and saber-toothed "tigers," while according to oral traditions held in veneration were also nonetheless understandably destroyed as a matter of course.

Even horses and camels being hunted down before reintroduced years later from Europe, Asia and Africa, where farming and animal husbandry technologies began developing early on.

So that by the time Spanish ships scudded into California's coastal waters, a migrant population had all but expended its wealth of big game animals while yet living comfortably and arguably more secure albeit without the trappings of their mammoth-hunting predecessors.

Giant condors still soaring upon those same thermals that daily summoned the fog, the occasional imperial mammoth presenting an oddity amongst a sea of elk, deer and antelope.

Elusive jaguar, panther and great brown bears yet present and in comparative abundance.

Nevertheless, mankind had most assuredly taken over.

With those first to inherit California having exacted profound effects upon it. Fashioning of their adoptive homeland a community largely free from predators, while expending potential livestock that might otherwise have been sustained even domesticated and farmed, as would be done elsewhere.

EDEN

Families settling amidst the rich and diverse ecosystems of California precipitated an equally colorful and varied prehistoric pastiche of cultural and linguistic traditions.

A milieu which seems to have originated cumulatively from seven or eight basic language stocks, each as disparate as English is to Chinese. Engendering some thirty-one distinct idioms, amongst which approximately 135 divergent dialects came to be spoken.

Genetic material referred to as mitochondrial DNA and passed down exclusively from mother to child suggesting emergence of such expanding diversity as being the result of singular populations splintering over generations into autonomous groups.

Linguists agreeing.

Subtle variance in physiognomies combined with this confusion of tongues betraying an Asiatic Diaspora identified collectively as American Shoshone.

Each Shoshone family facilitating evolutionary processes by marrying into and establishing new and separate populations.

Thus progressively isolating into distinct tribal groups courtesy of increasingly complex physical and linguistic barriers. With diversity of landscapes perhaps contributing further to proliferation of a society ultimately as fractured and disconnected as that of Old Spain itself.

Yet, where these first Californians never coalesced into anything resembling a united or nationalistic society, they remained, unlike their European counterparts, remarkably heterogeneous.

An accurate general depiction of such cosmopolitan community is, of course, impossible to render. As with Spain, its only common denominator remaining that of pervasive diversity.

Most often lacking complexity of social structure and scattered as they were throughout an equally complicated landscape, the majority existing in politically autonomous family (tribal) clans.

With anthropologists suggesting that concepts of land ownership, or personal ownership of anything for that matter, remaining marginalized if not inconceivable amongst most.

Stone Age Californians functioning peacefully under a common notion that certain precincts pertained to specific clans. And were not be trespassed against without explicit permission most often secured through an exchange of gifts or trade items paid as tribute.

Food supplies being plentiful, even in desert outlands that appear desolate and barren to the uninitiated, there remaining little call for trespass or confrontation.

Leading rather to development of a marvelous interfamily trade network and, for the most part, harmonious co-existence.

Events centering around tribal (family) interaction signaling celebrations. Oral traditions recounting feasting, dancing and song.

Each "tribe" consisting generally of far less, but never more, than one thousand individuals. Overwhich reigned either patriarch or in some cases matriarch.

Ruling caciques countered as check against totalitarianism by a council (puplem) of individuals deemed gifted and or wise.

Traditions reflecting a prevalence of democratic principals including widespread usage of the "ballot box" system for resolving communal discord.

When and where employed empowering each family courtesy of its own uniquely fashioned stone. Cast or withheld in matters of tribal concern.

Leaving issues unresolved until attaining a consensus.

Corresponding intransigence understandably forestalling installation of more progressive societies.

Tribal leadership, more often than not, being handed down from father to son or mother to daughter.

Yet such hereditary chains of command do not seem to have been mandatory. Communities selecting on occasion someone other than a direct heir to rule over them.

War when it did occur, was generally a pre-arranged affair between individuals. Victory going to the one first to slay his or her singular opponent.

Vengeful bloodbaths remaining all but unheard of.

Western observers accustomed to competition and obsessed with conquest and acquisitions subsequently perceiving this apparent disinterest in power and position with suspicion. While the reality of said state of affairs contributed monumentally to a prevailing, seemingly all encompassing peace.

Generally speaking the most prominent individual in every family group being not its political leader but rather a shaman, or priest (in popular vernacular-the medicine man). Who like tribal religious elsewhere throughout the Americas practiced totemic ritual. Identifying each child upon birth as sibling to some aspect of the natural world.

Organized instruction of children seeming to have been universal.

Shaman who were perceived as being in possession of an ability to act as intercessory both with totems (saints) as well as in the greater sphere of all natural elements courtesy of an ancient and hereditary birthright alone defining "religion" and or education for their people.

Having been "ordained," as were the sons of Aaron, into an ancient priesthood. And preoccupied with not only hallmark ceremonial rites associated with birth, puberty, marriage and death but daily rituals surrounding procurement of sustenance, exorcism of illness and maintenance of positive interactions with the unknown.

Artistic aspirations found their fullest expression in music and the dance. An infectious joy generated by dissonant intonations from rudimentary flutes and rattles often sustaining celebrants through marathon ceremonial events.

Tattooing was common. Giving expression to a strangely moving mythology of which the details have long since been lost. Three vertical lines on the chin often supplementing similar markings to the head, cheeks, arms and breasts.

A handful of artisans produced complex, polychromatic rock art, stone sculptures and pottery.

Yet amongst peoples who lived life in practical and basic ways it would be in the very practical art of basket weaving where they most excelled. Creating stunning and functional pieces for daily use.

Adept at harvesting Nature, most notably desert populations inhabiting the Colorado River Valley participated in deliberate and varied agricultural endeavors.

Elsewhere acorns, wild oats, rhubarb and roots serving most as dietary mainstays. Supplemented with a bounty of walnuts, wild fruits (apples, plums, cherries, peaches, filberts) and berries (blackberries, gooseberries, raspberries, currants and cranberries).

An infinite variety of herbs being employed not only

for medicinal purposes but in the preparation of fish, rabbit and various other small game.

Architecture throughout California while extremely rudimentary, was at once ergonomic and characteristically practical.

Families inhabiting the wooded north coast constructing traditional "teepees" of a sort fashioned from redwood planks, further inland of cedar and in the south with simple willows and tules (bullrushes).

Most significant structure in any given settlement being its temple or Vanquech (Van-qu-ech) with attendant sweathouse, wherein only adults received advanced religious instruction through tantric ritual.

Attire remaining most basic. Peoples in the north compelled to bundle up more frequently than those of the south. Which all did by fashioning capes out of elk, deer, rabbit or exquisite sea otter skins.

Northern families more often sporting moccasins, with tribes to the south wearing sandals. Beyond which men and children simply going naked. Hygienic concerns prompting women into wearing a two-piece apron, or tiki, fashioned from buckskin, shredded bark or in some cases plant fibers.

Smoking of native tobacco was commonplace. The prevalence of hallucinogenic Jimpson weed leading to proliferation of a significant drug culture.

Famously berated by Western observers as being backward and indolent, the fact remains that while all about stood natural resources beyond measure unexploited, yet in the midst of their own comfortable abundance, and with no need or want left unfulfilled, they simply languished happily and peacefully in isolated splendor.

Necessity as Galileo observed being the mother of invention, advanced technologies required to unlock California's treasures never developing. There was no need.

And when at the close of the Ice Age an effective door into California slammed shut by virtue of authentic isolation occasioned courtesy of encroaching deserts to the south and east and to the north a submerged land bridge, no further integration from more progressive cultures beyond occurred.

Whereupon scattered and isolated even from each other, most lived out their lives rarely venturing beyond the locale to which they'd been born.

When the mammoth disappeared there had remained elk, deer, antelope and rabbit enough. Endless varieties of oak assuring unfailing abundance of acorns, with vast seas of grass providing harvests of seed ad infinitum.

Along the coast flourishing so many lobster, clams, abalone, oysters and mussels that no one there could have ever gone hungry.

For localized specialty items families simply gathering routinely to trade. Salt, seaweed, dried fish, sea otter capes and jewelry manufactured from luminescent abalone shells purchasing elkhorn tools, deerskins, pinenuts and obsidian arrowheads.

It would appear then that these first Californians having lived out countless generations lost in time and surrounded with peace and plenitude, found no reason to search for ways of enhancing a system that continually nurtured and precipitated upon them unprecedented joie-de-vivre.

We ate
and slept,
hunted a little,
fought a little
and in all things took God at His word
not trying to interfere with His plans,
or improve His handiwork.

American novelist Willa Cather later observing how,

They seemed to have none of the European's desire
to 'master' nature,
to arrange and re-create.

They spent their ingenuity in the other direction;
in accommodating themselves to the scene
in which they found themselves.

This was not so much from indolence,
as from an inherited caution and respect.

It was as if the great country were asleep,
and they wished to carry on their lives without
awakening it;

> Or as if the spirits of earth and air and water
> were things not to antagonize and arouse.

So it was that where Montalvo had supplied his California with everything desirous to the heart of an aspiring Western adventurer, Nature running directly counterpoint bestowed upon California's largely eastern population all things necessary for attaining without strife a most desirable state of contentment. If ever there had been an Eden, surely this was it.

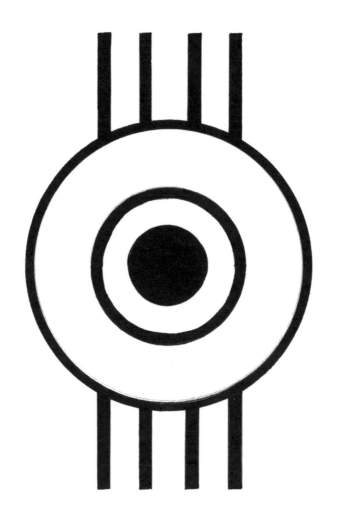

THE CHRISTENING

O f those many conquistadors about to hurl both themselves and their fortunes at the unknown quantity that was America none exhibited more daring and recklessness than he who as a little boy had gazed in wondering awe upon the spectacle of Cristobol Colon parading Indian retainees with their parrots and gold through the streets of Barcelona.

Dreams shape the lives of those they haunt.

A nightmare conjured by little Hernan Fernando Cortes prognosticating his ascendancy from would-be knight to Mexican god. Rendering him even more resplendent than Montalvo's Esplandian.

As an hidalgo Cortes gaining ready access to the prestigious University of Salamanca.

"Access" however not translating into social acceptance. This perceived gatecrasher from remote and impoverished Extremadura remaining a stark contradiction amongst an otherwise urbane and glamorous court.

Founding father of **New** Spain at first seemingly destined to remain ever an outsider. Neither students nor faculty suspecting for an instant the latent dream dancing even then in fourteen year old Fernando's head.

Stoic and by his own definition less than attractive, subsequent biographers painted diplomatic portraits:

The colour of his face was somewhat ashy
and not very merry,
his eyes having a somewhat loving glance
yet grave withal.

And had his face been longer
it would have been handsomer.

While in demeanor
he ever possessed the austerity of a grim soldier.

Personification of the harsh desert to which he'd been born, no one would ever have perceived in this undersized and otherwise common boy an embryonic capacity to become Spain's most celebrated and successful conquistador.

No one, that is, except for Hernan Fernando Cortes.

And so it came to pass. As quoting left and right from his favorite storyteller Garci Rodrigo Ordonez de Montalvo, young Fernando went on to alter the course of New World history forever.

An unprecedented career that began upon receipt of his Law degree from Salamanca at age nineteen.

Imaginative cunning and daring treachery displayed thereafter propelling him rapidly through a Spanish body politick to the very pinnacle of power in Colon's New World.

Where amidst a cutthroat environment he honed his natural leadership abilities with the professed piety and casual brutality that were to become

Hernan's trademarks.

Mastery both of Law and men facilitating acquisition of not only ranching interests on the island of Santo Domingo, but mining operations in Cuba together with a coerced and lucrative posting as Capitan General of the New World.

Placing him at odds with the King's appointed Governor of Cuba, Diego Velazquez.

Cortes in attempting to outmaneuver Velazquez inventing though never laying claim to a soon to be created position of Vice King (Vice Regal) or Viceroy.

As interim illegalities and the aspirations of Velazquez aside Hernan went on to assume full authority for his King in New World affairs.

Presumptuous effrontery that did not go unchallenged. The would-be king leaving many an enemy in his wake.

Regardless Hernan's stunning success remaining difficult even for a legitimate monarchy to argue against. In fact provoking the King through intimidation.

As by masterminding Mexico's conquest, Cortes alone produced a flood of gold and riches beyond measure back across the seas to Spain.

Zeitgeist forging his **New** Spain with confidence and absolute moral certainty regarding an inherent right and indeed divine mandate to do so.

This quintessential man of his Age proudly bestowing upon each new conquest terminology derived from the heroic poetry that served him as catalyst.

So it was then while plying the Pacific aboard his sailing vessel <u>Saint Lazarus</u> (San Lazaro) on May 3, 1535 in search of yet another mythic kingdom, juggernaut Hernan watched with much anticipation when a great "island" appeared upon the horizon.

Pragmatically ascribing the name La Cruz (The Cross) to a stark and forebodingly beautiful Lands End.

Whilst to his men directly, envisioning kingdoms filled with gold and populated by Amazons, suggesting the tantalizing anomaly as being rather CALIFORNIA.

Illiterate and gullible, most remaining convinced they were indeed skirting the very coast of Montalvo's fantasyland. Many keeping a look out for signs of magnificent cave dwellings and monstrous flying griffins while all felt compelled to press on in the hope of exploiting that which did not exist.

A real life Esplandian thereafter dispatching three ships under Francisco Ulloa with orders to carefully examine the entire coastline of **his** California.

Where upon sailing into what was subsequently christened the Red Sea of Cortes, Ulloa discovered waters rich with pearl-bearing oysters.

And eventually detected the Colorado River Delta.

Causing conjecture that Hernan's California was, in fact, not an island but rather one grand peninsula.

When in the midst of reconnoitering, Ulloa's ships floundered:

Wracked by wind and waves,
she (the ship <u>Santo Tomas</u>) began to take on water
so badly that those aboard could not keep it down,

according to what they told me,

shouting to me that they were sinking
and could not keep afloat.

God grant that this may not be true
and that they are all now safe.

Every man on board the <u>Santo Tomas</u> drowned.

Prompting Ulloa to send his surviving escort, the <u>Santa Aguedo</u> back with an update for Cortes while himself pressing on alone.

I have determined, with the ship <u>Trinidad</u>
and my few supplies and men to go on,
if God grant me weather,
and the wind will permit,
as far as I can,

And send this ship (the <u>Santa Aguedo</u>)
and these men to New Spain with this report.

God, whom may it please to advance
your illustrious lordship

in person and estate through a long period,
grant that our outcome be such as
your lordship desires.

I kiss your lordship's illustrious hand.

Whereupon Francisco Ulloa and his flagship the
Trinidad simply vanished into thin air.

Oral traditions of California's Cahuilla in the Colorado
River Valley attributing an ignominious ending to a
conquistador's tale.

Recounting how each year at flood stage the mighty
Colorado inundated vast tracts of otherwise arid
desert lowlands.

Sailing into and across seasonal Lake Cahuilla
(today's Salton Sea), Ulloa's Trinidad hoving to and
dropping anchor.

Apprehensive Cahuilla gathering cautiously on shore.

Only to be addressed through a Mescheca (Aztec)
interpreter by a white, bearded Captain Moreno,
claiming to be the Son of the Sun.

Indigenous history suggesting the query of a wary
chieftain who wondered why it was that the Son of
the Sun required interpreters when addressing his
own people?

Dismissing said impertinence Moreno persisting
rather with interrogating the suspicious cacique
concerning gold, eternal symbol of the sun.

Recommending that a generous gift of the same, should the Cahuilla be in possession of any, might serve as fitting tribute.

Southwest traditions having maintained that much of the gold used to adorn Aztec palaces had, in fact, been taken from northern mines.

Of course news concerning the exploits of Cortes had undoubtedly long since reached these Aztec/Tanoan brothers in the Colorado River Valley.

Where a cunning chieftain responded with claims that the Cahuilla were indeed in possession of great quantities of gold. But their king was old and frail and unable to come to Moreno.

Suggesting that most assuredly a handsome reward would await Moreno if, on the other hand, he should condescend to present himself before the ancient Indian monarch.

Blinded by greed a conquistador striking out for his host's village. Whereupon the divine pretender together with his entourage were summarily ambushed and slaughtered.

Leaving as curiosity an unmanned and thereafter plundered ship sitting marooned on a seasonally drained floodplain for eons.

Verbal tradition being such as it is, we are left to ponder the identity of Moreno. Was he, rather Ulloa, or did perhaps Moreno usurp control of Ulloa's expedition following an act of mutiny?

Additionally those well versed in California's Story recognize a curious cross pollination between what was perhaps Ulloa's <u>Trinidad</u> with the soon to unfold successful exploits of one Hernando de Alarcon.

Who under direct orders from his King retraced Ulloa's journey the following year. And in a grand ruse presented himself as Son of the Sun.

Alarcon did not disappear, however, but rather returned to tell the tale.

Meanwhile, court records subsequently filed indicating that following circumnavigation of California Ulloa re surfaced in Peru.

Yet Cortes, to emphasize the courage required for undertaking his death defying Conquista, offering elsewhere derisively in a court of law that detractors direct their questioning concerning California in particular rather towards a known to have disappeared Ulloa.

We are told that a ghost ship yet lies buried beneath the sands of the Coachella Valley, somewhere in the vicinity of a since expanded Salton Sea.

Attempts at maintaining secrecy concerning reports delivered to Cortes by the <u>Santo Aguedo</u> had failed. Hence Alarcon's sudden appearance upon the scene.

Californians being left with a curious amalgamation of out and out myth and equally questionable"histories," each written by individuals anxious to surpass the other in claiming more gold and glory.

Ultimately undone through treachery equal to that of his own Cortes himself being deported from New Spain and in chains, where he spent the remainder of his days attempting to reclaim both confiscated estates and entitlements, but to no avail.

Following years of feigning by the Crown legend providing us with a tantalizing chance encounter between King and conquistador on those same streets of Barcelona where long ago the glimpse of Colon's triumphal entrada had sparked Hernan's monstrous ambition.

Together at last, a maligned and abandoned Cortes stopping the monarch's carriage by placing his foot upon its step while insisting he be heard. Whereupon from inside the coach a voice demanding:

Who is this man that would dare detain the King?

To which a most unlikely Esplandian replied,

It is I,
your Majesty;
the man who gave you more riches
and kingdoms
than have come down to you
from all the kings of Spain.

Two hundred years of competitive discoveries each shrouded in secrecy followed. Leaving European cartographers confused concerning the true geographic configuration of California.

And where Hernan had attempted to conquer the same from its east coast, nemesis Antonio Mendoza, as his King's first duly appointed Viceroy of New Spain, opted rather to approach it from the west.

Meanwhile Montalvo's anonymous succedaneum penning yet another sequel to <u>Deeds of the Very Brave Knight Splendoor,</u> in which our champion and the mighty conquistador Hernan Cortes joined forces and subdued the entire New World.

CABRILHO

At four o'clock on the morning of September 28th in 1542 three Spanish ships spun from off a turbulent sea into the sheltering embrace of San Diego Bay.

Sailors knelling united by their Captain in offering prayers of gratitude for a propitious ending to an otherwise harrowing turn of events.

Three months had passed since the <u>San Miguel</u>, <u>San Salvador</u> and <u>Santa Victoria</u> sailed past Cabo San Lucas.

Thereafter becoming forestalled by contrary winds and currents. Tacking back and forth the tiny flotilla persisting, steadfast in its determination to chart California.

Nothing however could have prepared even these seasoned mariners for the unexpected atmospheric assaults broadsiding them on that fateful September morning.

When at around 2 a.m. hot blasts of wild and erratic winds inexplicably kicked up all of a sudden and seemingly from out of nowhere. Pummeling their vessels both from the southeast **and** southwest intermittently.

Sending frantic men startled from out of their sleep howling and praying, so certain were they of being undone by no less than the Devil himself.

A characteristic and quick response from Captain Juan Rodriguez,

> For whom faith was like air and light
> And the very breath with which he spoke

calming his frightened and disoriented crew. As together they petitioned Mary, Queen of Heaven, for divine intervention.

Seemingly she responded. As the elements fell suddenly still.

A rising sun revealing the headland and sand bar that had afforded unexpected and perfect protection from bizarre turbulence experienced beyond. And in which Rodriguez perceived nothing less than Mary's own sheltering embrace.

As floating upon a sea of glass he knelt with all to once again surrender their souls, this time in prayers of thanksgiving.

Little beyond scholarly conjecture is known concerning the early years of California's Juan Rodriguez. Even his birthplace and nationality remaining shrouded in mystery.

He was most likely born of humble parentage in or around Seville and subsequently appropriated by the wealthy Sanchez de Ortega household. Who cared for him in exchange for services rendered in and around the family's hacienda.

As thereafter Juan accompanied eldest son Diego

Sanchez to New Spain where destiny threw both men's fortunes together with those of Hernan Cortes and Pedro Alvarado.

Perhaps it was Alvarado who supplied an enigmatic boy with the nickname by which he would be remembered to history.

Portuguese slang meaning "randy little billy goat," Cabrilho being a term much bandied about amongst such camaraderie. Suggesting that a spunky Spaniard had somehow caught both the attention and affections of his superiors.

Cortes needing boats with which to control a Mescheca (Aztec) metropolis surrounded by water.

Overnight crossbowman Rodriguez becoming boatwright Rodriguez. It is not known whether Juan had ever built so much as a skiff beforehand.

And may well have been then and there perhaps on the Noche Triste (Night of Sorrows), when boats built by Rodriguez carried no less than Alvarado away from otherwise impending death, that this soldier of fortune garnered for himself both nickname and the noblesse oblige of his employer.

For immediately following said event during which all Spaniards where effectively driven out from Tenochtitlan (Mexico City) Rodriguez came to be identified rather as Cabrilho. And thereafter ascended rapidly into the heady heights of great power and wealth otherwise reserved exclusively for men of noble birthright.

However it came about Cabrilho suddenly found himself on a fast track to fame and fortune. First marching under auspices of Adelantado (Royal Developer) Alvarado into neighboring Guatemala.

And there granted great jurisdictions within the framework of a new kingdom independent from that of Hernan Cortes.

When Alvarado departed to challenge in Old Spain the absolute authority of Cortes over New Spain, ordering Cabrilho establish in his absence a Christian capitol for the Kingdom of Guatemala.

Aping Cortes, who was anything but a knight, naive "Randy" thereafter behaving as he presumed one ought by toppling pagan Mayan Stele at Copan to replace them with images of Mary.

Then not only founding, but twice relocating Guatemala's Cuidad Antigua while simultaneously herding thousands of Indian "infidels" into hastily organized schools for religious education.

As reward receiving upon Alvarado's return permission to "employ" those many new converts in the harvest of both cocoa and gold.

In which Guatemala abounded.

So it was that Juan Rodriguez awoke to find himself one of the wealthiest and most powerful men in America. And accordingly coveted both by Cortes and Alvarado alike.

With his new found fortune and fame remaining entrenched in an escalating power struggle between not only each of his former employers but newly arriving upon the scene as first duly appointed Viceroy of New Spain Sir Antonio Mendoza.

When all three men petitioned Rodriguez for assistance with staging the conquest of California an innately chivalrous and loyal soldier dutifully rejoining but to his patron Alvarado alone:

> He ordered that I should build him an armada
> while he was away in Spain,
> and so I built it.

Whereupon Mendoza, in a determined attempt to maintain control over the likes of Cortes and Alvarado, confiscated Cabrilho's armada.

With protests rendered mute even before reaching His Majesty's ears when Alvarado perished unexpectedly during an Indian uprising, allegedly being crushed to death under the weight of his own horse as presumably it stumbled and then fell upon him.

Whilst at Mendoza's recommendation, the King having ordered Cortes stripped of all honors and possessions.

So it was that as first Viceroy, Mendoza ridded Spain of both otherwise immensely popular and authentic threats to the monarchy's own sovereignty over a New World.

There is no honor amongst thieves.

Dealing with such thugs was nasty business. Disaster lying thinly veiled in the coerced arrangement subsequently struck between Mendoza and upstart Cabrilho, who in accepting a Viceroy's offer inadvertently signed his own death warrant.

To be immolated as but the first of many lives subsequently sacrificed upon the altar of a land that would one day yield more gold and treasure than Cortes, Alvarado, Mendoza or Austrian Habsburg heir to the Spanish throne Charles I could have ever imagined.

Hence on that fateful morning one year later Cabrilho found himself in San Diego.

Where his attempts at putting ashore were retarded by arrows served up generously from the bows of Indians anxious to forestall Spanish incursion.

A protégé of Hernan Cortes being quick in firing back, but not with crossbow and arquebus.

Cabrilho rather producing small ornamental crucifixes and articles of Spanish clothing as gifts.

Correspondingly obsequious Kumeyaay (Coo-me-ya-eye) explaining their previously hostile posturing as deemed warranted owing to reports being received from the interior of men not unlike Cabrilho who were presently engaged in killing Indians.

Sagacious Rodriguez recognizing he had just received a timely update concerning an Entrada staged by a royal appointee anxious to outdo renegade Cortes both in discovery as well as conquest.

As indeed at that very moment auspiciously dressed in full suit of golden armor Francisco Vasquez de Coronado rode at the head of Viceroy Mendoza's expeditionary forces into what is now the American Southwest. Seeking both legendary Cibola with its Seven Golden Cities and a beyond wealthy Gran Quivira.

As Cabrilho's ships sat listing at anchor their captain celebrated the feast day of San Miguel (Saint Michael) patron of his capitana (flagship). Ascribing the name of this Heaven's Champion for Good over Evil upon Mary's safe haven.

While gazing out across what is today San Diego at a coastline cloaked in oak and Torrey pine and teeming with antelope, penning for his jealous Viceroy a report he would not live to deliver.

In which special note was made of the striking contrast between this California and the austerity of landscapes encountered previously. Suggesting further that a gloriously opalescent world now unfolding before his very eyes might well possess rivers of gold and city/states not unlike those sought by the Golden Knight Coronado.

It was a hopeful captain and crew who six days later weighed anchor and hoisted sail to press ever northward, anxiously scanning with increasing wonder the palisades, beaches and wooded coastal valleys of sybaritic southern California.

While no griffins were spotted, big blonde bears and giant condors proved a common sight.

And where Amazonians seemed in short supply, yet the country appeared densely populated with presumably benign peoples congregated in large villages and, due to the affable nature of the climate, parading about naked as the day they were born.

Flames of fear flared anew however as the armada approached what is now Los Angeles. When once again all found themselves caught up in the grip of hellish, erratic winds. A giant billowing dome of smoke lingering out over the sea raining ash and hot embers down upon them.

Again they prayed. Again the winds subsided.

Cabrilho noting the anomaly in his ship's log as La Bahia de Fuego (Bay of Fire).

All struggling to interpret a landscape ablaze, fearful they might well be approaching some monstrous gatekeeper determined to prevent their accessing fantastic treasure or perhaps ushering them into the gates of Hell itself!

No sooner had the conquistador contemplated such ominous possibilities than did he spy unusually large villages comprised of very substantial houses. And found himself being encircled by dozens of canoes under the command of two colorfully adorned Chumash caciques.

Who came requesting by name an audience with the famous Captain Cabrilho.

Relieved to discover his solicitors were not Lucifer's minions but rather emissaries of southern California's most advanced indigenous culture, Rodriguez remaining understandably amazed that word of his arrival had already preceded him up the coast from what is now San Diego.

While as a boatswain expressing admiration for the caciques' fine navy.

Who responded with invitations for the Spanish to witness first hand how said tomols (outriggers) were constructed.

An offer Juan Rodriguez could not pass up. Putting ashore this time at what is now Rincon. Adjacent to a village he would later christen Carpinteria after its many fine craftsmen.

And was there invited to participate in a great conference being convened by local lords. During which Cabrilho found himself again brought up to date concerning Mendoza's Golden Knight, while hearing testimony that none amongst the Chumash had ever heard either of golden city-states or a place called Gran Quivira.

Rodriguez penning a missive the Chumash promised they'd deliver to Coronado. As payment for which he rewarded them handsomely in advance with clothing and religious tokens.

The curious, sometimes harrowing misadventures of Juan Rodriguez Cabrilho are easily interpreted by anyone familiar with Southern California's coastal waters.

Where the meeting of an icy southbound and tropical northbound current render travel difficult. Then all but curtailed by an added constant of southeasterly headwinds.

Arriving as he did during late fall and early winter, Cabrilho's tiny ships being further harassed by the natural often violent meteorological phenomena of a Santa Ana condition. Commonly referred to still as Devil Winds.

Occasioned when seasonal warming along southern California's coast reverses the otherwise routine ebb and flow of fogbanks by overheating normally cool air and thus sending it spiraling heavenward. Conjuring an atmospheric void into which hot air from inland deserts race.

The Santa Ana's tossing Rodriguez about at San Diego themselves no doubt responsible for transforming Los Angeles into a scene from out of Dante Alighieri's Inferno. As the complete lack of humidity occasioned only during this fluke onslaught of rapacious desert wind often even today fans otherwise containable domestic fires into mammoth conflagrations.

It is understandable then how one ignorant of the natural sciences behind said phenomena might perceive himself as being in the grasp of some monster or even at the very gates of Hell.

More awesome still would be the precipitous coastline encountered following Cabrilho's powwow with the Chumash. Where rainsqualls consistent with conditions surrounding a seasonally dominant Arctic current pounded his ships into an effectual retreat.

Recognizing what accounts compiled later by conquistador Herrera and navigator Urdaneta don't say, and further tipped off courtesy of observations from contemporary fishermen, reputable scholars are left with valid reason to dismiss as suspect all further progress reported by the expedition.

Rodriguez and his men were the first Europeans ever to behold a land as mysterious and hauntingly beautiful as that of Montalvo's fictional chronicles. Witnessing together the natural splendor of a semitropic paradise. Its sea of cerulean blue creaming in gentle surf upon vast sandy beaches. Yielding to the temperate rigors of those perpendicular mountains plunging into the sea.

Well versed in popular mythology and having themselves experienced presumably supernatural displays of wind, fire and encounters with strange peoples and beasts, the presumption that all were haunted by fear and intrepidation remains inescapable.

Cabrilho would seek refuge from rainsqualls at what he referred to as Possession (since renamed San Miguel in honor of his subsequently altered christening for what is now San Diego) Island. Where concerned sailors careened both vessels while taking on fresh water and provisions.

Herrera stating men reduced to eating but rotten biscuits arguing in favor of abandoning their enterprise.

Had a rift developed over whether or not to proceed? We may never know. What follows is a series of once detailed suddenly brief entries into the ship's log suggesting continued exploratory maneuvers, yet noting distances that don't make sense while leaving as conspicuous vagaries well known and readily identifiable landmarks.

With First Mate Bartolome Ferrer now writing on behalf of Cabrilho, describing today's Big Sur and Carmel as an "ice bound" wasteland that could only have existed in his imagination. While failing to make note of Monterey, San Francisco, the Farrallones or Drake's Bay.

Even more unsettling being the abrupt change in deportment amongst Cabrilho's crew.

Having gained his sobriquet for pluck and verve yet Randy ever maintaining a knightly decorum.

Displaying none of the chivalrous attributes otherwise demonstrated throughout this voyage, Ferrer not only no longer presenting gifts to the natives but contrary wise capturing four native women and two boys with which to pleasure and otherwise serve his men.

The fact remains that after presumably surviving tremendously high seas along an Arctic coast, during which each vessel became separated from the other, with all,

commending our souls both to God
and to the briny deep,

everyone found themselves reunited again at Possession Island?

Where First Mate Ferrer reports that Cabrilho suffered a fall and broke, according to various depositions taken later, an arm, a shoulder or a leg. From which the good captain is said to have contracted blood poisoning and died.

We are told that the conquistador was buried on January 3, 1543 in what some say was a leaden chest at an Island christened in his honor.

Eye witness accounts subsequently given in court corroborating the fact that Captain Cabrilho's final words were delivered in the form of an edict to First Mate Ferrer that he not turn back until either an Amazon kingdom or a legendary channel referred to as the Straits of Anian had been detected.

In subsequent reports delivered to Viceroy Mendoza, Bartolome Ferrer claiming to have faithfully carried out his Captain's dying orders. Presenting as proof the aforementioned log and charts.

Cabrilho's voyage of discovery was a massive undertaking. And succeeded with bringing vast new territories into Spanish ken.

Yet under said circumstances and regardless the effort was greeted at Mexico City with little enthusiasm.

As void of magical landmarks or kingdoms to plunder, Ferrer's reports leveled but a second strike against

Antonio Mendoza's efforts to surpass the glories of his nemesis Hernan Cortes.

For where Juan Rodriguez floundered, Coronado's enterprise had failed altogether. Solid gold armaments long since abandoned, Francisco wandering naked and lost somewhere in what is now Kansas amidst seemingly endless herds of strange"hunch-back" cattle.

Spain ever after referring to America's buffalo as rather cibola.

Whatever became of Cibola, or Gran Quivira for that matter, not to mention Cabrilho himself, will perhaps forever remain a mystery.

As for the suddenly devalued Island of California, how could Viceroy Mendoza have known that its rivers like those of Montalvo's fairytale were literally strewn with gold? Extensive redwood forests perhaps viewed by Ferrer constituting the finest timber ever known to man? Or that the coastal plains and valleys beyond those beaches skirted were among the richest and most fertile on earth.

Surely in chasing after myth Spain failed to recognize the wondrous reality Cabrilho had laid open before her.

Meanwhile disturbing accusations being leveled against Ferrer. Who following months of subjection to continuous danger and the pervasive peril of running aground on some unknown reef or shoal without any possibility for rescue, while further intimidated psychologically by displays of seemingly supernatural occurrences, may well have become frightened enough to carry out that which otherwise remains unconscionable.

Where modern study confirms daily distances reported in Ferrer's convoluted log and charts as having no basis in fact, early nineteenth century excavations during resort construction at Portuguese Bend near San Pedro harbor in Los Angeles reporting the discovery of a leaden casket in which was found:

a Spanish conquistador,
killed from a wound to the back of the head.

Conflicting evidence of a controversial stone inscribed with the initials JRC would subsequently be recovered at San Miguel in what is now Channel Islands National Park, where, nonetheless no verifiable evidence of the Rodriguez burial site has ever been located.

Pointing an accusatory finger across the centuries at individuals no longer present to defend themselves remaining unethical. Equally disconcerting, however, being the possibility of such heinous crimes escaping punishment.

That Ferrer ascribed his Viceroy's name (Mendocino for Mendoza) to the ambiguity of Cabrilho's sailing orders did not merit impunity.

And so determined the Royal Audiencia (King's Court) following a complete and thorough investigation. Testimony garnered from sailors present leaving such a pallor of doubt that rather than reward Bartolome and his crew all were summarily banished to obscurity if not certain execution as foot soldiers in a war then being waged against the dangerous Arucano Indians of Chile.

We may never know whether or not our hero was struck down by his own men. The truth lying buried in Chilean gravesites, amongst remains of individuals relinquished to anonymity by a suspicious sovereign.

AZTLAN

S tudents of Spanish American history have estimated that gold and other precious metals valued at close to 100 billion dollars in contemporary currency were spirited away during the Conquista. With in the advent of shipwreck and subsequent piracy as much as 10% of the same now lying at the bottom of the sea.

Hernan Cortez alone having lost a fortune even before his royal shakedown when during Tenochtitlan's siege jewels and precious metals were carried off by local high priests.

Their concerted efforts focused upon salvaging and relocating the same to its place of origin.

Legend having long maintained that Mescheca (Aztec) civilization began around a land-locked sea far to the north of Mexico in a land called Aztlan.

The foundations of which sat squarely upon seven chambers filled with the relics and riches of ancient America.

When expanding an empire Montezuma's predecessors recognizing the Valley of Mexico as but a replication of their homeland.

In the midst of its land locked lakes resurrecting their secret and sacred capitol city.

Once local ministers identified the threat that was

Hernan Cortes, launching a concerted effort to return both royalty and riches to the security of a northern stronghold.

Curiously and coinciding with tales of Aztlan and its seven chambers was a widely accepted legend developed during the Moorish occupation of Spain.

Concerning a Christian archbishop and six acolytes whom "God" rescued from encircling "infidels" by magically transporting them to a mysterious island. Whereupon stood seven cities so rich that even their streets were paved in gold.

The location of said cities remaining ever vague.

Belief in the existence of rich islands coupled with rumors of great Indian kingdoms and golden city-states keeping attentions riveted upon what yet remained the Great Northern Mystery of New Spain.

Adding fuel to flames of enthusiastic speculation being the inexplicable transference by cartographers of Coronado's wanderings onto reports drafted by Cabrilho.

So that mythic Quivira and Aztlan as Cibola's Seven Golden Cities suddenly appeared as though known to exist and in California.

With independent operator Juan de Fuca and apocryphal Bartolome Fonte each claiming successful circumnavigation of the same.

By which time Admiral of the Spanish Royal Navy

Francisco Gali had stepped forward to tender a more trustworthy yet incomplete appraisal.

When sailing east at the helm of his leaky, cranky caravel in 1584 he became swept up in a southbound oceanic current.

Which carried him to within two hundred leagues of California's fabled shore.

Being by the same course
upon the coast of New Spain,
under 37° 30',
we passed by a very high and fair land.

With many trees,
wholly without snow,

And four leagues from the land
you find thereabouts many drifts of roots,
leaves of trees, reeds, and
other leaves like fig- leaves,
the like whereof we found in great abundance
in the country of Cipango (Japan),
which they eat;

There likewise we found great store of seals;

Whereby it is to be presumed and
certainly to be believed,
that there are many rivers, bays and havens
along those coasts.

From thence we ran south-east,
south-east and by South,

and south-east and by east,
as we found the wind,

To the point called Cabo de San Lucas,
which is the beginning of the land of California,
on the north-west side,
lying under 22°,
being five hundred leagues distant
from Cabo Mendocino.

So it seems that amongst other interesting observations Gali had been the first to actually spy a Cape guessed at by Cabrilho's pilot Bartolome Ferrer.

Unless of course some other as yet unknown mariner slated past the anomaly without leaving behind any written account.

Still nothing indicating the existence of great kingdoms or golden city-states ever subsequently being noted or reported.

MANILA'S GALLEONS

early forty years would pass before even Spain itself came to grasp the enormity of Cabrilho's monumental achievement.

While Juan Rodriguez skirted California, Viceroy Mendoza having deployed Antonio Lopez de Villalobos at the helm of another Cabrilho built ship with orders to complete Colon's quest for an as yet unattained Orient.

Lopez succeeding in discovering an archipelago off the coast of China. Which he christened Philippines in honor Crown Prince Philip II.

And from whence Francisco Gali had sailed.

When Philip's father, Charles I (Habsburg's Charles V), grandson of King Ferdinand, retired to seek absolution in a religious cloister Philip ascending both as Spanish monarch and Emperor of Charlemagne's Holy Roman Empire.

And as such rousting out and pressing into service otherwise cloistered Augustinian Friar (Fray) Andres Urdaneta.

Who had prior to seeking Holy Orders accompanied Pedro Alvarado in America, where he'd served alongside Cabrilho during the conquest of Guatemala. Through avocation becoming an experienced sailor when soldiers of fortune with whom he traveled returned to Spain by way of circumnavigating the globe.

Once home a disillusioned mercenary like his King turning away from mayhem in search of penance and sanctuary.

Newly crowned Philip recognizing that few if any man alive knowing more about not only navigation but the waters of the Pacific then this soldier become sailor become Augustinian Friar.

So it was that Fray (Brother) Andres found himself being rousted from the monastery and posted by a King who controlled both Church and State as ostensibly Chaplain of Philippine-bound invasionary forces.

When in 1565 four warships manned by four hundred soldiers under the leadership of Miguel Gomez de Legazpi sailed from the Mexican port of Navidad.

Urdaneta had long since transcribed and carefully studied the papers both of Lopez and Cabrilho. By means of which this self- educated navigator managed to successfully conduct all safely across the Pacific. His acquired knowledge concerning tradewinds delivering them upon the scene following a voyage of less than three months duration.

Where Legazpi was quick in squelching opposition, which upon yielding left Spain with its long desired stronghold in the East.

King Philip then ordering built vessels big enough in which to transport much anticipated treasure back to Europe by way of Mexico.

Filipino shipbuilders responding by producing ships larger than the world had ever seen:

> Of an huge bignesse,
> so high that they resembled great castles.

Chinese navigators sympathetic to Brother Urdaneta's predicament informing him that to sail north out of the Philippines was to catch hold of that California-bound current encountered by Gali.

Which he did in company with Admiral Legazpi's grandson Felipe Salcedo. The two arriving back at Acapulco following a voyage of little more than four months duration.

This conundrum of an abstemious monk conducting a military operation that launched what quickly became the longest lived and arguably most successful trading enterprise in history but endemic of both Spain and the Age of Conquest.

Urdaneta's circular route having most assuredly been employed earlier by sturdy Chinese junks in an as yet little known cultural and economic exchange carried on between Asia and North America.

That which currents and tradewinds now facilitating being contrarily anything but obscure; driving a seemingly endless parade of monstrous treasure ships from one side of the Pacific to the other.

Considering all that which had transpired since the disappearance of Juan Rodriguez it is difficult to resist conjecture. Had Captain Cabrilho survived there remains little doubt he would have himself played an instrumental role in establishing Euro-Chinese trade.

As it was Cabrilho's heirs found themselves ruthlessly severed from participation in an enterprise otherwise facilitated by virtue of their father's own ships.

That American ship building efforts had proven not only outrageously expensive but now obsolete what with the enthusiasm of Filipino carpenters prompting Viceroy Mendoza's successor Don Luis Velasco to rationalize away costs incurred by and as yet unpaid to the Rodriguez estate.

Suggesting coldly that said effort conducted before his advent had been outlandish and regardless the fiscal responsibility of unauthorized renegades. And this despite the fact that in the end predecessor Mendoza as Viceroy had himself appropriated and pressed into service all ships in question.

Rodriguez necessarily having sunk his entire fortune into expediting Alvarado's orders to build said Armada. Establishing a costly Atlantic based headquarters in Honduras, from which take delivery of metalwork (anchors and equipment) shipped in from Spain. Maintaining thousands of Indian retainees employed to retrieve, pack and drag the aforementioned items through mountains and swamps overland where on the Pacific Coast he had literally carved shipbuilding facilities from out of the jungle.

Similarly funded logging, milling and tooling at Ixtapa placing Spain's second and by far and away grander (and yes more expensive) navy into what was then referred to as the great South Sea.

Velasco recognizing that he could now build eighty bigger and better ships in Manila for what it had cost Rodriguez to deliver thirteen, simply refusing repayment of debts incurred by former Adelantado Alvarado, who was dead, and Viceroy Mendoza, who had since been transferred to preside over just conquered Peru. Leaving Cabrilho's family overwhelmed with staggering debt to face eviction at the hands of indifferent creditors.

Shrewdly outmaneuvered heirs of arguably the last conquistador poising any threat to Royal containment of New World enterprise, the Rodriguez estate accepting Velasco's offer of a one way ticket back to Spain in exchange for ownership of Guatemala.

So it was that by disavowing fiscal obligations Don Luis as Viceroy of New Spain successfully annexed an entire Kingdom

(There is no honor amongst thieves).

While at the same time launching a new and glorious era of trade by replacing dangerous renegade conquistadors with subservient merchant venturers.

On June 1, 1578 the first of many wondrously grand galleons sailing out from Manila loaded to the scuppers with it's staggering inventory of spices, tea, musk, porcelain, ivory, camphor, sandalwood, silk, jade and jewels.

Picturesque in the extreme what with five decks, towering bow and even loftier stern, elaborately carved balconies, gilded statues and hanging lanterns. Three monstrous masts being rigged with enormous square sails upon which the royal coat of arms and an image of Philip's patron saint were painted.

Her maiden voyage reading more like a page from one of Robert Louis Stevenson's adventure novels.

As unable to resist such heady temptation, sailors-turned-pirates murdered the galleon's captain, dropped anchor at remote Caroline Island and proceeded with stashing ill-gotten goods by means of which all intended to return incognito as gentlemen of leisure.

When distracted would be bon-vivants left their ship momentarily unattended, honorable chaplain and cabin boy in collusion with a hastily recruited handful of guilt-ridden defectors raising anchor and sailing away, to leave twenty-eight criminals marooned on a desert island.

Subsequent ventures being placed under more careful scrutiny. As soon great galleons flooded New World and European markets both with seemingly endless supplies of much coveted merchandise.

The ships conveying said treasures garnering for themselves an equally rich and permanent place in the literature of adventure while transforming a subverted Spanish Crusade run amuck by juggernaut conquistadors into commercialism and consumerism on a scale previously inconceivable.

All of which precipitated incredible fortunes upon those lucky enough to receive trading concessions from the King.

Who alone claimed as virtual monopoly the world's first global economy.

Sitting supremely empowered as the envy of all Europe. And correspondingly its target. For even as Spanish poet laureate Felix Lope de Vega sang the praises of Philip's gaudy grandeur, English playwright William Shakespeare cautioned,

Greatness courts disaster.

NOVA ALBION

Scrawled alongside cartographer's indications of an Island called California was an oblique breech between New World landmasses identified as the Straits of Anian.

Such anomalies leaving contemporary students of American Explorations baffled.

During the mid sixteenth century English navigator Francis Drake reasoning that if said short cut existed it had to lie somewhere well north of Philip's New Spain.

And accordingly heading out armed with a commission from his Queen, Elizabeth I, to locate what all of England now referred to rather as the Northwest Passage. Intent upon introducing a decidedly British presence into as of yet exclusively Spanish Pacific trade lanes.

Drake's license from Elizabeth for moving on otherwise Ibero America carrying with it a startling and heady caveat.

As in addition to gathering information an otherwise legitimate mariner being ordered to,

Capture and plunder as much Spanish treasure
as possible.

Motivation behind such calculated aggression having little to do with commerce or British plans for colonial expansionism. Simply stated, Elizabeth was fighting for her life.

Less than one hundred years had passed since a successful rescue by Ferdinand and Isabella of both Spain and Catholicism from oblivion.

When their daughter Juana married into the powerful Austrian Habsburg dynasty Iberia becoming not only protectorate of but politically meshed with Charlemagne's Holy Roman Empire.

So it was that Ferdinand's grandson Charles found himself sitting both upon the throne of Spain and, as titular Charles the Great (Charlemagne), guardian and ruler of a decidedly Catholic amalgam.

Prompting Spain to adopt its habitual off the cuff reference of living life in service to,

Ambos Majistados

which is to say both Majesties, or God and the King.

Controlling as he did bodies politic as well as ecclesiastic rendering Charles supremely empowered. Which did not go unnoticed by prominent European families otherwise aligned.

Leading to a courageous and profound diplomatic indictment from Britain's Lord John Acton,

Power tends to corrupt.
And absolute power tends to corrupt absolutely.

In point of fact Charles' reign as King both of Church and State indeed being one of dictated Vatican warrants issued against any perceived threats to Spain, Rome or the Habsburgs.

Precedent for such heady co-mingling of authorities having been set in motion innocently enough by Charlemagne himself. And championed thereafter through Isabella's shared determination to protect Christianity from extinction.

Provoking her launching of Spain's infamous Inquisition. Which Charles leveled as his own personal and very lethal weapon against any and all dissidence.

Playing god on earth, ordering a litany of torture and executions on behalf of Spain and in collusion with Rome against not only Muslim and Jew but any Protesting Catholic (Protestant).

An ultimately guilt ridden monarch denouncing at age sixty both thrones to seek refuge in absolution through penance as a cloistered monk.

Yet in handing over unprecedented keys of heaven and earth to his son Philip, inadvertently unleashing a monster even more terrible then himself.

Philip fixating upon Charlemagne. Through an illusory genealogy referring to himself rather as Eldest son of the Church.

Then as such zealously accelerating his father's abandoned attrocities in a desperate attempt to contain mounting apostasy. And thus as,

Christ's firstborn

transforming all of Europe into a Naboth's vineyard.

Breaching the schism occasioned when England's Henry VIII denounced Rome in favor of instituting his own Church, by removing heir apparent Edward VI. Whose death under mysterious circumstances left Edward's sister, devoutly Catholic Mary Tudor, seated upon Britain's throne and promptly married off to Philip.

Philip and Mary effectively squelching the rebellion begun by Henry. Ordering clergy since married as per a heretic Church of England to dispense with their wives while demanding restoration of Catholic Mass in full panoply.

Any objecting religious being expeditiously burned at the stake. Of course mounting persecution against Protestants but bolstering their ranks. As by torching them Catholic Inquisitioners succeeded only in igniting a candle that has yet to be extinguished.

When Mary died unexpectedly Philip moved quickly to request the hand of her cousin and suddenly heir apparent Elizabeth.

Who, as a child of divorce deemed illegitimate in the eyes of Rome, maneuvered through a Catholic world while nonetheless understandably sympathetic with those harboring differing theological and political viewpoints.

Upon her ascendancy recognizing that she alone sat as the only monarch potent enough to stand up against Spanish domination through manipulation of the Church. Whilst understanding clearly the political advantages of remaining Catholic and in full communion with Rome.

Surely Pope Sixtus V would rectify the little matter of illegitimacy surrounding her birth should she tender assurances with regard to England's continued orthodoxy.

And there remained the menace of Elizabeth's devoutly Catholic cousin Mary Stuart as otherwise heir to England's throne. Who brought her own insurance with regard to religious unanimity and correspondingly protection from Spain.

Yet Elizabeth declined Philip's politically motivated marriage proposal while as an aside daringly breathing new life into King Henry's Church of England.

Reasoning afterall that she sat empowered as Queen of England only because of her father Henry and uncle Edward's since subverted English Reformation.

Still, openly opposing Philip was but to commit more than political suicide. As having herself dabbled with Anglicanism she stood to lose far more than mere sovereignty over the British Isles.

Accordingly fighting for her life Elizabeth as Anglicanism's rising star discovering in commoner Francis Drake a like minded and worthy champion.

Drake's father Edmund had been ordained a priest in the Church of Rome. When Elizabeth's father ousted

Catholicism and confiscated Tavistock Abbey, the priest married and sired son Francis.

Whom Father Edmund apprenticed to seafaring Uncle William Hawkins of Devon.

Neither rigid Catholic nor ardent Anglican, Hawkins attending either service depending upon his port of call.

So it was that Francis learned both to negotiate amongst foreign merchants and deal with officials from differing religious mindsets.

His acquired tolerance ending abruptly however upon receipt of news that Edmund Drake had been sentenced and burned at the stake by reinstated Catholic Tribunals for refusing to renounce an otherwise lawful under Anglican Church parameters marriage to young Drake's mother.

Burning with righteous indignation Francis and Cousin John Hawkins responding by attacking and plundering Catholic Spanish ships.

Experienced as he had become in matters of shipping and trade, Drake reasoning that if England was to forestall the atrocities and political aggressions of Catholic Spain she must somehow sever the pipeline of New World treasure and commerce that fueled it.

So it was that Francis sensed nothing of ambiguity or moral conflict in his Queen's subsequent charge to clandestinely capture and destroy anything Spanish and hence Catholic.

Imbued with this crusader ethic Drake beginning his reconnaissance of the Pacific Ocean in 1579 not by means of a Northwest Passage but around Spanish South America.

Where off the coast of Chile near Arica he sank his first Catholic ship.

And continued wreaking similar havoc while advancing northward.

Encountering a Manila galleon off the north central coast of Mexico.

Laden with twenty-six tons of gold, silver, jewelry and plate, the unsuspecting Plus Ultra <u>La Senora de la Concepcion</u> sailing unarmed.

His own ship <u>The Pelican</u> had been built for stealth. And thus with ease chased down and sacked what those who commandeered her referred to rather as the cumbersome <u>Cacafuego</u>.

Thereafter forcing Catholic shipmaster Antonio Morera to endure a prayer, by way of which Drake delivered Elizabeth's message to Philip.

Confiscation of the <u>Cacafuego's</u> cargo
is being executed by Elizabeth, Queen of England,
in the name of God in heauen,
so that God's people might be protected
from a king who presumes the right of dictating
to the Almighty.

Following which Morera and his men were each paid

with Spanish gold reales from out of their own confiscated strongboxes before obliged to seek "salvation" by swimming for a mainland looming but one mile off port bow.

Anglican privateers thereafter stuffing <u>The Pelican's</u> gullet with so much treasure as to jeopardize its soundness. Then rechristening her the <u>Golden Hinde</u> (Golden Grouper or Big Golden Fish).

Fearful his overloaded vessel might in fact break apart and sink, Drake opting to make landfall so as to stash excess loot and strengthen bulwarks. Which he did along the vagary of a far afield land of myth.

Of course Spain held no monopoly on lands of myth. The people who gave to Montalvo and the world such heroes as King Arthur and Merlin standing in possession of equally marvelous tales surrounding the landscapes of their own legend.

Handing down from obscurity a rich oral tradition suggesting those first to inhabit England having been led by a giant warlord named Gogmagog. Whom Trojan warrior Brutus subdued in battle.

Prodigy referring to themselves everafter as Britons after Brutus.

Britons christening their island home Albion (white banks), as alabaster cliffs,

> soared out of the Sea of the Franks
> along the Island's southwest coast.

After burying the crucified man/god Jesus Christ in his own tomb, Joseph of Arimathea setting off to proselytize amongst these inhabitants of Albion.

Countless otherwise pagans yielding before his missionary zeal.

Vowing as Christ's servants (Knights) to replace ignorance, greed and abuse of power with a new society founded upon the Christian tenets of

Love, valor and compassion.

This genesis of Knighthood evoked from a hauntingly beautiful country covered with misty forests inhabited still by goblins, pixies and dragons bestowing upon England its first civilized by Western standards and singularly transcendent community:

The castles of the knights
stand on hilltops
above the towns and villages,

And from these eminences
the knightly class protects the farmers and craftsmen
who toil diligently in the lowlands.

The country is rich in gold, silver and precious stones.
From which artisans and metalworkers fashion
extraordinary weapons and armour
for their knights.

Surrounding pagan kingdoms
grew to envy the richness of Albion
and made frequent attacks upon it.

Resulting in a state of almost continuous war
which had an unhappy effect upon its politics.

To such an extent
that the knights themselves
quarreled over concerns of military leadership.

As a consequence disunity arose.
Facilitating powerful pagan Pendragon's rise to
power.

Who in time
through military might,
magic and guile
came to maintain control over the knights.

When Drake's ship hove to and dropped anchor
alongside the soaring white cliffs of a bay that would
everafter bare his name, this Briton who would
himself soon be knighted for courage displayed
against a monarch no less threatening than evil
Pendragon, saw before him not Montalvo's California
nor even New Spain, but rather a new Albion.

And so christened northern California's pale
barrancas and misty forests,

And that for two causes;
the one in respect of the white bancks and cliffes,
which lie toward the sea;

the other, that it might haue some affinity,
euen in name also, with our own country,
which was sometime so called.

Spending thirty six days within the confines of what is today Point Reyes National Seashore making necessary repairs to the <u>Golden Hinde</u> whilst offloading and burying treasure for later retrieval.

During which time,

Our Generall

was approached by emissaries of a Coast Miwok hioh (chieftain).

Whose oration and horrific displays of self-mutilation suggested to Drake that the pagan population of New Albion had received him as though a god.

Miwok elders in fact mistaking pallid, white Britons arriving as they did in a winged and presumably supernatural vessel as, rather, ghosts.

Subsequent and frantic staging of ritual dirges being hastily carried out in hopes of exorcising the same.

Only after much wailing and bloodletting before perplexed Englishmen did they perceive their folly. Thereafter approaching Drake cautiously. Petitioning to touch and prod at him.

The cross cultural touching and prodding that followed so thoroughly enjoyed mutually that a bonnet of woodpecker feathers was placed upon Drake's head to announce his acceptance into the tribe.

An act interpreted by the Englishman as rather Miwok abdication of sovereignty.

Drake's Chaplain Francis Fletcher reporting that the indigenous population of New Albion had:

cheerfully relinquished all claim and title of their province to Her Gracious Majesty, Queen Elizabeth I.

And solemnized the occasion by presiding over California's first Anglican prayer service. Whereupon:

Our Generall caused to be set vp
a monument of our being there,
as also of her Maiesties and successors right and title
to that kingdome;
namely, a plate of brasse,
fast nailed to a great and firme poste;

whereon is engrauen her graces name,
and the day and yeare of our arriual there,
and of the free giuing vp of the prouince
and kingdome, both by the king and people,
into her Maiesties hands:

together with her highnesse picture and armes,
in a peece of sixpence currant English monie,
shewing itselfe by a hole made of purpose through
the plate;

vnderneath was likewise engrauen the name
of our Generall, etc.

Chaplain Fletcher's accounting containing full disclosure of Elizabeth's newest acquisition:

The inland we found to be farre different from the shoare,

A goodly country,
and fruitfull soyle,
stored with many blessings fit for the vse of man.

Fitted out with very large and fat Deere,
which there we sawe by thousands, as we supposed,
in a heard.

Then tossing out that which could not help but to rivet a royal's attentions,

There is no part of earth heere to be taken up,
wherein one does not find some probable shew of
gold or silver.

Not surprisingly then as she dined at Deptford Port on board England's first ship ever to circumnavigate the globe and following proclamation of the same as a monument to be preserved, Elizabeth listened with intent fascination whilst Drake proposed schemes for launching, courtesy of the four million dollars netted from a plundered <u>Cacafuego</u>, New Albion in that land of white cliffs, misty forests, oversized deer and his own buried treasure on the far side of the world.

A scheme undone however by secret negotiations carried on between England's ambassador to Spain and several of Drake's men. Each of whom conspired to secure Albion's treasures for themselves.

Elizabeth's response becoming the catch phrase of an escalating Cold War,

They should take who have the power.
And they should keep who can.

even before knighting Drake as champion of the realm.

With such deadly competitive maneuverings between England and Spain but underscoring a deepening rivalry that was to hold far-reaching implications even for a country, claims of an English knight notwithstanding, the rest of the world would continue to hail as California.

Spain having reached full flower quite literally ruling the world. Her cadre of brave and capable admirals, generals and merchant-venturers extending daily a global sphere of Catholic influence.

Staggering amounts of gold and other precious metals from across New Spain and Peru together with all the riches of the Orient via Manila bolstering an unprecedented economy.

Funding, amongst other things, construction of the world's largest building. From which Philip now presided over his globe spanning empire both as King of Spain and Emperor of Rome.

Denouement to such outrageous commercial success being the immortalization of Montalvo's fictitious Conquista as referenced in Miguel Cervantes' just released and timeless masterpiece Don Quixote.

A book which in essence ended the genre of often lurid romance novels even as Philip attempted to destroy all physical evidence of the same.

Charles had long since tired of seeing his very real Conquista sullied with terminology from fictional profanities scribbled endlessly across maps, charts and notes delivered to the Habsburg Palace.

Now from Spanish Escorial his fanatical son Philip not only banning reading of such deemed as pornographic literature but ordering it be burned.

With marvelous histrionics Cervantes casting Inquisitor Tomas Torquemada in the personage of Don Quixote's own book burning priest. Who having acquired a taste for the writings of fictional chronicler "Montalvan" in particular,

Verily neighbor, his is the best book in the world,

spared an otherwise condemned work from the pyre.

Curiously Montalvan's compositions so loved by the fictional priest being, of course, the most lewd and scandalous of all.

Prompting a fictional household to demand exorcism of Quixote's library, for fear of evil enchanters perhaps yet residing in said mischievous tome.

Cervante's would see spared Charlemagne, Roland and Amadis. Yet few bothered lifting a hand to rescue from Philip's wrath most texts torched. Where today even amongst the Spanish but a trifling are remembered.

Many of the romances recited so enthusiastically by Don Quixote having long since been swept from memory without any help from his housekeeper's broom.

Regrettably the very non-fictional Philip burning more than books. Perpetrating outrageous crimes against humanity. Shaking Christianity to its very foundations.

Presaging demise of Charlemagne's Holy Roman Empire what with growing ranks of Protesting Catholics rising up united against a maniacal King's insidious Inquisition.

Prolonged civil war in France had itself been largely responsible for rendering Spain and the Habsburgs supremely empowered. European rivalries older than history left emasculated and controlled under the sovereignty of an otherwise alien government now holding court on the Iberian Peninsula.

With the advent of Protestant reformers both in Germany and Switzerland aided in no small measure by the amorous propensities of Britain's Henry VIII, rifts already dividing Europe deepening.

Philip's petition for Elizabeth's hand in marriage prompting similarly politically motivated overtures for alliance with the British from the French.

Ultimately refusing Catholicism and Protestantism both, Elizabeth choosing instead to marry England, as it were. And thereby protecting British sovereignty.

An act which polarized European players. Across the continent religious banners like those of Medievel crusaders past being hastily paraded into battle, so many small-minded, easily manipulated men, touting conflicting messages of a conquering god fed them by various and sundry vested interests.

With most adhering to whichever dogma best served their own political agenda. Throwing the entire continent into a wasteful era of escalated warfare and destruction.

Rendering California a hideout for copycat Protestant and Anglican pirates, whose only purpose in plundering Catholic Spanish galleons was albeit under the guise of piety but one of personal gain. Transforming remote New Albion into an uncharted buccaneer ally alongwhich many a devout sailor met his ignominious end.

Knight of the realm Drake himself through annihilation of the Spanish Armada succeeding with bringing Philip's superpower to its knees.

There having ever been something ethereal with regard to Iberian domination of Europe and the World.

And when presented with a very authentic opportunity of reining in and securing global pre-eminence she capitulated through reckless arrogance.

Notorious Philip II serving as but the first in a succession of worthless favorites remembered to history as the Three Horrible Philips. Each of whom squandered Hispania's golden opportunity for establishing sustained domination.

In the end King Philip IV ruling and ruining the Spanish Empire.

Meanwhile a Protestant/ Anglican challenge so early playing itself out even in the distant arena of far-off

California presaging all that which was to follow.

The noble knight Sir Francis Drake of Britain having hurled down his gauntlet before a supremely empowered Spanish dragon.

Godsmacked Philip II as dragon on the otherhand remaining convinced that heretic Drake had discovered the Straits of Anian.

And sitting consumed with the fear that by way of which England might at any moment seize both Anian and Quivira to rein terror and destruction down upon his Pacific trade lanes.

When Philip's ambassador to the British alerted him of Elizabeth's plans for colonizing New Albion a publicly humiliated monarch thus compelled to take extraordinary actions. As doing anything less than shoring up control over New Spain in particular was to risk losing altogether his lucrative Euro-Chinese trade.

All of which lent extraordinary importance to previously sublimated California.

SAFE HARBOR

An exhaustive search for those imaginary Straits of Anian or Northwest Passage would preoccupy both Spanish and English explorations throughout the next century.

During which time merchant- venturers operating under license from Catholic Spain generated escalating profit margins through trans-oceanic trade with the Orient.

Meanwhile the hardships for men laboring aboard massive floating treasure ships proving innumerable.

Typhoons ever threatening, as did the dreaded scourge and cruel torture of scurvy. Starvation and thirst assured should any anomaly impose delay.

Off California cumbersome transports then but taunted by notorious "southeasters" threatening to drive them aground.

With the advent of French/Agnostic corsairs, English/Anglican privateers and Dutch/Protestant pirates monitoring like wolves a western horizon for the white sails of approaching opportunity rendering circumstances surrounding an already difficult proposition desperate.

Unknown numbers of galleons chased down and plundered. Countless terrified Catholics left shipwrecked and vulnerable to the dangers of a mysterious land occupied by equally secret peoples and beasts.

The extraordinary hike back to civilization in 1579 of men left marooned by Francis Drake bringing both problems of mortality upon the high seas as well as incessant piracy to the front doorsteps of a concerned Viceroy's palace at Mexico City.

> These white men in so strange a territory
> having been the amazement
> of a land filled with savages.

Prompting Don Martin Enriquez to respond with plans for reigning in mounting problems along an increasingly dangerous northwestern littoral.

So it was that even as Pedro de Unamuno prepared to depart from Manila at the helm of yet another vulnerable floating transport he received unexpected and confidential orders.

Phrased in the form of a request from Viceroy Enriquez that he risk lingering in California's pirate alley long enough to scout for well-positioned and safe harbors from which to secure Spanish commerce through installation of fortifications.

Dutifully Unamuno accepting an impossible commission. The impracticality of conducting investigative reconnoitering from the deck of a galleon not only void of defenses but so unmanageable as to require six men at the helm being obvious even to a layman.

And accordingly understandably cautious, sailing his San Anselmo with such timidity and so far afield that it wasn't until attaining Morro (Moor) Bay,

(Beware, there be Moors along the Coast)

that he even came within visual contact of California.

A cloud of arrows served up generously by resolute Costanoans curtailing attempts made thereafter to dock in what proved regardless an at best inadequate estuary. Either fearful of the great beast beaching itself upon their shore or perhaps already familiar with the sorts of characters such monsters divulged, local clans anxiously chasing the thing away.

Happily Unamuno obliging, what with his own anxiety concerning pirates, a crew already stricken by scurvy and reward from the Viceroy notwithstanding visions of gold coin awaiting him either way at Acapulco from merchants ready to purchase treasures stowed in his cargo bay.

Don Pedro's but sketchy report bringing Enriquez acute disappointment. Arriving as it did on the heels of news concerning pillaging off Cabo San Lucas by Drake's cousin, privateer Richard Hawkins.

In 1595 Don Luis Velasco as newly posted Viceroy anxiously extending a secret contract of his own. Galleon master Sebastian Rodriguez Cermenho responding by hastily recruiting assistance from navigator extraordinare Francisco Bolanos.

Who recognizing the importance of achieving Velasco's objectives agreed to risk everything-- and lost.

The tragedy of <u>San Augustin</u> commencing at Cape Mendocino when upon sighting land Bolanos determined to maintain visual contact with the same. Only to predictably find himself caught up by those often violent southeast gales.

Which at Drake's Bay no less ran his massive vessel aground. High surf pounding it to pieces. Scattering a fortune in beeswax, silk and fine porcelain across the beaches of what is today Sonoma County.

A distraught merchant venturer crowding seventy grateful-to-be-alive sailors into the small launch fortuitously thrown on board for the express purpose of coastal reconnoitering.

And in which all now conducted their increasingly perilous twenty-five hundred-mile voyage back to Acapulco. Shamefaced Bolanos regardless charting the coast gingerly skirted in route.

Dutifully maintaining copious notes concerning an equally gracious reception by Drake's Miwok together with his own numerous sightings of those unusually large deer (actually elk) reported previously by the English. Whilst purposefully dispelling any notion of a New Albion when comparing that which he beheld not with England but rather Castile.

A report subsequently delivered to Viceroy Velasco's succedaneum Gaspar de Zuniga Acevedo y Fonseca, the Count of Monterey.

Who identified immediately as sheer lunacy the deployment of massive tradeships out on exploratory maneuvers.

Yet compelled by King Philip III to,

explore and seize hold of California

ordered three small brigantines be built for the express purpose of charting and containing that which remained yet a snarl.

With departing Velasco urging Acevedo call upon as overseer for his carefully conceived operation an anything but common commoner by the name of Sebastian Vizcaino.

Who while soldiering had faced off with Protestants at Flanders in Spanish nether lands long before encountering them again upon the high seas along California's heatedly contested coast.

An opportunity presented thereafter to seek fame and fortune in New World trade having launched the ambitious country boy on a road to stunning personal fortunes.

When in 1585 Sebastian swung his Manila galleon the Santa Ana around Cabo San Lucas only to find himself face to face in a maritime standoff with England's Sir Thomas Cavendish.

Vizcaino's loss calculated in far more than surrendered merchandise. As after offloading captain and crew Cavendish left all marooned by cavalierly setting fire to their ship.

Still fortune seeming ever to favor Sebastian. Who watched as in the wake of a storm his burning galleon drifted ashore.

Flames successfully extinguished, Vizcaino conducting all safely back to Acapulco in little better than the burned out hull of a ship shot through with cannon balls.

His repugnance for the heretic Protestant now rivaling that of Drake's disdain for Catholicism.

And thusly fired both by religious ardor as well as a determination to protect his own vested interests, had approached Viceroy Velasco directly with an offer to explore, colonize and thereby stabilize California and at his own expense.

In exchange for which he requested but the right to develop and exploit a region otherwise filled with limitless possiblities.

Velasco's immediate attempt to appoint the self-made captain of commerce not going unchallenged by cabildos (councils) of well-positioned hidalgos each clamoring for their own opportunity to cash in on America.

As following the Cortes debacle, titled men in collusion with the Crown had established a now seemingly all-powerful Supreme Council of the Indies. Which from its headquarters at Seville maintained autonomous aristocratic control over all commercial enterprise carried on throughout both America as well as in the Orient by virtue of its required authorization with regard to selecting players whilst otherwise closely scrutinizing all royal appointees.

Understandably a commoner the likes of Vizcaino having no allies present on such a Council. Rather, sitting as impediments being wealthy and powerful individuals intrigued by his proposal and now determined to execute the same but without him.

And so to commandeer Sebastian's dream while ridding themselves of his presence arguing that this son of a sheepherder possessed neither the education nor necessary capital required for carrying out such grand schemes.

In truth Vizcaino's but modest by comparison resources and lack of formal schooling armed less capable critics with more than sufficient ammunition against him.

There was for example his simple and awkward approach to Christianity.

Exposed when commissioned to establish trade with Emperor Iyeyasu of Japan. Where unable to restrain personal passion for Christ, Sebastian informed the man esteemed by his own people as god incarnate that Catholic Spain's true desire was not merely one of developing commercial relationships but rather to be awarded an opportunity of bringing him certain knowledge concerning the one **true** God.

An impatient emperor sending his impertinent suitor back to New Spain carrying a curt memorandum addressed to His Most Catholic Majesty:

> Our countries are far apart.
> And navigation is difficult.

Pray do not come again.

Leaving even devotee Velasco with doubts concerning Vizcaino's diplomatic capacities.

Regardless the Viceroy testing his champion further by tendering contracts for establishing a fortified colony along the known to be difficult coast of Lower California.

And was not surprised when Sebastian promptly recruited missionaries to aid him with accomplishing an effectual spiritual conquest of the province as well.

At Puerto de La Paz this determined would-be knight of the old school together with his Christian emissaries finding themselves forced to abandon their but tentative beachhead at the point of a spear thrust menacingly by equally old school

pagan savages.

Characteristically resilient, Sebastian not hesitating to petition Velasco anew for permission to try again. Certain that given another chance he might yet subdue,

that which Cortes himself had twice failed to conquer.

Such tenacity and piety were awe-inspiring to a Viceroy who in passing his gauntlet recommended that successor Acevedo not only endorse but bankroll Vizcaino with funds from the Royal Treasury:

In addition to possessing a practical knowledge of
the South Sea
and being a man of even disposition
upright
and of good intentions,
he is of medium yet sufficient ability
(although I had feared it otherwise)
for governing his people.

And this is coupled with energy
enough to make himself respected by them.

GULLIVER'S TRAVELS

Sagacious enough to recognize at his disposal a man capable of facing down both Protestant pirates as well as pagan savages should either be encountered, Acevedo did not hesitate in recruiting, funding and presenting Vizcaino with what proved to be arguably the most beautiful ships ever to grace Oceanus Pacificus.

Each built for stealth yet all three, the <u>San Diego</u>, <u>Santo Tomas</u> and <u>San Vicente</u> spared nothing by way of ornamentation.

Nor would be Sebastian, who found himself draped not only in a regal uniform but also with entitlement as Capitan/General so as to outmaneuver detractors and thus facilitate further advancement.

Correspondingly the team Vizcaino himself assembled being equally impressive. Beginning with his recruitment of previously overlooked former pilot of the failed Cermenho voyage Francisco Bolanos (who arguably knew more about the California coastline than any other man alive).

And predictably Franciscan missionaries (four to be exact) so as to keep the entire endeavor spiritually on track.

All of whom together with a crew of one hundred and thirty five set sail in the spring of 1602 for a dangerously contested coast.

Arriving on the heels of their departure were orders from Seville demanding royal patents for the Count of Monterey's California enterprise be awarded rather to Marquee of Montesclaros Don Gabriel Maldonado.

Acevedo's bold response not attempting to disguise his own apparent sense of gleeful satisfaction,

Too late!
Lord Vizcaino is already on his way there.

Lord Vizcaino's miniature galleons spending six months waging battle against those headwinds and that contrary current that had so impeded the progress of Juan Rodriguez Cabrilho.

While additionally burdened with having to watch out for pirates.

The Viceroy warning Sebastian that Dutch Protestant Oliver Van Noort reportedly lie in wait for him somewhere north of Cabo San Lucas.

Gratefully Acevedo's champion caught no sight of his nemesis.

Still an enemy more deadly than buccaneers did attack, broadsiding the expedition with a vengeance.

Purple spots broke out upon our flesh.

Teeth were loosened in our gums.
Even so that, unawares, we spit them out.

While sharp pains
shot through our bones,
making us all the more sensitive to the keen,
cold winds.

Scurvy claiming the lives of eighteen men even before the little flotilla reached what is today recognized as Southern California.

Where on November 10th all three ships dropped anchor at Cabrilho's Bay of San Miguel. And immediately landed a crew for the express purpose of setting up hospital and obtaining fresh water, medicinals and whatever foodstuffs might be bartered for from,

naked savages,
besmeared in paint
and festooned with feathers.

As feast day for favored by Philip III Saint Didacus (San Diego) fell on the morrow, arrangements were made to conduct an appropriate observance.

During which and despite instructions contrariwise Lord Vizcaino changed the harbor's name from San Miguel to rather San Diego, in honor both of Saint and of his own somewhat battered capitana.

Vizcaino too detected the almost immediate and striking contrast between these landscapes which had so caught Cabrilho's admiration and those of the barren coastline skirted previously.

Seventeenth century southern California presenting a very agreeable setting indeed what with its:

forests of oak,
shrubs resembling rosemary in savor,
and many fragrant and wholesome plants…

mildness of climate…

excellence of the soil…

harbor abounding with fish,
flats with shellfish,
and woods with wild game.

Fray (Brother) Antonio de la Ascension further noting traces of golden pyrite in the sand at his feet on the beach, from which he quite accurately deduced the presence of gold in mountains surrounding.

Eyeing Eden with calculated fascination Vizcaino noting that San Diego presented,

an excellent location for a permanent settlement.

And in subsequent supplications both to the Almighty as well as Acevedo petitioned for an opportunity to launch the same.

San Diego being the kind of harbor a challenged Spanish monarch needed further north, in the vicinity of Cabo (Cape) Mendocino, where most galleons first came within sight of land.

More than six months into it and the adventure was just beginning for Sebastian's intrepid band of Iberian adventurers.

An adventure that would soon rival both in oddness and unsolved mysteries even the yet to be released fictional parodies of Lemuel Gulliver.

When at what is now Avalon on the Island Vizcaino christened Santa Catalina all eyed Cabrilho's Bay of Fire from afar.

And while no flames were visible, spiraling smoke from countless unidentifiable sources draped what is today Los Angeles with a veil of haze.

Vizcaino wasting little time himself in dousing the fire by again altering charts so as to bestow the name Bay of a Thousand Smokes upon Cabrilho's curiosity while simultaneously countering previous references of Hell when pronouncing upon its principal headland the name of Heaven's gatekeeper, Saint Peter (San Pedro).

Then discovering Santa Catalina to be populated by the white, blonde, blue eyed priests of man/god Chinigchinich.

Attempts made to locate he with golden hair who had descended from heaven like a bird yielding only the discovery of his temple.

In which Brother Antonio saw but a trick by the Devil to subterfuge worship of Heaven's one true god. Ordering that the shrine together with its phallic idol dressed out in sea otter skins and condor feathers be destroyed.

Whereupon anxious locals pled that Vizcaino take leave or risk his own destruction at the hands of pilgrims even then in route aboard a curious drogher.

Compromised Sebastian capitulating.

Only to be greeted off the coast of Santa Barbara by a flotilla of Chumash tomols conducting as escort colorfully draped in elk skins Indian King Matilija.

Who after boarding the <u>San Diego</u> enticed his guests ashore with a promise of,

       ten women for every man on board.

Scarlet-faced Ascencion insisting the chieftain's gracious hospitality be refused. Vizcaino countering to appease both chaplain and chief, with liberal distribution of religious tokens as an expression of gratitude for gracious hospitality extended by these peoples of the surrounding islands and coast.

From Santa Barbara northward the mysterious landscape disappearing completely behind a cloak of fog so dense as to render any investigation futile.

Seven days spent skirting presumably from a safe distance what is now Big Sur. With landfall remaining impossible to detect.

When at seven o'clock on the evening of December 16th a ponderous marine shroud lifted to reveal the magnificent moonlit sweep of Monterey Bay.

From their safe vantagepoint all observing great bears gathering on the beach to feed upon the stranded carcass of a whale.

In the light of dawn Spaniards witnessing herds of the

very big deer reported by Sir Francis Drake, which Vizcaino noted as being,

even larger than cows.

Meanwhile scurvy continued to plague the expedition. Having claimed fourteen more lives just since taking leave of San Diego.

Contrary headwinds and current, not to mention that damnable fog, too, persisting.

All of which had conspired to place the venture far behind schedule and, correspondingly, dangerously low on provisions.

So it was that giant beasts notwithstanding Vizcaino elected to put ashore.

Where beneath the canopy of a great oak California's would-be founding father established yet another emergency beachfront hospital. From which men were again dispatched to secure fresh water and whatever foodstuffs and medicinals might be obtained this time from resident Rumsen Ohlone.

Having arrived on the Feast Day of Santa Lucia, Brother Antonio accordingly making arrangements for conducting a celebratory mass. Following which Vizcaino convened an emergency council to assist him in determining how best to proceed.

All agreed they man the <u>Santo Tomas</u> with those disabled by sickness and send it back carrying a report to Viceroy Acevedo concerning the expedition's progress.

Which arrived at Mazatlan three months later with but nine of its thirty- man crew. Underscoring dramatically an already understood need for installation of that supply point and way station in California.

Meanwhile the <u>San Diego</u> and <u>San Vicente</u> forged onward. Again contending with a coastline obscured. Which perhaps explains why neither ship detected the narrow portal of a coastal sanctuary far grander than any Spain might ever have imagined. San Francisco Bay remaining undisclosed.

On January 12, 1603 Sebastian attaining Cape Mendocino. Which Viceroy Acevedo had noted as being more or less the expedition's northernmost objective.

With but six men well enough to keep the deck, and encountering,

so much rain and fog
as to throw us into great doubt whether to yet brave
going forward or to turn back,
for it was as dark in the daytime
as at night,

ultimately nature, and not a Viceroy's latitude, forcing the expedition into an effectual retreat.

As again lost in the fog while still waging war against disease Vizcaino turned about to hasten home.

Whereupon the <u>San Diego</u> became separated from the <u>San Vicente</u>.

Neither encountering the other again until February when both vessels wallowed in to the same small harbor near Mazatlan that had earlier received a similarly distressed <u>Santo Tomas</u>.

Of the less than glorious return Sebastian recording that his men arrived,

in the greatest affliction and travail ever experienced
by Spaniards; for the sick were crying aloud,
while those who were yet able to walk,
or to at least move on all fours,
were, nonetheless, unable to manage the sails.

God in pity conducting us.

Despite his own sustained injuries incurred when thrust from out of bed during high seas, Vizcaino setting off on foot to secure help from local villagers.

Nearly four more weeks passing before that which was left of the venture attaining Acapulco.

Faced with yet another in a long string of extremely challenging and failed enterprises, an indomitable man girding up his broken ribs to pen for patron Acevedo the most optimistic report possible.

Resulting in an arguably embellished treatise, with the fact remaining that Sebastian had to deliver a safe harbor somewhere in the neighborhood of Mendocino or risk any hope of further involvement from an openly hostile Council of the Indies.

Exaggerations concerning his portrayal of Monte-rey as,

a famous (meaning exceptional) harbor

in particular being directed at maintaining King Philip's attentions focused both upon Sebastian and California.

And predictably received by the Count of Monterey with great enthusiasm.

Breathtakingly beautiful, Monterey Bay is nevertheless not an exceptional harbor by any stretch of the Spanish imagination.

Nor had Vizcaino discovered it.

His navigator Francisco Bolanos already having reported the anomaly's existence seven years earlier. Yet, Sebastian had to "discover" something exceptional. And all things considered Monterey would have to do.

It was a ploy that worked.

Acevedo awarding Vizcaino command of the next Manila- bound galleon (franchises worth a personal fortune). With an understanding that his champion would use said windfall for the express purpose of returning to colonize both Monterey and San Diego.

Council members at Seville intent themselves upon controlling exploitation of the Orient as well as California thereafter employing every means available to forestall Vizcaino's receipt of said concessions. But without success.

That is until Acevedo found himself being transferred to serve as Viceroy of Peru. Whereupon supplemental funds from the Royal treasury earmarked for Vizcaino's enterprise found themselves redirected by Vice-regal successor Maldonado.

Who kept California's conquistador otherwise occupied with the far less expensive wild goose chase of searching after non- existent reputedly mineral laden Pacific islands.

Thereafter appointing,

the nobleman of less than noble birth

as alcalde (a civil posting akin to mayor/ justice of the peace) at Tehuantepec; smugly deeming said honor sufficiently grand for a sheepherder's son who had dared forestall entitlements otherwise due himself.

Vizcaino living comfortably, yet ever anxious concerning California.

All the while Viceroy Maldonado finding other more self serving ways in which to spend money allotted by the King for Sebastian's enterprise.

Such reprehensible behavior on the part of a Marquee but heralding more than a century of similar opportunism.

Enter the House of Bourbon.

Eighty years of continental warfare driven by a Protestant Reformation having all but undone the

Habsburg Dynasty, an allied with the Habsburgs Constable of Bourbon finding himself unexpectedly installed as monarch of not only France but Spain and much of Italy as well.

Under a Family Compact the Bourbons reigning over a Catholic world while themselves becoming increasingly dependent upon individuals capable of funding their own enterprises. Which many offered to do in exchange for patents to exploit for personal gain while simultaneously promising advancement of the Bourbon's Empire.

Of course the only objectives ever advanced seeming to be but enhancement of the personal fortunes of those making the promises.

So it was that while the Sea of Cortes would be plundered for its rich harvests of pearls, little if any efforts were made to otherwise colonize California.

With the extraordinarily expensive undertaking having itself been plundered by greedy Maldonado, a second bankrolling simply never materializing.

Sebastian dying awaiting allocated funding he would never see.

Yet although cruelly denied his hard-sought right to establish California nonetheless honored ever after by lasting nomenclature and the glamour he had himself ascribed to it.

With the Bourbon's realization that there were no Straits of Anian nor fabulously wealthy Indian kingdoms to be exploited, justification for additional expenditures on behalf of California evaporating together with it's own infamous fogbanks.

Leaving Vizcaino's "Island" of mystery and sensuous beauty to languish in an intermittent mist for another one hundred and sixty years.

Meanwhile mere mention of fabulous and far-off Monterey igniting with mounting enthusiasm all the pundits of Europe.

Vizcaino's California becoming so enmeshed in the public's mind with that of Montalvo's that as late as 1647 writer/historian Bisselius warning travelers to be wary of the great bears, giant deer and griffins inhabiting it:

And this is not a fable
but the truth!

Monterey itself, thereafter surfacing in that brilliant bit of satire, written to expose the antics of royal families not unlike the Habsburgs and Bourbons. As according to Lemuel Gulliver (aka Jonathan Swift) it stood adjacent to Brobdingnag (which, incidentally was inhabited by giants) and,

very near to the land of the Lilliputs.

Set in motion by Sebastian's own enthusiastic sales pitch, California's Monte-rey garnering accolades better applied to a sister and mammoth estuary, the presence of which remained either undiscovered or unreported.

As embellishments were magnified with each recounting and to such an extent that when Spain did return nearly two centuries later her cautious soldiers kept an eye out for giants and monstrous flying beasts. Iberian magistrates standing upon its very shore finding Vizcaino's exceptional harbor impossible to identify.

BLACK ROBES

Torn asunder by a Catholic Inquisition and otherwise ill conceived protectionist policies, Charlemagne's once glorious Holy Roman Empire collapsed. Rendering Spain in the aftermath of a Protestant Reformation divorced from not only its former alliance with the Habsburgs, but ultimately sustained loss of France and the Netherlands as well.

And while outright bankruptcy resulting from a grand scale family squabble remembered to history as the Seven Years War was successfully averted, yet the Bourbons as Papal protectorates by default awoke to find themselves in dire financial straits.

Where earlier Constable Bourbon had like the cavalry ridden to rescue a Habsburg controlled Catholic Empire during the reign of Charles V (by capturing both Rome and a renegade Pope), the eighteenth century debacle bequeathed King Fernando VI de Bourbon proving even more daunting and ultimately impossible.

Meanwhile preoccupied with maintaining control over her dwindling sphere of European influence while attempting to restructure the same, Spain's American concerns receiving little more than implementation of new measures by means of which to further exploit them.

In truth the Spanish no longer able to afford their New World Empire. Yet doomed to extinction without it.

When King Fernando's momentary and glorious flourish of political and financial realignment between Church and State ended with his unexpected descent into insanity, both an Iberian superpower as well as the Roman papacy standing authentically threatened.

Ascendancy of Charles III de Bourbon as Crown head of State and Pontifical protectorate proving if not providential than serendipitously fortunate.

For embodied within a man otherwise comedic in appearance was the extraordinarily rare combination of genuine piety, brilliant intellect and courage enough to deploy both against barbarism and ignorance.

Perceived at first as but the awkward, timid and potentially ineffective inheritor of not only Fernando's throne but quite possibly his insanity, this man otherwise referred to by a largely Hispanic constituency as Don Carlos ultimately proving to be arguably the most enlightened European monarch since Charlemagne himself.

Erstwhile anxiously undoing both Spain and Rome, emboldened politicos endorsing him only to discover that they had but unwittingly empowered perhaps the greatest earthly ally either ever had.

Charles tackling a seemingly endless laundry list of injustices beginning with his termination of Spain's insidious Inquisition. Stating simply that,

The Spaniards wish it so.

Such heroic displays of humanity proving but commencement of an unprecedented legacy celebrated today as The Bourbon Reforms.

Not since seventeenth century crusader Ignatius of Loyola, whose revolutionary Society of Jesus (Jesuits) assaulted head-on both the insanity of Spain's Inquisition as well as her blatantly exploitative New World policies, had detractors of Catholicism been caught more off guard.

Jesuits, or black robes after the simple garb each wore in solidarity, had demanded restoration of Christ to his rightful place in Papal politics.

A coup they would themselves achieve by standing up as Jesus in proxy against corrupt political and ecclesiastical leadership running rampant throughout both hemispheres.

Exposing in the process an evil web of long- standing conspiracy coursing its way into the very heart of Vatican City.

Then having met with stunning success presenting a very real prospect of one world government. Which of course had been Loyola's objective. And overwhich Jesus would ever prevail as king of kings.

Whereupon the Society found itself charged with,

dictating to kings

by peoples of differing viewpoints and understandably fearful of seemingly all-powerful Black Robes now holding sway over not only ecclesiastical matters but secular issues as well.

Monarchies across the continent countering by colluding to undo them.

While in anonymity as head of the House of Bourbon Don Carlos continued bankrolling Loyola's Holy Order.

The corruption Jesuits tackled had roots reaching back to Colon's discovery of America. When greed effectively shipwrecked arrangements fashioned previously between Church and State.

Beginning with circumstances surrounding subversion of a noble concept conceived by Queen Isabella as an Encomienda or Covenant Program.

A trusteeship intended to saddle Spain's conquistadors with sacred obligations to invest personally in the education, conversion (reduccion) and economic development of Indian monarchies as reciprocity for the privilege of profiting from said "improvements."

Most managing to manipulate through ridiculous interpretations of said Covenant outright subjugation of Indians placed under their jurisdiction as if not slaves than regardless victims of abject servitude.

Enter the Jesuits. Who through intervention sought to eradicate the corrupted system altogether. Which they did by appointing themselves as Trustees and thereby claiming both new and lost ground while brilliantly achieving the Encomienda's intent.

Jesuit methodologies aping concepts previously executed successfully during the reconquest of Iberia itself, when Rodrigo Diaz de Vivar (El Cid) countered through example the religious and political power struggle then tearing Spain apart by stationing missionaries along his frontlines with whom to install prototype outreach communities.

The purpose of such highly visible installations meant to dispel misgivings concerning otherwise intransigent motivations of conquest by eradicating cultural misunderstandings between Islam and Christianity through exemplary social exchange.

Facing off with their own "Moors," Loyola's Jesuits incorporating this noble concept as subsequently redefined by a decidedly Catholic Dominican Order to secure through positive outreach that which remained as yet untainted in the World.

A process of acculturation that came to be referred to as The Mission, through which Dominican, Jesuit and later Franciscan proponents provided for education, economic development and elevation in status of indigenous populations around the world.

Missionaries perceiving in America something far more precious and significant than the lunatic myth chasing of conquistadors.

Arming Indians with education, trade skills and exposure to high culture in order to level an otherwise disparaged playing field even as cutthroat, opportunistic European colonialism crashed down all around them.

Jesuit missions subsequently launched around the world being held in trust for the native peoples who conscripted to construct, live, study and worship in them.

Socio-political and humane efforts that resonated with the spiritual instincts of Eusebius Kuehn (hispanized as Eusebio Kino). Who at age thirty-six abandoned his distinguished career as professor of mathematics at the Bavarian University of Ingoldstadt to join forces with Loyola's Society of Jesus.

An anticipated call to labor in China never materializing.

Kino finding himself rather being dispatched off to New Spain. Where he arrived at Mexico City in 1687.

A boy raised in alpine Tyrol thereafter surprising even himself by the way he took to the range,

Quick as a duck does to water.

Subsequently working northern frontiers not only with supervision of Christian communities launched across what are now Arizona and Sonora but installation of as their means of economic infrastructure a prolific cattle-raising industry.

When mathematician- become- wrangler Eusebio approached his superior, Father Juan Maria Salvatierra, with a scheme to maintain as self-perpetuating all Jesuit Missionary efforts, Rome listened.

The proposed Pious Fund as subsequently drafted working proceeds donated by a handful of wealthy and generous Catholic patrons who perceived in fiscal soundness assurances that existing missions could themselves sustain proliferation of more missions.

With Eusebio's cattle ranching becoming the established economic mainstay of all such North American Mission "business." Which as promised by America's first cattle king kept the Pious Fund self-perpetuating.

So it was that in ten short years, hard-riding Padre (Father) Kino installed functioning mission ranchos (ranches) as far north as the Gila River in modern day Arizona.

Where outside of what is now Tucson he supervised construction of splendid Mission San Xavier del Bac.

Its extensive herds of cattle and troops of Indian cowboys standing as precursor for all that which was to follow in still far-off California.

Which Kino now advanced upon as but an intended stepping stone towards his long coveted China.

Armed with Salvatierra's commission sallying forth in 1697 to further explore the great northern mystery. Intent upon accessing directly that which most of the world yet perceived as being an Island.

The Society of Jesus having already installed a provincial headquarters on said "Island" at Loreto, from whence fifteen missions had subsequently been launched. Yet for whom all communications and supplies continued to be routed by way of the Sea of Cortes.

Saavy Professor Kino remaining convinced that California was not an island but rather a great peninsula. Having seen for himself an abundance of abalone shells and the like in the middle of an Arizona Desert.

And upon rafting the Colorado River in 1701 walked headlong into desert tribesmen who assured him that indeed the great Ocean lie but a few days journey hence.

Returning with said assurances to draw up a singular map that would stand for decades as **the** authoritative depiction of northern New Spain.

Which he forwarded together with a glowing report characteristically focused upon attaining the Orient, to Father Salvatierra:

I am of the opinion that
this California near the new-found land passage,
recently discovered,
might best be called Alta (Upper) California,
just as the preceding region...
as far as 30 degrees of north latitude,
might best be called Baja (Lower) California.

With the favor of Heaven,
if your Reverence and his Majesty
will give us workers and missionaries,

we must
all in good time
go forward
until we reach as far as Grand China.

And perhaps to the north of Alta California
we might be able to find a shorter road to Europe
by way of Grand China!

So it was that with such unbridled enthusiasm, the configurative geographic reality of California stood confirmed. Yet Father Kino, who had himself baptized more than 5,000 American Indians, would never see either China or hoped for missionaries with whom to advance upon California.

And when they did arrive, seventy years later, came clad not in universal Black but rather the Blue of Spanish Franciscans.

Meanwhile what with visions of encomiendas still dancing in their heads, Old and New World politicos sat poised to exploit Loyola's magnificent success.

So commenced a shell game between entities determined to force Rome's hand in parceling off all Jesuit mission communities.

With Don Carlos, who harbored no intention of granting outside access to the spoils of a transcendent Jesuit conquest, now unexpectedly standing in their way. And proceeding instead with inauguration of an autonomous American Indian commonwealth again to be mentored by the Society of Jesus.

In Spain at San Martin the King having successfully established not merely a Mission but rather an experimental prototype principality wherein he'd tested theories of self-government that would harbor far reaching implications for as yet untried Alta California.

Frustrated by Jesuit control and the Bourbon's alliance with said Society which in effect denied access to all others, covetous aristocrats responded by declaring open war both upon Don Carlos as well as the Jesuits.

Kino's Pious Fund having come to represent little more than the Bourbon Family's own personal fortunes.

Whose pious monarch as King of nearly half the world had set his sights upon installing what Rome referred to grandeloquently as The Millennial Kingdom of God; a perfectly conceived global community sitting poised to receive Earth's returning Messiah.

To achieve said social transcendence Don Carlos struggling elbow to elbow with the Jesuits in dragging Europe and the rest of the world out from under an unseemly centuries old morass of exploitative colonialization policies.

Jesuit mentors now awarding their communally developed and maintained ranchos, plantations, businesses and trades, not to an impatient aristocracy, but rather into the hand's of a Spanish monarch's newest subjects, vis-a-vis Indian novices (neophytes), whose lands and resources were held (like those of any other citizen's) in common with the King.

Envisioning Spain as recipient of enhanced trade through establishment of said Commonwealth, Don Carlos underscoring Jesuit labors with his equally inspired political framework as hammered out at San Martin. Dumbfounding all who had previously perceived the gawkish monarch as being inconsequential and easily contained.

Indians previously given access to nothing now together with the Bourbon Family in alliance with the Society of Jesus owning everything.

Outmaneuvered (indeed, hoodwinked) European aristocrats moving quickly to dethrone the intellectual visionary. Precipitating subterfuge on a scale so outrageous as to render simplistic the family squabbles of Machiavelli's Prince.

Threatening Charles with insolvency, which loomed over him only because he had, out of his own pocket, funded accelerated Jesuit enterprise. Rome standing compromised by powerful creditors both in Portugal and France now demanding the Vatican foreclose upon in lieu of immediate repayment all outstanding financial obligations.

With the Bourbons compelled by no less than Pope Clement XIII to accommodate said demand by expelling all Jesuits, so as to liquidate assets held in common with the Indians.

The coerced edict being delivered by Don Carlos himself to a shocked Christian brotherhood:

Because of weighty considerations
which His Majesty keeps hidden in his heart;
the entire Society of Jesus and all Jesuits
must leave the country (America)
and their establishments and properties
must be turned over to the Royal treasurer.

The entire sordid affair bringing Loyola's transcendent social experiment and corresponding threat of one world government to a screeching halt.

As without warning Jesuits found themselves summarily dismissed. Their Spanish ally standing helpless to intervene, what with the Church itself forcing his hand.

Never one to be dissuaded, secretly Charles assembling his most trusted family members and friends. And with them conspiring to rescue not only Spain but Rome's own grand agenda for world domination.

RECONQUISTA SEGUNDA

In wake both of Jesuit expulsion orders as well as near capitulation by the Spanish throne Father Kino might well have opined with consummate resignation, .

> God moves in mysterious ways;
> His wonders to perform.

Words while written forty years after Eusebio's death and by a Protestant minister nonetheless in vogue and familiar to continental Don Carlos for whom William Cowper's hymn <u>Light Shining Out of Darkness</u> resonated with deepest pathos,

> He plants his footsteps in the sea
> And rides upon the Storm.

Across the sea Spanish America having transmutated into a world of social irregularities startling as the vast region's divergent geographies. Alarming Hindu-like castes rendering all communities volatile. What with abject poverty and hunger stalking excess and gluttony.

From coifed and cotuiered Creole (native born American of Spanish or French descent) to naked, disenfranchised former lords of the land, inequity alone establishing itself as New Spain's singular common denominator.

A Jesuit presence providing the Western Hemisphere's only check against not merely segregation but absolute disparity between classes.

And when in 1765 that solitary presence was banished by Royal decree all social reform coming to an abrupt standstill.

Don Carlos recognizing in his global and very public humiliation but the backlash of Spain's own many sins.

Her terrifying Inquisition underscored by exploitative colonial policies having provoked Catholic factions into forging outside alliances with such organizations as a secret and secular Freemasonry.

Whose priesthood now stood determined to realign social priorities through both emasculation of monarchies and corresponding estrangement of religious from either commerce or politics.

Secular Christianity popularized by this eighteenth century movement referred to as The French Enlightenment breathing life into a new ideal regarding inherent rights and liberties. Advocating proliferation of free and independent capitalism.

Initially naïve concerning Masonry's mounting appeal, a caught off guard Don Carlos awakening to discover both himself and his court seriously compromised by the same.

Spanish Prime Minister Don Pedro Abarca de Boleo of Aranda secretly serving simultaneously both as Grand Master of Freemasonry having himself all but dictated Jesuit expulsion orders.

Only through acquiescence to concessions arranged between an abruptly enlightened King and a secular brotherhood powerful enough to authentically challenge even the Pope, did Charles manage to maintain on track his own transcendent agenda.

Wisely accepting without resistance Abarca's fiat as President of the Bourbon's Council on Reforms.

Endless manipulations aside, Charles going on to achieve extraordinary victories both at home as well as abroad. Maintaining against all odds by virtue of remarkable restraint Spanish Catholic control of the global limelight for yet one more generation.

Grand Master Abarca had although born at Aragon, yet as an hidalgo spent most of his privileged youth studying in Paris. Consorting with the likes of Rousseau and Voltaire.

His subsequent displays of arrogance as President of the Bourbon's Council on Reforms convincing modest and humble in the extreme by comparison Don Carlos but to accommodate Don Pedro's every extravagance. Thus knowingly providing a political interloper with rope enough to hang himself.

Which predictably Abarca did when a man who dared dictate to Pope and King next attempted imposing demands upon the Spanish people directly.

To prevent concealment either of weapons or identities ordering that subjects of the Crown no longer be permitted to wear otherwise cachet wide brimmed hats and trailing coats.

Whereupon Madrid erupted in riotous protest,

Enough is enough!

That this perceived to be French Count had even supposed he might legislate fashion but deepening mounting resentment against a man Catholic Spaniards now labeled as,

the Parisian traitor to both Majesties.

Wisely Don Carlos had withdrawn to his country estate before an outraged proletariat assaulted Madrid's Royal residence.

To contain mob violence and prevent the influx of dissidents Abarca responding by declaring Marshall Law. Dividing the Spanish Capitol into police jurisdictions. Blockading all roads leading into and out of the City.

For his own part Charles proceeding with extreme caution. All the while demonstrating,

an uncommon command of himself
on every occasion.

Wrote one royal observer,

He ever prefers carrying a point by gentle means
and has the patience to repeat exhortations
rather than to exert his authority even in trifles.

Yet, with the greatest air of gentleness,
he keeps his ministers and attendants
in the utmost awe.

Never for a moment does he forget that
he is the King;
nor does anyone else.

Meanwhile Monaco's Marquee of Grimaldi, Don
Carlos Francisco de Croix as Bourbon's Minister of
State Affairs quietly searching for an effective way to
counter Abarca's further meddling.

Discovering his glimmer of hope when finding himself
staring into the smiling face of a French Mademoiselle
while attending yet another soiree as proudly she
introduced her Andalusian-born husband Joseph
de Galvez.

Who had been lured away from Holy Orders by an
opportunity to study Law at the same grand University
of Salamanca that produced Hernan Cortes.

Quick in recognizing the value of a pious attorney to an
innocently righteous and correspondingly vulnerable
monarch presently countered on everyside by legal
wranglings, Croix without hesitation moving to bring
Galvez on board initially as his own personal secretary.

God moves in mysterious ways,
His wonders to perform.

So it was that Joseph found himself on a first name
basis with Don Carlos of Bourbon. Who came to think
of Croix's bright and devout young assistant as but his
own alter ego.

Ultimately bestowing upon the promising protégé
both knighthood and a charge that he serve as

Protector for the House of Bourbon.

Which Galvez accepted with a deep sense of honor and conviction.

Only to find himself summarily positioned as second most powerful man in what remained the world's most potent monarchy by virtue of a posting as his King's Universal Inspector General.

With full authority to act in the name of Don Carlos.

And thereafter presented in Seville before a Supreme Council of the Indies by similarly recast now as Viceroy of New Spain Carlos Francisco de Croix.

Both men then dispatched off to America there to carry out a heady and risky proposition.

At Mexico City the Bourbon Family Dream Team delivering as promised not only a Royal decree concerning Jesuit expulsion orders but the announcement that full investigations and restructuring of New Spain's administrative and financial infrastructure were to follow.

At the conclusion of which Galvez returned and proposed to an unsuspecting Council a laundry list of reforms ostensibly recommended by himself yet in fact as drafted in the Bourbon Family's own global effort to circumvent further opposition.

The sting of French betrayal had most wounded Don Carlos as it came from within his own family. Where advocates of the Enlightenment operating out of New

Orleans conspired openly to successfully undermine
Jesuit alliances. An incident referred to as it played
before English Americans as The French and Indian
War.

Treaties consequently signed at Paris in 1763 leaving
an otherwise Catholic Bourbon Family itself divided
over whether they should cede extensive territories to
a suddenly secular France.

Outmaneuvering not only Portuguese intervention
but these machinations of his own family, Don Carlos
startling Europe by unveiling what popular history
remembers as Spain's Second Grand Reconquest
(Reconquista Segunda).

Beginning at Madrid where he recruited otherwise
distracted aristocrats to re-establish Spanish/Catholic
domination of European and American science,
industry, commerce and the arts.

> Know that you do not gather to make
> pretty conversation,

he reminded volunteers.

> My desire is that you keep me informed
> of everything.

> That you see to it these affairs are taken
> care of promptly,
> whether major or minor.

> And that where possible justice be bent
> so as to favor the poor.

The result of said efforts transforming a Capitol beleaguered by political and philosophical harangues and now Marshall Law.

Introducing modern urban aspects to long dismissed as medieval Madrid.

Precipitating installation of Paseo del Prado as arguably the most fashionable promenade in all of Europe. Lined now as it was with elegant palaces and soaring portals opening onto public parks anchored by monuments celebrating Spanish greatness.

Prompting returning English tourist James Smith to record:

> The appearance of Madrid
> is grand and lively;
> noble streets, good houses,
> and excellent pavements.
>
> As clean as it once was dirty.

A successful makeover as orchestrated by Don Carlos serving as catalyst for copycat and privately funded Sociedades de los Amigos del Pais (Societies of the Friends of the Country) throughout Hispania.

In America Joseph Galvez not only opening the King's Academy of Arts and Sciences, but offering courses tuition free for all subjects of Indian derivation.

Which Don Carlos funded even as he rushed to rescue the debacle of his own forced estrangement from Jesuits and their Indian proteges.

Denouement to Charles' scheme being the reading of an investigative report before a smug and duplicitously secular Council at Seville by Universal Inspector General Galvez.

In which he suggested that while Britain's long considered threat to Spanish sovereignty over northern New Spain remained perhaps imaginary, Russia on the other hand sat poised to invade.

Informing shocked grandees courtesy of an attachment from his own secretary Matias de Armona as Spanish Ambassador to the court of Czarina Catherine the Great that Russian colonies had already been installed north of California.

And that furthermore Catherine fully intended to continue her expansionary scheme into the very heart of Spanish North America.

According to Armona,

Independently wealthy and well traveled Don Miguel de San Martin claims to have himself witnessed Muscovites trading with English American trappers on the shores of California.

In light of such revelations the Inspector General unable in good conscience to propose anything less than damage control by immediately consolidating and developing Spain's northernmost territories. Suggesting that doing less would be but to risk losing them altogether.

A calculated, bold and highly visible proposition, that

could not help but enhance international respect both for the Bourbons as well as Spain.

Joseph's report laden as it was with his King's own hidden agenda, placing an unanticipated set of circumstances upon the table before a stunned cadre of otherwise independent operators.

Who recognized that refusal of supporting the Bourbon's in making such an aggressive move might be tantamount to surrendering into Russian hands their own personal plans for New World conquest and exploitation.

As predicted, Minister General of the Council of the Indies Julian de Arriaga firing off his hastily drafted response. In which he all but demanded the King's instigation of a defensive offensive plan as proposed by Galvez if only to counter Russian aggressions in order that both the assets of Spain and Rome be protected.

Should the Crown fail to act,
those very lands that embrace the famous
bay of Monte-rey
might well be lost forever,
to not merely a foreign government
but the Eastern Orthodox Church as well!

At last Don Carlos had the very individuals guilty of manipulating both himself and pontiff right where he wanted them.

Brilliantly executed by a strategically placed and trustworthy Viceroy, his former secretary as Inspector

General and former secretary of said Inspector General as Russian ambassador, a satisfied King listened to the tenor of his own directives delivered back by way of a duped Council's petition.

Compliance with Arriaga's request meant reestablishment of Spanish dominion over the New World, realignment of the King and Pontiff and rescue for an agenda shared both by Don Carlos and the Society of Jesus.

Meanwhile an all but insolvent monarch recast himself as tertiary of a religious order famous for its adherence to vows of poverty and noted for successfully executing marvelous works without any visible means of fiduciary support.

So it was that the modest Franciscan brotherhood favored by country boy Sebastian Vizcaino found itself entrusted with keeping a regal Jesuit dream of new World Order alive.

Franciscan custodies to be established on the northernmost frontiers mirroring those founded previously by the Society of Jesus, in that each would secure dominion for both Majesties while keeping the same free from foreign invasion or independent colonialization.

Don Joseph Galvez setting off with orders in hand to launch the grandest enterprise of his Majesty's career.

From Loreto, capitol of formerly Jesuit California, directing promising Hijo del Pais (American- born of European extraction) Juan Bautista Anza in expediting a dicey and dangerous transference of jurisdictions.

Who not unlike Galvez had begun a suddenly high profile career preparing for ordination into the priesthood.

A devout Catholic soldier now struggling with the very painful task of rounding up and deporting all Jesuit religious from El Norte (Northern New Spain). Concerning which he subsequently recorded,

> Those who see the fathers passing through the
> villages on their way to exile,
> break into tears.

> All I can say is that
> a good King commands it
> so there must be more to it than we can know.

Opinions concerning reasons for the extradition vary as widely as the distance between heaven and earth.

What Anza could not know was that covert orders countering the purpose for said expulsion were simultaneously and obligingly being carried out in Mexico City.

Where Don Joseph Galvez had early on paid his first visit to the Franciscan Missionary College of San Fernando.

Upon whose Father President Francisco Palou the King's Universal Inspector General had come to depend for pertinent and sensitive information with which to successfully carry out on site operations.

Subsequently setting up as staging area for his monarch's grand ruse since fabled San Blas. Where Anza's Jesuit exiles found themselves passing the baton to Franciscans headed back in as advance guard for an extraordinary rescue mission.

Don Joseph positioning his own Secretary, Matias de Armona as first duly appointed Governor of the region.

Obligatorily teamed by Arriaga of the Council of the Indies who for all practical purposes yet maintained jurisdictions over New World operations with seasoned and secular public servant Gaspar de Portola as on-site Inspector General/ Commandante for the newly posted governor.

Heralding from independent Spanish Catalan, Portola's appointment all but politically castrating Galvez and his King.

Catalonians having themselves staged their own open rebellion for autonomy.

And from amongst whom the Council now recruited direct from Catalonia's capitol of Barcelona an army to accompany Portola.

Portola as an hidalgo envisioning all the rightful spoils of conquest due him in exchange for personally funding what he perceived as but a business venture.

Technically speaking legal jurisdiction over California lay in the hands not of Spain but rather Rome, by virtue of a Jesuit occupation paid for from out of the Pious Fund.

Yet and despite orders from Don Carlos to transfer the regions existing missions directly into Franciscan custodies, Portola placing each under the command of commissioned military officials.

None of whom attempted to sustain continuity with regard to operational Indian communities. All rather discarding novices while ransacking their respective properties in search of non-existent wealth popularly held to have been amassed and stashed by misrepresented Jesuits.

Only through dint of the greatest effort Franciscan Palou now as newly posted Reverend Father President of the region managing to rescue most but not all of California's existing mission communities.

Six months more of such 'administration,'

he reported to Galvez,

and there would have been nothing left at all overwhich to administer.

Portola informing Palou that while the King had instructed he transfer Jesuit missions over to Franciscan custodies they had instead been forced to post officers in charge of each as no Franciscans were on site at the time of his arrival. Furtively opining,

It is too bad we did not arrive at the same time.

Suggesting further,

But as I found myself without missionaries
I had to have recourse to military commanders.

Offering sardonically,

No doubt Inspector General Galvez
will restore governance of the Missions
to your Reverence.

So it was that to the chagrin of all Franciscans, Indian's
undone through expulsion of Jesuit mentors were
upon advent of their own arrival but again made to
feel the sting of Spanish duplicity.

Open rebellion and bloodshed would be swift
in following.

Tell me honestly,

wrote Galvez to Palou,

how much did that bandit of an administrator
get away with.

I promise you,
I shall know how to make him feel
the weight of my justice,
and see him disgorge his ill-gotten gains!

General Portola receiving a dressing down the likes of
which he had never expected following Don Joseph's
arrival at La Paz.

Who railed against otherwise independent operators
concerning the fact that with regard to California there

would be no private division of assets or grants of land awarded in exchange for services rendered. Even the ordered establishment of presidios or armed garrisons intended but to serve as temporary fixtures on an otherwise Indian playing field.

Upon realization that his appointment constituted little more than provision of guardianship over the equivalent to,

those damned Jesuit missions again,

Portola allegedly participating in clandestine subterfuge carried on by the Council even before a single Franciscan mission could be installed.

Meanwhile unsuspecting Franciscans moving ahead with renewed and concerted energies directed at rescuing from ruin the noble and temporarily shipwrecked agenda of Both Majesties.

While seemingly all the potentates of Europe could not dissuade Vatican City from giving Don Carlos its blessing, what with Rome's own domination of North America hanging in the balance.

Those opposed to restoration of said empowerment managing retraints, however, in placing a new harness upon both Charles and the Franciscans by insisting Rome's Pious Fund be administered by the Junta de Guerra y Hacienda (Board of War and Finance).

Thusly saddled with having to court an openly hostile treasurer for everything from barley to Church vestments nonetheless Father Presidents Palou and

Franciscan Commissary General of New Spain Manuel de Najera accepting their impossible task knowingly and with characteristic aplomb.

How does one protect established Indian missions while installing new ones when those in charge of funding for the same remain intent upon if not undoing altogether then limiting the same?

Palou and Najera did so by arranging for Inspector General Galvez to meet with a mystic of heroic mindset. Noted for being,

> peaceful as a dove
> and wise as the serpent.

New Spain's recognized expert on social reform and Christian utopianism, Dr. Junipero Serra.

To whom Sir Joseph was officially introduced outside of La Paz on February 11, 1768.

Already the northern frontier of New Spain had erupted in open rebellion as Jesuit novices attempting to protect their communities fought back against men poised to exploit them.

An intellectual who had himself together with the aid of Francisco Palou previously established arguably the most successful of all New World Indian Missions and under harrowing circumstances, Serra understood better than most the potency of forces now taking aim upon separating missionaries from their own successfully operating communities.

So it was that while Palou quite literally held down the fort in Old California, Dr. Serra found himself being mustered out and marched off to extend the reach of a temporarily floundering agenda.

All of which now sensitive to legal ramblings Don Carlos meticulously documented and filed away so as to leave unprecedented paper trails of evidence and financial records in his newly installed expressly for said purpose Archive of the Indies (Spanish America) at Seville.

Meanwhile Francisco Palou making Joseph Galvez to understand that Serra as his King's evangelist was the type of missionary who would seek martyrdom rather than surrender protection of mentored Indians in the face of political subterfuge or otherwise duplicitous mandates.

Suggesting that should Don Carlos burden this scholar with orders to achieve the impossible he reciprocate by lavishing upon an authentic crusader both protection and creative latitude.

Charmed by Palou's candor, Galvez remaining nonetheless unprepared for his subsequent conference with Serra.

When he caught himself staring into the large, seductive eyes of a man whom Francisco Palou had suggested be considered unquestionably worth his weight in gold.

Serra on the other hand seeing in the honest, open faced Inspector General but an answer to his own prayers.

Perceiving in said opportunity those marvelous workings of the king of all kings.

Who as far as Dr. Junipero was concerned had at that very moment delivered into his,

insufficient and unworthy hands,

a sacred mandate that he carry Christ's message of peace and through love salvation into the furthest recesses of California.

Of course accepting his posting as Reverend Father President of all proposed missions in what Palou now referred to as New California. Responding with characteristic enthusiasm intentions for installing no less than fifty such transcendent communities.

Delighting Galvez further. Who recommended rather that they get the first three utopian missions up and running before considering grander plans.

Go with the blessings of God
And of our Founder St. Francis,

writing newly posted Guardian of the San Fernando Missionary College Rafael Verger to Galvez and his vanguard of empire builders,

Go to work in the mystic vineyard of California.

Go with confidence and the assurance
that all will succeed
because you have Brother Junipero as your superior.

Meanwhile Governor's Inspector General/ Commandante Portola styling himself rather as,

Governor in Chief of this Peninsula of Californias,

only to be unsaddled thereafter by one whom a Catalonian grandee dismissed initially as being least significant to the operation's outcome.

The man Galvez referred to as merely Captain habitually sublimating Serra as but,

the missionary.

The missionary indeed who as juggernaut would go on, with a nod from Don Carlos, to all but subvert Portola's entire campaign into what Californians today remember only as,

The Sacred Expedition.

Rescuing from disgrace and infamy a beleaguered King challenged on every side by threats equally as ominous as those of Moorish caliphates.

Single-handedly epitomizing Catholic and Spanish integrity while at the same time fending off duplicity from both.

The installation under Franciscan Custodies of New California proving to be Spain's magnificent final chapter in a sometimes glorious oft times tragic American saga that had come to bridge more than three centuries.

And in which Sir Joseph Galvez found himself cast as last of the conquistadors.

TURNING POINT

n January 9th, 1769 an Entrada begun 160 years earlier by Sebastian Vizcaino lifted off.

Once again with the dispatch of three ships. And from Vizcaino's own Puerto La Paz. To be shadowed this time on land by two expeditionary forces marching north out of Loreto.

All of whom were to rendezvous at Sebastian's Bay of San Diego as orchestrated by Joseph Galvez, highest ranking and most powerful Spaniard to visit California since the advent of Hernan Cortes.

Out in front strategically placed Sir Vicente Vila of the Spanish Royal Navy sailing in command of a retooled and made resplendent former freight carrier dubbed San Carlos in honor of his King. Transporting in addition to its crew forty-eight military cadets from Catalonia together with arms and supplies enough for founding a new kingdom.

Cruising several weeks behind as piloto or master of the San Antonio being Admiral Juan Perez. Conducting both his crew and yet another squadron of soldiers recruited mostly from across New Spain.

Thought to be bringing up the rear drifting tiny by comparison San Joseph. Loaded to the scuppers not with personnel or arms but rather accoutrements gathered in by Galvez and Palou from across Sonora, Culiacan and Old California with which to outfit new churches at each soon to be installed Franciscan mission.

Fray Junipero Serra having in company with Galvez pronounced his blessing while concurrently beseeching Saint Joseph as seraphic guardian of the enterprise for protection.

Divine intercession that everyone affiliated with said enterprise would during the months ahead find themselves in desperate need of. As beyond obvious challenges of logistics the compromised monarch's Entrada soon floundered under a haze of duplicity.

Parodied innocently enough aboard his flagship San Carlos. Where outrageous displays of self importance tendered by Lieutenant Colonel Don Pedro Fages (Faa-hey) precipitated not only loss of life but open rebellion and near mutiny.

Rendering comedic equally vainglorious Juan Perez of the San Antonio who having served prior as master of a Manila galleon seemed disposed to hold court as though king himself,

> lording over decision making like the entire world gratefully awaited his every command.

Such arrogance combined with a blanket refusal to acknowledge errors in judgement costing the expedition dearly both in terms of time lost and wasted rations.

On the other hand traveling in company with proud Perez were dedicated military engineer and cartographer Miguel Constanso together with company surgeon and Bourbon Family intimate Dr. Pierre Pratt.

Each of whom accepted the chagrin of imperfect leadership without overlooking a wonderful nobility inherent in their undertaking. To collectively infuse the same with endless quantities of sorely needed enthusiasm and hope.

Healthy optimism in fact launched and personally encouraged by Galvez himself who harbored every intention of accompanying the expedition through to Monterey.

Croix arguing effectively against the taking of such a risk. Leaving Don Joseph rather to run the entire operation by remote control as it were. Accompanying each vessel out of the harbor aboard his own frigate the <u>Concepcion</u>, even sailing alongside the <u>San Carlos</u> to as far south as Cabo San Lucas.

Then personally bidding farewell and god's speed as northwesters swept the billowing sails of a hoped for successful conquest from his view.

Aboard the <u>San Antonio</u> Miguel Constanso recording sentiments no doubt shared by a King's Alter ego:

This enterprise,
desired for so many years,
begun many times with great preparations
and expense,
will undoubtedly be pleasing to the august
Monarch of Spain,
whose magnanimous spirit and religious piety,
heaven rewards,
by raising in his kingdom great and illustrious men,
in every station, Ecclesiastical, Military, and Politick,

who contend equally in executing the great charges committed to their eminent capacity and talents.

From myth to reality California was about to be baptized. Its conquest the culmination of centuries-old European dreams and failed aspirations.

And would harbor forever after within a conflictive soul something of Spanish greatness and altruism.

As an effort to install the noble and grand incarnation of a Spain that never was--the pious conquistador, the wealthy and gracious landowner, the truly holy clergy working synergistically with a King operating in accordance to Divine Will.

Such was the dream anyway.

With all of this hope piling up against an august geographic backdrop of equally mythic proportions-- the real California. A fantastic place created by Nature's own powerful hand. And populated with ancient societies harboring equally mystic propensities.

Who would soon come to expect so much from those sinners and saints fast advancing upon them. Flying as they were in the face both of changing world politics and Church policies.

An anachronism in their own time, this Crusader's stand against the eternal conflict between good and evil that to this day lingers enigmatically over the landscapes of all civilizations.

PART TWO

THE MISSION

SAN JUAN CAPISTRANO

At the heart of dynamic Southern California stands one of only two buildings still extant wherein mystic Fray Junipero Serra practiced his extraordinary hybrid of Christian utopianism.

Founded concurrently in 1776 with the United States of America, an inauspicious by comparison launching of Mission San Juan Capistrano signaling regardless a similarly high-water mark for the Spanish American experience. Subsequent construction of its cathedral-like great stone church representing in all of California Spain's grandest architectural statement.

Bells suspended from the more than one hundred-foot high campanario of that temple proclaiming a successful conquest both by Christendom's Pope and Spanish protectorate. An image of a rooster cast in gold and perched on top heralding the advent of a new day dawning.

Illumination emanating out from within its stupendously vaulted ceiling visible for miles. The lighthouse effect invoked suggesting a triumph of divine enlightenment over both spiritual as well as intellectual darkness.

Such regal, awe- inspiring imagery in plastered stone but the certain reflection of Franciscan Serra's own San Fernando Missionary College at Mexico City.

And when it all came crashing down in the aftermath of a terrible earthquake, Spain too seemed to shudder.

Modern visitors are greeted by a confusing maze of pathways as scattered and unfocused as the Empire inherited by Don Carlos de Bourbon.

Of the grand capitol building funded from the Spanish King's own largesse little more than a stretch of bougainvillea-draped wall and portion of the nave remaining.

Single most entrancing ruin in all of North America, one sensing here the eternal sheen of hope reflecting thwarted dreams since abandoned.

Today's generation having reconstructed adjacent the sanctuary as it once appeared. Paying careful attention to architectural detail while applying modern earthquake-tolerant structural engineering techniques and standards.

Corridors and arched cloisters connecting a great sleeping ruin with its grand reincarnation harboring countless treasures of profound historic significance, including the but modest by comparison chapel of Fray Junipero Serra.

Stumbling unsuspectingly upon this outwardly nondescript adobe building marked only by a simple plaque is to plunge headlong into and stand immersed with wondering awe.

Gold-leafed reredos, rising above a three hundred and sixty-year-old tabernacle of solid gold, suspending a timbered and tiled roof. All about circling an array of priceless Spanish and Indian art.

Bestowing upon unassuming construction ostentation intended to suggest nothing less than both the throne of God and very altar upon which Jesus Christ sacrificed daily through blood atonement for the redemption of a failed humanity.

While little of such splendor ever surrounded Serra, even this memorial remaining less than a modern knight of medieval mindset had hoped for.

Remarkable amongst men as is this chapel standing in the midst of its otherwise but historically interesting surroundings, Fray Junipero perceiving therein the actual presence of a god who's help remained ever eminent.

With innocent and childlike faith so abiding that when he prayed for miracles they inevitably occurred.

Rendering fearless the founding father of California. For he knew nothing of defeat.

Had not God in Heaven promised that His help alone would be sufficient for those who relied upon Him?

Asthmatic and further handicapped by an ugly ulcerated leg, an otherwise ascetically stunning giant of a man yet stood merely five foot two inches tall.

His enigmatically naive sophistication towering above the lives of most other religious both present and past.

He himself ever looking not upon outward appearances but rather inward, as if able to peer at the soul. Therein, as exemplified euphemistically by his outwardly unassuming adobe chapel at San Juan, lie true beauty and majesty. Therein he perceived the presence of "God."

His own soul casting a shadow of staggering and heroic proportions across the length and breadth of California.

Whereupon he intended to install dozens of mission communities, each mirroring in varying degrees of grandeur that which one encounters at San Juan Capistrano; the but twenty-one subsequently founded constituting regardless more than adequate cornerstones for his new and grander Rome.

Each yet bearing silent testimony to a brave and daring co-operative carried on between outcast European intellectuals and a savvy Stone Age people.

Who together with the selfless, unconditional love of this singular man ever coaxing their potential, championing their cause and tirelessly fending off their exploitation, walked in holy alliance across the bridge he himself provided them into the uncertainties of a modern world.

SERRA

Miguel (Michael) Joseph Serre was born at 1:00 A.M. on November 24, 1713 in the city of Petra on the Island of Majorca off the Spanish coast of Catalan. Proud Antonio placing a laurel branch above the doorway of his but modest home as prescribed by ancient custom so as to announce the arrival of his son.

Steeped to this day in tradition Majorca sharing with the Iberian Peninsula it's lengthy and complex past.

Hannibal ruling over it briefly prior to the advent of Christianity. And under whose standard recruits from an Island kingdom stormed Rome.

Julius Caesar later pressing Roman Majorca into service against Gaul (France/Western Switzerland) and the Britons.

When Rome fell, Byzantium then hearkening. Compelling native sons of an independent island kingdom into the Crusades; some marching off for a contested Holy Land, others responding to Spain's own struggle against the Moor.

Antonio Serre could not know that the tiny son cradled lovingly in his arms would go on to become Majorca's last great and arguably most controversial Crusader. Particularly what with doctors holding out little prospect for the frail infant's survival.

Margarita Ferrer having already lost two infants at birth. And accordingly on the outside chance that this babe too might perish an anxious husband making haste for Saint Peters Church, there to baptize his boy as per custom even before permitting its mother's embrace. That the soul delivered into her arms for however briefly might be untainted by original sin.

Though small and delicate, little Christian Michael did survive. Inadvertently displaying both the promise of seldom equaled tenacity and innate elan for life.

Asthmatic conditions persisted. As did the boy.

Simple parents of modest means soon grappling with not merely health care issues but how best to provide for Michael's self evident artistic and intellectual prowess.

So it was that Antonio petitioned for local Franciscans to aid with providing that which he could not.

Thus on the occasion of Michael's sixteenth birthday he began an extraordinary adventure that would see him crowned in the pantheon of Majorcan heroes.

As devotees of failed would-be knight Franchesco di Pietro, who during the Middle Ages launched a counter Crusade aimed at ridding the world of its unholy obsession with greed, power and conquest, Franciscans had grown to comprise a veritable army.

Their champion born in 1182 to the French wife of a wealthy Italian merchant. Franchesco (Francis) spending an indulgent youth free from moral restraint. Where as part of a, gay and reckless crowd,

he was remembered as having been,

the gayest and most reckless.

Amidst Holy Wars staged between Muslim and Christian any honorable son was expected either to conscript with the military or accept Holy Orders.

Flippantly Francis throwing his fortunes together with those of a Jerusalem bound army; the naïve, arrogant and coddled youth vaingloriously marching off ostensibly to defend Christendom.

Only to be abruptly incarcerated in but one of many minor altercations seemingly contrived to keep independently powerful Italian states, each manned with standing armies of their own, distracted from consolidating and thereby potentially usurping control over a politically ambitious Pope.

It was during said captivity that Francis succumbed to a prolonged illness.

And would be while slipping into and out of consciousness that he found himself pondering Life's mysteries.

Reassessment presaging a supernatural epiphany. Pietro di Bernadone's son claiming communion with no less than the living Christ.

Particulars aside a young playboy returning home transformed. Determined to stand up alone if needs be against the savage insanity of sending Christians off in the name of a pacifistic and loving Lord Jesus to commit murder as penance for their own sins.

Those in his hometown of Assisi who had accused Francis of cowardice for abandoning the battlefield standing consummately shamed. With the Gentle Knight as he came to be called quietly maintaining certain knowledge that "God" could not to be found amidst conquest and plunder.

Professing Christ himself having while ministering to all humanity otherwise lived life as but a simple beggar.

Then shocking family and friends with an announcement of his intentions to do likewise.

> Neither shall I wage war
> nor shall I toil for wealth

Turning his back upon a Pope shackled by vested interests, Franchesco divesting himself of not only a substantial inheritance together with the sacraments of the Church but even his very reignment.

Standing naked and vulnerable before all critics armed with nothing other than a courageous commitment to authentically follow in the footsteps of Jesus Christ.

> I am this day a new creation.

And so it was that this boy upon whom all the world's riches had ever been lavished threw himself at the mercies of that world. To depend, as had his hero Jesus Christ, entirely upon "God's" hospitality.

For he desired to acquire wisdom,
which is better than gold,
and to purchase prudence,
which is more precious than silver.

Franchesco's much publicized and magnificent display
of innocent humility succeeding in focusing the
attentions of both kings and commoners alike on a
singular path that leads to authentic happiness and
profound significance.

Be glad and happy,
showing that you rejoice in the service of the Lord.
And be becomingly courteous,

he told any who would listen.

Whoever may come to you,
be he professed friend or foe,
let him be kindly and hospitably received.

No matter how great you perceive his fault to be,
let him not depart after he has seen thy face
without having been shown God's grace.

Franchesco's counter Crusade of salvation through
simple living and unconditional love surviving the
political manipulations of Medieval Bishops, Popes and
Kings as but a timeless echo of Christ's own message:

Behold the lilies of the field.

They neither toil
nor do they reap.

And yet I say unto you
that Solomon in all his glory
was never arraigned such as one of these.

In the midst of so preaching on a singularly memorable afternoon Franchesco's discourse was overwhelmed by a cacophony of nesting swallows.

He paused. And capturing the imagination of all present requested the little birds be still just long enough for him to share with those assembled the words of Jesus Christ.

When the swallows fell silent so did the crowd. And thus remained until Francis had pronounced a blessing upon not only his brothers and sisters but those little birds as well.

There was something about this young man.

Not surprisingly such innocence was often met with scorn.

Yet those who scoffed at or ridiculed him made no attempt to otherwise "rescue" Francis from an implied,

Holy insanity.

Of his many detractors, biographer Thomas Celano suggesting,

It is futile for the wicked to persecute the man
who is striving to do what is right,
because the more such a one is abused,
so much the greater will be his triumph.

Dishonor,
as someone has said,
only serves to make the noble soul more resolute.

Francis sought refuge from ridicule at the ruined monastery of San Damiano outside of Assisi. Where clad typically in but a modest tunic and wearing sandals only when necessary he lived after the manner of abstemious Saint Anthony.

Assuming a three fold vow of,

Poverty,
Chastity and
Obedience to Christ's teachings

while encouraging others to,

Preach Jesus Christ always.

And when necessary
use words.

suggesting that they,

Give up your small ambitions.
Come and save the world.

The spiritual movement thusly launched carrying with it far-reaching and global implications. Ultimately transforming even then as yet unknown California.

A liturgy subsequently composed to honor him capturing perfectly the ethos both of Francis and of his mission:

Lord,
make me an instrument of Your peace,

Where there is hatred,
let me sow love,

Where there is injury,
pardon,

Where there is doubt,
faith,

Where there is despair,
hope,

Where there is darkness,
light,

And where there is sadness,
joy.

Grant that I may not so much seek to be consoled
as to console,

To be understood
as to understand,

To be loved
as to love,

For it is in giving that we receive,
It is in pardoning that we are pardoned,
And it is in dying that we are born
into eternal life.

Fearful of mass defections by Christians no longer seeking his counsel but rather that of a hermit living at San Damiano, Cardinal Guido Ugolino prevailing upon Rome to recognize and embrace Francis and his mounting army of disciples as but a separate yet Catholic Order.

So it was that on July 16, 1226 Pope Honorius III pronounced his papal blessing upon Assisi's famous beggar while setting Francis apart as father and founder of Franciscanism.

To which that beggar in consummate humility deferred, insisting rather that anyone wishing to follow him consider themselves as but the least of Christ's brothers (friars minor).

The Order of Friars Minor (ofm) as it came to be called afforded protection to those defenseless, solace to all in discomfort and food for the hungry while acknowledging every creation including the animals with unconditional love.

Through superlative example Franciscans succeeding in changing the world as they knew it, dragging Europe with its killers for Christ by the collar out of as it were the darkness of barbarism and into the holy light of compassion and unfailing humanity.

Such actions being the certain reflection of men who knew nothing of duplicity. As by preaching Christ only, rather than Christian dogma, Franciscans threw open wide the doors of Christendom to all mankind.

Muslim sultans bestowing upon them guardianship over shared sacred sites in a contested Holy Land. Compelling individuals of all faiths to reassess the authenticity of their own publicly professed piety.

Francis had succeeded in bringing the substance of Christ's exemplary life back to the heart of the matter. And by so doing effectively challenged every individual equally with his appeal to turn away from all forms of pseudo-religion.

Encouraging that humanity not focus upon meaningless conquests and acquisitions but rather the successful conquest of one's desires
for the same.

When Francis died in 1228 Cardinal Ugolino become Pope Gregory IX moving quickly to claim a revolutionary's counter cultural congregation by pronouncing sainthood upon their hero's head.

Ultimately even Queen Isabella insisting she be buried in but the modest tunic of a Franciscan.

With Don Carlos III now serving simultaneously both as monarch and Lay Franciscan brother.

Not surprisingly Little Michael Serra (Serre) as beneficiary of Franciscan care and schooling also ultimately desiring but to lead the simple and focused life of the Least of Christ's Brothers.

His petition to do so being denied, however. Father Guardian in the Majorcan Capitol of Palma assuming that because of Serra's diminutive stature the boy had lied concerning his age.

Deceit does not wear well under a Franciscan's habit.

When discovered that indeed Michael had not lied, but was simply extremely small and boyish for his age, a shamed Provincial yet deferring. After all there were the Franciscan's own famously rigorous vows of asceticism, which he conjectured might prove too difficult for one so frail and delicate of health.

Predictably the boy physicians prognosticated would not live to see his first birthday persisted.

Trademark integrity and tenacity carrying him through to full completion of his novitiate at age twenty-four.

Of that vocation Michael later recalling:

> I was almost always ill
> and so small of stature
> that I was unable even to reach the lectern,
> nor could I help my fellow novices
> in the necessary chores of the novitiate.
>
> However,
> with my profession
> I gained health and strength
> and grew to medium size.

The Franciscan brotherhood of San Bernardino in Petra had early on acquainted Serra with a chronicle entitled <u>Fioretti de San Franchesco</u> (The Little Flowers of Saint Francis). Michael becoming enamored with one of those little flowers (spiritual brothers) whom Francis referred to as Junipero,

a man of utter simplicity and celestial mirth.

God's own little jokester.

Himself possessed of a sunny, optimistic disposition, an otherwise sickly, undersized boy constantly forbidden from engaging in rigorous playtime with other children, often left behind to entertain the farm animals of his father's corral, Michael had ever accepted in good humor corresponding slights from sturdier lads.

Understandably identifying with little Junipero, who from retribution exacted ultimate triumph over each difficult situation dealt him through his own humor and good naturedness.

So it was that upon becoming a Franciscan Michael exercised the privilege of changing names. Opting to be identified rather as Junipero.

Colleagues regardless persisting in referring to him rather by a different sobriquet:

Knight of the Cross.

KNIGHT OF THE CROSS

Heir apparent to great estates in and around Palma bestowed upon his father by King James of Aragon in return for championing successful expulsion of all Moors from Majorca, Ramon Llull spent a privileged childhood engaging in but the outward display of chivalry at jousting tournaments and otherwise mock melee.

Many of which occurred in private bedchambers. As notorious for his infidelities he garnered for himself the rather lurid reputation of being a womanizer.

Subsequent fraternization with Franciscans prompting Llull's Quest beyond the superficiality of grand carnivals in an attempt to locate knighthood's true substance.

Having become convinced that authentic chivalry entailed far more than merely parading about as a glamorous mounted warrior in shining armor.

And succeeding with discovering the heart of the matter.

Whereupon Llull, like Franchesco (Saint Francis), threw down his sword and turned his back both on self importance as well as materialism to pursue penance and personal salvation through asceticism and contemplation.

Which resulted in his composition and release of an extraordinary tome, "Libre del Ordre de Cavayleria

(Book of the Order of Chivalry),"that both defined and set new standards for the art of chivalry, .

which is the glory of Europe.

Arguably the first manual ever written for the express purpose of instructing knights in ethics as well as etiquette, Llull's didactic "Book of the Order of Chivalry" is a wonderfully rambling work which in its wanderings establishes as knighthood's premise an educated, literate and secular lay priesthood. Expertise in bridging written word with iconographical expression but the result of his own unique life experience.

Which now became indelibly stamped upon every aspect of knighthood. Single handedly giving rise to a great and consummately secular cult nonetheless grounded perhaps as never before in Christian idealism.

Llull's book launching a rich cultural identity thereafter indulged in by men otherwise denied accessibility to priesthood and or the written word.

Chivalry as a direct result becoming more ornate, more concerned with symbolism, more aware of historical precedent, more ceremonious and in the face of egregious Papal politics, staunchly secular.

Advocating for example regular participation at jousts and tournaments otherwise banned by Church officials. Ramon deeming said exercises as essential for the honing of skills and development of physical prowess.

And just as Catholicism had with the rise of its own literate priesthood found a facility for embracing new movements such as that of the Franciscan Order, so now Chivalry through a medium of heraldic art and disbursement of knowledge facilitated courtesy of Llull's book reached out and consolidated men drawn to it from across a wide spectrum of aristocratic society and centers of otherwise remote secular endeavor.

Thus instilling a continuing vigor together with an infinitely variable range of religious sentiment. Transforming Western civilization's notion of Chivalry into increasingly complex and symbolic modes of expression and observance. Promoting general awareness with regard to the richness and potential of its own independent traditions.

And thereby becoming courtesy of this broad- based mythology not merely a literate and elitist but rather an open and acquired culture with full panoply of varied and popular art.

Llull rendering Scripture into relevant vernacular to advance the instruction of Chivalry itself. And by so doing successfully establishing upon the foundation of suddenly antiquated modes and procedures a young, vivacious and colorful concept of knighthood.

Ramon's pen alone giving rise both in and beyond Spain to a Secular Christian Order wherein one became a knight by virtue of an eighth sacrament administered not at the hands of a Roman Catholic King but rather from another knight previously ordained.

Popularizing the notion of an ancient Order. All of which led unwittingly to proliferation of Freemasonry.

Llull's course-altering anthology opening with the fictional premise of a squire being in route to his King's great court. Who finding himself wandering lost allegorically in the woods happens upon an old hermit absorbed with reading a book.

The disoriented squire inquiring after directions only to discover that this monk had himself once been a knight.

Ensuing dialogue exposing tremendous ignorance on the part of one about to be knighted with regard to knighthood's significance and correspondingly the Art of Chivalry.

Prompting a patient hermit to share particulars recorded in the very book he is presently reading by means of which Llull conveys his own ideology regarding the proper exercise of chivalry:

A knight is to be
courteous and nobly spoken,
well clad,
and one who holds open house within
the limit of his means.

Loyal to Christ
and truthful in all his affairs.

With hardiness, largesse and humility
being the principal characteristics by way of
which he is recognized.

While a number of Llull's passages suggested as inspiration the prose of Lancelot and Romance of Alexander, yet his own experience both as knight and Franciscan stood equally exposed.

And perhaps nowhere more so than in the ceremony of ordination as per his dictation wherein:

> The knight is bathed so as to recall his baptism,
> signifying a second cleansing from sin.

White linen undergarment girded about his loins to be worn as a constant reminder that he remain chaste.

> A two edged sword then placed in his hands
> thereafter to be employed by him
> as protector of the weak and upholder of justice.

The overwhelming success of Llull's "Book of the Order of Chivalry" brought with it both fame and notoriety. Which Ramon fostered through issuance of additional tomes.

Most memorable being a treatise dreamt up while contemplating his navel which he entitled "The Thinking Machine." Wherein Llull proposed a failsafe method for unraveling and or properly divining any unknown quantity and all mysteries.

Such brilliance was extinguished by stones hurled in ignorance from a Muslim Camp who perceived in Ramon but another arrogant Christian missionary.

Whereupon his native Majorca ascribed the name of its famous martyr to their own University. Which through scholastic endeavor and the prestige of a posthumous affiliation with Llull came to overshadow even Salamanca in continental recognition. Following receipt both of a degree in Philosophy as well as a doctorate in Sacred Theology Fray Junipero Serra found himself being awarded a professorship at the distinguished Lullian University.

At which time he acquired a replica of Llull's own Crusader's Cross, an emblem indicating a knight's willingness to himself be crucified as was Christ for humanity's sake. And in which Serra placed a relic of the martyred Franciscan.

Thereafter wearing the same about his neck and for the rest of his life.

So it was that around campus, as it were, colleagues took to calling Dr. Serra rather Knight of the Cross.

Said "Knight" in point of fact proving himself through deed and daily intercourse arguably the most chivalrous man any of them would ever meet.

Serra's own admiration of the Knight become Franciscan intellectual superceded only by a fascination with both Greek philosopher Plato and said visionary's protégé Aristotle.

Boundless imagination, an urbane sense of humor, the musicality in his voice, animated enthusiasm and flare for the dramatic, all would become Serra trademarks. And but the outward expression of true genius.

The eloquence with which he spoke leaving one associate emoting,

His sermon is worthy
of being written in letters of gold.

While teaching both philosophy as well as sacred Theology Serra found himself additionally pressed into service as Department Chairman for the studies of John Duns Scotus, whose formula for god centered community had served as inspiration for Sir Thomas More's famous fairytale Utopia.

Which had from the time Serra first read it fired his own desire to see the same installed. A proposition so daunting that few dared even dream about let alone consider.

But here was such a man. Who like Ramon Llull, Franchesco di Pietro, John Duns, Aristotle and Plato, could not be contained within the framework of conventionality.

It was while presiding as professor over the morning class on Sacred Theology that Doctor Junipero Serra found himself being introduced to a strapping and eager Francisco Palou Amengal.

Who came petitioning for admission into popular Serra's already crowded classroom. The friendship sparked then and there between them being immediate and enduring. Both men going on to dream great dreams and together.

Meanwhile unprecedented success both as theologian

as well as educator could not squelch Serra's longing for the opportunity of being cut loose in some field unplowed there to install that which daily he promoted but from the lectern.

Understandably reticent to embark alone upon such an uncertain proposition, the unbidden expression on protégé Palou's part for this same adventure bringing a brilliant little professor to tears.

They would do this thing. And they would do it together.

Ten years Serra's junior, Palou finding himself readily accepted for missionary work in the New World.

Junipero on the other hand becoming embroiled in controversy. His superior refusing to part company with Majorca's finest scholar. In fact to prevent separation, tendering anew a supposition that Serra was simply too frail for undertaking such an arduous assignment. Then indicting him further regarding even suggesting he be permitted to serve alongside Francisco Palou.

Thereby temporarily scuttling great plans.

But Serra, who understood Llull's "Thinking Machine," would as always prevail through exercise of his intellect.

On this occasion secretly circumventing the impediment by forwarding blind-copies of his petition directly on to an obstinate provincial's superior.

A tactic Serra would continue to employ successfully throughout what was to become his long and illustrious American career. And by way of which he ever guaranteed means of maintaining on track agendas otherwise beyond the grasp of small minds and Neanderthal bias.

So it was that a stunned provincial found himself not only overruled concerning objections raised with regard to sending Palou and Serra and together as missionaries by no less than Minister General of the Franciscan Order but furthermore embarrassed when directed to facilitate Dr. Serra's immediate posting as an emergency replacement for a stronger and younger recruit who upon confronting the prospect of trans oceanic travel expressed fear of the sea and now refused to serve.

In short order the dynamic duo were off for a scheduled rendezvous with their shared destiny. Serra at thirty-six and Palou twenty seven, each on the threshold of his best manhood, both to be challenged and countered for the rest of their lives.

Beginning at the port of departure when beautiful Serra found himself subjected to,

the excessive regard of his new superior.

Francisco immediately escorting his companion out of the friary to reside rather on board ship.

Only there to find themselves both being submitted to the Inquisition of an Anglican Captain. Who expressed open disdain for all things Catholic.

Countering characteristically with wit one ignorant statement from out of the Englishman's mouth after another, Serra quipping that the Captain himself stood in need of penance for having abandoned Holy Mother Church. Which but ignited his accuser's hatred and prejudice.

Who suddenly produced a knife and holding it to the missionary's throat threatened killing him. An act the

provocative bigot

all but unwittingly accomplished erstwhile by thusly provoking with his strangle hold Serra's latent asthmatic condition.

Francisco's intervention but bringing more threats from the knife-wielding mariner,

I'll throw both your bodies overboard
and proceed to London directly.
Who would know the difference?

To which Palou countered that as they each traveled under the protection of a Spanish passport, should either of them not be delivered safely at Cadiz, international repercussions would be certain to follow,

Our king will demand indemnity from your king
and you will pay with your own head.

Ultimately reason and the boys prevailing.

Surviving to face off against the darkness of ignorance again and again as knight-errants for Christ; each devoted as they were to Llull's ethics, Duns' vision and Franchesco's Counter- Crusade.

Exiting at Cadiz the Old World to take on the New.

Whereupon the <u>Villa Soto</u> upon which they sailed nearly sank mid ocean. Palou and Serra power praying to Saint Barbara, native daughter of Constantinople and accordingly patroness of all Crusaders, for her divine intervention.

After disembarking safely, Franchesco's knights surprised by a sudden and great noise exploding behind them. All in port watching with amazement as the <u>Villa Soto</u> broke apart and sank to the bottom of the harbor.

The boys carrying with them this memory of Saint Barbara's intervention throughout an extraordinary journey that ultimately landed them both in California. Where they would enshrine her memory for the benefit of future counter crusaders in a land even as yet outside their own ken.

A long an arduous road indeed. As Serra insisted upon following literally in Franchesco's footsteps who ever denied himself even the grandeur of riding upon a horse.

The two hundred and seventy-mile Trail of Cortes coursing its way from Vera Cruz through jungles and over mountains to the San Fernando Missionary College in Mexico City.

And upon which they were remembered as having set out alone and with nothing more at hand than,

a prayer book for luggage,
pomegranates for rations
and God as their guide.

It would be enroute that Junipero developed his profound spiritual relationship with Saint Joseph. An endearment that deepened thereafter following a singular night spent lost in the wilderness and without food.

When serendipitously Serra came across a family of modest means who without hesitation opened their home. Father, mother and child feeding and looking after him.

A grateful missionary being sent on his way the following morning supplied both with directions and a loaf of wonderfully satisfying bread.

It was bread that Junipero had tasted before.

At long last arriving in a modest village Serra sharing his experience concerning the hospitality of that family up the road. Only to be met with perplexed gazes.

But there is no family living up there on
that wild road.

Fray Junipero's spontaneous and unintended blasphemy,

Jesus, Mary and Joseph,

garnering a great round of laughter from the townspeople. His candor being evoked not from shock however, but rather devotion. Had he been attended to the night before by no less than the Holy family themselves?

It had in fact been their gift of bread which first gave him pause. For during his long hike with Francisco from Vera Cruz to Mexico City he had twice been rescued from near starvation by a stranger's gift of that same wonderfully satisfying bread.

When despite the great distances traveled between each earlier incident both Good Samaritans though dressed differently yet seeming to have been the same individual.

Had he perhaps been sent by Saint Joseph, to whom they had prayed for help. Or was he perhaps Saint Joseph himself?

Two crusaders keeping said experiences guarded safely within their hearts.

But there was one night when no intercession heavenly or otherwise occurred. And would be numbered amongst the darkest moments in Serra's life. During which Junipero sustained the leveling of a heavy cross upon his gallant shoulders in the form of an otherwise innocuous insect bite.

Scratching the irritation on his leg throughout an uneasy sleep. Awakening at dawn to find himself completely bloodied. The ensuing infection developing into an ulcerous open wound.

In characteristic humility Junipero accepting as the only stigmata of which he deemed himself worthy an ugly sore that would torment him throughout the rest of his life.

And although thereafter detained yet never deterred; deflecting with trademark cheerfulness those whom, as during childhood, foreverafter chided his slow progress. Quietly marching on to outdistance them all.

Endowing whimsical "Junipero" with a patriarchal dignity more reflective of Joseph. As unassumingly Serra nonetheless acquired along the way a paternalistic instinct towards everyone with whom he came in contact.

Everyone that is except Francisco Palou, who remained as before both soulmate and,

the governor of my heart.

Best of friends, as Plato suggested, sharing that which they have and that which they are with each other.

Blessed Junipero Serra's words, like those of seraphic Saint Francis, cutting pseudo Christianity to the quick.

To the one who is in love,
all things are compatible.

By the time Christian Michael arrived at Mexico City he had not only fallen in love with all humanity but grown spiritually to stand before them as the consummate brotherly Father.

Commissary General of San Fernando subsequently emoting,

Would that I had a whole forest of such
juniperos (junipers).

Yet again, and like Francis, while as a priest deserving
of attendant recognition Junipero ever deferring.
Insisting rather he be called upon not as Father but
merely Brother.

During the eighteen years that followed Brother
Junipero working tirelessly alongside Brother
Francisco, teaching and administering first to
compliment then later salvage utopian efforts
launched previously by Jesuit missionaries.
Who had themselves ever- stressed equanimity. Serra
readily recognizing the value inherent in their system,
while advocating further that,

love be prerequisite
and respect for all humanity mandatory.

The magnificent flagship community Santiago Jalpan
with its attendant mission church which he and
Francisco installed outside of Queretaro in semi
tropical North Central Mexico standing as a model for
the entire New World.

Still subsequent expulsion and exploitation both of
Jesuit developed novices and resources making any
such endeavors echo throughout the land with the
hollowness of a great lie.

Two boys from Majorca being quick in responding.

With Palou mustered out to serve as Father President
of formerly Jesuit missions in what was suddenly

devalued as Old California courageously advocating that Serra be given charge of extending the subverted agenda into as yet untried New California.

Which would allow fulfillment of Junipero's life-long dream to launch communities as envisioned by John Duns in the midst of worlds untried.

A selfless act and self-inflicted wound on the part of Palou, who then stood by helpless as his dearest friend marched off,

> Always forward,
> Never back

to lay the foundations for a decidedly new interpretation of civilization as per Llull, Franchesco, Duns, Plato and Junipero Serra.

Five long years passing before two devotees were to see each other again.

THE SACRED EXPEDITION

At two o'clock in the afternoon on April 11, 1769 a Spanish keel broke San Diego Bay's glassy expanse for the first time in nearly two centuries.

Captain Juan Perez nervously eyeing an empty harbor. Sir Vicente Vila having set sail weeks earlier and with whom he was here to rendezvous yet nowhere in sight.

Master of the <u>San Antonio</u> dropping anchor while refraining from going ashore. His instructions having been clear,

Run no Risks.

So it was that Perez made a decision rendered even more difficult by the fact that all aboard save two Franciscan missionaries lie deathly ill from scurvy.

In case of such an eventuality the orders of Don Joseph Galvez being that he remain twenty days before continuing on alone if needs be to Monterey.

Having himself initially overshot San Diego, arriving first at an archipelago off the coast of present-day Santa Barbara before suggesting the errors of Vizcaino's charts as transcribed by cartographer Cabrera Bueno, Juan Perez conjecturing publicly that Vila too had most likely made the same miscalculation. And perhaps sailed even further afield.

Mounting foreboding distilling upon captain and crew as days turned into what seemed an interminable two weeks spent listing at anchor.

When as if a ghost ship, what with no hands on deck, the errant <u>San Carlos</u> wallowed in and hove too alongside it's stricken companion.

From his afterdeck a distressed Perez ordering men over to reef sail and investigate.

Dead and dying discovered below deck bearing silent testimony to a nightmarish ordeal sustained.

When blown off course by adverse winds the <u>San Carlos</u> having floundered somewhere south of Panama. Then heading due north and northwest but with no making up for lost time or greater distance left to be traversed.

Enroute discovering casks containing the ship's drinking supply to have leaked, Lieutenant Pedro Fages then further detaining their advance as he desperately reconnoitered a little known coast in pursuit of potable water.

Soon every sailor on board falling ill from scurvy.

Leaving young Catalonian volunteer Jose Antonio Yorba, who had never before even been in a boat, to row ashore at Cedros Island and there attempt procurement both of water and sustenance.

Panic gripping hold of Yorba when the <u>San Carlos</u> unexpectedly disappeared from view. Overwhelming relief evoking tears of joy from a frightened youth once his ship reappeared upon the horizon.

Despite objections voiced against drinking the but brackish and malodorous water retrieved, Fages forcing all to partake. Whereupon plague swept through the galley, ultimately claiming twenty- four lives. With but four of Vila's crew surviving.

And to whom it seemed the disabled vessel had thereafter conducted itself into San Diego Bay.

Yorba, as one of but few even able to stand, carrying comrades ill with what surgeon Pratt dubbed,

Mal de Lo Anda

from off the afflicted San Carlos and into a makeshift hospital camp hastily assembled across from what are now the airship terminals of San Diego's Lindbergh Field at today's Spanish Landing.

Thereafter spending the next week digging graves in which to bury those fallen at since paved over and otherwise forgotten Dead Man's Point (H Street near Laurel).

When Mal de Lo Anda spread to infect men from off the San Antonio all efforts at San Diego focusing upon simply surviving long enough to receive overland contingents enroute.

With two or three men succumbing every day, many more failing to witness Gaspar de Portola's arrival.

Such triage not going unnoticed by curious Kumeyaay, whose main village of Cosoy lie little more than three miles distant.

As curiously they eyed said proceedings from afar. Remaining justifiably fearful both of these strangers and their affliction.

They would soon discover more valid reasons for maintaining but cautionary intercourse with the frail creatures tossed unexpectedly by the sea upon their shore.

Meanwhile and unawares a laconic Inspector/ Commandante General moving through the motions of conquest. Whilst complaining that cactus and scrub along what was suppose to have been an opened road reduced both his own uniform as well as those of the Royal Red Jacket escort to tatters.

Fray Junipero Serra enduring, with consummate resignation, endless slights and indignities at the hands of indifferent leadership,

From my mission of Loreto
I took along no more provisions for so long a journey
than a loaf of bread and a piece of cheese,

for albeit my mission
I was treated
as a mere guest
to receive the crumbs
of the royal soldier commissioner,

whose liberality at my departure
did not extend beyond
the aforementioned riches.

Lack of co-operation let alone respect repeatedly
compelling the missionary to his knees; as did a
patient Franciscan's troublesome leg, which became
ghastly inflamed shortly after departing Loreto.

At Mission San Francisco Xavier Brother Junipero being
reunited briefly with confidant Francisco Palou. Who
upon sight of his comrade's affliction pled out of fear for
Serra's life that he forego the expedition.

Aware that were he not present Portola might abort
mission installations altogether, Serra responding
with characteristic sang froid,

Let us not speak of that.

I trust God will give me the strength
to reach San Diego,
as He has given me the strength to come thus far.

In case He does not,
I will conform myself to His most holy will.
Even though I should die on the way,
I shall not turn back.
They can bury me wherever they wish
and I shall gladly be left among the gentiles,
if it be the will of God.

Which afforded Palou little consolation. Who out of
love conspired further to detain Serra by playing upon
his friend's aversion towards preferential treatment.

Arguing effectively that should Brother Junipero continue so disabled his handicap might well delay and otherwise place undo burden upon the Indians with whom he traveled.

And thus succeeded in convincing Serra to send Portola on ahead. Which Junipero did while insisting he would overtake the Royal guard after allowing for but a few days respite.

Palou spending the next three days employing his cunning together with any and every salvo available in a concerted effort both to reduce the swelling of Junipero's leg and convince his companion to bow out of the enterprise.

Neither endeavor meeting with success.

As well enough or not Serra insisted upon being underway before losing altogether any hope of ever catching up.

Junipero's leg remaining yet so horribly swollen as to render even standing let alone walking impossible.

Compliant Palou arranging with fourteen-year-old Joseph Maria Verqerano to accompany Serra as aid and manservant.

Who after dutifully positioning and strapping Brother Junipero atop a mule set off alongside muleteer as medic Juan Antonio Coronal to overtake the entrada.

Leaving Francisco sobbing openly from agonizing heartache.

Serra calling back over his shoulder,

See you in Monterey!

Palou's tearful response,

See you in eternity,

invoking Michael's tears.

But not lessening his resolve.

A note arriving upon the heals of said sad departure ostensibly from the King himself as addressed personally through Galvez to Palou affording some comfort.

Most assuredly God in heaven
will not only see to good Father Serra's recovery
but to his arrival at Monterey,

there to perform the work
to which he has been ordained,
if not predestined.

Meanwhile and despite great difficulty Brother Junipero overtook Portola. Painful inflammation in his leg persisted. As did he.

Riding more than a month ahead of the Royal Red Jackets was trail blazing Corporal Joseph Francisco Ortega, who together with pick wielding Jesuit schooled Indian novices extended a Camino Real (King's Highway) across untried territory.

And upon which Captain Fernando Javier Rivera y Moncado conducted his squadron of for the most part Mexican Soldiers each dressed out in de rigueur as habiliments full leatherjacket "armor" fashioned from layered cowhide. Further armed with broadsword, short-musket (trabuco) and bullhide shield.

Mounted cavalry afforded the additional protection of leather chaps designed to protect legs and thighs from brush and chaparral while riding otherwise similarly equipped but for the additional accoutrements of lance securely holstered to sidesaddle.

Grey robed Franciscan Brother Juan Crespi accompanying mule driving, provision carrying Jesuit novices themselves each in white muslin shirt and pantaloons of Jesuit mission manufacture.

An awesome procession to be sure. Exceeded in grandeur only by the second contingent marching several weeks in arrears. What with its Royal Red Jackets conducting Portola together with Serra and acolytes dressed out as personal escorts for a life-size statue of Mary, Queen of Heaven, in their habits of celestial blue.

A magnificent and arduous affair.

Frequently the barren outland traversed forcing both companies to bivouac without so much as fuel enough for campfires.

The erratic weather conditions of Baja California subjecting leather-clad cuirassiers to hot days without so much as a drop of water only to then inundate them with sudden and torrential monsoon rains.

But it was the caterwauling of a mountain lion that most discomforted the advance guard. Ever shadowing them. Keeping all on alert and ill at ease. Repeatedly jettisoning spooked livestock pell-mell into a wilderness from which they could not be recovered.

Rivera had like Portola come to perceive in his marching orders but a call to serve as escort for the Franciscans. And accordingly not only conducted all maneuvers in a perfunctory manner but maliciously withheld rations from Brother Crespi's novices after suggesting falsely that supplies were running dangerously low.

So it was that Christian Indian volunteers found themselves left effectively marooned what with nothing to eat and in hostile territory.

Rivera arriving in San Diego sans Indians and in remarkably good condition on May 14.

Any inclination towards celebration being tempered, however, with his realization that horrendous misfortune had swamped the expedition's navy.

Meanwhile, as Palou had predicted, Serra's handicap further delayed the second company. Still it was Brother Junipero's determination to gather up all novices found left abandoned in Rivera's wake that slowed Portola's advance down to a crawl.

Having determined previously to establish in route a supply depot at what was subsequently christened San Fernando (after Serra's Missionary College) de Velicata, loss of beasts of burden (scared away by the lion) and cast off Indians prompted Rivera to if not by design than of necessity leave there behind far more provisions than anticipated. And all certain to be required for sustaining still impossibly far off San Diego.

Stumbling across Rivera's immense depot in the desert, an incensed Father President of the Missions of New California insisting that time be taken to convert such blatant effrontery against both Christian Indians and Franciscan missionaries alike into not merely a warehouse but rather the expedition's first Mission.

Defiantly challenging otherwise abandoned novices to remain and there focus efforts upon transforming said site into both a temporal as well as spiritual oasis. Suggesting further that this effort would but help to bridge the great expanse between communities of their own in the south with those that they would, denigration aside, regardless soon themselves help found further North.

Arbitrary political and ecumenical boundaries drafted years later leaving Mission San Fernando Velicata aligned with the histories and traditions of Baja California. All but forgotten to the grand story unfolding in Alta (New) California, yet standing as first in Padre Serra's since celebrated chain of new communities.

Of their march ever northward Portola would record,

Never have I seen a more frightful country.

Serra, on the other hand, noting in said advance but an adventure that read like a verse straight out of Saint

Thomas More's Utopia:

> For under the line equinoctial,
> and on both sides of the same
> as far as the sun doth extend his course,
> lieth, quoth he,
> great and wide deserts and wildernesses,
> parched, burned, and dried up
> with continual and intolerable heat.
>
> All things be hideous, terrible, loathsome,
> and unpleasant to behold;
> all things out of fashion and comeliness,
> inhabited by wild beasts and serpents,
> or at the least wise
> with people that be no less savage, wild,
> and noisome
> than the very beasts themselves be.

While fully expecting both to witness as well as construct that which More forthwith suggested in his brilliant fantasy:

> But a little further beyond that,
> all things begin
> by little and little
> to wax pleasant;
> the air soft,
> temperate, and gentle;
> the ground covered with green grass;
> less wildness in the beasts.
>
> Until at the last
> shall ye come again
> to people, cities, and towns

wherein is continual intercourse
and occupying of merchandise and chaffare,
not only among themselves and with their borderers,
but also with merchants of far countries,
both by land and water.

To find citizens ruled by good and
wholesome laws;
that is an exceeding rare and hard thing.
Rehearsed here are divers acts
and constitutions
whereby cities,
nations, and countries,
and kingdoms
may take example to amend their faults,
enormities,
and errors.

Standing at the same latitude as Mother Spain, Dr. Serra had presumed that New California should therefore prove equally agreeable for successful installation of agricultural technologies employed at home.

And accordingly with aid from both Galvez and Palou had gathered together those self same seeds, vegetables, flowers, cattle, sheep and even chickens.

In said assertions Junipero was not to be disappointed. Articulating through his journal the marvelous, subtle transition of geography and environment encountered as he marched ever northward into a land,

nearest the earthly paradise.

As while yet amidst stark desolation the perceptive padre caught his first faint scent of New California's moisture -laden air.

Thereafter witnessing rocky desolation yield to a realm of rich grasslands sweetened with the fragrance of anise (wild licorice).

Green marshes opening into park-like oak woodlands carpeted with the gold of poppies and blue of lupine.

Everywhere grapevines clambering with abandon into high out-stretched arms of giant alisos (sycamore trees).

Lavender plumed artichoke lording over an otherwise veritable herb garden.

All about rambling tiny pink roses.

> While I am writing I have before me a branch of these roses of Castille, the Queen of all flowers.
>
> Upon it are three full-bloom roses and others in bud.

Diminutive yet stunning flowers, these in particular carrying Michael back across half a world and home to Spain. Validating in his own heart the fact that stretched out before him lie his ultimate field of labor. Indeed, a land as beautiful and laden with potential as that of Sir Thomas More's fairytale.

And to his further delight geographically speaking even similar in appearance to Mother Spain.

For in trekking across open, grassy plains and hills burnished gold beneath a perennial sun, he beheld but the reincarnation of Iberia's central plateau. Perceiving Valencia's own sweeping Mediterranean coastline in his approach to San Diego.

Proclaiming the bay wherein sat two Spanish ships riding at anchor,

Truly beautiful to behold,
and worthy of the fame
Cabrilho and Viscaino had each ascribed unto it.

Distant mountains rising above plains populated with herds of wild sheep, deer and antelope seeming to a Majorcan but the certain reflection of Spain's own grand Pyrenees.

Truly New California proving to be quintessentially New Spain.

A revelation which brought Serra great solace. For he sensed having come full circle to arrive with contentment back at home.

But it would be the Californians themselves who truly stole his heart.

I found myself suddenly amongst twelve of them,
all males and grown,
except two who were boys,
one about of 10 years, and the other of about 15.

I saw that which I had hardly managed to believe
when I used to read it or they told me of it,

which was their going totally nude,
as Adam in Paradise before his sin.

So they go, and so they presented themselves to us,
and we conversed a long while;
without there being perceptible in them
in all that while,
though they saw us all clothed,
the least blush for being in that manner.

I praised the Lord,
I kissed the earth,
giving His Majesty thanks
that after so many years of desiring them
He had granted me to see myself among them in
their land.

I put my two hands on the heads of them all,
one by one,
in token of affection;
I filled both their hands with dried figs,
which they at once began to eat;

And received with signs of much appreciating it
the regalement of a net full of roasted mescal
and four fish
which they presented to us.

Their affability now declining to familiarity,
for if in sign of affection
we put our hands on their heads or shoulder,
they did the same to us,

And if they saw us seated,
There they sat close to us.

Here upon this clean slate void of any vestige of the Old World, untainted by those scandals of the New, Serra recognizing a population in possession of sufficient innocence with which to successfully inaugurate an authentic Utopia.

Such grand dreams all but terminally shattered however when, on June 29th, he marched headlong into the death camps that were San Diego.

There to discover half the men from both ships having perished. And with supplies left behind in Velicata, severe shortages of rations jeopardizing survivors. Placing the entire enterprise on the brink of disaster.

Personal devastation consuming him when in addition to said complications he was apprised of the fact that soldiers had already rounded up and sexually exploited Indian proteges even before a would be Christian utopian had been given the opportunity of introducing any of them either to Plato or to Christ.

In an instant romance giving way to an overwhelming sense of desperate isolation.

MONTE-REY?

S talked by tragedy a petulant Portola grew anxious concerning wrapping up his floundering military operation. Which required that he proceed forthwith to Monterey.

And so arbitrarily replaced Vila's deceased crew with his own Red-jacket guard. Ordering them to set sail immediately.

Sir Vicente objecting. Arguing that soldiers were not sailors and could not possibly commandeer his ship.

In acquiescing Portola then demanding Perez set sail in the San Antonio for La Paz, ostensibly to secure both a second crew as well as additional and sorely needed supplies.

Whilst determining to continue the advance but as a single grounded company.

Leaving Admiral Vila with his orphaned San Carlos at anchor. And Serra otherwise alone to pick up the pieces and care for the sick.

It would be during the Inspector/Commandante's absence that Vila the knight joined Serra the Franciscan in subverting what ravages of nature aside both men recognized as but proliferation of a hidden agenda designed to undo both Majesties.

Dispatching their own call for help back down that just blazed "Camino Real" to Francisco Palou at San

Xavier and thence on to Galvez directly.

Then, following Portola's departure, gathering invalid sailors and soldiers to witness the founding of Mission San Diego on the anniversary of Spain's great victory against its last Moorish caliphate. Accordingly adding to said christening "de Alcala," which is to say "of the fortress" in reference to Granada's Alhambra.

At his Mission San Diego de Alcala the Crusader remaining confident. Knowing that Sergeant Joseph Ortega, in whom he'd discovered yet another ally, marched at the head of Portola's advance guard and with both Friars Juan Crespi and Antonio Gomez in tow. All three committed to the spiritual conquest of California.

Antithetically riding Don Pedro Fages together with now but seven Catalonian volunteers. And Fernando Rivera whom as per Serra's arrangement found himself bringing up the rear, behind and in the dust of said caravan, as commander not of Spanish soldiers but rather fifteen Christian Indian muleteers.

Roughly paralleling routes shadowed today by Interstate 5 (north from San Diego to Los Angeles) and Highway 101 (from L.A. north to Monterey), this tiny band of Iberian "conquistadors" traversing the golden Pacific slope of a charmed province. Enroute grappling with interpretation of landscapes at once exotic and yet strangely familiar.

Southern California's overriding Island being quick to introduce itself, when fording a river at the Acjachemem (Ah-Hotch-ee-Mum) village of Hutukna

(Who-too-ka-na), European troops were thrown to the ground by a terrific earthquake.

Fray Crespi recording that the tremor:

> lasted about half as long as an Ave Maria,

> and about ten minutes later it was repeated,
> though not so violently.

Recording then how without hesitation an Acjachemem Ateateech (priest) responded promptly by addressing each of four directions. Leaving a Franciscan to understand that earthquakes were not an altogether infrequent occurrence in these parts.

The Acjachemem proved friendly and hospitable. Their chief imploring that his Spanish guests stay and,

> share in the rich bounty of our good land.

Meanwhile Fray Crespi articulating amazement concerning what he could only perceive as a general lack of modesty amongst all Californians thus far encountered. Describing the simplicity of women's raiment, while noting an otherwise,

> very manly fashion
> on the part of the men
> simply to go naked.

There on the Feast Day of Saint Anne a Franciscan in the midst of several thousand nude Indians conducting a most unusual Holy Day Celebration.

And during which Crespi christened river and Acjachemem village Saint Anne (Santa Ana) of the Earthquakes.

Then pressing into the hand of its priest, who otherwise refused payment for courtesies graciously extended, his gift of a small crucifix.

Following which Portola stepped off to hasten across a great basin teeming with antelope.

Crespi proclaiming the grassy expanse Our Lady, Queen of the Angels. Pronouncing upon the river traversing it Portiuncula (Little Portion), a term of endearment for San Damiano, which had served as sanctuary to his seraphic father Saint Francis.

All along the way rallying Tongva in chorus,

    yelped and hollered like so many coyotes.

Portola understandably guarded, nonetheless finding himself once again being received hospitably this time at Yangna (today's Los Angeles).

    One who spoke as with the voice of authority

conducting his curiously overdressed visitors to an extraordinary swamp where Fray Crespi recorded witnessing bitumen (actually tar) bubbling up from underground petroleum deposits.

Catalonian boys raised on Montalvo's fairytales shaken when presented with bones of hideously fanged monsters recovered from a murky cienega (marsh).

On the Feast Day of Santa Monica Portola headed due north to cross a low range of mountains.

And upon descending marched headlong into a country densely settled with many large towns.

To thereafter parade across land- locked valleys wherein great blonde bears were confronted seemingly at every turn.

Bones of strange beasts encountered at Los Angeles notwithstanding apprehensive soldiers did not see any griffins.

Yet faced off nonetheless with an equally frightening prospect of seemingly endless mountains sliding into the sea.

Chronicler Crespi recording:

It was a sad spectacle for us,
poor wayfarers,
tired and worn by the fatigues of the long journey.

For all of this tended to oppress our hearts,

But, remembering the object to which these toils
were directed,
and that it was for the greater glory of God
through the conversion of souls,
and for the service of the King,
whose dominions were being enlarged by this
expedition,
all were animated to work cheerfully.

Entering the Salinas Valley near what is today Soledad the Entrada then spending six days tracing its river. To arrive at their final destination.

Which remarkably Gaspar refused acknowledging, when gazing across vast dunes he suggested that if this was indeed fabled Monterey it had subsequently become filled in with sand!

Arguing further that the packetboat <u>San Joseph</u> which had been sent directly and should have long since arrived was similarly nowhere to be seen.

Fray Juan Crespi wondering,

> Without being able to guess the reason,
> we were all kept under hallucination,
> with no one daring to assert openly
> that the port we beheld before us
> was indeed Monterey.

Portola's official report being more succinct,

> At Punto Pinos (Point of Pines) there is no port.

Ignoring assertions concerning the nonexistence of that which stood before him Crespi planting a large cross there in the dunes while together with Brother Gomez dedicating Monterey to Jesus Christ.

Miguel Costanso recording:

> All the officers voted unanimously
> that the journey be continued,
> as this was the only course remaining open to us,

for we had hoped to find--
through the grace of God--
in the much desired port of Monterey,
the packetboat <u>San Joseph,</u>
which might relieve our needs;

and,
if God willed that in our search
we should but wander and perish,
we would have performed our duty towards
God and man,
cooperating to the death
for the success of the undertaking
upon which we had been sent.

So it was that despite having obtained their objective the expedition continued its march. Only to find themselves lost in a spacious forest where stood,

rank upon rank of sheer,
ruddy trunks of giant timber
before this unknown to Spaniards,

which Crespi christened Palo Colorado or Redwood.

From Half Moon Bay Portola spying afar off the white cliffs of Drake's Nova Albion. Clearly having ventured too far north.

When both trailblazing Ortega and soldiers dispatched to procure venison each returned that evening bearing reports of a gigantic oceanic causeway not indicated on any known chart, everyone in the little band rendered perplexed.

On the morning of November 4th Portola surmounting a redwood clad rise above what is now the community of Palo Alto to gaze spellbound upon,

An inland sea,
a new Mediterranean,
stretching northward and southward
as far as the eye could reach.

Further exploration revealing the great and quiet bay beneath him all but landlocked,

so near together were the two titanic pillars
of its one gate,
opening onto a sunset sea.

Crespi marveling that of this landmark discovery Portola reported laconically having,

found nothing,

leaving us in doubt
as to whether we could find anything further on.

And sensing both duplicity and the reality of a hidden agenda as hinted at by Serra, could not help but smile.

For in Portola's folly of refusing to acknowledge Monterey he had most assuredly been divinely manipulated into delivering a miracle.

His duplicitous,

hallucination

which had kept all in a quandary, the,

hallucination

that compelled him to press on, but brought resolution to a debate conducted months earlier between Father President Serra and Inspector General Galvez concerning the King's oversight in proposing establishment of Franciscan Missions both at San Diego and at Monterey, without dedicating either to Saint Francis.

If Francis wants a mission,

quipped Galvez jocularly,

> let him cause his own port to be discovered
> and we'll put his mission **there**.

Crespi's eyes twinkling, as with a sly smile he recorded,

> This port which of course we promptly named in
> honor of our most holy and seraphic father Saint
> Francis is very large and without doubt
> could contain not only all the armadas of our
> Catholic Monarch
> but also all the ships of the world.

Insisting further to Portola that,

> This is the harbour of our father St. Francis.
> And we have left Monterey behind.

When Gaspar countered by suggesting they continue the advance all voting unanimously against him.

Advocating instead a speedy return by way of Monterey to San Diego and at once, as having traveled further than anticipated without any sign of <u>San Joseph</u> the expedition was running dangerously short of what had been, from the outset courtesy of Rivera, but meager provisioning.

Illness imported from off <u>San Carlos</u>, too, having dogged them. Sixteen men losing enroute the use of their limbs.

Transporting disabled soldiers on tepestles (litters) dragged behind mules having been at best a dangerous proposition. What with livestock constantly spooked by the sudden appearance of everything from jack rabbits to grizzly bears.

Even Portola having endured the indignity of being so transported.

Ohlone Indians remedying his predicament by instructing that he counter the ravages of disease by gorging on wild blackberries-- which the Commandante did. And promptly recovered.

Whilst convalescing near a huge Indian temple constructed of timbers and tules at what is today California's magnificent Filoli Estate, Gaspar weighing his options.

Recalling in a letter written years later:

> In this confusion and distress, friend,
> not under compulsion from the Russians,
> but from keen hunger,

which was wearing us out,
we decided to return to San Diego,
for the purpose of recuperating our strength
by means of the provisions
which we judged would soon arrive there
on the San Antonio.

In order that we might not die meanwhile,
I ordered that at the end of each day's march,
one of the weak mules which carried our baggage
and ourselves, should be killed.

The flesh we roasted or half fried in a fire made
in a hole in the ground.
The mule being thus prepared,
without a grain of salt or other seasoning--
for we had none--
we shut our eyes
and fell to on that scaly mule (what misery!)
like hungry lions.

We ate twelve in as many days,
obtaining from them perforce all our sustenance,
all our appetite,
all our delectation.

At last we entered San Diego,
smelling frightfully of mules.

The reverend father president said to me,
as he welcomed me back,
'You come from Rome
without having seen the Pope,'
alluding to the fact that we had not found
the port of Monterey.

Meanwhile at San Diego disease had continued taking its toll. Leaving sick to tend to the sick, those dying to bury the dead.

Kumeyaay not having been as forthcoming as the Ohlone with regard to sharing their extensive knowledge of medicinals. Serra left but to perform daily the sacrament of extreme unction. Commending each man lost to

God's grace and mercy,

while reminding all present that lives thus surrendered were not sacrificed in vain, but rather, to be rewarded elsewhere.

Intuitively Brother Junipero had sensed a need for heightened security. So it was that in Portola's absence and disregarding Rivera's recommendations,

the missionary,

ordered relocation of his entire encampment to a hilltop deemed more strategic.

Those strong enough aiding by cutting down alisos and gathering reeds from the San Diego River adjacent with which to erect modest housing and fortifications.

Vila mustering Spain's royal standard in from off the San Carlos to be hoisted high above this first European settlement on the West Coast of what is today the United States.

Mystic Serra ringing but the single bell in his possession while blessing with holy water a wooden cross placed to indicate an intended church.

Displaying upon a makeshift altar his life-size image of Mary-Our Lady of Bethlehem.

Which coincidentally just happened to be the exact same Portuguese influenced interpretation of her that had calmed Cabrilho's troubled heart when in San Diego so many years earlier.

Now as before evoking similarly profound veneration from sailors left to confront their own mortality. Comforted as they were by an image with which they were most familiar.

How providential, thought Serra, that he had brought this specific portrayal of Mary overland with him.

Behind his crude- made-splendid altar showcasing a magnificent painting of Mary-Mother of Light, depicting the Virgin holding baby Jesus in one arm whilst with her other lifting an Indian child towards heaven.

Powerful icons eliciting from Kumeyaay women offers to suckle with their own breasts the beautiful infants portrayed.

Mary's presence reminding all that they were in the service not only of both majesties but the mother of their god, whose noble mission was that of rescuing from darkness every child born into this world.

Each day as he overlooked the magnificence of Southern California's gentle wilderness, Serra sprinkling holy water, ringing his single bell and singing the Te Deum.

Majorca's own Knight of the Cross opening that proverbial door through which California might access, with a blessing from Christianity's god, the terrible uncertainty of European colonialism fast approaching.

And against which both Crusader Serra and these innocents were about to do battle.

THE MIRACLE

I t would be at San Diego when Serra proved himself an authentic hero. His unbounded faith and if not receipt of divine revelation then uncanny ability to ferret out deception he alone preventing abortion of nascent California.

Thereby staying the course and correspondingly setting tenor for all that which was to follow.

Single-handedly assuring that what proved Spain's final Conquista be defined not by the brutality and bloodletting that had come to underscore three centuries of European meddling in New World affairs, but rather for its innovative social pioneering and unfailing humanity.

Serra being no youthful dreamer when at fifty-six he set out to impose his idealized interpretation of Christendom upon an unsuspecting frontier. Steadfast as fictional King Utopus in a determination to bring:

> the rude and wild people
> to that excellent perfection
> in all good fashions, humanity, and civil gentleness
> wherein they now go beyond all people of the world.

This subsequently re-occurring quest for social transcendency, set in motion by Serra, foreverafter permeating California's story.

As perhaps nowhere else in all the world did a land and a dream come to find themselves so inextricably intertwined; both reality and a pervasive ideal perennially perceived as being one and the same.

What with blue robed Franciscans cast as philosopher/king mentors launching nothing less stupendous than a Spanish intellectual's interpretation of Plato's Republic.

Peaceful progressives far removed from war and tyranny and greed. Offering themselves as embodiment of the selflessness required for sustaining such societies. Accepting vows that denied personal access to the rewards of their own conquest. Efforts made representing rather payback to God for having already bestowed upon them gifts of life and the promise for eternal salvation.

California's founding fathers harboring but one ambition; to elevate through education and otherwise provide for the advancement of those amongst whom they'd been called to serve.

Willingly accepting even martyrdom in return.

Splashing imagery of the pelican across thresholds to their modest abodes. Who through piercing its own skin nurses with blood, fledglings otherwise unable to reach food stored for them in their mother's gullet.

Benefits to Don Carlos on the otherhand for piety manifested through facilitating said Franciscan effort being both goodwill and exclusive rights of developing trade garnered from a subsequently beholden constituency.

Rome's reward to be the ongoing proliferation of its own grand agenda aimed at salvaging from ruination and self-destruction a World gone amuck. With the intent to see installed by close of its second thousand years a globe spanning Millennial Kingdom of God.

Momentary precedent for such dreams had shined luminously in the Caribbean, across Patagonia, deep in the jungles of Guatemala and throughout a Sonoran frontier.

Forced expulsion of its Jesuit architects by those understandably fearful of one world government occasioning the subsequent skirmish to prevent disinterested and thereby competitive parties from forestalling said agenda in favor of renewing expansionary policies of privatized colonialism.

Despite great cost and much sacrifice Don Carlos vowing that California as a Kingdom of Spain would entertain no outside interference from any vested interests other than those of his own.

And stood not merely determined but defiant concerning Catholicism's agenda to convert and thereby impart salvation both in this world as well as the next through Christian sacraments and a Greek education.

Correspondingly bestowing at his own expense upon those deemed most impoverished the gifts of literacy and applied technologies together with an introduction to Western Art and athletics.

Meanwhile as hunger, fear, disease and discouragement undermined all efforts surrounding inauguration of the

WEST OF THE WEST

self-governing Indian commonwealth envisioned by Don Carlos, it would be Brother Junipero alone who kept that flame of Plato and Christ alive.

One hundred and fifty men, more than half of the expeditionary forces dispatched to New California in the first place, having died; most from "Mal de lo Anda" as introduced courtesy of the San Carlos.

Thirty-eight more interred at San Diego during Portola's brief absence.

Kumeyaay willing to trade whatever they had in exchange for anything Spanish exploiting a demoralized and sexually frustrated soldiery itself placating fears of impending mortality by seeking solace through promiscuity.

Indians who through submission acquiring all the trappings of an exotic culture rendered the envy of their peers. Provoking those unwilling to surrender yet equally desirous of securing similar booty.

So it was that when a but modest guard skiffed over to prevent theft of sails and rigging from off the San Carlos, emboldened Indians leapt the parapets of an improvised camp. And in appropriating provisions at will left dying men unable to protest stripped naked of all possessions lying exposed in their tents.

Shots fired from the ship to frighten away thieves but sparking their wrath made manifest in a cloud of arrows.

One projectile nailing Brother Juan Vizcaino's hand to a door he had rushed to close.

Another piercing Joseph Maria Verquerano's throat. Striking an artery. Which when draining into the boy's windpipe, drowned him in his own blood. Whilst he pled, between gasps for air, that Serra administer absolution.

Brother Junipero, in so doing, made to witness a terrible and excruciating death as he cradled the lad in his arms.

Soldiers hastening back to the scene firing another volley of musket shot. This time into the crowd directly.

Serra power praying that both parties be spared further casualties.

Still the Kumeyaay were successfully disbursed only after several more of their own ranks had been killed. Precipitating overwhelming guilt upon those knowingly culpable for instigation of said confrontation through their own lack of moral restraint.

Who now out of shame dared not confess concerning circumstances surrounding the debacle. Unwilling to inform "Father" that because of personal indiscretion's not only Indians but Joseph Maria had died.

Fray Junipero already comprehending fully the vacuum of prehistory in which he now knelt.

It was in fact this critical and all-important element of innocence that rendered California a valid candidate for receiving authentic civilization as envisioned by John Duns.

And so to instantly atone for sins committed Serra demanding he be whipped publicly and severely as proxy penitent for the cowardly acts of others.

When embarrassed soldiers refused, a grieving father forcing all to witness self-mortification as in simulating Ramon Llull's martyrdom Michael beat himself nearly to death with a stone.

At dawn of the following day few other than Serra remaining convinced they would be in California long enough to inaugurate any sort of society, transcendent or otherwise.

Altercations with Kumeyaay were followed by a failed harvest of but hastily planted corn which having quickly fallen victim to birds and wild animals now yielded little in the way of sorely needed sustenance.

Circumstances rendered desperate by an apparent disappearance of the packetboat San Joseph.

So that when Portola returned to announce he had failed in his attempt at locating Monterey all perceived the enterprise as having come to an end.

All that is except for Michael Serra.

Who after conferring privately with confidant Crespi, remained convinced pugtilious Portola had indeed identified Monterey. And furthermore questioned openly why it was that a ship carrying accoutrements needed for installing churches seemed to have vanished into thin air?

Which prompted Sir Vicente Vila's contribution that even now Perez carried orders that he sail directly on to this Monterey which had not been found.

And that Rivera whom Portola had just dispatched ostensibly to retrieve supplies stashed at Velicata would in fact not return but continue on to Loreto without looking back.

No longer merely suspicious, Serra knew that powers intent upon subverting all Catholic endeavor, covertly operating so as to introduce rather a secular colonialism, were at play against both Majesties.

Indeed having purged the America's of missionaries, power players backing Portola on the Council of the Indies harboring no intention of seeing installed more State controlled religious. Hoping instead to secure a second chance at conquest funded privately and without the meddling of king or Catholicism.

Cognizant of those inexplicably exiled Jesuits, determined to prevent similar subversion against the Franciscans, Serra in quiet desperation pouring out his heart and soul to heaven.

One hundred and sixty six years had come and gone since the Count of Monterrey announced Spain's intentions of establishing a Catholic kingdom of California. Should failure to do so occur again and at this late juncture a perspicacious missionary recognizing that its spiritual conquest would in all likelihood never again be undertaken.

And while accordingly admonishing phlegmatic

Portola to stay the course- hold fast- await both
heaven's intervention and the arrival of one or the
other or both of the supply ships

Always forward,
Never back

moved quickly to outmaneuver plans previously
devised contrariwise.

Assuring the Governor's Inspector/Commandante in
no uncertain terms that should he withdraw,

the missionary

would himself remain behind to effect a spiritual
conquest alone if needs be.

Meanwhile, Serra's own previously dispatched plea for
help had long since reached both Palou and Galvez.
Who unbeknownst to Portola were already in the
midst of mounting a rescue effort.

Faced with Junipero's obstinance, a surreptitious
operative inventoried and suggested that under
strictest of economies should the expedition hold out
at San Diego until March 20th they might yet abort
and make for a hasty retreat.

Accordingly proposing to knowing Serra that if
supplies did not arrive by the aforementioned date
either from Perez or Rivera (neither of whom had any
intention of returning to San Diego) all would be
forced to quit the new kingdom.

Never had Michael doubted for one minute whether or not his own prayers for success were being heard in heaven on high. And now could not help but smile with a realization that Portola's ultimatum just happened to fall one day after the feast of California's seraphic patron Saint Joseph.

Perceiving in this coincidence assurances with regard to divine intervention.

Recognizing soon to be posted as Governor Portola as but errand boy for a secular and heretic New World cabal operating in collusion with the now Masonic controlled Council of Indies prompting loyal Sir Vicente Vila's pact that he commandeer Serra personally regardless of the outcome on to Monterey.

Clandestine correspondence from the missionary concerning said strategies both thrilling a royal patron and comforting Palou. Serra was alive, as was the enterprise.

There would be little time to spare what with Portola's deadline fast approaching.

Requesting that all join in a nine-day vigil of prayer and supplication for divine intervention from no less than Saint Joseph, Serra who was now himself afflicted with Mal de Lo Anda regardless insisting upon abstaining from either food or drink throughout.

By means of which he successfully shifted men's attentions away from an impending retreat to focus rather upon their own deep-seated Catholic faith.

Each morning at sunrise the weakened religious rallying his vanguard of Christian soldiers and sailors with communal recitation of special prayers.

Such theater resulting either through divine intercession or synchronicity of chance in an occurrence that rendered even agnostic Portola astounded.

When on the Feast Day of Saint Joseph an emaciated Franciscan gathered all about him to offer up one final appeal.

At dusk on that same day a curtain of heavy marine air shrouding San Diego's coastline suddenly parting. Whereupon an ecstatic Serra shouted that he could see the San Antonio, hull down, as if a great white-winged angel, just beyond the harbor.

Leaving men unable themselves to see anything at all scratching their heads. And suggesting the missionary had in his weakened state begun hallucinating.

When one by one others proclaimed excitedly that they, too, could see the sails of a ship.

An evening of mixed elation and quandary quickly dissipating into general disbelief however when all realized that if they'd seen a launch it had most assuredly passed them by without stopping.

And so it had. But as Captain Juan Perez approached the archipelago of Santa Barbara in his race northward to Monterey a crewmember alerted him that the San Antonio had mysteriously lost its anchor.

To proceed into an unknown without any ability of stopping was but to court disaster. And knowing that an extra anchor courtesy of the orphaned San Carlos sat in San Diego where he could purposefully beach his vessel along a gentle sandbar with which he was already familiar, Perez made an abrupt and unanticipated U-turn.

In the meantime before a duped Portola, Serra convincing those present that whether real or imagined, the vision of San Antonio's sails was most assuredly a sign from no less than Saint Joseph sent to encourage patience.

And now armed with full support of Catholic troops, frustrated an Inspector/Commandante by leaving him little alternative but to further postpone departure.

For what turned out to be yet another remarkable test of faith "the missionary" knowingly gambling away Portola's schedule for successful retreat.

Five days later, when the San Antonio did crash land into those open arms of a spiritually conquered entrada, it would be difficult to determine just who was more surprised to see whom; with one exception.

Never had Serra's faith in the Almighty wavered. Nor had his own efforts to assure success.

Informed of events as they transpired aboard the San Antonio, Brother Junipero throwing his arms up in the air to declare that Saint Joseph had himself reached out and grabbed hold of Perez, by dispensing with that anchor, and thus dragging him back to San Diego.

Nor had anyone failed to notice that the <u>San Antonio</u> arrived accompanied by an extraordinary escort. The winds sweeping salvation in the form of a supply ship being laden with thousands upon thousands of swallows.

Every Catholic present recognizing in these little birds but the symbolic emissaries of Saint Francis. Suggesting furthermore cognizance on his part of their effort. A sign that he, too, was looking out for them from the Holy Courts of Heaven on high.

So it seemed to all assembled that day in San Diego as if Francis and Joseph had both made their presence felt.

Most being convinced they'd beheld a miracle.

Portola detecting something else.

Perez handing him letters from Galvez. The King's Alter Ego did not believe in harbors that disappeared anymore than did the Franciscans. Assiduously suggesting that a would-be Governor get on with his assignment.

Never again would Portola underestimate Serra's brilliance or leadership abilities nor his extraordinary connections.

And obliged to conduct a second march on Monterey insisted Brother Junipero accompany Juan Perez personally aboard the <u>San Antonio</u>, suggesting Monterey might be more readily discernible from a seaward approach, while quipping that with a "saint" on board,

God himself will most assuredly point it out to us.

Otherwise pedestrian Serra agreeing to indulge in a boat ride whilst Portola struck out again down his now familiar trail. Both parties to rendezvous at the cross planted by Fray Crespi on that beach hypothetically above Vizcaino's illusive bay.

Disappearance of the packet boat <u>San Joseph</u> remains if unresolved then suspect. As do the particulars surrounding a sparing Council and King represented on site by Portola and Serra.

What stands certain is the fact that for the rest of his life Fray Junipero would celebrate the 19th of **every** month as Saint Joseph's Day.

Those subsequently joining the Franciscans in California marking an annual appearance of Franchesco's little swallows with fiestas and prayers.

Surprisingly aligning as solidly as Saint Patrick with his Ireland or Germany and Saint Boniface not Joseph but rather spiritual interloper Serra to California and the Story of its founding.

MONTE-REY!

nxious that he might redeem himself Portola shunted a second expeditionary force off to Monterey.

The seasonal verdigris of California's landscape setting them adrift upon a surreal canvas splashed with every conceivable shade of green.

Such enchantment noticeably impacting exhausted yet esthetic Spaniards. For whom death itself seemed suddenly vanquished together with the tawny topography of summer's drought. As all about amidst a riotous explosion of wildflowers stretched the world resurrected.

Upon arriving in Monterey a compunctive Inspector/Commandante not only agreeing to recognize Vizcaino's harbor but even managing identification of the very oak underwhich equally challenged survivors had themselves convened nearly two centuries earlier:

twenty paces from a small spring,
at high tide its branches almost sweeping the waves.

The <u>San Antonio</u> arriving one week later.

Serra setting foot on what was to become both home and final resting-place. Seeing in this arguably most dramatic convergence of land and sea on earth but an even lovelier rendition of his own native Majorca.

And to Palou penning,

> This is indeed the famous harbor
> discovered by Vizcaino in 1603;
> it has not changed.

> As for saying why the first expedition did not find it,
> this is not my affair.

> The great thing is that we are here.

From the branches of Vizcaino's grand oak Fray Junipero suspending two bells. In its shade raising a second cross, configuring another makeshift altar and displaying anew his life-size <u>Mary-Our Lady of Bethlehem</u> together with the painting <u>Mary-Our Lady of Light</u>.

And there on Pentecost, birthday of Christendom, lighting dozens of candles, singing the Te Deum and sending sweet smelling incense adrift upon a spring breeze.

Blessing Spanish standards mustered in from off the <u>San Antonio</u> whilst Portola proclaimed Monterey future seat of California government. Then dedicating the site to seraphic patron of Don Carlos III, San Carlos Borromeo.

Soldiers weeping openly as following burial of yet another, Alexo Nino, Serra remembering each and every fallen comrade by name.

From afar Chief Tatlun of Ixchenta viewing such powerful ceremony with wonder filled eyes.

His people already having attributed supernatural powers to the cross planted earlier by Fray Juan Crespi. Avowing that but to touch it was to dispel pain and illness. While insisting that each night the magic token assumed gigantic proportions. Standing luminous in the dark.

When blue-robed mystic Serra erected yet a second cross and placed beside it nothing less breathtaking than the image of a beautiful goddess Tatlun experiencing euphoric hope.

Hope for the liberation both of himself and his people from an insidious syndicate of religious who by virtue of claiming as manifestations of their own supernatural powers every pain and illness known to man successfully overruled his authority while exacting compliance to their every whim.

Tatlun enthralled as he witnessed the auspicious arrival of something newer, bigger and already perceived even by the Rumsen Ohlone people of neighboring Tamo (Monterey) as being more powerful.

Recognizing in this spiritual challenger but a potential ally.

Might this new wizard provide him with the very real possibility of overcoming a hated oligarchy of sorcerers who through unscrupulous intimidation held all of Tamo and environs hostage?

So it was that where the Kumeyaay at San Diego had attacked, and Monterey's local Rumsen Ohlone fled, Tatlun boldly embraced Serra openly. Anxious to align himself with one who through the healing miracles of a cross had already manifested both power and benevolence.

Humbled by such an unprecedented reception, Serra thereafter assuring Tatlun that he was not himself a magician. And that he possessed no powers with which to heal the sick or ailing. While acknowledging rather that Jesus Christ, whom the cross represented and whom he himself served, could not only heal the body but save the ethereal soul.

Culture clash and conflicts were inevitable. Nevertheless the love affair between Serra and Tatlun's people, in whom a grateful Franciscan himself recognized powerful allies and ever after referring to them as Saint Joseph's emissaries, proved genuine and lasting.

So it was that the village of Ixchenta became identified rather as San Jose (Saint Joseph).

Leaving Fray Junipero convinced that had Christ been given this same opportunity of demonstrating pure love to the Kumeyaay at San Diego before seeing them subjected to European vice they too might well have responded as favorably. And now prevailed upon Portola to not only make his exit but take with him all military personnel.

Already opting out of an exercise he could no longer manipulate, nonetheless the Governor's Inspector/ Commandante refusing even to consider aborting the politically sensitive presence of a Junta controlled military.

And responding rather by refusing to permit Serra's founding of his Monterey mission anywhere outside a precipitately installed Royal Presidio designed to provide the protection Franciscans neither wanted nor deemed warranted.

Regardless while soldiers engaged in raising fortifications for what would one day replace Loreto as California's new provincial capitol, Fray Junipero Serra and his volunteers from San Jose (Ixchenta) making quiet preparations for construction of an elaborate temple elsewhere.

At San Diego Serra had come to depend upon the assistance of fourteen- year old Kumeyaay O-o-nil.

Who on his own demonstrated a determination to break the code of Spanish language. And so despite continual altercations with soldiers persisted in shadowing the priests.

Such lively curiosity having warmed Serra's heart.

Himself the consummate linguist, Fray Junipero had previously managed translation of both catechism and prayers into the Pame tongue spoken by his novices back in Mexico's Sierra Gorda.

Yet facility with Mallorquin, Catalan, Spanish, Latin, English and various Indian idioms aside Serra finding himself completely stymied by California's extraordinarily complex pastiche of languages.

A dilemma he overcame by identifying an almost insane indigenous fetish for European garb,

I have a hard time understanding their
mania for clothes,

Fray Junipero recording,

They jump out of their skins,
as the saying goes
for any bright colored cloth.

If I had given the Franciscan habit to all
who asked for one,
there would already be extant
a large community of blue-robed friars
residing in Alta California.

They even pester me for my spectacles.

So it was that Serra rewarded O-o-nil's persistence by lavishing upon him all the trappings of a Spaniard's wardrobe. Then, outfitted to the nines in leather cuirasses and boots, placing the boy astride a mule.

All of which elevated him in stature as well as status and correspondingly enhanced his sphere of influence.

In return for which O'o-nil served Serra faithfully as interpreter. Who in the aftermath of losing Joseph Maria perceived yet another gift from a compassionate god.

Here was one of California's own who could go before him to pave the way for spiritual redemption.

And in memory of he who had found favor as Christ's most beloved, christened little O-o-nil rather John (Juan) the Evangelist (Evangelista).

At Monterey Serra bestowing upon little John (Juanito) yet another commission.

Spend all day playing with the gentile children.

Which was to say those children who were not Christian.

Each evening Juanito teaching Doctor Junipero words he had learned from the boys and girls of neighboring villages.

So that by the time construction was completed on a temporary church inside the Presidio, missionary Serra found himself armed with enough of an Ohlone lexicon to begin ministering.

Whereupon he commenced in earnest the fulfilment of a lifelong dream if not his destiny to flood some territory as yet untried with the illumination both of education as well as transcendent Christian precepts.

The impossibility of mastering this country's many languages stood overshadowed only by the difficulty presented in attempting to bring Serra's gift as it were to people scattered throughout a landscape as variegated as they themselves.

So it was that Fray Junipero focused rather upon bringing California to the gift.

And if Church is to be considered theater then that which Serra staged can only be described as religious spectacle.

Beginning with his parading of Mary accompanied as she was by her vanguard of Franciscans in blue flanked by a Governor's Royal Red Jacket brigade into the new country.

And where Portola had blown off witnessing the show prepared for San Diego he found himself standing uncomfortably center stage at Monterey next to a man even he now recognized as being not just any missionary but rather The King's own personal evangelist extraordinare.

Who, understanding the teaching value of artistic form, ever called upon his own natural abilities as a showman in carefully staging everything from dress to salutation.

Having discovered that occurrences as singularly compelling as the display of a cross or pealing of bells precipitated crowds, accordingly incorporating unorthodox even flamboyant style into already ostentatious Catholic ritual.

Each altar regardless of how small bearing many candles. Every structure no matter how modest dressed out in elaborate and colorful banners illustrated with Bible stories.

At services Serra performing what Franciscans referred to as Stations of the Cross while underscoring the same by singing in beautiful Gregorian chant each step in succession.

To teach love he was love.

Shaming perpetrators of evil acts into submission and riveting congregations by repeating his display at San

Diego of self- mortification. Beating himself repeatedly and savagely as surrogate penitent for the wrongdoing of others.

Magician or not, Serra's methods having the desired if not magic affect of gathering large crowds. Thousands choosing to take counsel from this man who above all else remained consistently genuine and pure of heart in his dealings with them.

Leaving even Portola to ponder conjecture surrounding America's greatest missionary, San Francisco Solano, of whom it had been suggested given flute or violin might well have single-handedly conquered the entire continent.

Of course Serra's conquest as Knight of the Cross was at best misunderstood by the likes of Portola.

And not to be confused with conquest in the traditional sense. His Quest rather, to see education prevail over ignorance- virtue over vice, being leveled at both Indian and Spaniard alike.

So charismatically executed in fact that, much to the chagrin of a Supreme Council's American Junta, many on-site government and military personnel, amongst them both Ortega and Yorba, having succumbed.

Which of course in short order provoked powerful independent operators intent upon removing both King and Pope from the California arena of commercial and colonial exploitation altogether.

Meanwhile word that New Spain's westernmost

frontier had at last been secured through establishment of two Franciscan missions and two royal presidios prompting a call for worldwide celebration.

Don Carlos employing the same devices of showmanship subscribed to by Serra, in captivating his own European constituency.

As amidst cacophonic bell ringing, High Mass and elaborate processions Spain flaunted a successfully inaugurated Conquista. Never suspecting it was to be her last.

Viceroy Carlos Francisco de Croix circulating *urbi et orbi* a report in which following recital of vain attempts made previous to occupy the famous harbor at Monterey he quoted conquistador Galvez.

Who for the edification of Catherine the Great and King George of England proclaimed Spain to be solidly entrenched between the thirtieth and thirty-eighth degrees of north latitude:

Two of His Majesty's vessels
lie at anchor in San Diego harbor at this moment.

As for Monterey,
there is a strong garrison there,
abundantly supplied with artillery and
munitions of war.

Last month,
when the San Antonio left this port,
the Presidio and the Mission of San Carlos
had food supplies for a year in their storehouses,

without counting the provisioning
that would be necessary
for the establishment of the next Mission,
San Buenaventura.

As early as this coming October,
the same vessel is to go back to Monterey,
freighted with a tremendous cargo
and carrying thirty Fathers from San Fernando
who will be going to found other Missions
in these rich and vast regions
that lie between Old California
and the harbor of San Francisco.

According to what is told us
by Captain Portola
and the missionaries who have
explored the territories,
they are peopled by Indians so peaceable
that our Spaniards are as safe there
as they are in Mexico.

The Reverend Prefect of the Missions,
who is on the spot,
adds that these good natives have
already promised to entrust their
children to him,
to be brought up in our holy Faith.
This worthy and zealous friar has been so kind
as to describe to us the solemn Masses
which he has sung
since the arrival of the two expeditions,
and the magnificent Corpus Christi procession
over which he presided on June 14 last.

All this is a clear manifestation that God is with us,
and that it is He who has brought our undertaking
to a successful conclusion.

Left unmentioned were one hundred and fifty dead,
loss of the <u>San Joseph</u> together with its cargo and crew,
Indian uprisings at San Diego and most significantly
Portola's previously issued orders to withdraw.

Also unheralded was Serra. As per the missionary's
own request.

I do not wish that there should be any
mention of me,
except in relation to the blunders
I may have committed.

Out of respect for the desire of his personal friend,
Don Joseph Galvez but acknowledging a humble
servant without identifying him by name. While
similarly refraining from accepting credit of any kind
for his own numerous personal contributions to
the effort.

Even while Minister General Julian de Arriaga of the
Supreme Council of the Indies presented Don Gaspar
de Portola as Spain's hero of the day.

Inspector General Joseph Galvez, Viceroy Carlos
Francisco de Croix and the King on the other hand
sending prayers in clouds of incense and cathedrals
filled with candles to Saint Joseph and to Saint
Francis, for and in behalf of not Portola but rather their
gregarious and tenacious little missionary.

Who sitting at California in the improvised structure Gaspar had begrudgingly permitted be built to serve as Mission San Carlos, recorded commencement of the complete and total social transformation he envisioned into historic context by inscribing upon the frontispiece of it's first book of records:

FIRST BOOK
wherein are entered
THE BAPTISMAL RECORDS
of the gentiles
who have become Christians
of this Mission San Carlos
of the Port of Monterey
which belongs to the Apostolic Missionary College
of San Fernando of Mexico,
and is conducted by the missionaries
of the Seraphic Order
in so far as its spiritual needs are concerned.

It was founded at the expense
of our Catholic Monarch
of both Spains,
Lord Don Carlos III,
whom God keep,

And administered on the orders
and full commission of the Most Excellent
Lord Don Carlos Francisco de Croix,
The Marquis of Croix,
and present Viceroy and Captain General
of this New Spain.

By Most Illustrious Lord Don Joseph de Galvez,
member of His Majesty's Council and Cabinet

in both the Royal and Supreme Council
of the Indies,
Superintendent of the Army
and Inspector General
of this New Spain.

It is conducted by the Franciscan religious
of said Apostolic College,
and was begun on the most solemn day,
Pentecost Sunday, Feast of the Holy Spirit,
on the third of June of the year 1770.

Its first ministers were the Fathers Preachers
Father Junipero Serra, President,
and Father Juan Crespi,
both sons of the holy Province of
Mallorca in Europe,
and apostolic missionaries of the said
Apostolic College of San Fernando of Mexico
for more than twenty years.

And this he wrote following a day spent working side by side in the fields planting crops with his missionaries and Indian allies.

California's adroit magician going on to overcome daily predicaments encountered as if by magic through sheer ingenuity.

Blessed in the arena of agriculture and animal husbandry courtesy of historic fraternization with more advanced Moors, Serra considered himself fortunate to count amongst his inaugural cadre men raised in Majorca and on the farm.

Their value to California's founding father as an onsite font of agrarian knowledge proving inestimable. And leading to many long lasting successes.

Still it would take a season of failed crops before even these farm boys identified clearly coastal California's otherwise predictable Mediterranean cycle of light winter rains followed by summer's drought.

As when the abundance of that first spring disappeared suddenly, a critical crop yield stood dead in the fields.

Whereupon as if Robinson Crusoe's Friday, Chief Tatlun came forward to provide Serra's fledgling experimental community from the land's own self-perpetuating natural bounty.

Apprehensive concerning such open parlance between Spaniard and Indian, a departing Portola leaving strict orders that each soldier refrain from his use of weaponry and munitions.

Placing an outright ban on hunting for lack of shot and shell.

And all this so that the same might be available in the advent of some future altercation.

Subsequently Lieutenant Colonel Pedro Fages overseeing but the occasional slaughter of a grizzly bear. With each animal taken supplying much coveted meat and in abundance.

Following months of subsistence level existence, word that the San Antonio had again returned as prescribed and laden with provisions prompting a spontaneous celebration at Monterey.

Yet curiously Admiral Juan Perez sailing this time under orders forbidding him to venture any further north than San Diego.

Sensing subterfuge anew, Serra racing south.

Where he leveled both barrels of his incredible personality and heroic faith at Perez in stating the obvious; that while but a modest guard sat encamped at San Diego the entire expedition all in dire need of supplies remained starving at Monterey.

Leaving Perez to pose the rhetorical question,

Whom do I obey, You or the Council?

before dispensing with his orders and together with Reverend Father President of New California slating northward to rescue the Entrada for a second time.

At San Diego Serra discovering that Galvez had shipped not only extra seed for planting, together with sufficient tools for harvesting an anticipated bounty but ten new missionaries with whom to further the harvest of souls.

And that Palou had secured and forwarded replacements for all religious accoutrements lost together with the packet boat <u>San Joseph</u>.

Including amongst other things an extraordinary gift from Viceroy Carlos Francisco of gold vestments manufactured in Mexico from Chinese silk.

The incongruity of a missionary dressed in robes so ragged as to render himself nearly as naked as his native constituency handling such magnificent garb commanding a peculiar effect upon all present. Inordinate awe resulting from the pain of pressing need occasioning extended silence.

But it was yet another gift that so touched Michael's heart as to elicit from him a flood of tears.

When upon opening an offloaded crate shipped by Don Joseph Galvez, Serra came face to face with an exquisitely carved statue of Saint Joseph.

The message communicated being clear.

Brother Junipero would treasure this tribute, ostensibly from Don Carlos himself, venerate it on the 19th of every month and keep it close to him for the rest of his life.

The Santo standing vigil over his tomb even to this day.

I WISH THAT I COULD FLY

rusader Serra had successfully prevailed against every attempt to undo the installation of missions in California.

Portola exiting directly aboard the <u>San Antonio</u> and emerging following a ten year torpor of clerical oblivion as Governor not of California but rather urbane Puebla.

His departure being chased by a curious letter from Governor Matias de Armona to Serra directly wherein the seemingly timorous adjunct warned,

> This unbridled desire of yours
> to plant missions in the new land,
> when there are not enough soldiers present to
> protect them does nothing but tempt the Devil.

Following which another compromised official found himself being transferred-- from Loreto back to Mexico City.

With the disappointment of Armona and Portola behind him, Galvez rallying to raise high a curtain on his majesty's newest theater of operations. Commencing with importation of those ten missionaries sent for the launching of five additional missions.

Such confidence proving premature, however. For in replacing Armona and Portola with Don Phelipe de Barry (Bar-ee) as Governor and already on site Lieutenant Colonel Don Pedro Fages as Governor's

Inspector/ Commandante both King and Pontiff discovering they had but endorsed yet another openly hostile administration.

As quick to register personal objections regarding residing at Monterey, or in his words,

a wilderness filled with savages and missionaries.

Barry insisted upon remaining amidst the by comparison relative comforts of Loreto. His decision leaving Don Pedro Fages dangerously empowered by default.

Of whom both soldiers and Indians now referred to rather as El Oso (The Bear).

And this not because he'd rescued through procurement of bear meat meager troops poised on the brink of starvation.

Which, incidentally, Fages never ate. Leaving both military and missionaries to subsist on ursine flesh and supplemental fruits and berries as provided by Tatlun, while as if the "King's anointed" dining lavishly upon what little remained in his Royal Bodega (storehouse).

To be sure, as was customary, Don Pedro had himself purchased most of those same provisions. A time honored gesture done in exchange for title and privileges tendered by the Crown.

Nonetheless, such blatant inequity running counter to a Spaniard's sense of Chivalry, but eliciting mounting contempt amongst the ranks.

Emergency provisioning shipped thereafter and paid for courtesy of Don Joseph Galvez rendering as inexcusable any further proprietary actions on the part of Fages.

Still medical officer Pierre Pratt finding himself left begging for access to chicken soup denied men lying near death. And this, Fages claimed, in the name of economy. Yet again while he himself consumed the same liberally and daily.

On bended knee Pratt arguing that soup was the only weapon available in his arsenal against a life-threatening malady from which even he himself suffered. But to no avail.

Serra's intervention being inevitable and inevitably successful.

Pratt and others dying regardless.

Receipt of reports concerning a subsequently compliant Don Pedro supplying sick and dying men with chicken soup, or anything else requested, but for a price, and that courtesy of said extortion garnering everything he fancied from his already impoverished soldiery, jettisoning Serra into an indignant rage.

Adding fuel to the flames being registration of a complaint from Catalonian volunteer Jose Carillo. Who'd discovered that his beautiful new musket purchased in lieu of cash as compensation for services rendered had upon catching a commanding officer's fancy been appropriated from off an inventoried San Carlos.

Serra as advocate threatening to file suit on Carillo's behalf and courtesy of alliances with Galvez before no less than the King himself, whereupon Fages returned the firearm to its rightful recipient.

Notoriously conservative in expressing compliments or handing out rewards, inordinately liberal with the whip when exacting often unreasonable compliance to military regimentation, disgruntled troops on the brink of insurrection had good reason for referring to their commanding officer as rather "The Bear."

Fifteen of whom abandoned ranks. All vowing they'd kill Fages should he pursue them rather than be submitted to his retribution.

But it was Serra's emissaries, and not a despised Commandante General who came after them; determined to rescue frustrated young men from their otherwise impossible predicament.

Listening attentively as each boy demanded better treatment and more food. Understanding clearly a longing to return home, yet as honorably discharged soldiers.

Counseling his "children" concerning countless unknown dangers lying between impossibly far off Spain and their hideouts in the redwoods near present-day Watsonville and elsewhere amongst the oak groves at what is now El Cajon.

Pledging to secure both amnesty for acts of desertion and forbearance from punishment should they but agree to return. Giving assurances that Serra's authority to make such promises carried behind it the full weight of both Majesties.

Each company accepting Fray Junipero's offer returning under Franciscan escort to Monterey and San Diego respectively.

Whereupon only a stern dressing down from the King's evangelist kept Fages from administering immediate disciplinary action.

Serra referring to "The Bear" rather as but

a ridiculously little man.

Who by way of actual physical description was in fact both robust and hirsute. Which fascinated smooth skinned Indians, having deduced that because this man killed and presumably ate so much bear meat he had himself become as hairy as a grizzly bear.

Prompting incessant petitioning as an object of their fascination to satisfy curiosity concerning his perceived sexual prowess. Offering in cuckold their wives and daughters. Which but taunted a man already saddled with irrepressible libido.

Serra soon discovering Fages whilst out "bear hunting" otherwise leading soldiers in riotous orgies. Spanish boys surrendering even their uniforms in exchange for sex and consequently running around naked as the Indians they'd compromised.

Jettisoning Brother Junipero himself on a bear hunt after Don Pedro's own famously furry hide.

An emblematic dilemma compounded further by uninhibited sensuality on the part of California's indigenous population understandably problematic for a Franciscan whose own response to Eros was one of flagellating himself senseless with a strap.

Still Crusader Serra could not stand by passively objecting whilst his newly posted partner in empire building trampled upon virtues so diligently touted to a hard-won congregation of Christians.

And while never advocating celibacy argued that regardless Lieutenant Colonel Fages as Governor's representative maintain an exemplary standard of comportment and decorum before and on behalf of both his own men and the Franciscan's converts.

After rounding up a tribe of naked Spaniards, encouraging that they sanctify sexual relationships through conversion of and marriage each to his respective consort. In return for which thereafter arranging with the King, through Galvez, to provide every compliant soldier with land and livestock enough for sustaining a family.

Young Captain Jose Antonio Yorba being first to seek Serra's proposed sanctuary for the carnal man. Three other boys, according to records maintained both in Monterey and at San Diego, following suit.

Such intermarriage, however, while not uncommon on the frontier yet flying in the face of European sensibilities.

And at a time when Mexico City itself remained rigorously segregated, did not go unchallenged from nearest reigning diocesan prelate, the Bishop of Guadalajara. Who registered disfavor by denying Serra dispensation to confirm Church membership upon California's Indians. And thus prevented their ascension beyond baptism.

Dismissing as racist a Bishop's less enlightened perspective Brother Junipero simply continuing to encourage and bless interracial unions.

While simultaneously appointing none other than Don Pedro Fages as godparent of an Ohlone child baptized at Monterey.

So it was that a reckless Spanish hidalgo found himself bound before Christianity's god as guardian of little five-year-old Ni-ku- become Bernardo de Jesus.

The successful arrangement working its intended magic. Stimulating in otherwise playboy Don Pedro paternalistic tendencies towards responsible manhood.

Humble and by virtue of Franciscan covenants sworn to a life of not only asceticism but chastity and obedience to Christian precepts, Serra could not help but perceive in the actions of men such as Fages and the Bishop of Guadalajara mere consequences of otherwise good souls shackled by an egocentricism fostered through exposure to affluence and great privilege.

And determined, then and there, to rescue not only California but simultaneously salvage Don Pedro Fages from the sins of his fathers.

He would begin by shutting down Mission San Carlos at its present location inside the presidio of Monterey. Transporting but meager accouterments (Saint Joseph's statue and all) away from the less than sterling example of a sexually frustrated soldiery, to establish his virtuous community across the Carmel River, at a site near where it stands today.

Similar actions subsequently being carried out at San Diego. When arriving upon the scene Francisco Palou moved Mission San Diego de Alcala as per Serra's request three miles up river, "officially" so as to take advantage of better farmland. Purposefully placing distance between the Presidio and baptized Christian innocents.

Lastly Junipero fired off a letter to Don Pedro's wife, Countess Dona Eulalia de Callis. By way of which he informed the genteel lady that her husband had been pronounced earthly guardian of an Indian child. Suggesting further she join her spouse in California so as to better safeguard his lordship's soul from purgatory.

Understandably, where even Governor Barry refused taking up residence in remote California, a Countess would, quite naturally, likewise object. Nor was Eulalia thrilled to hear that, by association, she was now godparent to an Indian.

Her own sensibilities overwhelmed by such prospects, and harboring no intention of leaving an estate and life of privilege to consort with "heathens" on an isolated frontier, the Countess de Callis reacting by submitting rather a petition to the Junta de Guerra y Hacienda

(Board of War and Finance) that her husband be removed from the California exercise altogether.

Infuriated both with Serra and Eulalia, Fages dispatching his response to said Junta directly. In which he railed against the Reverend Father President's sexual proclivities and otherwise overzealous denouncement of good men exhibiting nothing more heinous than "normal" tendencies.

A concurrent communiqué to his wife endorsing her reasoning that she not consider joining him. Encouraging Eulalia to enjoy the amenities afforded her special status as wife of a Royal commissioned officer presently on a fast track for future advancement.

One revealing line to the Junta exposing his participation in pellucid schemes to subvert and privatize Franciscan operations. When advocating losses incurred at California be offset by closing down costly San Blas.

Arguing that in lieu of said installation contracts be issued for private interests to establish commercial overland supply routes and at their own expense.

And this even as Governor Barry denied Franciscans access to provisions left behind and still warehoused at Velicata. Suggesting he lacked authorization to release the same.

Overland supply routes while desirable could require years to establish. Curtailment of regular shipments from San Blas during the interim would effectively starve out Franciscan operations.

Knowingly an astute King witnessed how as if on cue Minister General Julian de Arriaga began placing pernicious demands upon Franciscans while at the same time undermining Galvez through character assassination.

His campaign first to oust the Bourbons and thereafter divest Franciscans of their new country already having been launched in collusion with Galvez's own Secretary, Miguel Jose de Azanza.

Who as shipping clerk of the San Joseph had no doubt himself been personally responsible for its disappearance.

And now by orchestrating a classic game of Spanish Prisoner drew into question his employer's mental stability through duplicitously tossing the proverbial pearls of a righteous man before swine.

Galvez like Serra being that rare sort of individual possessed of enthusiasm and genius sometimes perceived by those less gifted as madness. "Madness" by means of which otherwise ordinary men accomplish miracles.

So it was that the second most powerful man in the world found himself denounced publicly for laboring under a delusion that he maintained personal contact both with Saints Francis and Joseph.

And whilst under said "holy" insanity perceiving himself as being protector of the House of Bourbon.

Galvez, of course, standing guilty on all accounts.

Adding fuel to said fire being his own marvelous often dramatic actions taken following the bloodbath occasioned when rich men who through engineering expulsion of the Jesuits had rendered vulnerable working class Indians and underpaid troops to sort out contradictions.

Ordering that in exchange for compliantly risking even their very lives in order to restore law and order on behalf of those otherwise culpable of conjuring chaos each volunteering soldier dictate his own salary from the Board of War and Finance!

Meanwhile emphasizing before humble and broken mission Indians their King's egalitarianism and aggressive program of social reforms aimed directly at curtailing the sort of exploitation to which they'd all just been subjected by virtue of coerced Jesuit expulsion orders.

Emphatically driving home his point as had Saint Francis by divesting himself of rank, pretense and elegant uniform to stand naked before them.

Such a magnificent demonstration of consummate humility while horrifying to men of the Council regardless galvanizing ruthlessly evicted and disenfranchised Indians. Who to their absolute endearment listened attentively as Galvez implored that they forgive a shamefully proud aristocracy, maintain steady resolve and hold fast to their own Christian hopes and dreams.

That together with their King they would transcend the indignities being heaped upon them both by unrighteous men,

> You are yourselves due all the respect inherent
> in the royal bloodline of Moctezuma,
> which you must rightfully claim.

> Rest assured that Mary, Our Lady of Guadalupe,
> is ever mindful of your struggle.

> She sees the insolence sustained both by yourselves
> as well as your King.

Such "insolence" on the part of Joseph Galvez, of course, precipitating down upon him a flood of wrath from an insulted aristocracy.

Who responded by sabotaging his every campaign to put down open rebellion along that formerly stable Jesuit frontier through misappropriating and or purposefully misdirecting both men and munitions.

Prompting an Inspector General's tongue in cheek response that the Board of War and Finance might be better served if it ceased posting Council appointed sons of noblemen and supplied him instead with uniformed Guatemalan apes.

Laughter evoked by such candor being heard all the way across the Atlantic to Madrid. The common people of New Spain belonged to Joseph Galvez.

Effecting damage control, Secretary Azanza rushing to circulate his employer's outbursts under Royal Seal as though official mandates.

With each successive order proving more outrageous and damning then the last.

None, however, carrying with it Don Joseph's signature--none, that is, except for the last. Which read as coerced,

> Jose Galvez,
> insane for this unhappy world;
> pray God for him
> that he may be happy in the next.

In truth driven to the point of broken health by constant deceit and double cross from political forces hell-bent against his King, an heroic man found himself being packed off to Spain a declared lunatic.

Which of course spelled sudden disaster for Serra.

Meanwhile Galvez through Viceroy Carlos Francisco issuing **and signing** charges of treason against and orders to arrest Miguel Jose Azanza.

Whereupon and before he could respond Croix, too, found himself abruptly retired by the Council.

And no sooner had Galvez and the Marquee been extradited than did Serra find himself standing face to face with this same subversive beast.

Perhaps it was divine intervention, as Fray Junipero would later claim that an unlikely protege was unwittingly installed as succedaneum to Croix. Even as if by heavenly decree the days of Minister General of the Supreme Council of the Indies Julian de Arriaga drew abruptly and unexpectedly to a close.

For against all odds the Bourbon's noble experiment would be rescued from shipwreck.

Meanwhile Don Fernando Rivera had at long last returned not from Velicata as promised but rather Loreto. And not with supplies but rather an army of thirty- six soldiers. All of whom now sat idle at Monterey while purposely dilatory Fages, claiming insufficient manpower, refused permission to found even the third mission as prescribed by no longer upon the scene Inspector General Joseph Galvez.

Arguing that to do so would be but to render vulnerable an inadequately protected coastline.

Savvy and belligerent Serra setting about installing not one but two communities and inland far removed from the sea.

Mission San Antonio standing less than a day's march from Monterey. San Gabriel Archangel gracing those promising mission fields discovered at what is now Los Angeles.

Such maverick efforts not going unchallenged.

As returning from Mission San Antonio to his relocated Mission San Carlos at Carmel unaware of all that which had come down politically in the capital of New Spain, brazen Brother Junipero discovering a pair of disturbing letters awaiting his perusal.

The first being from Mission San Gabriel. The second a cedula signed at Mexico City by newly appointed Viceroy Antonio Bucareli.

San Gabriel's missive containing horrific news. Soldiers subsequently posted by Fages presumably to protect Serra's missionaries standing guilty one of raping a woman, the other of raping the woman's son.

Husband and father of the victims just happening to be Chief Tao ati of neighboring Tobiscanga. Who while inspecting an experimental Christian community was made to witness the aforementioned and brutal sexual assaults.

Before being shot dead at point blank range while fending off both his wife and son's assailants.

His head then severed and thereafter placed upon a post outside the entrance to Serra's newly founded mission.

Reports submitted thereafter to Don Pedro (Fages) by Rivera suggesting that such actions had been taken in order to ward off threats of further aggressions on the part of local Tongva warriors.

Such barbarous acts purposefully committed by Fages' soldiers, of course, but taunting an entire consortium of clans. Thwarting all Franciscan effort. Leaving two young Spanish missionaries outraged and now living in fear for their own lives.

Fages responding by ordering a stockade be thrown up to enclose the mission. Then instructing Rivera even as he pledged support for the missionaries that a guard be posted to deny all Indians entrance.

Rendering Franciscans who had installed their mission but to serve the Indian incredulous.

Don Pedro then cavalierly reporting that due to chaos reigning at an unauthorized and recklessly installed Mission San Gabriel, the King's otherwise prescribed founding of Mission San Buenaventura had been necessarily aborted. Proclaiming his presumed triumph over a now labeled as subversive Serra.

Which Brother Junipero's second letter would reveal.

Under aviso from Governor Barry's Inspector/ Commandante Don Pedro Fages the Board of War and Finance was ordering San Blas shut down. No longer were supply ships to sustain experimental Franciscan communities in California.

Palou consoling Serra later with,

> A hostile Council has always repudiated
> the Utopias of the Visitor General (Galvez).

Then came the charges of Serra's own insubordination with regard to matters concerning dissident soldiers and establishment of unauthorized mission communities.

A new Viceroy advising that the missionary consider himself dismissed from California altogether.

> You may remain if you so choose.
> But only in a subordinate capacity to that of

Governor Barry's Inspector/Commandant.

On the heels of this fired off and effective death sentence to the Bourbon's "Noble Experiment," newcomer Viceroy Bucareli receiving letters of his own both from Joseph Galvez and Francisco Palou.

Each of which suggested Mother Spain owed the very success of its California enterprise entirely to Serra's steadfastness alone while exposing duplicitous actions dictated by the King's enemies not only against Franciscans, but towards Galvez and the Marquee de Croix as well.

Knight of the Sacred Order of Malta Antonio Bucareli realizing at once that he had been duped. And now seeing through muddy waters clearly the events surrounding his own unexpected posting as Viceroy.

Complete illumination regarding the entire sordid matter arriving in the form of yet another letter. This one from Don Carlos himself, in which the King stated offhandedly that were it not for Fray Junipero Serra there would be no California. Which of course sent Bucareli into near panic.

Having grasped the enormity of a scenario that had occasioned abrupt retirement of Don Galvez and the Marquee of Croix both to result in his own unanticipated appointment Bucareli would later recall:

> I had dismissed a revealing comment
> made by the retiring Marquee de Croix
> when he suggested offhandedly that
> as potentate of Mexico

I prepare myself
not to be surprised
by the sudden and unannounced arrival
of my successor.

Brilliant yet unassuming Bucareli had, like his King, been perceived by a seemingly all- powerful and presumptive Council of the Indies as weak and malleable. The revelation of which but prompting him to respond with a combatative enthusiasm equal to that of Portola's "missionary."

The memorandum rushed to Don Joseph Galvez who had purposefully forestalled his own deportation long enough to arrange a hoped for opportunity of communicating directly with Carlos Francisco's successor, containing Antonio Bucareli's pledge to serve both majesties:

with all my strength
my talents and my life,

satisfying the protector of the House of Bourbon. Who then hurried his recommendations on ahead to Don Carlos.

Suggesting that having read and taken to heart the new Viceroy's pledge, extraordinary and immediate actions place Bucareli's lifelong companion and confidant, highly decorated and distinguished royal officer Alejandro O'Reilly as head of the Board of War and Finance.

Whilst by return mail warning both Bucareli and O'Reilly that Minister General Julian de Arriaga of the Council of the Indies, and not Charles III, was courtesy of said Board effectively running their New World circus. And having armed them with such knowledge, admonishing further that they protect each other. And so united proceed with caution.

At a previously scheduled and grand reception hosted to welcome the new Viceroy, Bucareli had been snubbed by clerics disgusted with a secular and heretic Council's dismissal of Galvez and the Marquee. No bells being rung. No Mass celebrated.

The new appointee left sitting for hours only thereafter to be escorted into a hall where not one individual stood to greet him, nor extended a congratulatory hand in fellowship.

Bucareli accepting said humiliation with consummate obeisance.

The King's own confessor Father Eleta at last breaching an awful silence only to discover that Sir Antonio was not in cabal with the Council but rather an innocent and presumed puppet of the same.

Whereupon a second and grander reception being arranged, during the course of which such an outpouring of love occurring that at length the unassuming Viceroy prevailing upon all present to refrain from causing him further public embarrassment.

A letter from his King encouraging that Bucareli maintain on track the marvelous work begun by Don Joseph Galvez and the Marquee de Croix would follow.

Unable as he was to retrieve his own cedula since

dispatched to Junipero Serra, an enlightened Caballero (Knight) hastily drafting another, in which he beseeched the Reverend Father President's forgiveness while requesting that said illustrious scholar and dedicated pioneer stay on in California and indefinitely.

Junipero, of course, having no way of knowing that this second missive was being hurried on its way to him. And as with the ill-informed clerics at the capitol could not ascertain his new Viceroy's true nature.

After enduring long hours in yet another Gethsemane, a discouraged Crusader deciding to accept what he perceived as "God's will" with quiet resignation. But only upon receipt of full disclosure and in person from this Bucareli himself.

And so set off for San Diego accompanied by little Juan Evangelista, there to secure passage on a soon to be sailing south <u>San Carlos</u>.

Upon receipt of word concerning Serra's actions Don Pedro Fages hastening to catch up with and escort him so as to monitor said situation.

Enroute Michael absorbing the essence of every village, every person, every tree, every blade of grass, every beast and every bird; quietly fearful he might never see any of it again.

Expressing his anxiety with regard to attaining Mexico City and thereby hopefully resolving California's dilemma in a single line scribbled hastily to Palou,

I wish that I could fly.

A HOUSE DIVIDED

O f sixty-two Viceroys who reigned over New Spain none left more profound a legacy or fonder memory in the hearts of his constituency than Knight Commander of the Holy Order of Saint John of Malta, Antonio Maria Bucareli.

Who administered according to the ideas of his King,

which were in and of themselves noble.

Manifesting unfailing benevolence while so doing and without ever seeking profit for himself.

The Order championed by Sir Antonio had according to tradition been founded by Christ's own John the Beloved. Who as per Christian lore yet walked the earth, and for whom as knight errant men the likes of Antonio Bucareli felt disposed to sacrifice all that they possessed, even to their very lives if needs be.

Secretly Don Carlos increasing by twenty thousand pesos his new Viceroy's otherwise but modest salary so as to accommodate the many charitable overtures directed at Indians, those otherwise in need and missionaries serving either and funded by said knights.

Bucareli's own illustrious Spanish/Italian lineage embracing cardinals, dukes and pontiffs. So it was that a posting as governor of Cuba had come as no surprise to anyone.

His sudden promotion as Viceregal on the other hand catching even Minister General of the Supreme Council of the Indies Julian de Arriaga off-guard.

Who had it not been for ill health might well have successfully sabotaged this second attempt by the Catholic King to recapture control of New World operations.

Fray Junipero Serra's death defying dash to meet with the new Viceroy at Mexico City nearly costing that King's missionary his life. Illness overtaking him and little Juanito both.

He was half-dying when I saw him arrive here,

writing Bucareli,

but the apostolic flame burned within him,
making an extraordinary impression upon me.

California needed a miracle. As did a now desperately ill evangelist who had prior to this pow wow with the new Viceroy received extreme unction from his brothers at San Fernando Missionary College.

Typically Serra would have his miracle. The California experiment being sustained. And this because Sir Antonio perceived in Brother Junipero's presence a mandate as it were from none less than John the Evangelist to rescue through him the agenda of Both Majesties.

Two men cut from the same cloth,

Serra as least of the Brothers of Christ with Bucareli as Knight-errant for Christ's beloved, forging then and there an immediate alliance.

Which they subsequently maintained by pummeling into honorable compliance colleagues of questionable loyalties with more than 4,300 letters, all copied to their King. Broadcasting each oath made and every action taken so as to prevent duplicity.

The period during which Sir Antonio Bucareli ruled
was an uninterrupted sequence of peace
for New Spain;

For it seemed as if Providence wished to reward
the virtues of the viceroy
by scattering upon his subjects
everything that contributed to their well being.

He was one of those men
whose memory will never be erased
from the heart of the Mexican people.

His administration a clear example
of what this land was capable of being,
when a man of integrity and intelligence
resolutely undertook the difficult task
of developing both its natural and human resources.

For ability and high character
Bucareli stands out as one of the greatest men
in the history of New Spain.

Far from being a narrow bureaucrat,
he was capable of a broad point of view

which grasped both the patent and
the underlying problems
of the entire viceroyalty.

A well-developed sense of perspective
was one of his most marked traits,
enabling him to see matters as they were,
but not checking him from taking measures
to circumvent possible ills
which to him
did not appear greatly threatening.

His letters show him to have been simple,
straight forward,
unselfish,
clear-thinking,
and sincerely religious,
without a shadow of conceit or pretence,
and even without great personal ambition,
except to perform his duty to the full.

Finally,
he was keenly interested in the problems
that he encountered,
and was an indefatigable worker,
and these characteristics,
joined to the rest,
make it clear why he achieved such success
in the face of difficulties that would have
proved insuperable to a less capable ruler.

Feigning power and position Bucareli had from the
beginning requested that his heady mantle be
transferred to friend and coadjutant Alejandro
O'Reilly, who had, in fact, openly sought said office.

Regardless, Sir Antonio's extraordinary efforts and authentic dedication garnering but escalating praise from Don Carlos who correspondingly refused parting company with such a champion.

So it was that Bucareli's temporary posting drew into a long-term and collaborative administration. During which he would eventually find himself serving alongside soon to be returning as Universal Minister General of the Supreme Council of the Indies Sir Joseph Galvez.

And like Galvez finding few concerns so captivating as the thrilling experiment being carried out under the auspices of Don Carlos and those Franciscans in New California.

A fixation first riveted following that unexpected knock upon his door by no less than Crusader Serra himself.

Bucareli listening spellbound as an eloquent scholar expounded point by point upon everything from military procedures to horticulture to the installation of community as prescribed by John Duns.

When launching the new country Fray Junipero had requested one hundred missionaries with which to found fifty missions.

The man must be out of his mind!

responding Reverend Father President of the San Fernando Missionary College (and fellow Majorcan) Raphael Verger. Who then blasted his colleague for embarrassing the Order in front of no less than King Charles by even suggesting such a thing, as Franciscans stood possessed of neither the means nor the one hundred men.

Now Serra requested one hundred soldiers!

He would explain. Fages was forestalling all expansionary efforts by arguing that the Junta (Board of War and Finance) had supplied him with neither the means nor men enough for protecting new installations.

Reiterating to Viceroy Bucareli that while he personally neither asked for nor wanted protection, nonetheless if the Junta intended both to control expansion **and** maintain military installations, then as Father President of the same he would insist upon being sent one hundred soldiers. Good Catholic soldiers.

Each of whom must come accompanied by his wife and children.

For most assuredly such an army of Christian soldiers would overwhelm the likes of on site saboteurs while serving through example as civilian missionaries to the Indians.

Delighted at Serra's acumen, Bucareli would arrange through confidant O'Reilly, who now sat as commander in chief of said Junta, to see that California got its troops.

Now with regard to overland routes by way of which to service her,

Yes, by all means establish them

argued Serra; but not at the expense of a critically necessary San Blas connection.

Pointing out through simple arithmetic the unsound nature of a proposal underway to shut down California's all-important staging area.

Illustrating that were the Viceroy to gather every mule in El Norte (the Northwest Territories) there could not be assembled enough livestock with which to convey sufficient provisioning for sustaining New California.

You do the math!

Nor could Doctor Junipero resist taking this opportunity of informing Bucareli that both Portola and Fages had themselves decreased said stable by feeding the same to their soldiers and without compensating Franciscans, to whom the beasts rightfully belonged, for their loss.

Stressing that amidst such acute shortages common sense dictated proposed overland supply routes be up and running before Mexico City even consider shutting down California's only dependable source of provisioning.

With equal acuity Fray Junipero stating each of his other grievances against Don Pedro in particular, suggesting poor example and countless improprieties as being themselves responsible both for dissension in the ranks and insurrections amongst native populations.

Recounting for Bucareli atrocities committed most recently at San Gabriel, and rumors of mounting threats from the Kumeyaay at San Diego; agonizing over the fact that given integrous leadership such confrontations need never occur amongst an otherwise gentle people.

Then pleading for repatriation of five Catalonian volunteers who tired of soldiering wished only to return home but with dignity.

Bucareli applauding Serra for his insight, his iron will and his candor. Clearly those attempting to intimidate a monarch had equally underestimated that monarch's missionary.

They had also failed to recognize the heroic spirit behind an otherwise demure Bucareli.

Who upon realizing that while the Council openly endorsed their King's agenda, they regardless conspired endlessly to if not control than contain it, vowed with the missionary and the King to launch covert operations of his own.

California would have more missions together with additional presidios manned by family men of proven character.

Serra himself instructed to compose for the same what has since become heralded as an Indian Bill of Rights.

A legal instrument containing thirty-two points of law constructed so as to govern California in accordance with those principles upon which the King himself had founded it.

Meanwhile not only would San Blas be retained, but its operations supervised by a harbormaster reporting directly to Sir Antonio Bucareli.

Loreto would remain as seat of government for all of California and carefully monitored through strict adherence to established protocol for the keeping of accounts and filing of reports and again directly with the Viceroy.

Additionally Serra was to have his one hundred Catholic soldiers. Together with their wives and children.

For serendipity being such as it is, Bucareli had just received a related petition from Captain Juan Bautista Anza.

The man who, like Galvez, had begun his since illustrious secular career rather in seminary studying to become a priest.

When upon receipt of news that Apache raiders had murdered his father,

> He put down his prayer book
> and took up the sword.

And since garnered distinction for honoring both his father and his god by demonstrating in otherwise military campaigns a disposition towards employing diplomacy over open warfare.

Prompting his earlier recruitment by Galvez to aid with carrying out Jesuit expulsionary orders. Following which Anza had been dispatched alongside Fernando

Rivera into California as a leather jacket soldier, thereafter accompanying Portola on both attempts made at founding Monterey.

Joseph Galvez now returning as Marquee of Sonora instructed to set Sonora-born Anza on a fast track for advancement by installing the promising young officer as commandante over the Royal Presidio at Tubac outside of present day Tucson, Arizona.

Where he sat swapping stories concerning Jesuit extraditions and adventures in New California with Franciscan Father Francisco Garces. Who like Galvez recognized in this quietly energetic soldier a genuine passion both for Jesus Christ and for the California experiment.

Having himself traveled extensively throughout the borderlands of New Spain, Garces possessing full knowledge of Jesuit Father Kino's charts. Which he shared with Anza. Giving assurances that New California could be accessed without too much difficulty even directly from Tubac.

Juan Bautista responding by petitioning the new Viceroy for permission to mount, at his own expense, a second Entrada into California; this one overland and from Tubac.

Such was the business that had brought him to Mexico City on the heels of Fray Junipero Serra.

Bucareli would arrange for both men to meet; in California.

Serra endorsing said proposal. While cautioning Anza and Bucareli that ready access from Sonora might accelerate an unwanted introduction of the secular colonialism festering there.

Bucareli countering while arguing the inevitability of future exploitation by endorsing acceleration of efforts to arm the Indians against said eventualities through more aggressive installation of mission communities.

Granting his Franciscan full jurisdiction over California with rights even to veto military decisions when and where effecting the Indian population while simultaneously adopting Anza's proposal to,

Open the road.

Overwhich Captain Juan Bautista would himself conduct an army of sympathetic families to assist as soldiers, artisans and teachers with the work of education and conversion envisioned by Serra.

Sir Antonio in collusion with confidant O'Reilly further insisting that because said operation facilitated military agendas it be funded not from out of an all but empty Pious Fund, but rather with monies supplied courtesy of the Board of War and Finance.

All energies were to focus upon still vulnerable San Francisco. Where Anza's families would together with the Franciscans install a strategic and model community designed to address the needs of both Majesties.

Erstwhile transferring Don Pedro Fages away from California, leaving Fernando Rivera as effective on-site Inspector/Commandante, until Anza could finish with founding San Francisco.

Whereupon the capitol would be moved from Loreto to Monterey, and Anza then posted as Governor.

Brother Junipero returning to California convinced that,

> God himself
> has played like an organ
> those who underestimated Bucareli.

Anza, on the other hand, having been raised in a realm of tough frontier politics, arriving back at Sonora filled with misgivings. Serra's expressed concerns regarding secular colonialism haunting his every thought.

Never had he been able to banish completely the nightmare of escorting Jesuit mentors away from a paradise that had been their own Utopia. Now he could not help but question the wisdom or lack thereof behind lying vulnerable yet another country obviously ruled by innocents.

Surely the self-fulfillment of indigenous populations everywhere seemed by nature an inherent right. Yet inevitably here as elsewhere intervention on the part of a more aggressive culture remained imminent.

Anza's philosophical struggle being endemic of the Age; as doing nothing would but render populations vulnerable to exploitation by others deemed less noble.

Meanwhile still of concern to Serra was the establishment of that mission and royal presidio between San Diego and Monterey as initially prescribed by Don Joseph Galvez.

Under a Viceroy's Reglamento, which Serra had himself constructed, the Reverend Father President now standing in possession of

Loco parentis

or power of attorney with regard to representing Indians and otherwise overruling on their behalf even local governors and military officials.

And holding ultimate authority in decision making concerning the placement and founding of all mission installations.

An unnerved Fages receiving word that missionary Serra had effectively circumvented both his own military authority as well as that of Governor Barry by approaching directly not only the Viceroy but head of the Junta General O'Reilly.

Whose orders canceled plans of closing down the port of San Blas by removing it from Military jurisdictions and furthermore binding it as a Department of the Kingdom of Spain over to the Viceroy directly.

O'Reilly then announcing creation of his newly conceived,

Division of Interior Provinces,

overwhich the King's champion Don Joseph Galvez, as both Universal Minister General of the Supreme Council of the Indies and Marquee of Sonora, would control everything other than California along the northern frontier.

When word that Bucareli had commissioned Juan Bautista Anza to conduct a second grand Entrada into California from those same Interior Provinces, not only Barry and Fages but Fernando Rivera reading clearly the writing on the mission wall.

Meanwhile Sir Antonio undoing all efforts to starve out Franciscan missionaries by dispatching double the amount of supplies previously requested by Don Pedro Fages.

Never again were any of California's volunteers to endure the pang of hunger or restraint occasioned by a lack of essentials.

From San Diego Rivera firing off a missive to Fages at Monterey alerting him of the fact that not one but two ships had just put in. And loaded with both foodstuffs and additional soldiers, accompanied by wives and children all of whom were to be posted at Monterey.

And that two more ships privately funded by Catholic benefactors of the Pious Fund were even now enroute from San Blas to reconnoiter at San Francisco directly for the express purpose of continuing explorations northward so as to expedite Franciscan expansionary efforts there as well.

The Road between Carmel and Mexico City thereafter

ever kept hot with messengers carrying an endless stream of correspondence directed at apprising Viceroy Bucareli of details, progress and any insubordination as Serra's contained rage found healthy expression through calm, steady and focused action.

Whilst an infuriated, circumvented triumvirate that was Barry, Fages and Rivera attempted to sabotage said correspondence, by if not preempting then altering the same.

Which but exposed their duplicity. For as always the missionary employed his old trick of sending blind copies to everyone involved in his operations.

Meanwhile President Rafael Verger at the San Fernando Missionary College having installed Palou at Monterey as pro-tem President of New California in Serra's absence now for reasons unknown attempting to preempt their reunion by plotting Serra's reassignment as Reverend Father President of the College at Mexico City.

Apprised of said machinations Fray Junipero making his hasty exit as if that proverbial thief in the night.

To yet prevail and with Palou over a house divided.

REASSESSING THE DREAM

I n the wake of course altering events at Mexico City Juan Perez received command of a new frigate outfitted specifically for servicing California. And aboard which sailed on its maiden voyage out from San Blas both Fray Junipero and Juanito Evanglista.

Thus concluding Serra's two-year foray into the Halls of Power.

During long hours spent gazing opaquely at an endless horizon Michael ruminating endlessly over his Odyssey to the rhythm of the sea.

He'd surprised even himself with previously untried capacities as an attorney. A man otherwise schooled in things spiritual and philosophical drafting working legal instruments subsequently endorsed almost as dictated to the Board of War and Finance. Ultimately seeing bestowed upon himself as architect all but absolute authority over his Kingdom of California.

Beginning and ending with the Junta's full recognition of Indian rights to said Kingdom.

Such that concessions of any kind could not be made without Franciscan mediation. Serra alone being left to accommodate and regulate even military involvement proposed by the Junta.

If deemed not good for the Indian, power players standing overruled by legal father under Spanish law

Serra as guardian of the same.

Who had next insisted upon and received adequate pay with which to hire only the highest caliber of military personnel.

All of whom would acknowledge Indian autonomy through Franciscan Custodies even when administering punitive operations.

With the King providing additional inducements at Serra's request of land allotments and stipends in order to lure married couples capable of assisting as teachers and skilled artisans with education and the development of trades.

In fact while drafting Serra's Indian Bill of Rights sympathetic Bucareli having complied with all but three of the Reverend Father President's recommendations.

Wary regardless, Brother Junipero understanding better than most that vicious cabildos capable of restraining even the King would never take dictation from his Viceroy.

Additionally there had been the cautious Franciscan's meeting with a politically ambitious (and gluttonous) archbishop at Guadalajara concerning postponement of rights to confirm Church membership upon California's Indians.

And in whom he witnessed but,

the divine profaned,
the King offended and God completely forgotten.

The Bishop's sidekick seated as intermediary,

an angry prince with blood on his hands.

What could a missionary know of greed, cynicism, belligerence or bellicosity?

California society as envisioned by Dr. Junipero Serra seeming but the ultimate ironic mockery of such revelations. Certain of undoing political skullduggery, backstabbing and duplicity.

California. A land whose knights would all be Franciscan counter crusaders. Their castles rather temples to god.

Yet even armed as he now was with government sanctioned Reglamentos, how could simple missionaries and Indians possibly triumph in the face of such peripheral debauchery?

Comprehending fully the timelessness of humanity's common struggle against a diabolical evil as old as the race itself, Serra pondering the words of Plato and of Aristotle. Each of whom had themselves attempted exorcism of depravity through installation of a code of ethics.

He contemplated Franchesco di Pietro's determination to conquer iniquity through asceticism and obeisance.

And reflected upon his own daily struggle to eradicate if not evil then the world's passions and all selfish ambitions. Only to now discover himself regardless at this very moment and perhaps more so than ever consumed by both.

Michael loved Jesus Christ. Who through forcing introspection taught the principle of love without condemnation.

And it would be ultimately by following Christ's example that this hopeful dreamer found his answers:

> To the one who is in love
> all things are compatible.

True love being defined as selflessly embracing the problems of another. There was simply no other course of action available except to level genuine love passionately and ambitiously as his own secret and superior weapon against apathy and hatred; reasoning that to do anything less was to sacrifice not merely his soul but that of California's as well.

> I am nothing,
> yet with the nothingness that I am
> I shall assist God,
> who whether I act or not,
> WILL save the world from itself.

In donning Franchesco's habit Michael had long since laid aside even his own identity. Declining ever after any personal recognition, honors or rewards.

With nothing to hope for, standing empowered by nothing to fear.

And blossomed like the proverbial flower in an otherwise stark and hostile wilderness.

I stand unoffended
for I am not worthy even of offense.

But for the sake of My Lord and Saviour Jesus Christ
who stands insulted and profaned,
I shall not remain shackled and silent.

I shall love,
as did He
without restraint.

And with this love as my weapon
undo even the Devil himself.

Curiously Antonio and Maria Serre had christened
their boy after the Archangel who in defense of
humanity ever faced off against evil.

Now as never before Serra needing Archangel
Michael's help. Staring out across an expanse of sea as
vast as his own feelings of inadequacy summoning
divine intervention by reciting an exorcist's prayer:

St. Michael the Archangel,
defend us in the day of battle;

be our safeguard against the wickedness
and snares of the devil.

May God rebuke him,
we humbly pray,
and do thou,
O' prince of the heavenly host,
by the power of God,
cast into hell,

satan and all the other evil spirits,
who prowl through the world,
seeking the ruination of souls.

Amen

As a Doctor of Theology Serra understood clearly that mankind had since the days of Cain and Abel proven itself capable of horrendous sin. Amply demonstrating time and time again a willingness to destroy not merely the aspirations, dignity and freedom of individuals but those of entire societies and races as well.

All of which led to a conviction concerning humanity's need for salvation from itself that had compelled Michael into the missionfield.

Now a seasoned evangelist, Fray Junipero journeying back into California resolved to never again become disheartened, regardless of certain opposition.

His thoughts suddenly returning to Majorca. To his one sister Juana, brother-in-law Miguel, their two daughters and little son Miguelito, whom Serra had ever referred to rather as "Mike."

He considered his parents. Were they still alive, he wondered?

For Serra the single most difficult challenge of his life had not been standing up against New World heretics and prevaricators.

Such palling by comparison when placed alongside the sacrifice of leaving behind family and Majorca forever.

Isn't it enough

his mother had insisted,

that you are a doctor of philosophy
and a lecturer
and the most renowned man of God
to come out of Petra?

Aren't you doing enough for God?

Why can't you stay here
where you can visit us
and bring a little more happiness to what is left of
our lives?

she had demanded whenever
he broached the subject.

Is it required that you go and preach to savages
and perhaps lose your life,
when you have already given twenty years
to God's work
here on the Island,
and could well give twenty or thirty more
without leaving us.

A man famed for his eloquence could tender no satisfactory response. Ultimately deeming it best not even to try. And accordingly leaving without so much as saying goodbye.

Only after his ship having sailed did a cousin as pre-arranged deliver Michael's written adieu to family and friends:

Hail Jesus, Mary and Joseph!

Farewell, my dear Father!
Farewell, my dear Mother!
Farewell, my sister Juana!
Goodbye Miguel, my brother-in-law!

Words cannot express my feeling
as I bid you farewell.
I wish I could communicate to you
the great joy that fills my heart.
Surely you would encourage me to
always go forward
and never turn back.

The Office of an apostolic preacher
is the greatest calling to which
you could wish for me to be chosen.

Filling three pages with lines written closely together, Serra expressing as best he could the love felt for each of them individually.

Begging that they forgive his cowardice in not confronting them, while imploring that they instead rally spiritually to sustain him through prayer as one unworthy and thus privileged to serve.

Asking that Juana and her husband comfort his parents, live together in harmony and take care in raising their children.

Recognizing that as he would never see any of them again correspondingly closing the letter as if to be read at his funeral,

May the Lord bring us together in Heaven.

When compared with heaviness of heart sustained from such a daunting farewell, dealings with the likes of Portola and Fages had been a breeze.

Mike? He recalled the last time he'd written to his nephew. It had been while making preparations for heading into the Sierra Gorda outside Queretaro:

> The holy mandate is now sending there
> this miserable sinner,
> who is your uncle,
> together with Father Francisco Palou.

> I recognize my uselessness and incompetence
> for so great an undertaking.

> But God is able,
> even through the agency of nothing at all,
> to achieve works which resound to His glory.

Mike adored Miguel and Francisco. And to their delight had gone on to become not only a Capuchin Franciscan but one noted for excelling both in mathematics and architecture.

Which led to thoughts of Serra's beloved Francisco. Laboring nobly and alone for nearly five years outside of Loreto. Sensing anew the joy of knowing that even now Palou was himself already in Monterey and awaiting him.

Lastly Michael considered the duplicity both he and Palou had encountered, seemingly at every turn, while attempting to do neither more nor less than carry out the edicts of Don Carlos as delivered to them by Joseph Galvez.

In contemplating the nature of their own shared dream Serra remembering all those who had insisted he and Francisco were if not naive and overzealous then stark raving lunatics. Which brought to mind the words of his favorite novelist Miguel Cervantes,

> After all, what is madness?
>
> Maddest of all is to see life as it is
> and not as it should be.

Surrendered to such musings a humble Franciscan fancying himself Sancho Panza, before accepting with resignation the fact that he had indeed been cast rather to play the role of Don Quixote in a dramatic comedy long since scripted by hands unseen.

And reflecting upon his ascent many years earlier of the hill Bonany near Petra, in Majorca, remembering how alone in its ancient shrine he'd bid a silent farewell to family, friends and all that with which he had ever been most familiar.

> Divine Ruler over all men;
> may what I see with my eyes
> and feel in my heart today,
> be multiplied countless times over
> through the wide reaches of this troubled world.
>
> Pour Thy rich blessings upon this shrine
> which so eloquently speaks for a common

brotherhood of all people
living in peace and humility.

Eternal One, who rules without favor
the hearts of all men,
grant to each of us a consecrated power
to dignify this brotherhood
by devoted deeds of understanding and friendship.

Surely then our hearts may cherish an abiding hope
that through Thy wonder-working ways
there will yet dawn a day of never-ending peace;

Thy Kingdom come on earth.

Never again would Fray Junipero Serra even consider voluntarily backing away from California. As surely no one less than his god had directed that he alter course and abandon loved ones and life in Majorca to himself champion at this moment the propagation of enlightened global fraternity.

And while comprehending fully the overwhelming odds stacked against such dreams recalled those stunning lines of Cervantes,

It does not matter if you win or lose.
It only matters that you follow the Quest.

Penning himself,

Where there is love, miracles are always nearby.

To effect yet another miracle Serra deciding somewhere out on the open sea that he must assume complete control over every aspect political, ecclesiastical, militarily or otherwise with regard to California's state of affairs.

So it was that upon discovering Captain Juan Perez sailed under orders forbidding a docking at San Diego, Serra demanded regardless the ship <u>Santiago</u> do so. As Council be damned, beginning at San Diego he intended to confer in person and privately with each of his missionaries.

So it was that around four o'clock on the afternoon of March 13, 1774 an action that wound up placing Juan Perez and all involved under investigation at court saw the <u>Santiago</u> hove to and drop anchor in the port of San Diego.

And so it was that Reverend Father President Junipero Serra met in private conference with fellow Majorcan confidant Luis Jaime (Hi-may) and his companion Vicente Fuster (Foo-stir) at successfully relocated away from the Presidio by Francisco Palou Mission San Diego de Alcala.

Thereafter selecting the site for a new base of Franciscan operations at San Juan Capistrano.

Then walking on to relocated by Palou Mission San Gabriel and a secretly arranged rendezvous with just arriving overland from Sonora Captain Juan Bautista Anza.

Serra maintaining this iron- grip and hands on control over California for the rest of his lifetime. And some would suggest everafter.

TUBAC AND BACK

Slated for closure immediately following the extradition of Galvez, had it not been for Serra's unexpected intervention a fledgling Franciscanland would have withered and died on the vine. California's occupation then transferred over to privately funded concerns.

For whom Captain Juan Perez should have delivered at a Monterey void of Franciscan leadership, supplies and equipment with which to further the secularist exploitation of San Francisco.

Serra's unexpected return from Mexico City shocking the harbormaster at San Blas. From whence had Fray Junipero not shown up Perez would have sailed on only to discover doppelganger Francisco Palou in Monterey as pro-tem Reverend Father President.

The perplexed admiral facing court-martial for insubordination regardless. When despite strict orders mandating otherwise he thereafter permitted Serra's disembarkation at San Diego.

Meanwhile, no sooner had Rivera arrived in Monterey not to reinforce but replace Fages then did those reasoning they remained nonetheless still in control of the situation find themselves dealing with an equally resolute Francisco Palou.

And even before legal proceedings against both Perez and Fages (and in short order Rivera) could begin, Fray Junipero whom neither Junta nor Council of the Indies could control nor contain, having managed to confer personally and in private with every one of his missionaries. Keeping a covertly scheduled rendezvous with Anza and secretly selecting the site (San Juan Capistrano) for his new base of operations.

All before reaching Monterey where Rivera was doing everything within his power to preempt perpetuation of an agenda suddenly centering upon the advent of Juan Bautista Anza.

Serra's clandestine pow wow with the man celebrated as peacemaker amongst North America's most savage tribes, having been of particular importance to the Franciscan Order. Who fervently prayed for his installation ultimately as Governor of their new country.

Characteristically chivalrous in displaying courtly Spanish grace Anza being quick to garner Serra's favor. Two California enthusiasts sitting up all night around a campfire discussing every aspect of the enterprise.

Anza's guide from Tubac being a fugitive of the debacle at Mission San Gabriel.

Who after seeking retaliation for his murdered chieftain found refuge together with eight disenchanted defectors amongst the Cahuilla. Thereafter joining a resistance movement launched against the Spanish by historically hostile desert tribes.

At Tubac surreptitiously volunteering to escort Anza across an uncharted desert.

When the sun rose on January 30, 1774 Captain Juan Bautista awakening to discover his guide gone and himself marooned amidst a trackless sea of sand dunes.

With great difficulty Anza managing to get all back on course only then to face off with tattooed giant Olleyquotequiebe.

Fortuitously Anza traveled with Franciscan Garces. Who had met Olleyquotequiebe before.

A trail-blazing missionary famed for traveling the frontier,

> with no other escort than his guardian angel

assuring an intimidating chieftain in delicate dialogue that wunderkind Anza wished only the privilege of passing through Quechan country, so as to access California.

Astute Anza voluntarily offering payment in return for facilitating said favor. And further solidifying the pact subsequently forged by presenting Olleyquotequiebe with a brightly colored sash and necklace made of silver coin struck with the image of Don Carlos.

Fray Garces later recalling how the giant stared with wonder and amazement at Anza's gift,

> having neither eyes enough to look at it,
> nor words enough with which to express
> his gratitude.

So began a great friendship between California's would-be Governor and the King of the Quechan.

Whose women so delighted the Spaniards as atop mounts of their own they pranced about like true Amazons.

Or as Anza explained,

> The people who live on this Colorado River
> are the tallest and the most robust that I have seen
> in all the provinces.

And their nakedness the most complete.

That he spiked his long hair with mud lent to Olleyquotequiebe the rather peculiar aspect of a walking palmetto. Anza's men dubbing him Captain Palm Tree (Capitan Palma).

Juan Bautista on the other hand bestowing upon Capitan Palma the more dignified and Christian name of Salvador Carlos Antonio in honor of Christ, Don Carlos and the Viceroy. Suggesting that Olleyquotequiebe had courtesy of his intervention single-handedly saved not merely himself but Spain's enterprise as well.

Terrain west of the Colorado River proved even more treacherous than lands previously traversed. Anza sending back to Olleyquotequiebe for safe keeping seven men together with thirty-five pack mules, sixty-five head of cattle and a hundred and forty horses.

Overwhelmed by such a display of trust, the Quechan

taking great pride in accommodating their new friend's request.

When the sun set on Tuesday, March 22, 1774 tolling bells at Mission San Gabriel welcoming a trail weary Anza and his modest expeditionary force into the enthusiastic embrace of both Brothers Fermin Francisco Lasuen and in from San Diego Vicente Fuster.

An overland trek begun so many years earlier by Father Eusebio Kino from Mission San Xavier del Bac to the great South Sea at last completed.

Anza, following his brief rendezvous with Serra, and Fuster returning directly so as to orchestrate for California a second and decidedly single-minded Entrada.

ANZA

 charade of endless petty quarreling between

pompous and arbitrary Rivera

and

elusively defiant Fages,

concerning everything from which horses belonged to whom to how best each might sublimate Franciscans defined the course of events preceding Anza's arrival.

Don Pedro (Fages) then sailing away without ceremony on a southbound <u>San Antonio</u> to accept promotion into the newly fashioned Department of Interior Provinces.

Prior to which in anticipation of promotion Don Fernando (Rivera) having purchased a large hacienda on the outskirts of Loreto. And quite understandably not pleased with the sudden prospect of staying on as Inspector/Commandante pro-tem at Monterey.

Personal aspirations centering around serving perhaps even as Governor of California but from Loreto preempted by the advent of youthful upstart Anza provoking acceleration of his efforts to see Franciscan California aborted.

Which Rivera attempted by planting seeds of dissidence at every turn.

Beginning with his fraternization of newly arriving upon the scene from Old California Fray Fermin Francisco Lasuen. Whom the Inspector/Commandante insisted serve not as a missionary but rather in the capacity of chaplain for his Royal Presidio.

Which of course flattered the nonetheless perceptive Lasuen. Who soon recognized Don Fernando's appeal as nothing more than a ploy to establish alliances before an anticipated deportment of all but priests affiliated with a military presence.

Of particular concern to Lasuen's traveling companion Francisco Palou was the fact that Anza would be returning accompanied by dozens of families all in need both of food and shelter.

When it became obvious that Rivera had no intention of fulfilling orders received from Bucareli concerning the establishment of anything other than a prescribed presidio at San Francisco, Serra's protege feeling compelled to take matters into his own hands.

Venturing alone to negotiate with local chiefs concerning installation of not one but, as per Junipero, two missions.

Prompting threats of incarceration from an outraged Don Fernando. Who upon discovering said insubordination ordered that Palou cease and desist.

Palou countering with recitation of his mandate from the San Fernando Missionary College that he function in Serra's absence as Reverend Father President of the Missions of New California.

Then himself blasting Rivera for failure to follow through with orders from the Viceroy that San Francisco be prepared for receiving families arriving otherwise under jurisdictions of said College.

When Don Fernando still refused assistance, Palou simply continuing his efforts so as to have all things in readiness for the new arrivals.

Who departed from Tubac on October 23, 1775 as part of a large-scale migration the likes of which North America had never before witnessed.

Twenty families, two hundred and forty individuals in all and more than half of them children. Led by since promoted Juan Bautista Anza together with his hand selected escort of eight seasoned soldiers gathered from across Sonora.

California's second grand Entrada was underway. And did not travel far before confronting its first tragedy.

As one day into the march Maria Ignacia Feliz Pinuelas began suffering premature labor pains. Ultimately opting sacrifice of her own life in order to deliver Caesarian,

> Save the child,
> or we shall both die.

On a single day grief stricken husband become father/widower Jose Vicente Feliz burying his wife and baptizing his son Jose Antonio Capistrano at Jesuit Father Kino's now Franciscan Mission San Xavier del Bac.

A sortie of Apache raiders administering the expedition's second and heavy blow. Rallying as they did as if from out of nowhere. Scattering livestock to the four winds.

Each remaining horse compelled to carry not one but two or three children.

Anathematic being Anza's glorious reunion with Olleyquotequiebe.

Who had assembled stores of beans, pumpkins, corn, wild wheat and more than a thousand melons for the express purpose of hosting his friend's entourage and under the shade of ramadas built expressly for their comfort.

Presenting Anza personally with caches of highly prized dried fish.

Whereupon Juan Bautista removed from a saddlebag an elegant military uniform modeled after that of his own and custom designed to fit the giant.

This stunning outfit having been prepared with the hope that Olleyquotequiebe might accept an invitation to serve as ambassador for Don Carlos.

Explaining to this King of the Quechan that his own Spanish King was sincere and genuinely pious. Then requesting permission to leave behind brothers Francisco Garces and Thomas Eixarch for the express purpose of installing in their midst a model Franciscan community.

Such respectful petitioning garnering Olleyquotequiebe's wholehearted consent.

The desert silence thereupon shattered by hearty cheers, laughter, howling and applause as a naked giant donned regimental blues. His smart black bolero sporting its piece de resistance- the palmetto shaped insignia cast in gold and designed by Antonio Bucareli himself.

An unorthodox ceremony followed by feasting, dancing and song banishing fear and uncertainty surrounding a centuries-long standoff between Spain and Indians of the desert.

Like Serra, lay Franciscan Juan Bautista desiring with all his heart to facilitate a lasting triumph of good over evil.

Recognizing in Olleyquotequiebe but another Montezuma. And standing determined to see that under his watch integrity and trust prevail.

Anyone offending an Indian in anyway,

he announced to all assembled,

will not have to wait
for sentencing from the Church or the King.
For I shall deliver punishment on the spot
and with my own sword.

So it was that Garces and Eixarch remained behind.

Fray Pedro Font staying with the expedition as chaplain, historian, cosmographer and unanticipated burr under Anza's saddle. Exhibiting a fanaticism void of reason or compassion no doubt motivated by some odd twist of professional jealousy.

For in all things a man heralded throughout the frontier as Indian fighter behaved more like Saint Francis than did most Franciscans.

Yet while paradoxically exacting discipline often through violent displays of physical punishment and intimidation. And subsequently finding himself left to endure Franciscan Font's constant criticism of a nonetheless magnificently executed operation.

Successfully conducting his most extraordinary caravan of men, women and children across the vast wastelands that separate Sonora from bucolic California.

In surmounting those heights that wall off the fabled country, families under armed guard marching beneath great stands of giant oak and pine. Where on Christmas Eve another of ultimately three children born in route arrived.

Anza celebrating the occasion with song, dance and liberal distribution of spirits.

Prompting a display of outrage from Fray Font over not merely the proposition of drink, music and dance but on this holiest night of the year.

In eloquent silence El Capitan, as his company endearingly referred to Anza, eyeing Font. Then after a long pause requesting respectfully that his chaplain baptize the boy immediately.

Which, piously, Font did.

Overcome from exhaustion and alcohol, the little company then retiring and sleeping soundly.

Whereupon snow began to fall.

Most of Anza's pioneers hailing as they did from semi-tropic northern Mexico never having experienced a white Christmas. And were understandably frightened upon awakening to the sight of something so odd, wet and cold.

Fear distilling into terror when, marching thereafter against an icy wind and snow flurries, all were suddenly thrown to the ground by a terrific earthquake.

Font quick to portend a ridiculous notion of further seismic activity and surreal supposition that they might never be warm again as divine punishments for the flippant manner with which all had dismissed Christmas.

Snow turning to rain. Thereafter warm and glorious sunlight dispelling darkness and eliciting from the caravan an audible and collective sigh of relief.

When in that glorious light of late afternoon unique to California's south country Anza's expedition beheld for the first time a fantastic flower-strewn landscape with its open park-like oak woodlands and rivers bordered by alisos, cottonwoods and troops of fan palms.

Completely banished behind snowy, shaking granite battlements being the deserts they had conquered in gaining access to an Eden.

As per orders from Bucareli, Juan Bautista now discarding frontier attire to don a regal Royal blue uniform with gold brocade not unlike that presented earlier to Olleyquotequiebe.

Having balked at such ostentatious display when first proposed back in Mexico City. Viceroy Bucareli insisting,

> Whatever honest men
> such as yourself might think,
> sometimes
> the difference between commonness and majesty
> is nothing more than gold buttons on royal blue felt.

> And as you may well prove
> the closest association to Don Carlos
> that California will ever see,
> it will not hurt you to show the Californians
> more than your own
> magnificent and natural dignity.

As if on cue each of the Entrada's families following suit, changing into the fine chemises, rebozos, mantas and hats provided them by their King. Lending magic to an already extraordinary arrival. Never had California beheld such proceedings.

So it was that with piety and in dignified couture lay volunteers passed through the doors of challenged Mission San Gabriel Archangel on January 4, 1776.

Only to be greeted by news concerning open insurrection at San Diego.

Rivera predictably expressing indifference concerning the affair. Anza understandably determining that he should take leave of the San Francisco bound expedition long enough to himself intercede.

Families having come to look upon their Capitan as someone more saintly than mortal weeping openly at this sudden and unexpected parting of the ways.

Ensigns (Sergeants) Jose Joaquin Moraga and Juan Pablo Grijalva left to conduct a heartbroken entourage ever northward whilst Anza rode south to San Diego.

Rivera being anything but delicate about expressing annoyance concerning said "interference," not merely at San Diego but with regard to the entire California theater of operations.

Even going so far as to suggest having received orders from Bucareli that he cancel the San Francisco project altogether. Recommending either Anza's cavalcade remain at San Gabriel or return to Sonora.

Anza sending them on ahead to Serra regardless.

Rivera had lied, as Juan Bautista suspected and would soon discover.

Ultimately neither Rivera nor Anza being present at San Francisco's conflicted founding. Nor would be Fray Junipero Serra.

Who subsequently arranged for said ceremony to be repeated. A momentous feat in light of the fact that despite Bucareli's assurances Franciscanland's future yet stood hanging tenuously in balance.

As it was tiny San Francisco in little more than a decade standing serene and successful, lorded over by a Spanish castle of sorts from which Sergeant Moraga came to serve in Anza's stead as commandante. With Don Carlos even planning development of a Royal Deer Park in which to showcase those really large deer (actually elk) reported earlier both by Vizcaino and now Francisco Palou.

While far to the south at San Juan Capistrano foundations were laid for construction of the grandest Christian temple in all of California.

Those first messengers to be dispatched by way of Anza's overland route arriving at Mexico City late in 1776 bearing news concerning the founding of San Francisco and San Juan Capistrano both.

Temporarily sidelined Joseph Galvez responding by laughing out loud.

Reflecting upon his somewhat insolent response tendered previously to an impetuous little Franciscan, who had insisted Saint Francis be honored in California.

Serra now standing in possession of his Bay for Saint Francis (and not just any bay, but the grandest of all bays) and his desired if challenged Mission of Saint Francis as well. And all of this while Galvez's own proposed Mission San Buenaventura remained as of yet unfounded!

Sir Joseph would receive even more stunning news and direct from the Royal residence.

Meanwhile stoic Rivera riding south in silence alongside Anza, never suspecting for a moment that he would not live to see New California again.

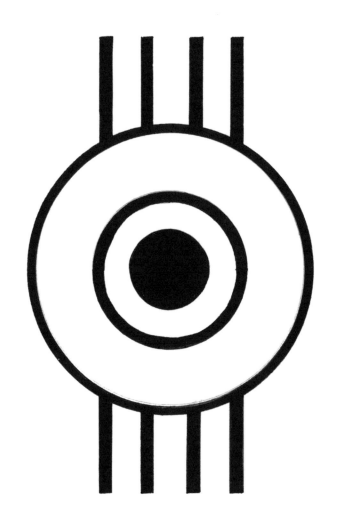

CHINIGCHINICH

S erra's stunning success and corresponding reductive effect with regard to a secular Spanish coalition intent upon divesting the Bourbon's of their Catholic monopoly over possibility laden California made similarly uncomfortable an onsite Indian oligarchy.

Who in possession of their own agendas were like the Junta and Council not inclined to sit idly by passively surrendering.

Throughout much of California the god of all humanity had ever been referred to in respective dialects as Chinigchinich or Star Man.

Who propitiously appeared in the advent of famine and political discord to inquire from great multitudes assembled what they wished most to achieve. And being pleased upon hearing expressed desires for peace and abundance, suggested that,

You are not capable,
nor can you do what you think or wish to do
on your own.

I am the only One who has power,
and I will give it to you,
so that you might have the peace
and abundance you seek.

I am the way.

WEST OF THE WEST

According to accounts maintained orally
Chinigchinich "dogmatised" on this wise,

> Dancing before the crowds adorned in robes
> of black, white and red
> He chanted his history
> of having come from the stars so as to teach them
> those things of which they were ignorant.

After dancing a considerable time then pausing to
separate the chiefs from amongst their people.

Out of teaming throngs selecting a great council.
Whom he endowed with powers for summoning the
rains, coaxing grain from the earth, subduing every
wild beasts, healing those afflicted and otherwise
performing many other desirable and noble tasks.
Making it understood that this "priesthood" he
imparted be passed on through successive generations.

Upon his departure imploring the people to seek out
those in possession of same priesthood for advice and
relief from life's burdens.

In the event of a scarcity of food, or any infirmity,
admonishing that they dress as had he and in
humility kneel together with said "elders" when
calling upon him.

That should they do so their wants would be
relieved. The sick would be cured and the hungry
receive sustenance.

Furthermore instructing adults concerning how best
to raise their children, before reiterating in dance the

rules they must observe in order that peace and abundance might be everlasting.

Then assuring them before ascending heavenward that,

> To those who have kept my commandments,
> I shall give all that they ask of me.

So revered was this Star Man that to Serra's day the faithful upon perceiving any good fortune or blessing expressing a spontaneous,

> Guic Chinigchinich,

which is to say,

> Thanks to Chinigchinich, who has given this to me.

Suddenly circulating in Serra's wake coming news that a monster by the name of Ouiot (We-ott) had appeared in the marshes of Puvanga (Long Beach). Claiming to be none other than Chinigchinich incarnate. Suggesting having descended from heaven as an orphan (for so this man first appeared amongst them), and in the form of a man/god not unlike Jesus Christ. Threatening countless oaths against and misfortunes upon the heads of anyone who dared turn away from him.

> Those who obey not my teachings,
> nor believe them,
> I shall punish severely.

> I will send unto them bears to bite
> and serpents to sting.

They shall be without food
and afflicted with many diseases.

Developing an open alliance capable of eradicating
Christianity altogether, what with displaced shaman
priests and sorcerers now rallying around their own
and potent messiah figure.

Who accompanied by his legions portending
calamities upon the heads of any who so much as
uttered a prayer to Jesus Christ, frightened many away
from Brother Junipero.

Serra understanding clearly the dynamic of this new
challenge. And deploying as his own weapon the pure
love of Christ in an effective counter attack.

So as to prevail against not only a shaman's
incantations but the still far greater danger of an
opportunistic Spanish aristocracy.

Serra standing ever vigilant against threats both
foreign and domestic.

His own greatest fear not being Star Man but rather
the fatuous if not deliberately belligerent acts of a
political machine already guilty of betraying Christ
through eradication of Jesuit Utopia.

Apocryphal tales recounting such things as a visit from
inland tribes who presented Christian Serra with gifts
of raw gold.

News of which Brother Junipero kept hidden even
from his brothers, so fearful was he that California

might in an instant stand undone by the same fate that had befallen both Mexico and Peru should word concerning presence of the highly coveted metal be broadcast.

Recognizing in his novices a treasure far more precious than gold, this beautiful little man who according to Indian suitors spoke with Jesus Christ directly, warning those bringing him golden tribute that yellow metals were but the fire of a powerful dragon. And were not to be touched lest by so doing the monster be disturbed who if awakened would destroy them all.

Vulnerable as Franciscans were both to a hostile Junta and Council and now mere mention of Star Man one begins to catch a glimpse of the courage displayed by Serra and his handful of potential martyrs.

Still shaman making every effort to dissuade through fearful spells and threats of bear attacks and snake-bites could not contain mass defections. Nonetheless rumored insurrections remained a constant.

Then came word that inhabitants of villages welcoming visiting Franciscans were being randomly slaughtered.

Mission communities correspondingly fearful of reprisals for everything from maltreatment by an individual Spanish soldier to the appearance of illness, either of which would be promptly attributed as testament to but the vengeance of Chinigchinich.

There had never been more than two Franciscans stationed at any given mission installation. Five to ten soldiers comprising an at best but modest guard.

Most assuredly even the bravest of hearts yielding to many a sleepless night.

Unlike his own god, Junipero himself could not be omnipresent.

Circumstances were critical. If a military presence was to be maintained on site Serra insisted it behave in accordance with Christian precepts or risk reaping the wind.

Mercifully Brother Junipero's steadfast petitioning for reforms having fallen upon the sympathetic ear of Viceroy Antonio Bucareli.

So it was that Commandante General Don Pedro Fages had been ostensibly banished through promotion into the Department of Interior Provinces. Thus facilitating an entrée for Juan Bautista Anza.

Yet with interim Rivera refusing co-operation of anykind.

In the midst of said reorganizational nightmare, a singular tragedy exposing glaring disparity between Serra's agenda (as dictated by Charles III) and that of the Supreme Council of the Indies (as carried out on site by Rivera). Galvanizing Viceroy Bucareli's personal commitment to his Franciscan champion forever.

Having from the beginning struggled against all odds at San Diego, Serra being elated to receive in Christian baptism both local Kumeyaay chief Pocoet and his brother Armquich. As in response many Kumeyaay then taunted followers of Ouiot-become-

Chinigchinich by similarly accepting the Christian sacrament of baptism.

At San Diego Fray Luis Jaime honoring Pocoet's own position of political importance in correspondingly appropriate ceremony. During which the Franciscan christened his new protégé Carlos, after the Spanish King, while bestowing upon brother Pocoet the name of Saint Francis.

Shaman aligned with a Chinigchinich pretender moving quickly to counter further apostasy by luring both Pocoet and Armquich back. Offering promises of not only supernatural powers through ordination to the priesthood but political control over an amalgamated consortium of clans.

A damp chill gripping the air when on the night of November 5, 1775, six hundred devotees of Ouiot together with an ambiguous Pocoet emerged in full war paint of black, white and red from out of the marshes at Nipaquay (now Mission Valley) to attack Mission San Diego. Even as similar legions led by Armquich surrounded the Royal Presidio situated above Cosoy.

Commandante Ortega being away at San Juan Capistrano, there to assist Fray Fermin Francisco Lasuen with launching Serra's much anticipated Utopian Capitol.

Outside of the San Diego Presidio Armquich setting a signal fire indicating readiness to his brother upriver at the mission. Then curiously taking flight without inflicting damage.

Even more baffling being the fact that routine evening communications conducted between mission and presidio by means of bells and bugle calls were curtailed. While neither fire nor murderous shrieks all under the light of a full moon aroused a single soldier from slumber when hundreds of insurgents descended upon and erased Mission San Diego de Alcala from off the face of the earth.

Fray Vicente Fuster recalling for a subsequently convened court charged with sorting out the bloody affair how,

Amid the yelling and firing of guns,
half-asleep, I hurried out of the building,
hardly knowing what was going on...

Flying all around me
were more arrows than you could possibly count...

There we were
surrounded on all sides by flames.

Hoping to calm a riotous melee
my companion Luis Jayme stepped into the fray
expressing but his habitual admonition:

'Amar a Dios, mis ninos
For the love of God, my children,'

In response to which the Indians fell upon him.
Stripped him to his underwear.
Shot him through with arrows.
And then clubbed him to death.

Employing mission buildings as barricades Fray Fuster himself rushing to rescue Commandante Ortega's two sons who had been left in his care. With but five soldiers bravely defending a community of more than three hundred.

Reported Fuster,

That night seemed as long as the pains of purgatory.

Flames illuminating a ghastly scene of murder and plunder garnering no response from the Presidio. Ultimately terror simply slipping away into the darkness.

Clearing smoke on the following morning revealing once beautiful Mission San Diego in ruins; its whitewashed facade marred by fire, contents plundered, campus in shambles, hacienda torched and livestock scattered to the four winds.

A day passing before Fray Vicente locating the pulverized body of his thirty-two year old companion Luis and the remains of not one but two Mexican teachers together with an unknown number of novices. All martyred.

Yet and despite the blind eye cast by a Presidio absent its loyal Catholic Commandante, damage inflicted promptly contained again by a synchronicity of chance that cannot help but suggest divine intervention.

When on the very next day two ships, each laden with supplies and soldiers, sailed into San Diego Bay. Even as they dropped anchor Juan Bautista Anza marching in from off the eastern desert at the head of ostensibly two hundred and forty one Christian soldiers.

Disciples of Chinigchinich not merely unnerved but terrified by this seemingly supernatural and immediate response from Jesus Christ himself.

Meanwhile upon receipt of the news and fearful of further uprisings Commandante Ortega ordering shut down just founded Mission San Juan Capistrano. Riding forthwith on to fulfill a difficult task of delivering news concerning the debacle to

Father.

Who upon being informed smiled, and with tears in his eyes, responded,

Thanks be to God.

NOW WE SHALL SHOW THEM
CHRIST'S LOVE AND FORGIVENESS.

Ortega never forgot that moment, or the fact that Serra saw even in this bloody sacrifice but another gift from a kind and loving Saviour.

God has provided us with an opportunity
to undo the followers of vengeful Chinig Chinix
by embracing them with unconditional love.

Without hesitation Fray Junipero as Reverend Father President pronouncing clemency upon all those who had perpetrated said atrocities.

And understanding clearly the issue at hand, instructing Rivera against taking punitive measures of anykind. Ordering rather that all efforts remain focused upon winning back anyone who had sought to destroy the community of Christ.

Communicating anew to the Kumeyaay that this mission, like all others, was entirely theirs for the taking.

Ortega seeing to it that Serra's pardon and invitation to come and further exploit everything including the concept be delivered.

Brother Junipero's wisdom in extending amnesty rather than attempting the impossible task of exacting retribution diffusing a bomb that might otherwise have erased altogether in bloodbath his entire Experiment.

Given the immediate and serendipitous appearance of powerfully armed reinforcements with means at hand for seeking revenge, insurgents throughout southern California could not help but to marvel at the humanity displayed in this Christian response.

And led by a penitent Pocoet, abandoned in droves, vengeful and unforgiving shaman fundamentalists. With volunteers showing up ready and willing to rebuild and restore Mission San Diego.

Word of the debacle and subsequent détente would be slow in reaching a Viceroy's Palace, what with Fernando Rivera running interference.

Who argued that the entire incident need never have occurred if only Serra had maintained his mission adjacent to the security of San Diego's presidio.

And upon greeting Ortega thereafter in San Diego disavowed Franciscan authority to extend amnesty or otherwise afford sanctuary of anykind to perpetrators of the attack.

With Anza's protestations being dismissed as insubordination on the part of an inferior officer. As were the career threatening actions taken by Ortega when he, too, attempted preventing Rivera from initiating punitive measures.

Refusing to be dissuaded Don Fernando himself marching into an improvised sanctuary at the Presidio and personally arresting and extraditing both Pocoet and Armquich. Ultimately stripping and whipping them senseless in public display.

Before canceling all efforts being made both to rebuild Mission San Diego and inaugurate Mission San Juan Capistrano. And this despite the fact the sailors present aboard each of Bucareli's ships had all volunteered to remain and help with said reconstruction efforts.

Rivera ordering them on to San Francisco then mandating further that they dispense with the building of missions there as well. Instructing all to focus energies upon construction of but the Presidio alone.

For such effrontery Serra demanding nothing less than Rivera's excommunication.

And when at long last in receipt of Fray Junipero's mysteriously delayed correspondence regarding the entire affair, Bucareli complying.

Even going further by seeing to it that not only Rivera but still holding court in Loreto Phelipe de Barry be held accountable and accordingly dismissed from the Governorship and similarly excommunicated.

Curiously no actions being taken against troops stationed at the presidio. Who under oath in subsequent litigation claimed neither to have seen nor heard that which they could not but have helped both to see and hear.

All of which simply cleared the way as if by unseen hands for delivering California's political leadership into the protective care of lay Franciscan Juan Bautista Anza.

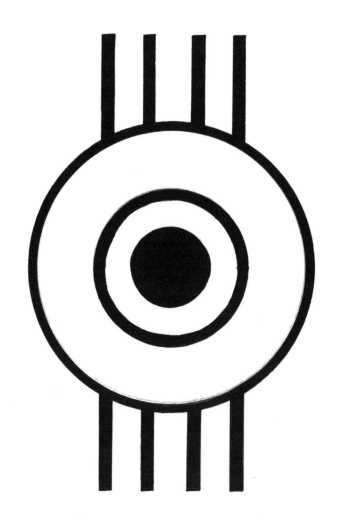

SABOTAGE

ow often the grand designs of great dreamers are but outwardly espoused while covertly opposed by jealous pretenders.

Fernando Rivera had no doubt under direct orders purposefully detained if not secretly thwarted Franciscan progress of any kind in New California. The auspicious arrival of gate crashing Juan Bautista Anza adding fuel to a fire set deliberately by those intent upon destroying Church and State monopolies maintained between Rome and the Bourbon Family.

And now detaining at Mission San Gabriel Catholic lay volunteers anxious to settle in San Francisco. Suggesting that their enterprise had been canceled, their promised stipends curtailed.

When regardless they insisted upon fulfilling the venture Rivera then objecting with a conciliatory,

What is the object of your going there,
unless it be but to tire yourselves uselessly,

I explained to you that I have looked
well into this matter
and have informed his Excellency that
there is no site suitable for founding a community.

To which Anza had responded,

My friend,
I am going where I have been sent,

and shall fill a bottle with
the water of that estuary,
cork it well,
have Fray Pedro (Font) here certify
to its genuineness,
and present it to the Viceroy.

Who has bidden me aid the Franciscans
with founding a community as near the sea as I can,
so that the possession of that port may be
assured to Spain.

The unexpected turn of events at San Diego rendering
said discussion academic.

Father Antonio Paterna at Mission San Gabriel pleading
for Anza's intervention. Juan Bautista responding,

I have no authority in California
except to see my company
through to their destination
at San Francisco,

A distressed missionary countering with:

You have the authority of God
to save innocent men from being murdered.

The subsequently awkward teaming of Rivera and
Anza exposing in no uncertain terms two openly
diametric agendas still polarizing New California in a
singularly brutal tug of war.

Times had changed. The world had changed.

Freemasonry in particular having given rise to an unprecedented ethos both of Individualism and of Nationalism.

With every man perceiving himself a king. Or at least presuming entitlement to the same inherent privileges of as John Locke put it,

> Life, liberty and the pursuit of real estate.

Tossing men the likes of Fray Junipero Serra and Capitan Juan Bautista Anza unwillingly into an ideological maelstrom.

At Mission San Gabriel Fray Antonio prevailing upon the man whom Bucareli had dispatched not only to bridge Sonora and California but a widening breach between divergent political aims.

Who after enduring more than a week of waiting for even acknowledgment of his presence from Rivera, sent a letter by courier to the grandee sitting camped within site of a Mission from whom all hospitality had been refused.

Anza's messenger returning bearing Rivera's written response,

> San Diego is a pigpen.
> If I had a thousand troops to clean up the hills,
> its pagan beggars would still breed a nuisance.

To which Anza fired back via courier,

> San Diego ought to be defended or abandoned, Sir.

Spanish lives, if not the lifeline of the empire itself,
are in jeopardy there.

Rivera responding with a single cryptic line,

Is this the opinion of the Viceroy?

A disgusted Anza replying,

It has been months since last I saw the Viceroy.
And then we had matters other than San Diego to
discuss- even if we had known about the trouble there.

Rivera responding with another note,

I have thought of abandoning San Diego.

Anza countering,

Were you sent here to defend
or to abandon California?

The absurd dialogue carried on by way of penned
correspondence between two men sitting within sight
of each other continuing thusly for two days.

Never did Rivera fail to answer Anza. Yet never would
he register any sign of sympathetic concern,

Good God, sir!
When a place is impossible to civilize
it is better to abandon it.

The priests have themselves failed
to make any headway with the Indians.

The military cannot discipline them.
What do you do with incorrigible animals?

Anza replying,

My people in Sonora
have fought the Apache
for three generations, Sir,
but we have not abandoned Sonora.

To which Rivera bristled,

In the name of all the sacred saints in heaven,
why do you not stay in Sonora then
and let us deal with our own problems?!

Peering at Don Fernando's tent from his window in
the Mission, a now impatient Anza tersely scripting,

We are here
under orders from the Viceroy of New Spain
to aid San Fernando Missionary College
with securing the Bay of Saint Francis
and to establish a land route
from Sonora to California, 'Governor.'

But if you need assistance at San Diego
I stand ready to offer it.

Following which Rivera and Anza set off together for
San Diego but in silence.

Where at the Royal Presidio Juan Bautista bunked
with in from aborted San Juan Capistrano Fray
Fermin Lasuen.

Both men sitting idle for days awaiting orders that never materialized.

El Capitan musing over a prescient letter from Fray Pedro Font concerning Rivera's cryptic dismissal of San Francisco,

> There is no use in going there,
> as we should gain nothing by it.

Anza's companion of the Trail proclaiming contrariwise and jubilantly,

> This is indeed the harbor of all harbors.
> Nature's true masterpiece.

> Much beautiful country have I seen in my lifetime,
> and many noble anchorages;
> but nothing to surpass these safe
> and spacious waters
> with their commanding heights.

> A city built here might rival any seaport in Europe
> both for splendor as well as security.

Anza now contemplating that which at San Diego Rivera had dismissed as but a pigpen.

Marveling over it's gentle grandeur, softness of air and subtle beauty.

Here also was treasure enough to entice any monarch or emperor. Rivera knew this. Anza knew that Rivera recognized this.

Surely those same private interests that had forced Jesuits into exile were somehow responsible for the bellicosity displayed both by Governor Barry and Inspector/Commandante Rivera.

Clearly no one sitting on a Council in Seville or Junta at Mexico City wished to see California developed by and for Indians, Rome and the Bourbons.

Anza ruminating endlessly in his mind over the words of Rivera's final missive at San Gabriel,

> You and the priest (meaning Serra)
> join to peddle a fantastic dream
> to His Excellency.

> Then you speak as though
> it were His Excellency's own favorite intention.

Tertiary Franciscan Juan Bautista's stern response having been delivered as if by a father to his impertinent child,

> While you are in a Franciscan country, Sir
> you are subordinate to the Franciscans.

> I need not remind you that
> the Spanish people here present
> are to go out of their way
> to be friendly to the Indians,
> that by our example
> we might achieve much good.

> May God go with you to San Diego.

Left to reflect upon the extraneous efforts he'd taken to keep Anza and Serra apart, having even gone so far as to place Brother Junipero under all but house arrest at the Royal Presidio in Monterey, Fernando Rivera now dared not leave Franciscan golden boy Juan Bautista behind.

Who after witnessing public lashings of Indians seemingly made purposefully more brutal out of spite for his own presence, whilst repeatedly being enjoined in sexual overture by coerced Kumeyaay, sickened of the proposition altogether.

Perceiving Franciscan California as but a goal so beyond the reality crashing down all around him as to render any hope of its successful installation well outside the realm of possibilities.

Having experienced early on the agony of forcefully evicting Jesuit missionaries from similarly subverted dreams, Anza thoughtfully reexamining that which he'd again experienced just since meeting with Viceroy Bucareli.

And subsequently explaining to Serra,

I simply cannot bear
to participate in a repeat of La Paz,

To which an ever-optimistic utopian responded,

No effort
given in the service of our Lord
is wasted.

The Kingdom of God on earth
is built of small stones
laid one upon another.

Anza's response revealing the depths of
his disillusionment,

Yes, Father, in your view.
But your time is counted in eternities,
mine in days, weeks or months.

My work must show results now,
or I shall be pushed aside
and left to die in the desert,
as it were.

Serra intending to encourage a devoted Christian with,

To die in the service of the Master,
is in itself a reward.

Regardless, having been countered on every side by
Rivera's unscrupulous efforts to sabotage both
Franciscans as well as himself, Anza would not be
dissuaded. Ultimately refusing even a personal plea
from Brother Junipero that he accept his arranged for
posting as commandante of the new Royal Presidio at
San Francisco with Governorship to follow. Opting
rather pursuit of advancement outside and far
removed from the political intrigues and
complications of a viciously coveted country.

Serra conceding, but not without placing a major
impediment in Anza's pathway to default. Reminding
his lay brother of vows concerning obedience to the

Order. Then instructing that Brother Juan Bautista first return and together with Olleyquotequiebe tender forfeiture over to the Viceroy at Mexico City in person.

So it was that during the spring of 1776 Anza and Olleyquotequiebe stood before Sir Antonio who received each man with enthusiasm and characteristic equanimity.

Even before Anza voiced his resignation O'Reilly promoting him as California's highest-ranking officer in return for having opened the road and successfully orchestrating San Francisco's founding.

Pledging bonuses not only for Anza but to each of his men.

In response to Serra's conspiracy Bucareli having conceded,

his presence,
good judgement and talents,
which I have now seen close at hand,
confirm me
in the positive opinion
which I have had of him
ever since the time
when he first stood before me
to propose the exploration.

But it was by virtue of said "good judgement," that Anza recognized a covetous cabal and not magnanimous Bucareli or the precious brothers of Saint Francis as wielding ultimate control over California's future.

And accordingly expressing in no uncertain terms his preference for engaging sorties of Apache warriors on the battlefield rather than being subjected to the malevolent, deceitful, backstabbing political arena of potential commerce into which California had already become mired.

Bucareli, unable to change a perceptive and honorable man's mind, capitulating. Granting Anza's request that he be returned home and there serve alongside Galvez as highest ranking military officer (Commandante de Armas) in the Interior Provinces.

Yet ordering that from hence he accommodate the needs of Franciscan Fathers Francisco Dominguez and Sylvestre Escalante both of whom were then dispatched to open a road between Monterey and Santa Fe.

Meanwhile Bucareli plying Fray Junipero with more than new ships and supplies.

Buried amongst sacks of wheat, barley, tobacco, sugar and coffee freighting a beautiful silver Monstrance gilded in gold. By way of which the Viceroy communicated to his missionary that authority from the Bishop of Guadalajara to confirm full membership together with the attendant Gift of the Holy Spirit required for participation in Communion upon his growing congregation of California novices would soon follow.

Serra's response mirroring that of Olleyquotequebe's when presented by Anza with a Royal pendant,

Our joy was great
when we took off the coverings
and looked and looked at it
with wondering eyes.

That was the good news. Next came the bad.

With Barry dismissed Rivera shamed and Anza disillusioned, Council member Phelipe de Neve having been placed in charge of New California through default.

Poising a threat so monstrous as to dwarf by comparison all Council appointees combined to date.

Minister General of the Council of the Indies Julian de Arriega having died unexpectedly. Sir Joseph Galvez posted as successor and inroute yet not due back in New Spain for upwards of a year. Leaving operative Neve with an unprecedented window of opportunity and Serra correspondingly facing his worst nightmare.

SIR JOSEPH TO THE RESCUE

In a mad dash to install secular colonialism presumably upon behalf of the Council and before that Council's Royally appointed successor could arrive to run interference for the Franciscans, Governor Phelipe de Neve breaching protocol broke every rule on the books.

Without mandatory sanctions from King or Pope countering by virtue of his authority as appointed Governor similarly imposed plans of a presumptive Serra to establish the San Francisco Bay area's second mission with installation rather of a secular municipality.

Whilst issuing orders to forestall and replace Serra's now two proposed missions along the Santa Barbara channel with a single and secular settlement instead.

Then from his comfortable Governor's mansion at Loreto ordering excommunicated Rivera back to California post haste with both secular colonists and armed reinforcements, while suggesting, under a guise of attempting to solidify the region without taxing Serra, his program be launched to convert previously established missions into similarly chartered municipalities independent of Franciscan custodies.

While as a backhanded complement to Serra personally, christening the first such colony Saint Joseph (El Pueblo de San Jose).

Serra was not amused. Where presidios had been tolerated pueblos being outright illegal intrusions as

SAN JUAN CAPISTRANO.

3

1. A 15th century Spanish knight as rendered
   by military historian/artist Angus McBride.
   © Copyright 1980 Osprey Publishing Ltd.

2. Portrait of Junipero Serra as crusader
   Saint John of Capistrano. Commissioned by
   Serra and executed at Mexico City in 1774 by
   noted artist Jose Paez. Reproduced here courtesy
   of Bellerophon Books, 36 Anacapa Street,
   Santa Barbara, California 93101.

3. Grizzly bears on the beach at Monterey.
   Painted by Prinz Von Maximilian Weid.
   Reproduced here courtesy of the Bancroft
   Library, University of California, Berkeley.

4. Mammoth Hunters at Rancho La Brea in
Los Angeles. Painting reproduced here courtesy
of the George C. Page Museum.

5. Awahnechee village of "Chucka," in Yosemite
Valley, as rendered by Raymond Dobb Yellana,
Reproduced here courtesy of the Bancroft
Library, University of California, Berkeley.

6. Inauguration of Christian community amongst
the Chumash at "Cieneguitas." Painting by
Henry S. Ford. And reproduced here courtesy
of the Santa Barbara Museum of Natural History.

5

CALIFORNIA

VIII

WEST OF THE WEST

9

10. Mount San Jacinto lords over a gentile
    (non-Catholic) mission-era settlement in this
    stylized Currier and Ives interpretation of Southern
    "California's Central Coast." Reproduced here
    courtesy of The California Historical Society.

11. James Walker's famous rendition of
    "Roping the Bear." Reproduced here courtesy
    of the California Historical Society.

12. Classic portrait of a "Californio," as depicted by
    James Walker. And reproduced here courtesy of
    the Specialized Libraries and Archival Collections,
    University of Southern California, Los Angeles.

but veiled means of introducing a colonial and secular presence that ever led to exploitation of Indians and was regardless strictly forbidden in California by order of Don Carlos himself.

Neve's actions in fact giving the impression that Spain's King had permitted his promise to California's Indian population concerning non- interference from the outside world be broken.

Jeopardizing overnight everything missionaries had and were presently sacrificing even their very lives to achieve.

Governor Neve's aggressive stance signaling but the beginning of an accelerated conflict predicted by Anza.

On the heels of news concerning San Jose's founding, Fray Junipero receiving the new Governor's hurried edict ordering conversion of all Franciscan mission communities ten years or older into subdivided colonial jurisdictions and this on the tenth anniversary of both San Diego de Alcala and Mission San Carlos Borromeo's founding.

In response to which the San Fernando Missionary College filed a twelve-page legal suite against both Neve and the Board of War and Finance.

That document quickly making its way to the desk of Charles III. His Majesty being reminded by Commissary General of the Franciscan Order Rafael Verger that as a result of said actions the Crown by virtue of previously made promises forbidding any colonial participation in California now stood in breach of contract. The Order of the Least of the Brothers of Christ addressing their complaint with an emphatic and urgent R! (Rey!).

Calmly R, as in ever even-tempered Don Carlos, dictating his response:

Do not worry.
All will be as was pledged.

At this very moment Sir Joseph de Galvez
is being installed at Seville,
himself to serve as new Universal Minister of the
Supreme Council of the Indies.

He will see to it
That His Majesty's promises are kept.

R!

Meanwhile, as letters were ferried from New Spain to Old Spain and back again, Serra simply ignoring Neve's schemes. Moving ahead as planned with proposed for the same site Mission Santa Clara. Upon arrival Galvez promptly endorsing establishment of the same.

But not before ordering the arrest and incarceration of his malicious former Secretary Miguel Jose Azanza.

Thereafter Serra receiving even more good news from Sir Joseph. The Bishop of Guadalajara had recanted and sent a previously withheld Papal Bull from Rome authorizing Fray Junipero to perform confirmation duties otherwise reserved exclusively for ordained prelates. So that a Franciscan missionary might solidly anchor the soul of his novices to an enterprise they had themselves engendered through gifts of the Holy Spirit and daily communion.

There remained but one problem. The much anticipated authorization carried with it an expiration date. Limiting practice of privileges extended therein to but three years. Curiously it had taken three years for the authorization to arrive?

And accordingly Governor Neve issued an aviso insisting whereas the time for which Serra had been authorized to perform confirmations having expired said license was therefore to be considered null and void.

Wasting no energy attempting to decipher whether chance or subterfuge had forestalled delivery of the Bishop's edict, Serra simply countering with his own assertion that three-year entitlements could only reasonably commence upon the date of their receipt.

And on that day, June 29, 1778, performing but the first of 5,308 confirmations, by bestowing full membership into the Holy Mother Church upon seven year-old Junipero Bucareli, whom he had himself baptized and christened following his return from Mexico City.

Serra would lose his trusted ally at Mexico City when stricken with pleurisy Antonio Bucareli died in April of the following year.

Meanwhile as Marquee of Sonora and Universal Minister General of the Supreme Council of the Indies Galvez continued to monitor and spare California as best he could further treachery; having already politically separated both it and the northern frontier from powerful entities in the government of New Spain sitting poised otherwise to exploit.

Additionally taking extraordinary measures to shore up his Interior Provinces while reinforcing Anza's inroads by replacing on site commanding officer Hugo O'Conner with confidant Carlos Francisco de Croix's nephew, Teodoro, as Inspector-Commandante/General of consolidated and decidedly separate jurisdictions.

Who was given to understand that as a Department of the Kingdom of Spain California remained extremely important to Don Carlos,

> His Majesty orders me to reiterate to Your Excellency
> the charge that you view those establishments
> even though outside your jurisdiction
> yet with the preference and attention
> which their importance to the King merits.

All should have gone well. And would have gone well were it not for the installation of Martin de Mayorga as Bucareli's successor. Who unbeknownst to the King had earlier participated openly with Miguel Jose Azanza in undoing Galvez.

So that now when petitions from Don Joseph to Teodoro Croix on behalf of California were forwarded innocently enough on to Viceroy Mayorga with Croix's disclaimer that as Inspector Commandante/General of the Interior Provinces he held neither jurisdiction over nor access to the Pious Fund, Mayorga in deference simply discarded them.

Meanwhile Neve conspiring endlessly to convert California into an arena of secular endeavor. Announcing his mandate that any new mission founded be forbidden from offering instruction or launching commercial enterprise. Which as Mayorga was running interference but succeeded in undoing everything previously engineered by Serra.

Shackling missionary efforts with an austerity extreme even for Franciscans. Croix providing out of his own budget but for two correspondingly ephemeral outposts to be established along Anza's overland route.

Purisima Concepcion and San Pedro y San Pablo the first (and only) California missions not located along the coast, additionally sharing a dubious distinction as installations void of communal infrastructure. Each consisting rather of little more than a simple parish church.

Thusly divorced from the purpose for their founding, both while extravagant gifts on Croix's part yet bestowing nothing more than superficial window dressing upon an already delicate proposition.

Palou expressing the Order's gratitude thusly,

> If we are to confine ourselves
> to saying Mass and preaching
> we may as well remain at Mexico City
> and save the King further expense.

Vulnerable targets like sitting ducks perched atop bluffs overlooking Capitan Palma's prized pasturage along the

Colorado River Valley, this presence of these two tiny churches making a mockery of the otherwise grand social experiments they were intended to anchor.

With Father Garces maintaining a guarded triumph by dutifully paying rent to Olleyquotoquiebe as arranged by Anza and previously endorsed through Viceroy Bucareli.

In California proper Bucareli had prior to his demise expedited paperwork setting into motion installation of Galvez's own favored and yet unfounded Mission San Buenaventura. Together with an attendant royal Presidio and now at Serra's request second Mission (Santa Barbara).

Political interloper Neve conspiring to abort both in order that another colonial municipality be chartered instead.

Before said window of opportunity closing and together with excommunicated Rivera managing to recruit colonists and soldiers from across Sinaloa and Sonora. Whom in the absence of deceased Arriaga and not yet upon the scene Galvez he'd then jettisoned into New California.

Better to act now
and beg forgiveness later.

So that even as Serra made plans to not only at long last found Mission San Buenaventura but launch Mission Santa Barbara and before Galvez could be apprised of circumstances as they existed at present in California two privately funded companies disassociated with Franciscan Custodies marching headlong into the province.

Neve further ignoring

that lunatic Galvez

by canceling the installation of Mission Santa Barbara altogether while issuing orders against founding any future Franciscan missions.

Serra's sense of looming disaster heightening upon receipt of news arriving overland from Anza's Tubac concerning the fact that Inspector Commandante/ General of the Interior Provinces Teodoro de Croix was refusing to provide Fathers Garces and Eixarch monies with which to mollify the Quechan. Arguing that funding for such need be provided them by a now recognized as subversive Viceroy Mayorga whose Board of War and Finance courtesy of arrangements made at the outset monitored Pious Fund expenditures.

And that similarly he'd endorsed Commandante Rivera's decision to refrain from tendering Olleyquotequiebe tribute in exchange for use of the "Anza" Trail.

Ever anxious to blight the names of Anza and Serra both, an excommunicated Rivera sitting commiserating with Don Pedro Fages at Tubac. Where combined flagrant disdain harbored by two exiled players for not only Franciscans but Capitan Palma and any other empowered Indian sparked what quickly exploded into California's single greatest disaster.

Traveling together with Rivera's soldiers being several hundred head of cattle. Which Don Fernando then purposefully parked in the Quechan farmlands (today's Winterhaven), there to fatten on Olleyqoutequiebe's crops, before herding them off towards far distant coastal grasslands.

When confronted both by Father Garces and Olleyquotequiebe regarding such effrontery, Rivera insisting that the pasturage like his livestock belonged to Don Carlos.

Then seizing upon the opportunity as on site superior ranking officer and using insubordination for his excuse dismissing and publicly stripping Capitan Palma both of rank and uniform.

While announcing that the King would, as he put it:

no longer submit to Indian larceny.

Tribute will no longer be paid
on lands that already belong to the Spanish Crown.

Horrendously humiliated Olleyquotequiebe refusing consolation from Fathers Garces, Eixarch and visiting Father Barreneche.

Meanwhile Neve's California bound colonists had crossed the Sea of Cortez from Sinaloa on July 17th, 1781. And proceeded overland up the peninsula to Mission San Gabriel. Where they expected to rendezvous with Rivera and his Sonoran soldiers and livestock and together found a presidio and secular colony at Santa Barbara.

Weeks passing before all present in coastal California receiving news concerning the tragedy that had befallen not only Rivera but both Colorado River Valley missions.

When, anxious to overwhelm the Franciscans yet desirous of seeing all livestock well fed, Rivera had dispatched his armed caravan while suggesting he would once again bring up the rear as ordered by Serra those many years earlier. But only after allowing his cattle to fatten on Indian pastures for yet another week.

When Santa Barbara bound troops disappeared over that western horizon hundreds of incensed Quechan descending upon an arrogant, unsuspecting Spanish officer. To exact from him their own imposed and heavy tribute.

In one fail stroke erasing two fledgling missions from off the face of the earth. Brutally massacring Fernando Rivera, his private guard of thirty men and three Franciscan missionaries. A handful of women and children present being abducted and carried off to remote hideouts. Livestock driven pell mell into the desert and slaughtered.

News of the unexpected debacle horrifying Neve and Croix. Both of whom deflected blame for the incident upon of all people Anza. Alleging that Juan Bautista had misled them into presuming a pacifity on the part of Capitan Palma that resulted in their misjudging an actually tenuous state of affairs still extant along the Colorado.

It would be Don Pedro Fages who raced from Tubac to the Missions, burying bodies and recovering kidnapped women and children as he went. Subsequently informing Galvez **and** Serra concerning his failure with regard to locating any sign of the Franciscans.

Years passing before former Quechan neophytes leading Aztec- become- Administrator of the Interior Provinces Jose Antonio Figueroa to a small garden of flowers blossoming in the midst of sand and creosote. Where heartbroken Olleyquotequiebe had laid to rest his innocence together with the bodies of three missionaries.

After attempts at dissuading outraged warriors from harming the priests, a shamed Indian ambassador recounting how Father Garces had naively feigned petitions to flee from assassins in route with,

First I must finish my chocolate.

Garces, Eixarch and Barraneche each subsequently shot through with arrows before being clubbed to death by an enraged mob not even Olleyquotequiebe could restrain.

Arriving upon the scene from Old Spain to receive word of circumstances surrounding the California related incident Galvez demanding as per Serra's precedent set at San Diego that Inspector Commandante/General of the Interior Provinces Teodoro Croix extend full amnesty and otherwise restrain from exacting retribution from the Quechan.

Even as Croix dismissed the debacle by suggesting that all had but taken dictation from nothing more sinister than the fiscal bottom line. And accordingly under said set of circumstances, what with a heightened need for security both to maintain open the road and to rebuild the missions, felt it most expedient simply to close everything down altogether.

Why was Anza not surprised.

Nephew of his trusted colleague or not, Galvez too left pondering the suggested banality of Teodoro's motivations.

Plagued anew with suspicions, yet opting to dismiss Croix as one incapable of such intrigue. And hence inculpable. Casting his glance further afield at Mayorga. Accepting with resignation the Viceroy's suggestions that he quit both desert missions and close down Anza's overland road.

Meanwhile safeguarding connections between the Interior Provinces and California rather by orchestrating Juan Bautista's posting at Santa Fe in the capacity of Governor over what is now New Mexico and from thence funding efforts to link Anza's jurisdictions up with those of Monterey.

While further identifying Neve as ringleader and correspondingly ordering he abandon Loreto and move in as it were with Serra at Monterey or face immediate retirement.

Thus a political operative found himself compelled to leave behind the insulation distance had afforded.

To be delivered first at Southern California where his two unauthorized Santa Barbara- bound expeditions had swamped Mission San Gabriel.

Discovering at San Diego that Serra's favored Joseph Francisco Ortega had long since intervened. Having conducted Rivera's military attaché on to Santa Barbara. And with them already established what proved to be the last Spanish Presidio built anywhere in the world.

Following which the faithful soldier was himself installed without registered objections from Neve as its first commandante.

Who nonetheless refused delivery of Sonoran colonists over into lay Franciscan Ortega's hands. Conducting all eleven families elsewhere and with them on September 4, 1781 personally directing the founding not of Santa Barbara but rather secular Los Angeles.

As Governor then ordering that Franciscans supply these founders of his Pueblo de Nuestro Senora, La Reina de Los Angeles with livestock and other necessities as replacement for all that which they'd lost while ostensibly under the protective care of desert Missions La Purisima Concepcion and San Pedro y San Pablo.

Such impudence being accommodated. And while two municipalities now existed, nevertheless through the co-operation of Ortega in particular Serra managing to successfully reign in Neve's threat upon Franciscan sovereignty.

Eventually, in Santa Barbara (as at all presidios), retiring soldiers together with their wives and children moving out of the barracks and onto lands corresponding with the Hacienda Royale.

Inadvertently conjuring an effective colonial presence of their own. With the controversial community of Santa Barbara petitioning for and receiving what proved to be the last municipal charter issued under Spain in what is now the United States.

Yet unlike San Jose and Los Angeles, Santa Barbara perpetuating the philosophical premise behind their monarch's dream, surviving to themselves become the Franciscan capitol of a continously countered concept.

In the meantime, having anticipated but increasing interference from a hostile Government, Fray Junipero moving quietly to expedite full removal of Utopia's capital away from closely monitored Monterey.

CHRISTIAN UTOPIA

he tour du force of a reunited Serra and Palou proved not merely historic but miraculous. Aided as it was with the reappearance of Sir Joseph Galvez.

Who prior to facing extradition earlier had requested Reverend Father President Rafael Verger dispatch all forty-nine missionaries then residing at the San Fernando College off to California.

Verger having responded by sending but those first ten, arguing that,

> Not every man is ready to go.
> Not every man is willing to go.

This type of pettiness if not outright insolence now standing preeminently overruled what with the King's Alter Ego back in town. A steady supply of Franciscan crusaders arriving at Monterey just as fast as Palou and Serra could arrange for their deployment.

Whilst Galvez recognizing Serra on a bad day as being of more value to both Majesties than an army of missionaries on their best days.

As where others lost courage Brother Junipero found strength in but hope alone.

Royal observers opining that the missionary and Marquee might well have successfully traded places. For in stubborn determination and sheer genius both stood equally matched.

Most of the missionaries Serra received were less than thirty-five years old. Their average tour of duty being ten years.

Letters home revealing young, optimistic often gloriously extroverted individuals laboring cheerfully alongside Indian proteges both at the lectern as well as in the field.

Everyone ate, studied, worked,
and worshipped together
for the common good.

Community as Doctor Junipero Serra installed it fitting nicely within the parameters of Saint Thomas More's fairytale UTOPIA as templated by Franciscan John Duns.

And now blossoming like a beautiful and exotic flower along the California coast.

Yet despite success Serra's constant obeisance instilling in the hearts of those alongside whom he labored not merely latitude towards and a deep and abiding love for their Father President, but the kind of initiative achievable only where integrity is coupled with acceptance. Spawning the effective management integral to execution of any far- flung and otherwise dangerous proposition.

So it seemed that missionaries under Serra's jurisdiction accomplished more than squadrons of similarly disposed men elsewhere.

Criteria for selecting new mission sites were manifold.

Foremost consideration being an area's potentiality for interested participants.

Beyond which such things as dependable water sources, readily available timber both for lumber and firewood, agriculturally suitable soils and pasturage upon which to farm and run livestock all remained essential.

Agribusiness being the economic foundation for Utopia.

And carried out on a communal basis, with everyone working to clear land, install irrigation and drainage systems and then cultivate, harvest and process.

To facilitate expansionary schemes and fulfill promises of reuniting Serra and Palou, Galvez had earlier on arranged for Franciscan surrender of Lower California's formerly Jesuit Missions over into Dominican Custodies.

Neither Palou nor Serra being made aware of said sacrifice until after the fact in order not to compromise either.

Still opposition ever countered Galvez,

California is poverty-stricken
and can ill afford further expansion.

Serra supplying Don Joseph with an appropriate response,

He who trusts in God shall not be confounded.

So it was that even during Brother Junipero's race to Mexico City back in 1772 the determined missionary had paused long enough to found Mission San Luis Obispo de Tolouse and with nothing more at hand than two bags of flour, three bags of wheat, a box of brown sugar and but one courageous missionary (Fray Jose Cavaller).

To whom ironically Indian women impregnated by Fage's bear hunting troops had happily offered up for baptism infants otherwise ordered destroyed by an outraged chief.

Whereupon Cavaller found himself undone by flaming arrows. Which twice burnt mission installations to the ground.

From such tenuous and dubious beginnings San Luis Obispo now standing as a model for all outreach communities.

Returning Serra suggesting that Cavaller and his new companion Juan Salvo attempt the manufacture of fireproof tile roofs.

Without so much as a mason, contractor or tile maker amongst them young missionaries up and down the coast setting to work experimenting. And eventually discovering local materials with which to produce solid and exquisite tiles.

Soon monstrous ovens in which to fire brick and even a furnace for manufacturing metal tools being installed.

The results of which were awe-inspiring.

Set off splendidly against either native sandstone or whitewashed adobe, complemented further by heavy wood beams, through trial and error Fray Junipero's volunteers inventing what the world today heralds as California's signature architectural style.

Adaptation to the peculiarities of an unlikely Eden's variegated geography and microclimates by amateur Franciscan engineers favoring simplicity resulting in the construction of straightforward rather than ornate buildings.

A decidedly Moorish influence of rounded arches and colonnades nonetheless embellishing each with interior courtyards and extraordinary waterworks.

So that California as a new Rome stood uniquely Franciscan in appearance; a hallmark of elegant austerity in frontier American design.

With contemporary students left to ponder an experiment rendered even more breathtaking when considering the fact that those fashioning the same had themselves never seen architecture beyond its most rudimentary applications.

Soon the provincial capitol at Monterey as well as a regional headquarters in San Diego each assuming their trademark look.

Across the distance of time seeming ever so to have been; architecture as indigenous of a benign natural landscape as its aliso, fan palm or oak.

Serra's blueprint calling for establishment of dozens

more such communities up and down the northernmost extension of New Spain's ever expanding Camino Real.

Each to serve as nucleus or campus through which courtesy of education and acquired trade skills volunteers might go forth to set in place a new and grander civilization.

And through which Stone Age society was given the opportunity of accessing a modern world.

With Franciscan mentors providing themselves as examples.

Serra himself perceiving secularism, or in his terms "godlessness," as ever having been the true failure of Sir Thomas More's Utopia. A sentiment shared by the author himself who for so advocating had paid with his head.

So it was that in the heart of California's Utopia stood its temple. To which as the single most important edifice of the community special attentions were devoted.

Far more than symbolic, the presence of this sacred sanctuary representing what Serra and More both identified as being a previously missing key that would unlock social success in this world as well as salvation in the next.

Unlike since marginalized and canonized More, Serra enjoying the benefits of operating hypothetically at least beyond the reach and far removed from jealous monarchies. And thereby discovering the latitude required for constructing such a world.

As inside every California temple sat the throne as it were and altar before which even Don Carlos acquiesced.

And accordingly interiors of the same were made resplendent with all the richness and grandeur an otherwise humble constituency could contrive.

So it was that whitewashed mud exteriors came to house exquisite imagery more suitable for a royal court.

Or as one European tourist upon the scene emoted,

Truly gorgeous
and rendered all the more so
encountered as it is
in such an otherwise remote country.

Ultimately the evolutionary incarnation of Serra's troubled Mission San Gabriel Archangel reflecting in miniature Cordova's own great Cathedral.

New structures both at Carmel as well as in San Diego assuming similarly toy-like dimensions, while yet invoking grandeur and nobility.

With such architectural aspirations symbolizing a triumph of California's artistic soul.

Meanwhile an inner cloister or courtyard adjacent and around which were arranged classrooms and workshops formulating Utopia's heart and housing its mind.

With manual labor as per John Duns and Thomas More both enshrined as the noblest of all occupations.

Students being encouraged to accept training in practical trades required for developing modern community.

Carpentry, blacksmithing, spinning of wool, weaving and sewing, tanning and otherwise working leather, field cultivation, harvesting and ranching together with the manufacture of ceramics, soap and candles all offered up as courses taught to interested pupils.

Soon beyond each campus standing clustered not merely housing for two Franciscan missionaries but the homes of married couples with their children.

As communities met with greater agricultural success, granaries and bodegas being constructed to contain the bounty of a shared enterprise.

With one soldier selected by the missionaries serving as civil servant or Alcalde, himself attended by a mayordomo (steward) nominated from amongst an Indian proletariat to oversee the mandated police presence of from four to eight military personnel.

Innovations being hard-won. Soldiers as alcaldes of Franciscan communities and Franciscans as political scientists or farmers left to learn by way of countless failures.

But the richness of soil and affable climate yielded bumper crops.

Abundance of food bringing with it forgiveness through success and correspondingly contentment.

Soon imported olive trees, date palms, citrus and cuttings for grapes garnishing staples of grain, corn and beans with luxurious embellishment.

And whereas but marginal triumphs were achieved in the propagation of bananas, cocoa and coffee, efforts to raise semi tropicals and Mediterranean crops on the other hand rewarding Serra handsomely.

Native plants soon being crowded out by glamorous exotics imported from as far away as Africa, China, South America and the Canary Islands.

Alongside California's wild roses flowering varieties introduced from around the world.

The mesmerizing effect of all this evoking admiration from those few outsiders fortunate enough to happen upon such wonders:

> Within Mission walls the Adam's figs
> spread their broad leaves between
> the apples and pears.

> The gold of the oranges
> mingling with the red of the cherries.

Coastal California's fertility and magnificent climate thusly proven, it was not long before each mission stood in possession of vast haciendas encompassing well ordered vineyards and orchards, sweeping fields of grain, large scale vegetable gardens, rows of cotton and hemp and seemingly every flowering ornamental known to man.

All sustained by an ingenious infrastructure of extensive irrigation canals, reservoirs, and gristmills.

With affiliated and similarly modern laundries and even pressurized bathing facilities. Water splashing and gurgling through open tile ditches lending delightful lyric to each Shangri-la.

And whereas Sonora's rangelands had been sparse at best, the luxuriance of California's sea of grass sustaining not only cattle but various breeds of sheep and fine horses.

Imported stock increasing in such numbers as not to be contained. Ranging freely over and into the broad plains and marshes of California's interior. Mingling with elk, antelope and deer on what became in effect virtually one vast pasturage.

So it was that the northernmost extent of El Camino Real came to be bordered by ever expanding and well-maintained Indian ranchos and haciendas. Each Franciscan-mentored settlement assuming the picturesque aspect of a large Spanish garden, from which rose the temple that anchored all success to the Cross.

News of which made its way around the world courtesy of global Franciscan fraternity.

The Order itself had in the aftermath of European Crusades been left to care for sacred sites in a contested Holy Land.

From whence bags of mustard seed were now gathered and shipped to San Diego courtesy of Franciscans who had heard tell of Brother Junipero's marvelous experiment in far-off California.

Which as Serra traveled up and down the Camino Real he sewed. Until his Utopia stood traversed by a singularly brilliant floral thoroughfare of beautiful yellow blossoms.

At California as in Sir Thomas More's fairytale, each mission's jurisdiction being laid out such that:

> the precincts and bounds be so commodiously
> appointed out and set forth,
> that none of them all
> hath of anyside less than twenty miles of ground,
> and of some side also much more.

> None desire to enlarge the bounds of limits,
> for they count themselves rather
> the good husbands than owners of the lands.

Blessed by nature and developed through gentle enterprise, not surprisingly Mission landholdings going on to generate phenomenal surplus.

With the Pious Fund revived, fiscal success being plowed in to building not only more missions but homes, gardens and individual animal husbandry efforts for the benefit of each and every Indian opting to join any given Franciscan community.

Neophytes (novices) consisting of all those who accepted not only baptism but confirmation into the Church.

Novices once sustained on marginal subsistence now dispensing from mission bodegas, courtesy of their own endeavor, weekly allotments of beef, lard, maize (corn), beans and more.

While annually receiving new clothing and blankets of their own manufacture.

Ships returning from Monterey and San Diego soon sailing into San Blas laden with milled grain, wine, oil, hemp, hides and tallow. All to be exchanged for books, foundries and other essentials necessary for sustaining accelerated growth.

Meanwhile, as per both Plato and John Duns,

men wise and well experienced,

representing each experimental mission community, gathering annually at San Carlos (today's Carmel),

because it standeth just in the midst of the Island,
and is therefore most meet for the ambassadors
of all parts of the realm;
there to entreat and debate of the common matters
of the Land.

Even as construction on a twice forestalled new and grander capitol progressed with shared high hopes at and for San Juan Capistrano.

AMAR A DIOS

Marching headlong into fields of towering hollyhocks Serra had upon returning to Carmel from Mexico recognized immediately that Mission San Carlos stood in possession of a new gardener. And one aware of his personal affection for these stately flowers which he always referred to rather as Saint Joseph's staff.

Only Francisco Palou Amengal would have thought to plant them for him.

His old friend greeting him with,

See you in Monterey!

Chief Tatlun too had been present as part of a grand reception organized by Palou.

During which emissaries of Saint Joseph insisted two old friends join them in ceremonial dancing. Which they did and to the accompaniment of much laughter and joyful howling.

Palou and Serra both seemingly ever able to prevail and subdue even the most circumspect. And this they accomplished through the exercise of authentic love. Seeing but a certain reflection of themselves in all humanity. Dispensing with differences. Embracing similarities.

So it was that where Fages, Rivera and now Neve perceived but a base and exploitable animal in every

Indian, two men from Majorca recognized and acknowledged instead their equals.

Personal observations of Palou and Serra regarding Indians being replete with comments concerning fine stature, kind deportment and delightful conversations. Courteous, charming, gentle and gifted but a few of the many traits each ascribed to them.

As to their attractiveness,

wrote Serra,

I cannot find words with which to properly express it.
They have stolen my heart.

Such commentary rendered startling when compared with contemporary portrayals left by men of lesser insight,

The physiognomy of these Indians

writing a soon to appear upon the scene Russian official,

is ugly,
stupid, and savage.

One myopic Englishmen adding,

They seemed to have treated
with the most perfect indifference the precepts,
and laborious example,
of their truly worthy
and benevolent pastors;

whose object has been to allure them
from their life of indolence,
and raise in them a spirit of emulous industry;

which, by securing to them
plenty of food and the common conveniences of life,
would necessarily augment their comforts,
and encourage them to seek and embrace
the blessings of civilized society.

Deaf to the important lessons,
and insensible of the promised advantages,
most still remain in the most abject
state of uncivilization;

and if we except the inhabitants of Terra del Fuego,
and those of Van Dieman's land as being human,
then these Indians of California are certainly a race
of the most miserable beings I ever saw
possessing the faculty of human reason.

Contrariwise Friars Junipero and Francisco recognizing in them both intelligence and innocence. Accepting their painful honesty as a necessary ingredient for establishing truly exemplary society.

One wonders concerning the Indian perspective regarding this spectacle of two Spaniards directing armies of religious and soldiers together with growing ranks of their own in constructing amongst them a new and extraordinary social order.

Somewhat petite, almost feminine in appearance, with swarthy complexion and large black eyes, an otherwise strikingly masculine Serra captivating if not intoxicating most all with whom he held intercourse.

Eternally warding off inner demons of his own by observing a life of rigorous penance through bodily chastisement.

Dressing in horsehair undergarments when deemed necessary. Whipping himself mercilessly with a leather strap if the aforementioned garment failed to abate his animal lust raging ever within.

Such honest displays of passion and penance engendering loyalty amongst an ancient culture which understood only authenticity and revered integrity and above all else the attendant courage to not merely sustain pain but also accept defeat.

So it was that where most present remained unable even to interpret Serra's mission concept, none ever failed in comprehending the crusader himself.

A man who addressed every individual respectfully and, as best he could, in their own tongue. A man who himself attempted to live the virtues he advocated.

And as a result thousands came to venerate and follow after him. With in some cases entire villages abandoning tradition to throw their fortunes together with the beautiful little Majorcan who loved them completely and without condemnation.

When at San Gabriel understandably incensed Tongva stood determined to expel any semblance of Spain, a waylaid Brother Junipero baffling would-be assassins by facing death at their hands with but joyous anticipation.

Intervening testimony on the part of Juan Evangelista concerning this sorcerer who confronted arrows and spears with a smile leaving many completely disarmed.

This man is neither vengeful nor threatening.

He is the kindest,
most compassionate and greatest gift
ever sent to us.

Guic Chinigchinch!

Serra surviving said ambush near Olon (today's MissionViejo). Arriving at the hoped for site of his proposed capitol city San Juan Capistrano accompanied by yet another army of interested and potential converts.

On numerous occasions similarly disarming men determined otherwise to kill him. Who upon meeting Junipero lingered in hopes of securing both forgiveness as well as his magic blessing.

Such popular adoration proving far too much for a man who ever maintained that,

I am nothing.
My sins are too great.

His mounting army of admirers charmed by Serra's constant frustration with what they perceived as but natural and healthy inclinations.

A grateful pastor recalling how,

Tears welled up into my eyes
when I saw with what good will they ever came to
my assistance.

Walking along the road with me
they would break out into song each time
I started a tune for them.

And would come up for me
to make the sign of the Cross on their foreheads.

All are as friendly as can be
young and old crying out:

Amar a Dios, Padre Viejo!
Viva Jesus!
Because you love God, Old Man!
Hail Jesus!

Serra's inherent greatness and corresponding notoriety spreading up and down and across California like the blush and abandon of springtime.

And where most disagreed with his philosophical and theological viewpoints many regardless hailing him respectfully as "Father" of their own volition and against Serra's protests.

Spanish soldiers and missionaries similarly reprimanded by one who insisted rather he be addressed merely as "Brother."

Regardless the Least of Christ's brothers called to serve as missionaries so very far away from home recognizing in their Reverend Father President a consummate

Spanish patriarch. Both spiritual and temporal leader, imparting inspiration through courageously exemplary displays of integrity and humility.

Garnering equal veneration from the halls of power. Where Galvez marveled at Francisco Palou's reports relating, in ever expanding superlatives, the superhuman effort being conducted to implant permanently upon California's soil a singularly transcendent society for and in behalf of both majesties.

See to it that the new missionaries come well
provided with patience, charity and good temper,
for they may find themselves rich in tribulations.

challenging Serra, in a written appeal to Rome for more "troops,"

But where can the laboring ox go
that the plough will not be heavy to drag
And unless he drag it, how shall the seed be sown?

Rome witnessing from afar as their own

little Indian

dragged that proverbial plow up and down and across California to reap for them a great harvest of souls.

Each morning at sunrise,

writing Palou,

all are enjoined in singing a hymn
and by means of which everyone

is called to the church.

Where recitation of the catechism
and prayer,
is followed by a lesson;

And then, in the huge patio,
before the church,
distribution of supplies takes place.

This is followed
by the gathering together of children
five years and older,
those studying the catechism
and those who are candidates for marriage.

Children marched off to school. Where daily they
received instruction in Spanish, general principals of
reading and writing and if so inclined such things as
art, music or the basics of arithmetic.

Whereby all began training as skilled laborers
and artisans.

Attaining full status as novices (neophytes) upon
receiving the Sacraments of the Church.

Such daily enterprise interrupted at noon by dinner
and a two-hour siesta.

Afterwhich the morning routine was resumed.

Children and catechumens returning to their studies.
Novices each to his or her respective task.

Late afternoon bells signaling an end to yet another day of significant existence. Whereupon most gathered to visit, engage in sport, music or otherwise share camaraderie on a central plaza.

Where Franciscan Stations of the Cross were staged weekly.

Torchlight parades in honor of Mary being conducted every Saturday night.

Seasonal mystery plays and feast day processions further highlighting this gathering place of new community.

Overwhich wherever possible Serra himself presided. Annually preaching a hundred or more sermons.

Culminating with Christmas. During which Brother Junipero dressed everyone up; children as angels, young men like seraphim, tribal chiefs for Magi and women donning the costume of shepherds or would be saints. Novices and gentiles arriving from miles around to witness and or participate in pageantry on a scale never before dreamed of.

Returning from whence they came greeting each other, as did Serra, with,

Amar a Dios.

Because we love God.

CHECKMATE

Galvez brought to a close the brutal chess match carried on between Serra and Neve. And this he accomplished by promoting the secularist operative into his Department of Interior Provinces overwhich he himself as Marquee of Sonora and Universal Minister General of the Supreme Council of the Indies maintained complete control.

Anza refusing further participation in the California Experiment, Brother Junipero now conspiring openly to see returned since chastened and presumably humbled Don Pedro Fages:

The officer Don Pedro Fages
is to be believed
when he states that he sinned not out of malice
but because he was lacking in knowledge
and in reflection,

submitting Reverend Father President Serra,

In addition to the religious service I have given
to my college or the apostolic institute
in working for these missions
for God and obedience alone,
I consider that I have also perhaps accomplished
something in behalf of the king,
for the role I played,
be it little or much in the conquest of these lands.

I have walked among soldiers,
I have been in the midst of perils,

And I have suffered want.

In a word,
I have done what I could.

Now, Your Excellency,
if this calls for some merit in military service,
I apply, cede, and renounce
in favor of Don Pedro Fages
all my service and merits,
without him knowing anything about it.

Nor indeed has he asked me for any such thing.

Rather, I am doing this of my own will
and of my own spontaneous action.

Let not the world know,
rather let it be as if the world did not know
that this useless religious has done any service
to the crown
and let all be accredited to Don Pedro Fages
as if he has accomplished everything on his own,
while I with the help of God
shall try even to increase his merits
while my life lasts
provided obedience does not cut short
my work here.

Moved by Serra's letter, ailing Bucareli having
responded with,

You may know that an action so pious,
upright, and religious
as Your Reverence has manifested in your desire

to be of service
to this interested officer shall receive
my studied attention.

Paperwork instigated thereafter would upon Don Joseph's return attain the desired result.

With Loreto's jurisdictions being transferred over to Monterey. Placing both under one single and cooperative administration.

So that peace might reign across the entire expanse of California. Where in El Norte now stood eight self-governing mission communities. Each contrasting markedly with surrounding Stone Age villages as thriving centers of Christian outreach. Attracting thousands to a lifestyle the likes of which no native Californian had ever before seen nor even contemplated.

The death of Antonio Bucareli in 1779 having dealt a terrific blow to Serra and his missionaries when attempts by powerful concerns in Spain yet determined to contain Galvez installed Martin de Mayorga as new Viceroy.

Who immediately plunged the government into secrecy by halting his predecessor's precedent of copious and open correspondence.

Individual missionaries across California unexpectedly receiving personal notes directly from the office of Viceregal. And strategically flattered willfully responding openly and hastily as per his request with regard to input that but facilitated Serra's undoing.

Stemming this new and rising tide of subterfuge Galvez taking extraordinary steps to see his own brother Matias posted in Mayorga's sted.

Who ascended as Viceroy in 1783.

Tragically Joseph and Matias both dying the following year.

In an ongoing effort to safeguard Don Carlos prior to his untimely demise Joseph having saddled the Council with mandatory acceptance of Matia's son and trusted nephew Bernardo Galvez as Viceregal successor. To which status Bernardo ascended in 1785.

And successfully maintained on track the agenda of Both Majesties, being remembered everafter as

The Triumphant Sun.

Expediting Serra's plans, Don Joseph Galvez had long since overruled former Governor Neve's orders forbidding the proliferation of California missions. Ordering instead an immediate founding along the Channel of his forestalled Mission San Buenaventura and Serra's Santa Barbara both.

Brother Junipero having previously dedicated a chapel built at Ortega's hastily thrown together Royal Presidio in Santa Barbara, from which he attempted to monitor and maintain a virtuous sphere of influence amongst and between Neve's imported soldiery and the local Chumash.

A difficult proposition in light of past failures nonetheless made easier courtesy of Commandante Ortega's own convictions and intercessions.

Who upon receipt of Neve's overruled edict facilitated Serra's plans for launching each previously forestalled Channel Mission.

While elsewhere both at San Jose as well as in Los Angeles nearly all Neve's would-be minions finding themselves rounded up and employed by or similarly engaged with the Franciscans in since founded Mission Santa Clara and Mission San Gabriel respectively.

So complete Serra's triumph that French visitors arriving upon the scene conveying to Governor Pedro Fages amazement over the fact that not a single colonist existed anywhere in all of California.

Indomitable Fray Junipero dedicating Mission San Buenaventura on Easter Sunday in 1782. Regrettably California's champion Galvez had not lived long enough to hear tell of this twice forestalled triumph.

As for Serra it was to be his ninth and last.

REQUIEM

gainst all odds the Galvez family had achieved a guarded success. With missionary Serra as knight- errant in California managing to stave off colonial expansionism otherwise prescribed.

Yet ultimately but postponing exploitation for another generation.

Perceptive eyewitness Hugo Reid in from fledgling English America appraising if awkwardly a miracle discovered thusly;

It was something, surely,
that over thirty thousand wild, barbarous,
and naked Indians
had been brought in from their savage haunts,
persuaded to wear clothes,
accustomed to a regular life,
inured to such light labor as they could endure,
taught to read and write,
instructed in music,
accustomed to the service of the church,
partaking of its sacraments
and indoctrinated in the Christian religion;

and that this system had become self-sustaining
under the mildest and gentlest of tutelage;

for the Franciscan monks,
many of whom were highly cultivated men,
who had been soldiers, engineers, artists, lawyers,
and physicians

before they became friars,
always treated the neophyte Indians
with paternal kindness,
and did not scorn to labor with them in the field,
in the brick-yard, the forge, and the mill...

When I view the vast construction
of the mission buildings,
including the churches, the refectories,
the workshops, the granaries,
the materials which were sometimes
brought for many miles
on the shoulders of the Indians,
I cannot deny that the Franciscan
missionary monks
had the wisdom, sagacity, and patience
to bring their neophyte pupils far forward
on the road from barbarism to civilization.

Nor that these Indians were not destitute of capacity.

In fact, "these Indians" constituting the very cornerstones upon which and for whom Serra's new and grander Rome had been built. As romantic monuments to Utopian idealism, relics of the same forcing introspection still.

To sit in the muffled adobe chamber furnished out with but one chair, table and bed of boards from whence Fray Junipero conjured the cultural majesty he bestowed upon California, and therein contemplate his anticipated and outwardly meager reward is to confront both heroism and a nobility rarely encountered during any Age,

If I have my health,
a tortilla and some vegetables,
what more do I want?

What Serra wanted and indeed succeeded in attaining remaining threatened from within as well as without. The manifesto of all utopia's everywhere continuously undone by man's inherently nonconformist nature. Which Serra having long since surrendered to his Order could neither consider nor comprehend.

Portending calamity being the deaths both of Joseph and Matias Galvez. When predictably politicos scrambled with renewed vigor to access California's developing treasure chest of natural resources and trained labor force.

Seeking to shake loose the ironclad grip of Fray Junipero which yet safeguarded said kingdom from all outside exploitation.

Anxious to slay but another dragon, yet suffering from ill health, Serra calling upon still strong and youthful Palou. Who consented to himself journey at the Reverend Father President's request to Mexico City. And there defend again all that for which the Least of the Brothers of Christ had labored under threat of martyrdom to see installed.

Palou taking leave of stewardship over Mission San Francisco presumably just long enough to as Serra's bombardier engage in a battle from which ultimately he would never return.

Anticipating this long and treacherous diatribe, and given his failing constitution, Serra recognizing that in all likelihood he would not live to witness Palou's certain triumph.

Physically vulnerable and by virtue of a disposition towards self sacrifice now facing at his own instigation this loss of Francisco's companionship for yet a third time, Fray Junipero prevailing upon Christ in prayer that he be spared the unthinkable isolation such separation would occasion.

Secretly commissioning manufacture of a redwood casket in which to have himself buried without bother even as,

> conspiring angels prepared to escort
> Blessed Father Junipero
> away from the pains and sorrows of this life.

Palou, just in from San Francisco, shocked by off-handed questioning concerning arrangements for Brother Junipero's interment.

> But the Venerable Father President
> is improving in his health,

protesting Francisco. Whereupon a soldier present contributing,

> The good Father always seems well
> when he is singing
> and at prayer.

> But he will not recover,

and is certain to die soon.

Overcome at hearing such commentary and on the eve of sailing away to Mexico City no less, Palou unexpectedly facing not merely the possibility of losing California but his dearest companion as well.

Riding in port being the ship <u>Favorita</u> upon which as Serra's emissary Francisco had been scheduled to depart. At ten o'clock on the morning of August 27th, 1784 its captain Juan Espinoza together with Chaplain Salvatierra calling personally upon the now famous,

Old Man of California.

Announcing that they wished to present him with a baritone bell brought from Peru as their gift for Mission San Carlos. To which Brother Junipero inquired,

Shall I be able to hear it?

Chaplain Salvatierra proposing it be delivered on the morrow. Serra responding,

Senores,
then I shall not hear the voice
of the new bell from Peru.

I shall not be here tomorrow.

Later that same day Palou administering rites of extreme unction and receiving a last confession from his companion. Who in a moment of overwhelming fear and loss Francisco steadied through recitation of all those with whom Serra was about to meet.

Rehearsing name by name everyone from Francis and Llull to Jesus himself.

Michael had long since raised a crusader's cross outside the door of his room at Carmel. Before which ever since throughout the day or night he knelt in prayer.

Sharing their deep and abiding devotion to Christ, both men kneeling together at the foot of that cross experiencing what each perceived as divine intercession. When unseen hands bestowed complete forgiveness and the peace of atonement.

Even as Francis and Joseph stood waiting
to receive him
Christ Jesus already embracing and sheltering him
from fear.

Thereafter singing beautifully the communion hymn of Saint Thomas, Serra turning and suggesting,

Vamos ahora a descansar.
Let us now go to rest.

Then holding tightly the Crusader's cross ever worn about his neck, lying down and without so much as his blanket, for he had already given it away, slipping into that sleep from which one does not awaken.

His final words spoken softly in Mallorquin to Francisco alone.

So it was that at two o'clock in the afternoon on August 28th, 1784 Francis gained the companionship of an exceptional little Indian,

with Palou left holding tightly to his breast the great love of his life, himself sustained by a room filled with "Saint Joseph's emissaries."

Salvos fired from both ships at anchor in the harbor answering back a death knell tolled by mission bells.

That California yet constituted the ends of the earth aside, this passing of its venerable Crusader not going unnoticed even beyond what was no longer but the vagary of Northwestern New Spain.

As a community transformed by Brother Junipero descended upon Monterey the empire that yet held sway over half a world mourning communally.

At Carmel the seemingly endless procession taking five days to file past Serra's redwood casket. Many depositing as homage a California rose.

Rendering Michael resplendent in his beautiful blue robe floating as it were upon a sea of pink blossoms.

Palou maintaining constant vigil, so as to prevent devotees from divesting the body of every last bit of clothing. Ship's surgeon Juan Garcia observing,

Better a small piece of cloth
from that holy man's reinment
than all the medicines in my infirmary cupboards.

To whom Francisco presented Serra's linen handkerchief, whilst otherwise imparting as best he

could bits of hair and habit. Before interring Fray
Junipero beneath the tile of a sanctuary floor strewn
with flowers and washed clean by tears.

To the accompaniment of thousands chanting and
wailing the eternal pounding of Carmel's surf but
steps away serving as fitting requiem.

No longer would California hear the musicality of
Michael's voice when tenderly greeting one and all with,

Amar a Dios.

or counseling,

To understand all
is to forgive all.

Which through his praxis had won them all.

Characteristically dismissive of insult, ever looking
to the example of Jesus himself, who even when
nailed upon the cross expressed but compassion for
his executioners,

Forgive them, Father,
For they know not what they do.

Serra's death on a far distant frontier foreshadowing
the anything but obscure demise of lay brother Don
Carlos de Bourbon in Madrid.

Did you think
I was going to live forever?

quipping Charles to family members gathering around his bedside during those final hours.

Count Abarca's successor Don Jose Moreno, Count of Floridablanca, approaching the gentle monarch cautiously with a request for pardon not only for himself but on behalf of all those who had conspired against him. Which Don Carlos dismissed kindly and without a moment's hesitation,

> It did not require this extremity for me
> to forgive them.
> They were forgiven in the moment
> of doing me injury.

Don Carlos like Fray Junipero being buried in but the simple habit of a Franciscan. And remembered for having resurrected, if only temporarily, a revival of Spain's former grandeur. Which because of them both glimmered even from a far- off in California.

Those fortunate enough to have interacted with the likes of magnificent yet humble Charles and humble yet magnificent Junipero never again encountering their equals.

Visions, Jonathan Swift suggesting, being the art of seeing things invisible, most grappling with but feeble comprehension of the dreams shared by this King and his evangelist. Struggling regardless and whole-heartedly to aid in launching a society the concept of which ever alluded even themselves.

Given philosophical carte blanche from Europe's most enlightened monarch, a single missionary successfully shaking off six thousand years of semi-barbaric Western Civilization to successfully implant, upon a remote and golden shore, the foundations of utopian idealism. His aphorism,

Always forward
Never back

inspiring, haunting and challenging California still.

Serra's heady mantle as Reverend Father President would be placed upon the shoulders of Fray Francisco Palou who neither desired, nor in light of his loss, felt capable of sustaining said office. Yet accepted while petitioning for a successor.

As Father Fermin Lasuen at the request of Palou journeyed north from Mission San Gabriel to assume jurisdictions, Francisco preparing at long last his siege on Mexico City.

From whence he would everafter prevail ably for Serra in one court case after another as Reverend Father President of the San Fernando Missionary College.

And while forced to witness California divided like Caesar's Gaul into three distinct political entities yet at the end of the day managing to see New California maintained under his own umbrella as president of said College and hence safe from exploitation.

Throughout the course of which Francisco channeled his overwhelming sense of personal loss through writer's quill. Penning a powerful biography subsequently published and presented to heir apparent King Charles IV.

And thereby keeping both Serra and his dream alive as it were to counter the indifference of a new and distracted Spanish monarchy.

PART THREE

CALIFORNIA
PASTORAL

LASUEN

I t would be voiced abroad that no one in all the King's domains shed more heartfelt tears of sorrow over the loss of Reverend Father President Junipero Serra than did Don Pedro Fages.

Who having been installed as Governor of California had since taken up residence together with his wife Eulalia and son Pedrito at Monterey.

A fact which Palou savored as but the fulfillment of Serra's own scheme to see an older and wiser bear restored and with honor.

Fray Junipero having always loved Don Pedro. Orchestrating his banishment but to stave off failure of the Noble Experiment and correspondingly rescue Fages from naive arrogance.

Positioning him in a face off not with benign Californians but rather warring Apache. Hoping thereby to exact humility and instill prudence.

What Serra could not know was that departing Governor Neve had in the absence of Galvez hobbled incoming Fages with an impossible list of program changes:

No new missions are to be built.

Existing missions must no longer give instruction in agriculture, trades or religion.

Installation of colonial settlements
is to be encouraged.

Soldiers must not fraternize with priests.

Indians must receive stiff punishment
commensurate to their infraction.

The idea being very old school.

Such Indians as were not hostile at first
thusly being provoked to hostility,
that there might be an excuse
for plunder, destruction, carnage,
and especially for the seizure and branding of slaves.

Reformed Don Pedro as Serra's hoped for champion
could not have arrived at a more pivotal moment. Nor
could he have been better prepared for that moment.
Superficially acquiescing before an unsuspecting Junta
while conveniently ignoring Neve's laundry list. What
with his own heart and soul now decidedly aligned
with the Brothers of Saint Francis.

Encouraging installation of new missions while
personally recruiting additional artisans with whom
to instruct more Indian novices. Having seen
enough of greed and treachery, he too now longing
for establishment of a world as Serra envisioned it
could be.

California's first family being greeted upon their
arrival at San Diego with as much revelry as the little
outpost could muster.

Culture shock understandably taking its toll on the Countess Dona Eulalia. Who to begin with was caught unawares concerning the fact that California's natural dress was little or no dress at all.

Interpreting overwhelming displays of nudity as but an indication of extreme poverty. Prompting enthusiastic and immediate efforts to distribute from out of her prodigious wardrobes items with which to clothe those she deemed most destitute.

Alerted to a one-woman charity program operating out of his own offloaded luggage, Pedro hastening dockside. Where he succeeded with restraining the Countess only by informing her that should she continue such patronage they would themselves be compelled to walk about naked as the Indians, as there was no place in all of California from which to procure otherwise suitable attire.

Countess Fages sustaining her second shock following arrival at Monterey. Where having literally stepped down from the proverbial castle in Spain, she simply could not abide moving into entirely unacceptable living quarters provided by the Presidio.

Inappropriate housing together with an endless parade of naked Indians showing up outside her door to gaze upon a refined member of the gente de razon (social elite) driving Eulalia to utter distraction.

Despondency becoming rage upon discovering her husband dallying with nine-year-old handmaiden, Indizuela.

The subsequent tirade elicited by yet another of Don Pedro's sexual indiscretions but echoing Serra's own misgivings of more than a decade earlier.

Refusing acceptance of her husband's argument that nine and ten year old children were considered adults in California and that regardless such consensual forays were but meaningless recreations, the Countess of Calli insisting rather her family not be compelled to remain another day in the midst of such barbarous depravity. Demanding instead their immediate return to Mexico City.

Bound by Serra's personal pledge concerning Don Pedro Fages, Franciscans moving quickly to intervene.

Dona Eulalia finding herself moving up to reside in the grand by comparison Mission San Carlos Borromeo. Where she remained until more suitable accommodations could be provided.

Don Pedro on the other hand left to live alone at the Royal garrison. Where after successfully countering yet again his wife's efforts to see him expatriated, rendered as penance payment out of his own pocket for construction of a sorely needed and beautiful new chapel within the Presidio.

Before its altar pledging anew to civilize himself if only Eulalia would remain at his side and in Monterey.

Orchestrating said proceedings being newly installed as Reverend Father President of the California Missions Fermin Francisco Lasuen.

Whose own placement in an otherwise uncivilized outland seemed if not unfair then harsh penance for one so urbane and vivacious. Visitors from society's highest ranks noting how incongruous this strikingly dignified five foot four, blue eyed, blonde of florid, pockmarked complexioned gentleman seemed here at the edge of the world.

Still Lasuen never registering more than a singular complaint,

> For me the solitude of my occupation
> is a cruel and terrible enemy
> which has struck me heavily like a blow.

Modest criticism from one who had endured the pangs of unconscionable isolation at Mission San Francisco de Borja in Old California when after bestowing his blessing upon departing Portola and Serra on that first march northward from Loreto he found himself left behind to endure five years without so much as a single missionary companion.

Lasuen's love for the native peoples being unquestionable. And beyond reproach. Alone together with them at San Francisco de Borja having not only rescued Jesuit efforts but subsequently handing over to Dominican Custodies the most successfully transformed of all Indian missions.

Regardless it is not difficult to imagine the loneliness of an otherwise intellectual left to labor without countryman or colleague.

Fray Francisco Palou rescuing him. When in route to

his own long awaited reunion with Serra at Monterey he retrieved Lasuen. Traveling together with him under escort from Joseph Francisco Ortega into a new land and old fellowships.

No sooner had the two arrived however then Fermin finding himself in the middle of California's political maelstrom.

Governor's Inspector/Commandante Fernando Rivera refusing to attend mass at the Mission. Insisting rather that Lasuen remain in Monterey and not as missionary but rather chaplain of the Royal Presidio.

It had not taken long, what with his own contradictorial marching orders, for Lasuen to recognize the extraordinary challenges being endured by Fray Junipero.

A sophisticated missionary quickly seasoning in this arena of duplicity and subsequently savvy concerning seemingly endless indiscretions.

Officiating with restraint. Compassionately determined to see virtue prevail.

So it was that the prescribed remedy of such a priest as confessor to aberrant Governor Fages had been quick and inspired.

Serra early on perceiving in Lasuen this presence and patience of Job, and accordingly wasting little time with assigning him to potential laden yet troubled from the beginning Mission San Gabriel.

Where as anticipated Fray Fermin met each crisis with characteristic resourcefulness. To see San Gabriel emerge and surpass all others both in prosperity as well as political tranquility.

Yet there was to be no resting on one's laurels. Lasuen instead finding himself ushered south as proxy for Serra at the founding of all- important Mission San Juan Capistrano.

When in the wake of troubles in San Diego a most ambitious project for which Fray Fermin seemed the most appropriate director became regardless temporarily scuttled.

Lasuen remaining at San Diego until 1785. From whence he found himself being called back not to Capistrano but rather San Carlos, there to serve as Serra's successor.

In route touring each community and interviewing every missionary as he made his way north to assume command of an unprecedented legacy.

Lasuen was, like Sebastian Vizcaino, the son of a Basque shepherd. Who having recognized early on his boy's "gift," ushered him into the safety of an abbey. There to begin a long circuitous route that led to this posting as Reverend Father President of New California.

Where together with now co-operative Don Pedro Fages he supervised steady proliferation of missions until as in Utopia,

none of them would stand distant from the next
above one day's journey afoot.

With Fages conducting exploratory forays into San
Francisco's East Bay as well as the San Joaquin Valley
in anticipation of anchoring the same through
establishment of more missions.

Who otherwise, at Lasuen's recommendation, threw
himself into horticulture as a distraction. Don Pedro's
orchard of more than six hundred exotic fruit trees
becoming the pride of Monterey.

The pride of California however soon standing not at
Monterey or San Juan Capistrano as expected but
rather in Santa Barbara.

Where Fray Junipero had dramatically countered
Montalvo's queen Calafia by coercing the symbolic
surrender of her pagan country into Saint Barbara's
hands. Which he accomplished through calling upon
Constantinople's favored daughter in grand public
ceremony to serve as Crusader patroness of what
proved to be his final earthly venture.

The subsequently unsurpassed architectural beauty of
Mission Santa Barbara as completed by Lasuen in
1786 a befitting memorial both to patron Saint and
founding padre.

Serra's confidant Joseph Francisco Ortega aiding as
Commandante at Santa Barbara in forging an
ultimately magnificent alliance between efforts of the
Royal Presidio and those of a mission previously
forestalled by Neve.

With this singular community born amidst conflict surviving troubled waters lying yet ahead to replace both Carmel and San Juan Capistrano as Capitol of Franciscanland.

Further fending off colonial incursions of anykind, Lasuen moving ahead with resurrection of Fathers Garces and Eixarch's Colorado River Valley mission, La Purisima Concepcion. Not in troubled desert hinterlands, but rather north of Mission Santa Barbara. Where in 1787 he breathed anew the breath of life into said establishment on a site adjacent to Chumash Laxshakupi.

To be followed in 1791 with his founding of both Missions Santa Cruz and Nuestra Senora de La Soledad.

Still Lasuen's watershed year lying yet ahead. When in 1797 he dedicated four new simultaneously installed and fully functional communities. One of which would become the largest mission ever established anywhere in North America.

GUESS WHO'S COMING TO DINNER

As a means of providing for California's entrée into the world of chaffare Don Carlos III had early on decreed that all Manila galleons put in at Monterey.

To outlanders such as the Californios (California born Europeans) these monstrous in the extreme, picturesque treasure ships providing breathtaking touchstones with a distant and glorious Mother Country.

Each forecastle and stern
rose three and four decks above the low waist.
And were made of material thick enough
to resist musket shot.

The lower part of the hull was also
out of measure strong,
being framed of planks and ribs foure
or five foote in thicknesse.

The hull was slender compared to the small round
trading ships,
being in length three times the width at the waist.

But instead of having streamlines,
the prow was wide and blunt
and smashed heavily through the waves
to the great detriment of speed,

the largest galleons presenting

such surface to the wind
that difficulties of steering were quite formidable,
sometimes requiring six or eight men
to handle the wheel.

Many of the galleons were painted and gilded
in the most dazzling fashion.

The bulk of such decoration was on the stern,
the pride of the ship,
from which she was judged.

The sails, too, were painted
with elaborate designs,
such as the arms of Leon and Castile,
crosses,
crowns,
the lion guardant
or portraits of the saints
after whom the vessels were named.

Each year it seemed vessels grew larger in size. Culminating with launching of the nine hundred-ton <u>Bigonia</u>.

Royal decrees notwithstanding only rarely did Californians catch a glimpse of such floating grandeur. Most galleon masters approaching no closer than Cortes Bank situated some one hundred miles west of what is today Southern California.

Penalties for noncompliance providing inadequate deterrence amongst already wealthy merchants understandably disinterested with a province void both of hard cash and significant tradegoods.

On that rare occasion when some galleon in dire need of repairs did obey orders and layover, unsuspecting merchants discovering for themselves the existence of a living breathing fairy tale.

With crowds of Californios, Spaniards and Indios (brothers in God 'En Dios' or Indians) anxiously gathering from far and wide so as to catch an exhilarating peek at a materialism otherwise unknown.

The carnival- like atmosphere occasioned rivaling Holy Day celebrations elsewhere.

Following wine, dancing and song, merchants finding their vessels voluntarily re-stocked with not only materials for repairs but copious amounts of fresh produce, meat and brandy and all without demand for repayment.

Of course Latin largesse preventing a ship's supercargo from doing anything less than reciprocating. Gifts of spices, fine linens, shawls and porcelain dinnerware being bestowed upon an otherwise penurious clientele.

Aside from which California counted only upon the markedly less extravagant yet far more predictable arrival of its Old San Carlos, which while not so ostentatious was received nonetheless with equal ceremony.

Spanish silver and gold coinage remaining all but unknown to California, El Principe, as locals dubbed the Old San Carlos (meaning Prince of and or errand boy for its King), providing necessities in exchange for drafts against pay due customers either from government stipend or Pious Fund.

Each year the "Prince" returning to San Blas laden down with increasing wealth from off developing missions.

Escalating abundance that did not go unnoticed in either the Capitol of New Spain or Peru. And soon drawing favorable reports even from previously circumspect galleon merchants.

With rumors concerning California's newfound wealth catching the rapt attentions of far-flung ports. Luring into its harbor a bon vivant the likes of which Monterey had never before beheld.

When on the morning of June 6, 1786 Governor Fages found himself being apprised of two foreign vessels listing at anchor off shore.

The coast shrouded for nearly a week in dense fog, no one being certain as to just exactly how long said ships had been sitting there. Nor was anyone able to ascertain from whence they hailed.

Correspondence received earlier providing the only clue. Viceroy Bernardo Galvez having informed all governors concerning a scientific expeditionary force under the direction of French Count Jean Francois Galup de La Perouse presently circumnavigating the globe.

Should this personal friend of the Bourbon family per chance show up in any Spanish jurisdiction he was to be accorded every hospitality.

Suspecting that his two mystery ships might well be those of globe trotting La Perouse, Governor Fages dispatching Admiral Estevan Jose Martinez out to investigate and either ward off or welcome sailors otherwise in trespass.

Who upon boarding an extravagantly outfitted <u>La Boussole</u> and <u>L' Astrolabe</u> discovered not only La Perouse but a distinguished cadre of scientists, navigators, cartographers and physicians.

Having been commissioned by French King Louis the XVI de Bourbon, and now half way into a four-year enterprise on par with space exploration programs of today, this voyage of La Perouse representing the huge investment of not merely monies but national pride.

It's mission:

To explore new lands,
investigate trade possibilities,
report on the activities of other European powers

and in some cases boldly go where presumably no man had gone before.

Fitted out with every scientific instrument available, and staffed by not only the aforementioned technicians but troops of artists tirelessly sketching events experienced and items encountered in a monumental effort to appraise the planet.

Even the French King's gardener, Mr. Collignon, being counted amongst team members onboard. Himself busy gathering, sorting and cataloguing information concerning exotic edibles and potential crops while at the same time introducing European seeds, roots and cuttings.

This Age of the Amateur representing as it did the dawn of scientific pursuit.

A wide-eyed Esteven Martinez standing before Fages to deliver his report replete with descriptions of marvelous ships full of reference books, plant and animal specimens and scientific paraphernalia previously unheard of.

Fages accordingly readying California to receive its first cause celeb.

La Perouse recording:

> At noon our longitude was 124°52'.
> I could see no land,
> but at four o'clock we were enveloped in fog.

> We knew that we could not be far from shore,
> for several land birds flew around us,
> and we caught a gyrfalcon,

his playful reference to yet popularly held notions that California was populated by griffins.

> The fog continued all night,

continuing La Perouse,

> and the next day at ten in the morning
> we perceived the land very foggy and very near us.

It was impossible to make out what land it was.

I approached within a league of it,
and saw the breakers very distinctly.

Our soundings were twenty-five fathoms.
But though I was certain of being in Monterey Bay,
it was impossible to distinguish
the Spanish settlement
in such thick weather.

At the approach of night I stood out to sea again,
and at daybreak stretched in for the land,
with a thick fog which did not disperse till noon.

I then stood along the shore at a very little distance,
and at three o'clock in the afternoon
we got sight of the fort of Monterey
and of two three-masted vessels in the roadstead.

The contrary winds obliged us to come to an anchor
two leagues from shore,
in forty-five fathoms,
muddy bottom;

The next day we anchored in twelve fathoms,
within two cable lengths of the land.

The commander of the two vessels spied,
Don Estevan Martinez,
sent us pilots during the night,
both he and the governor of the presidio
having been apprised by the viceroy at Mexico
of our expected arrival.

Martinez thereafter conducting ashore in launches a glamorous entourage. Jean Francios witnessing with surprise and delight scores of Indios, Spaniards, Californios and Franciscan religious assembling to receive him.

An extraordinary two-month conversation that ensued between Fages and a French savant steeped in natural sciences constituting the most engaging and intellectually stimulating verbal exchange of Don Pedro's life.

Who provided La Perouse with full access to Provincial Archives such as they were. Where the French Count took particular interest in former Governor Phelipe de Neve's preempted plans for launching California colonialism.

As Pedro and Jean Francois sat interviewing one another over fine French wines and California brandy messengers racing up and down the Camino Real relaying invitations for all to attend an official reception.

Which provided Dona Eulalia with her opportunity to orchestrate the grandest dinner party California had ever hosted.

On June 12, 1786 four hundred Spanish officers, soldiers, clerics and alcaldes sitting before tables laden with beef, roast fowl and rack of lamb. Vegetables and fruits of every variety imaginable having been assembled from amongst the mission communities.

All served up together with special soups and salads, dairy desserts, wine, tea and chocolate.

Belying the fact that California had prospered considerably since those days when Eulalia's husband fended off its starvation by sustaining the enterprise on ursine flesh.

Everyone assembled dining to the accompaniment of a full mission orchestra and choral. After dinner displays both of Spanish and Indian dance lending further enchantment to an already magical fete.

During which La Perouse shared news concerning the great wide world beyond California. Only to himself sit spellbound as Californio storytellers imparted their knowledge of pagan gods, gigantic redwood trees and ferocious grizzly bears.

Thereafter penning his official report:

A lieutenant colonel,
who resides at Monterey,
is governor of both Californias.

His jurisdiction is more than
eight hundred leagues in circumference.
But his real subjects consist only
of two hundred and eighty-two mounted soldiers,
who form the garrison of five small forts
and furnish detachments
of four or five men
to each of the twenty-five Missions
or parishes
into which Old and New California are divided.

These slender means
are sufficient to secure the obedience

of about fifty thousand wandering Indians
in this extensive part of America,
who otherwise continually change their residence,
following the season of fishing or hunting.

Nearly ten thousand have embraced Christianity.

Loreto,
the only presidio in Old California,
is on the eastern coast of that peninsula.

It's garrison consists of fifty-four horsemen,
who afford small detachments to fifteen missions,
the duties of which are performed by Dominicans,
who have succeeded the Jesuits and Franciscans.

About four thousand Indians,
converted and assembled in these fifteen parishes,
are the whole fruit of the long apostleship
of the different religious orders,
who have succeeded each other
in this painful ministry.

Northern (New) California,
notwithstanding its great distance from Mexico,
appears to me to unite infinitely more advantages
for the forming of missions
than does Old California.

Its first establishment,
which is San Diego,
dates only to the 26th of July 1769.
It is the presidio farthest to the south,
as San Francisco is farthest to the north.

This last was built the 9th of October 1776;
that of the channel of Santa Barbara
in September, 1786.

And Monterey,
at present the capital and chief place
of the two Californias,
on the 3rd of June 1770.

The harbor of this presidio was discovered in 1603
by Sebastian Vizcaino,
commander of a small armed squadron
based at Acapulco,
by order of Viscount de Monterey,
Viceroy of Mexico.

Since that time the galleons,
on their return from Manila,
have sometimes come into this bay
to procure refreshment
after their long passage.

But it was not until 1770
that the Franciscans established
their first mission here.

The Spaniards give the name of Presidio generally
to all their forts in Africa as well as in America,
that are situated in infidel countries;

the term implies that there are no colonists
but simply a garrison residing in the citadel.

New California,
notwithstanding its fertility,

does not yet possess a single European colonist.

Don Esteven Martinez,
Lieutenant from the department of San Blas,
in the province of Guadalajara
further explained
that the government maintains
a small marine force in that port,
subject to the orders of the Viceroy of Mexico
(as opposed to the Council of the Indies)
exclusively.

It consists of four corvettes of twelve guns,
and a schooner,
the particular destination of which
is the supply of the presidios of California
with provisions.

The piety of the Spaniards
has hitherto maintained these missions and presidios
at a great expense,
with the sole view of converting and
civilizing the Indians,
a system much more worthy of praise
than that of those avaricious individuals
who appeared to be invested with national authority
for no other purpose than to commit with impunity
the most atrocious barbarisms.

The Viceroy is at present
the sole judge of every dispute
between the different missions,
which do not acknowledge
the authority of the Governor at Monterey.

This Governor is merely obliged
to supply these missions
with military force
when they demand it,
but as he has effective military power
over all the Indians,
particularly those of the rancherias (villages),
and moreover has the command
of all the detachments of cavalry
which reside in the missions,
these different relations
very frequently disturb the harmony
between the military and
the religious government.

But the latter possesses sufficient influence
in the mother country
to in all cases prevail.

These affairs were formerly brought
before the Governor
(Commandancia General)
of the Inland Provinces.
But the new Viceroy,
Don Bernardo de Galvez,
has united all the powers in his own person.

The gardens of the governor
and of the missions
were filled with an infinity of plants
for culinary use,
which were furnished us in such abundance
that our people had in no country
been better supplied with vegetables.

It would be in referring to kingdoms such as Spain as rather "nations" that a disciple of the French Enlightenment exposed his deference to freemasonry.

Whose agenda calling for estrangement of Church and State from Commerce had already launched the birth of nations.

Materialism and not mysticism to be the sounding timbre of Modern Times and nationalism its religion.

Reverend Father President Lasuen himself having early on identified this shift in social and political consciousness now threatening Utopia's very existence.

With a new fusion of ideologies advocating self-fulfillment and commercialism stacking the odds against deemed as backward Indian principalities.

And accordingly prompting accelerated intervention by Franciscans anxious to elevate, enlighten and thereby in anticipation maintain as level an otherwise increasingly disparaged playing field.

Not surprisingly men such as La Perouse, who advocated replacement of empires with nations united not by monarchies but rather unregulated commerce, would perceive the but guarded pace of developing utopianism as if not oppressive then antiquated.

And, discounting altogether the notion of Indian "nations," saw in California but a missed opportunity for more enlightened foreign-venture capitalists to move ahead with commercial exploitation. While cryptically suggesting that, primitives

installed by the Franciscans as,

captains of their own destiny

lacked both mental as well as physical capacity to develop any kind of a practical government whatsoever.

The awkward stupidity of the Indians
offering up as geniuses of the country
not men like Descarte or Newton
but rather he who could enlighten his age
and countrymen
by teaching them that four and four make eight,
which is a calculation beyond the reach of a great
number of them.

The French Count's indictment further suggesting that such,

degenerate humanity

might be compelled to action only through administration of corporal punishment. Even going so far as to equate the marvelous communal aspect of Indian mission life as rather something akin to a colonial plantation whereon taskmasters exacted a work ethic and little else through liberal employment of the whip.

Poetically inferring that one could almost hear the crack of a black slaver's whip while touring Mission San Carlos.

That the very people who lived and worked on what Jean Francois identified as plantations were themselves its owners eluding him altogether; as did the peacefully progressive plodding pace of their collective endeavor.

Unable even to fathom those he had deemed the world's lowest class of humanity as having themselves engineered the same.

And in advocating outside exploitation continued,

A new branch of commerce
may here procure to the Spanish nation
greater advantages than the richest mine of Mexico.

The healthfulness of the air,
the fertility of the soil,
and the abundance of every kind of fur,
for which China is a certain market,
afford to this part of America
incalculable advantages over Old California.

There the unhealthiness and sterility
can never be compensated for by a few pearls,
which must be industriously sought
at the bottom of the sea.

Then in council with Lasuen following a thorough examination of former Governor Neve's proposals for California, expressing his own concurrent desire to see the new country thrown open for colonization.

Whilst advocating global divestment by the Church of all mission enterprises.

Of Fray Lasuen personally La Perouse reporting,

Father Fermin Lasuen,
president of the missions of New California,
is one of the finest men I have ever met,
anywhere.

I cannot find words to tell of his gentleness,
his kindness,
and his love for the Indians.

While concerning California's mentors in
general adding,

The monks,
answering our different questions
left us ignorant of no part
of the government
of this religious community,
For no other name can be given
to the administration they have established.

They are the temporal
as well as the spiritual governors,
the products of the earth being entrusted
to their care.

This government
is a true theocracy for the Indians,
who believe that their superiors
have immediate and continual communication
with God,
and that they cause him to descend every day
on the altar.

Upon returning from said investigations La Perouse finding his ships provisioned to the scuppers with fresh fruits, produce, meat and brandy. For which his "backward" Brothers in God refused all payment.

Never had nor would Jean Francois ever again encounter such a community. Nor could he begin to grasp the philosophical precepts and social structure that had created it.

Sailing away on the morning of September 24th 1786 shaking his head. Lamenting what he could only perceive as but a senseless waste of splendid resources.

Both the <u>La Boussole</u> and <u>L' Astrolabe</u> later vanishing and without so much as a trace somewhere in the South Pacific. But not before La Perouse having forwarded his extensive reports and collections on to Paris.

Which resulted in publication of a ponderous forty-four volume oeuvre entitled <u>Historie Naturelle</u>, lending it's own enlightenment to a world sitting poised yet again on the verge of great changes.

Whilst Francois himself resided either at the bottom of the sea or perhaps on some tropical island amidst a community not unlike that happened upon in California. Far removed and safe from laws of the jungle inherent with social changes previously so adamantly espoused.

OLD ENGLAND RETURNS

ix years would pass before California again played host to yet another entourage of European dignitaries.

During said interim however there coming to exist along her coastline an ever increasing and decidedly foreign presence.

Russians conjured to spurn a belligerent Supreme Council of the Indies now engaging openly in blatant violation of Spanish Trade Laws with Indios and Californios alike as an illegal harvesting of sea otter pelts developed. For which ready markets had been found amongst the Chinese and in which California abounded.

Nor had such an abundant and exploitable cache of furs gone unnoticed by Britain's aggressive Hudson's Bay Company. Themselves muscling in on what England still referred to proprietarily as rather New Albion.

A report for Mexico City from concerned Governor Fages regarding said illicit trade meeting with news heading into Monterey announcing the fact that England and Spain stood positioned anew on the brink of yet another war, this time over mutually held claims to America's northwest territories.

French Count La Perouse himself having noted previously that as far as Spain was concerned:

Northern (New) California,
of which the most northerly settlement
is that of San Francisco,
in latitude 37°58',
has no other boundary,
according to the opinion of the governor
of Monterey,
than that of America.

And our vessels,
by penetrating as far as Mount St. Elias in Alaska,
did not reach its limits.

Regardless, unable as she was to challenge Britain's naval superiority Spain ultimately capitulating. Conceding England's right to colonize territories not presently occupied.

In the midst of such political maneuverings Don Pedro Fages finding himself returning to Sonora as Inspector Commandante/General of the Interior Provinces.

With Jose Antonio Romeu posted as succedaneum. Who arriving at Monterey in deplorable health prevailed upon Commandante Josef Dario Arguello of the Royal Presidio at San Francisco to officiate unofficially in his sted.

Romeu dying less than two years later, on April 19, 1792. Ashamed at having failed to triumph over his illness and correspondingly ever unable himself to govern, insisting he be buried without ceremony or distinction and in an unmarked grave outside the precincts of Mission San Carlos.

Compassionate Fray Fermin Lasuen ignoring such humble posturing. Marking the interment of a nobleman undone with appropriate religious and civil observance.

Meanwhile Arguello continuing his unofficial reign as Governor with all now awaiting the arrival from Mexico City of Romeu's successor Jose Joaquin Arrellaga.

When in the midst of such transitions Californios received a second extraordinarily outfitted entourage of foreign luminaries.

Two British ships, the <u>Chatham</u> and <u>Daedalus</u>, sailing unannounced into San Francisco Bay on November 1, 1792.

With none less than arguably the most powerful and distinguished military officer in the world, Admiral of the British Royal Navy George Vancouver, riding at the helm.

Himself received by an unsuspecting California not with military pomp and circumstance but rather,

A priest of the order of St. Francisco,
And a sergeant in the Spanish army.

Vancouver recounting his impromptu reception thusly,

The reverend father expressed,
and seemingly with great sincerity,
the pleasure he felt at our arrival,
and assured me that every refreshment and service
in the power of himself or mission to bestow

I might unreservedly command;
since it would be conferring on them all
a peculiar obligation to allow them to be serviceable.

The sergeant expressed himself
in the most friendly manner,
and informed me,
that in the absence of the commandante,
he was directed on our arrival to render us every
accommodation
the settlement could afford.

We attended them on shore after breakfast,
where they embraced the earliest opportunity
of proving,
that their friendly expressions
were not empty professions,
by presenting me with a very fine ox, a sheep,
and some excellent vegetables.

The good friar,
after pointing out the most convenient spot
for procuring wood and water
and repeating the hospitable offers
he had before made in the name of the fathers
of the Franciscan order,
returned to the mission of St. Francisco,
which we understood was at no great distance,
and to which he gave us the most pressing invitation.

The British admiral in fact being generously hosted
not only at both the Royal Presidio and Mission San
Francisco but by a South bay amalgam of San Jose and
Mission Santa Clara.

Irking his hosts with habitual references to California as
rather New Albion. Nor had it gone unnoticed that he
seemed ever to be making copious notes concerning
such things as "Saint Francisco's" seriously deficient
armaments and insufficient military manpower.

In typical British understatement summing up the Bay
of Saint Francisco was but,

as fine a port as any in the world.

Then going on to report, in an exhaustive treatise
subsequently filed with the British Crown, that,

The most important of all blessings,
health,
is here treated with great indifference;

The climate of the country,
has the reputation of being as healthy
as any part of the world.

While of the country's Franciscan overseers suggesting,

If I am correctly informed
by the different Spanish gentlemen
with whom I conversed on this subject,
the uniform, mild, and kind-hearted disposition
of this religious order,
has never failed to attach to their interest
the affections of the natives,
wherever they have sat down amongst them:

this is a very happy circumstance,
for their situation otherwise

would be excessively precarious;

as they are protected only by five soldiers
who reside under the directions of a corporal,
in the buildings of the mission
at some distance on the other side of the church.

Vancouver, like La Perouse, failing to perceive the
inherent capacities of Serra's Indian proteges,
describing them in terms even more disparaging than
those of the French Count,

Deaf to the important lessons
and insensible to the promised advantages
afforded them by the Brothers of Saint Francis,

suggesting folly on the part of Franciscans for so
thoroughly believing in their potential.

Of the Royal Presidio and with greater interest
Vancouver noting,

It possesses no other means for its protection
than a brass three-pounder (cannon)
mounted on a rotten carriage.

The Spanish soldiers composing the garrison
amounted,
I understood,
to thirty-five,
who with their wives, families,
and a few Indian servants,
composed the whole of the inhabitants.

Aware that the world's foremost naval officer was in San

Francisco and taking inventory, Commandante Arguello sat anxiously awaiting word at Monterey concerning the whereabouts of Governor Jose Joaquin Arrellaga.

Who arriving on November 22nd to discover California's defenses completely compromised, understandably flew into a diplomatic rage.

It would be whilst hunting quail and gossiping over,

one hogshead of wine,
and another of rum

with,

the Spanish speaking citizenry of New Albion

when England's most decorated naval officer and his California escort Sergeant Salvador Sal received an abrupt and angry reality check from now upon the scene Governor Arrellaga. Who ordered that all courtesies being extended to the British cease. Then furthermore demanding Vancouver make his mandatory appearance at Monterey as required by treaties recently signed between the two world super powers. And at once.

Despite this sudden about face, San Francisco loading Vancouver's ships with beef, mutton, fresh fruits and vegetables, for which all payment was refused. Contrariwise retaining their honored guest just long enough for him to attend a grand feast for which two bullocks had already been slaughtered. Festivities continuing well into the night.

Never had Vancouver been hosted more graciously. And out of reciprocal respect rather than compunction dutifully headed south thereafter to keep a previously scheduled appointment in Monterey.

Anticipation of Old England's arrival prompting an unprecedented display of Spanish naval might. Spanish Admiral Alejandro Malaspina's two ships the <u>Descubierta</u> and <u>Atrevida</u> upon which Governor Arrellaga had himself just arrived intercepting and blockading the British admiral.

Arrellaga before departing for California having been ordered to accept Spanish surrender of all Northwest Territories over to England. And understandably holding as suspect the fact that no less than Admiral Vancouver had himself already breached said treaties which mandated that British ships in California waters stop but once and only at Monterey.

Convinced of if not open covert operations then espionage, under no circumstances would Arrellaga permit the departure of this presumed spy without first subjecting him to a thorough interrogation.

So it was that in the humble office of California's Governor a regal Admiral Vancouver endured dressing down the likes of which he had not been accustomed. And made to understand that overtures of hospitality extended at San Francisco aside British subjects were not welcome anywhere in what remained politically Spanish California.

Defending previous indiscretions Vancouver suggesting:

I had been given to understand,
not only that I should be hospitably received
on this coast
by the subjects of the Spanish crown,
but that such information
of the progress of my voyage
as I might wish to communicate
to the Court of Great Britain,
would be forwarded by way of Saint Blas
by officers of His Catholic Majesty
residing in these ports;

And that I was instructed to make a free
and unreserved communication
of all discoveries made
in the course of my researches,
to any Spanish officer or officers whom
I might chance to meet.

Then producing a letter so stating from Viceroy Juan
Vicente de Guemes Pacheco,

To certify him (Governor Arrellaga),
that I did not intend any deception.

Cedula notwithstanding distraught Arrellaga ordering
Vancouver tender a full report listing every Californian
with whom he'd engaged in social intercourse.

Which the Admiral did. Only to be instructed
thereafter that he remain on board his ship and await
the Spanish Governor's response.

In the meantime from a position offshore British naval
officers continuing their inspection, now of both

Monterey's Castillo and Royal Presidio:

On the outside,
before the entrance into the presidio,
which fronts the shores of the bay,
are placed seven cannon,
four nine and three three-pounders, mounted;

These, with those noticed at St. Francisco,
one two-pounder at Santa Clara,
and four nine-pounders dismounted,
form the whole of the artillery.

These guns are planted on the open plain ground,
without any breast work or other screen
for those employed in working them,
or the least cover or protection from the weather.

Such, I was informed,
was also the defenseless state
of all the new settlements on the coast
not excepting St. Diego,
which from its situation should seem to be
a post of no small importance.

The four mounted cannon,
together with those placed at the entrance
into the presidio,
are intended for a fort to be built
on a small eminence
that commands the anchorage.

A large quantity of timber is at present in readiness
for carrying that design into execution;
which,

when completed,
might certainly be capable
of annoying vessels lying in that part of the Bay
after a landing was accomplished;

As the hills behind it might be easily gained,
from whence the assailing party
would soon oblige the fort
to surrender,

nor do I consider Monterey to be a very tenable port
without an extensive line of works.

Vancouver's contemplated strategies revealing clearly
England's lust.

The presidio
is the residence of the governor
of the province,
whose command extends from St. Francisco,
southward along the exterior shore,
to Cape St. Lucas;

And on the eastern side of the peninsula
of California,
up that gulph to the bay of St. Louis.

The rank in the Spanish service,
required as a qualification to hold
this extensive command,
is that of lieutenant colonel.

With condescending British sarcasm Vancouver adding,

Whether the governor interfered in the common

garrison duty
I know not.

Then continuing:

A lieutenant and ensign,
sergeants, corporals, &c.
resided also in the presidio;

The establishment of which I understand
was similar to all the rest of the province,
but was incomplete in consequence
of the recent death
of the late commander (Romeu).

By this event, Lieutenant (Josef Dario) Arguello,
properly the commander at St. Francisco,
as being senior officer,
had taken upon himself the government.

And had sent the alferez, or ensign
(actually sergeant), Senior Sal,
to command at St. Francisco;

Which post we understood
they were severally to retain,
until another lieutenant colonel
should be appointed by the government.

By what I was able to learn,
I did not consider the number
of soldiers who composed the garrison
as exceeding one hundred,
including the non- commissioned officers.

From this body
detachments are drawn
for the protection of the neighboring missions;

The remainder,
with their wives and families,
reside within the walls of the presidio
without seeming to have the least desire
for a more rural habitation
where garden ground and many comforts
might easily be procured,
at no great distance from the seat
of the establishment.

This seemed to be composed entirely
of military people.
At least we did not see amongst them
those of any other description.

The few most necessary mechanical employments
were carried on in an indifferent manner
by some of the soldiers,
under permission of the commanding officer.

Days passed before Vancouver received his response
from Governor Arrellaga,

On Monday I received from Senor Arrellaga
a reply to my letter,
in which he was pleased to compliment me
upon my ingenuity;

and thanked me for having given him
the perusal of the viceroy's letters.

In vindication of himself he said,
that there was no royal order
for the reception of our vessel,
like that produced by Monsieur de la Perouse.

Spain's representative going on to insist that under no interpretation of the letters presented could Vancouver have presumed any right to make port but once in California and then only at Monterey.

Stating further that such irregularities required no less than a full inspection of both British ships and by the Governor himself. Which were then knowingly ordered off loaded along a coastal cattle-slaughtering ground notorious for its stench.

Disgusted with this display of insolence the world's highest-ranking naval officer dispatching off to Reverend Father President Lasuen a missive petitioning intervention from he whom California recognized as true reigning prelate.

Then with no response forthcoming simply sailing away.

Stopping thereafter at Santa Barbara. Where Arrellaga notwithstanding Vancouver found himself again received graciously. Franciscans even offering to ready for retrieval at San Juan Capistrano any supplies an Anglican brother in Christ might yet stand in need of for his long voyage.

The embarrassed Admiral expressing appreciation yet deferring.

Sailing rather directly to San Diego. Where Commandante Antonio Grajero informed Vancouver of orders received in advance of his arrival forbidding even the selling of water to Englishmen.

To an Englishman's relief, Admiral Malaspinas sailing in behind him with noneother than Father Lasuen on board. Who had prevailed upon the Spanish naval officer, himself in route back to San Blas, to facilitate a Reverend Father President's intercession on behalf of both California and its most distinguished guest.

Of Lasuen's appositeness Malaspinas recording:

Among those who could with
the most judgement and knowledge
make some interpretations,
Fray Lasuen, of the order of San Francisco,
president of the missions of New California,
without doubt deserved the first place.

He was a man who in Christian lore, mien,
and conduct
was truly apostolic,
and his good manners and learning
were most unusual.

This religious had with good reason merited
the esteem and friendship of both French and
English commanders
and the majority of their subordinates.

Of Vancouver's unexpected conference with Lasuen at San Diego the Admiral recording,

Father Fermin de Lasuen,
president of the missions of New California,
is one of the most worthy of esteem
and respect of all men
I have ever met.

Interestingly the Englishman perceiving an in fact but 56 year old Philosopher/King as being rather 72. Lausen's own writings on said subject acknowledging that,

Already I am an old man
and completely gray.

Vancouver not failing to recognize, harbored in the personage of said sage, California's greatest treasure. Witnessing further how,

His sweetness of temper,
his benevolence,
and his love for the Indians is beyond expression.

Ecumenical Lasuen reminding Admiral Vancouver that stores of supplies sat awaiting his retrieval should he desire them at not so distant San Juan Capistrano.

Again Vancouver declining. This time himself offloading,

a handsome barreled organ

which he proffered as England's contribution to a proposed "cathedral" he presumed planned for Carmel. An instrument thereafter delivered as intended for the great stone church soon to be constructed at San Juan Capistrano.

Concerning California Vancouver in his report to the
British Crown surmising,

The mode originally adopted,
and since constantly pursued,
in settling this country,
is by no means calculated to produce
any great increase of white inhabitants.

These benevolent fathers
are the corporeal
as well as spiritual physicians
of all the Indian tribes.
Their conduct appears at all time
to be regulated by their college at Mexico;

And they seem, in most respects,
nearly independent of military subjection.

The scarcity of spirituous liquors,
and the great regularity of the inhabitants
in food and employment,
induces a life of temperance;

The number of natives, at this period,
who were said to have embraced
the Roman Catholic persuasion
under the discipline of the Franciscan missionaries
in New Albion,
and by the Dominicans throughout
the peninsula of California,
amounted to about twenty thousand.

Their progress towards civilization
seems to have been remarkably slow;

and it is not very likely to become more rapid,
until the impolicy of excluding foreign visitors
shall be laid aside,
and an amicable commercial intercourse
substituted in its room;

by which system new wants become necessary,
new comforts would be introduced
and new industry stimulated.

And concluding by posing if not a threat to
California's mentors then this challenge,

The Spaniards, in doing thus much,
have only cleared the way
for the ambitious enterprizers
of those maritime powers,
who in the avidity of commercial pursuits,
may seek to be benefitted
by the advantages which the fertile soil
of New Albion
seems calculated to afford.

By the formation of such establishments,
so wide from each other,
and so unprotected in themselves,
the original design of settling the country
seems to have been completely set aside,

And, instead of strengthening the barrier
to their valuable possessions in New Spain,
they have thrown irresistible temptations
in the way of strangers
to trespass over their boundary.

A certain proportion of the natives have,
by indefatigable labour of the missionaries,
been weaned from their former
uncivilized savage way of life,
and are become obedient to social forms,
and practices in many domestic occupations.

All these circumstances are valuable considerations
to new masters,
from whose power,
if properly employed,
the Spaniards would have no alternative
but that of submissively yielding.

TROUBLE IN THE
FIELDS OF THE LORD

S pain having blinked in her New World standoff with England, a weakening monarchy then forced to endure but the first of many ensuing indignities.

Riding to the rescue at Monterey being Knight of the Order of Saint James, Sir Diego de Borica. Who arrived upon the scene directly from Seville accompanied by his wife and daughter in 1794.

To discover ensconced anything but strife. Indeed, seemingly rather a Plato's republic. The triumphal expression of John Duns flowering even as time and tide had turned to sweep both the political influence of Spain together with her frontier utopian schemes away.

Wrote unsuspecting Governor Borica,

> To live long
> and without care
> come to Monterey.
>
> Capitol of the most peaceful and
> quiet kingdom in the world,
> here I find myself more comfortable
> than in any of the courts of Europe.
>
> The climate is healthful;
> not too hot, not too cold.

There is good bread,
excellent meat
good fish,

And above all else good humor,
which is worth even more than all the rest.

That same year at Popeloutachem, some thirty miles distant from a new Governor's residence Reverend Father President Lasuen launching Mission San Juan Bautista.

Prompting Borica's order that Californio's follow suit with provisioning of classrooms and teachers for their own children.

Dreams of such cosmopolitan societies existing together in sublime harmony remaining too grand for the minds of most.

Myopic La Perouse and Vancouver both while espousing Enlightenment yet failing to grasp the prevailing joyous simplicity each had witnessed first hand in California.

Western civilization otherwise focusing upon materialism and personal ambitions rendered unable but to misinterpret and accordingly misrepresent resistance on the part of Franciscan mentors and their,

most miserable savages,

to divide up or parcel out that which said "savages" and missionaries identified rather as,

Heaven on Earth.

Themselves authors of a now marginally successful, revenue generating trading partner.

For so California had become. And on its own, without European meddling beyond that of Spanish missionaries tutoring Indians. With all income generated through but intermittent trade from what La Perouse referred to rather as "plantations" ever being plowed back into the further expansion of those same self-sufficient communities.

Sir Diego Borica himself observing that far from stockpiling non existent gold reales, Franciscans sworn themselves to vows of poverty had built homes for families while setting in place the foundations of one new mission after another. Hypothetically until,

> Christian fellowship shall embrace
> not merely California
> but the entire globe
> as one grand, singular community.

Spoken like a true knight.

It is not surprising that those less enlightened than California's Mission Indians had failed to grasp the grandeur and altruism inherent with such a Republic.

At Mexico City Francisco Palou successfully thwarting efforts intent upon transferring the same from out of Franciscan hands. Fermin Lasuen effectively containing on-site attempts being made by powerful cabildos to introduce colonialism. Overseeing installation adjacent to privately held San Jose of Serra's proposed Mission San Jose. Whilst elsewhere checking any possibility for expanding El Pueblo de Los Angeles by closing it in with the founding of Mission San Fernando Rey de Espana.

Both Indian coup de tats occurring in 1797.

Still, political storm clouds ever drifting in from out of the Old World would not be forestalled.

The grand reconquista launched by Don Carlos III having ended abruptly in 1794 with ascension of his son Don Carlos IV. Whose ministers remained focused upon competition rather than co-operation.

A mindset that would ultimately undo both their king and California. Striking the final fatal blow to Spain's floundering global monarchy.

Of which at Madrid the father of Latin American independence, Simon Bolivar recorded,

> Our King (Don Carlos IV) is a fool.
>
> And overly influenced by his wife,
> Queen Maria Luisa.
>
> Their son Ferdinand a spoiled boy
> with a wicked streak of cruelty.
>
> They live together in stylish excess
> and rule with a moral laxity and disinterest
> that has rendered them
> the scandal of Europe.

Endless outbreaks of revolution against the aforementioned inferences of autocratic abuse but exacerbating staggering debt yet dogging the Bourbons. All of which prompted Don Carlos IV to introduce extraordinary and unprecedented actions.

Lands otherwise ever held in perpetuity by the Crown ordered either sold or granted to private parties and or creditors as fiscal remedy. Spanish soldiers in particular receiving tracts of real estate in lieu of delinquent salaries.

Under a guise of "doing what is best for the people," a frantic Spanish King selling off acreage in order to raise monies.

Following suit, his ambitious Marquee of Branciforte as Viceroy of New Spain all but destroying Bourbon family designs upon California.

Franciscan custodies suddenly broadsided by a new and concerted effort to install secular colonization where previously only the monarchy had stood to profit.

So it was that Spain's final act of imposing colonialism anywhere in the Americas took place curiously in of all places closed from the same California. As orchestrated by,

One of the worst men
ever to disgrace a country.

With Colonia Branciforte leaving a decided stain upon otherwise but marginally blighted landscapes.

Catching both Lasuen and Borica completely off-guard. Each left to deal with not only arriving upon the scene colonists but news concerning their King's willingness to settle delinquent wages and retirement pensions due military officers in California through a mission secularization scheme.

Don Pedro Fages having himself unwittingly pushed this envelope ten years earlier when awarding retiring Colonel Juan Jose Dominguez concessions for establishing a private ranching enterprise on lands adjacent to the Pueblo of Los Angeles

Dominguez together with his partner Manuel Guiterrez having sought permission to remain in California. Suggesting they might there sustain themselves as ranchers.

Dominguez and Guiterrez then running cattle on properties abandoned by Tongva who had opted rather to join the experimental Christian community of Mission San Gabriel.

Never before in California had private interests been awarded a royal patent for developing or exploiting properties above and beyond establishment of former Governor Neve's illegal under Spain's own laws, highly contested by Rome, contained by the Franciscans and subsequently absorbed into the Missions, twin municipalities of San Jose and Los Angeles.

Nor had tracts of land ostensibly awarded to Dominguez and Guiterrez been inconsequential. Corresponding in dimension with allotments for the establishment of communal missions.

Were it not for the fact that Dominguez and Guiterrez were themselves intimates of the Franciscans and well liked by local Tongva such concessions would never have been tolerated.

As it was Palou heatedly opposed from afar the precedent such grandiosity established. Invoking laws drafted previously to protect Indians while filing suit from Queretaro on behalf of them in the face of said breach.

Fray Francisco's fears were not unfounded. His suit as subsequently filed notwithstanding, nineteen retiring soldiers now requesting privileges in return for having marched with Serra and Portola into the new country.

Without hesitation Don Carlos IV upon receipt of the same settling accounts due by presenting both status as Soldados Distinguidos (Soldiers of Distinction) and concessions for stock and lands suddenly ordered surrendered by Franciscan custodies.

Such Royal largesse but resurrecting conceptually Spain's heinous encomienda system. And successfully introducing long forestalled interference from private vested interest partners.

Presaging dismantling altogether of Franciscan Custodies and exploitation of a now trained and skilled labor force, Don Carlos IV next ordering activation of former Governor Neve's proposed scheme to divide and distribute every mission community ten years or older.

Betraying honorable soldiers who had themselves given the strength of their best manhood to establish a utopian community. Such actions but taunting them with the irresistible opportunity of becoming rich through blatant exploitation of their own legacy.

Spain's track record concerning coexistence of mission communities with private encomiendas remaining an uncontestably dismal failure.

All ranchos and haciendas throughout California aside from those pertaining to each Presidio had ever been held and developed communally for and in behalf of the Indian alone.

Parceling out a beanfield to one and two cows for another as Phelipe de Neve had prescribed was but to introduce concepts that no one, least of all mission novices, had ever conceived of nor been prepared for.

Such rationale but undoing the hybrid communistic society installed.

So it was that Franciscans the world over protested what they recognized as but Spain's blatant infringement upon the rights of California's Indian peoples.

Disavowing outcries Don Carlos IV facilitating installation of two private estates on the outskirts of Monterey.

Both of which were promptly set upon and burned to the ground by an incensed Indian community.

Even at its zenith the Franciscan's noble experiment embraced fewer than 10% of California's indigenous population. Such meager numbers of budding laborers and intellectuals, having nonetheless fulfilled each and every one of their objectives, remaining understandably disinterested with regard to dissolution of said accomplishments in exchange for but a stab at competitive capitalism.

And in perceiving a sudden shift of Spanish agendas now perpetrated once merely peripherally intentional acts of violence with increasing vigor. Fueled as they were by mounting concern amongst the gentile (non Christian) majority regarding this precedent of introducing private estancias (estates).

Franciscan mentored community itself suddenly being perceived as harbinger of Spanish duplicity and accordingly falling under attack.

Missions since Serra having greatly multiplied. Their farms and pasturelands now extending across vast tracts of coastal terrain. All of which from the outset had ever prompted complaints from pagan families concerning everything from decimation of grass seed harvests to displacement of the wild game upon which most still depended for sustenance.

Some countering said trespass by appropriating for personal use mission cattle and horses from off the ranchos together with fruits and vegetables out of the haciendas.

Such pillage perceived by the padres as not only marginal but understandable,

To understand all
is to forgive all.

But with the inauguration of private Spanish estates, that which had once been accommodated as but an annoyance quickly escalated into nothing less than civil war between novice and gentile Indians.

Under the pallor of heightened fear recanting Diego Borica opting to move his family from out of harm's way. Don Jose Joaquin Arrellaga being rushed back and reinstated as Governor.

Who characteristically took quick if unreasonably forceful action.

Soldiers restrained earlier under Governor Neve from assisting Franciscans with,

rescuing

novice fugitives from certain

purgatory

now finding themselves being routinely dispatched to round up and imprison anyone, novice or gentile, for even the most ludicrous of but alleged criminal activity committed against mission institutions otherwise being marginalized anyway by a shift in official Spanish policy.

Under the pretext of teaching renegades a lesson, Arrellaga's state of prevailing martial law but fanning the flames of open rebellion both from without as well as within the mission communities.

So it was that trouble flared up in,

the Fields of the Lord.

A Franciscan country standing unnerved by ever increasing contradictorily punitive military engagements.

The term Utopia being derived from Greek and meaning "No Place," in state of fact said ideal, which dictates survival be achieved and progress attained not through aggressive exploitation by the fittest but rather through co-operative endeavor, remains without precedent in Nature.

So it seemed Serra's Utopia, too, like all such schemes before and since would remain as but an elusive goal at best.

With all out war against it now commencing not surprisingly first amongst desert tribesmen and Tongva, both of whom had felt early on the sting of Spanish duplicity.

When grandsons of Olleyqoutequiebe appeared like thieves in the night; setting fields and grasslands associated with both private estates and Indian missions alike ablaze. Driving great herds of cattle and horses off into the desert.

Utopia standing paralyzed.

At enigmatic Los Angeles, Californio Corporal Jose Maria Pico receiving word concerning more than eight hundred insurgents in route and intent upon destroying a decidedly non- Indian community.

With but four soldiers at his disposal, Pico dispatching

neophyte runners off to Monterey, petitioning help from any and all who might hurry to his aid.

Returning from a successfully squelched uprising along the Carquinez Strait, where would have stood not a private estate but rather another mission had California's noble experiment remained on track, Governor Arrellaga only to be confronted with Pico's mayday and hence racing southward in response.

Along the way indiscriminately rounding up any Indian, Catholic or otherwise, if perceived as poising a threat.

Franciscan intercession prompting Governor Arrellaga's subsequent move to draft indignant, falsely indicted neophytes into the King's army, both as a means of making amends as well as to better arm missions against future attacks.

In a scenario reminiscent of equanaminous Anza, scaring up bits of Spanish uniforms together with copious offerings of good food as compensation for assistance with keeping the province stable.

Tentative peace between Californios, Mission novices and gentile Indians settling in across a land yet burgeoning with unprecedented promise. Still, halcyon days proving short-lived.

Where insurgents had failed to dissuade Christian converts, plague occasioning mass defections. As next an invisible and unassailable epidemic of small pox swept across the country.

The deadly assault at San Juan Capistrano in particular beginning on December 24, 1805. When tiny six-month old Marcel Pajao was snatched away. Fourteen month old Geronimo Nu and seven-month old Modesto Juimovit dying two days later.

By May of that same year an insidious virus having extinguished at San Juan alone the lives of one hundred and sixty novices, together with countless gentile Acjachemem for whom no records were kept. In some cases decimating entire families.

Shaman from across California quick to pronounce said scourge as but the judgement of Chinigchinich being leveled against all those who had embraced Jesus Christ.

Desperate Franciscans countering through an appeal to these same local religious for aid in exorcising the invisible demons.

Whereupon a novice at Mission Santa Barbara undergoing Franciscan sanctioned treatment from her Chumash shaman for small pox claimed in the process to have been visited by Earth goddess Chupu. Who, she asserted, insisted that all renounce Catholic baptism and bath in,

the tears of the sun,

or suffer certain death.

Chupu's cult gaining stature proportionate to the increased tolling of mission bells announcing dirge after dirge.

So as to dispel an oppressive aire of melancholia and thereby hopefully deflect defections, Franciscans ordering incessant tolling of requiem bells not only at Mission Santa Barbara but up and down the coast dispensed with altogether.

With neither incantations of shaman nor prayers of the priest succeeding in eradicating disease, a state of despondency descending upon California.

Yet it would be from what must have seemed the depths of hell itself that Utopia attained its most noble stature.

When on the afternoon of September 7, 1806 following a year long assault from smallpox, faithful novices and curious gentiles gathered together with Governor Arrellaga, his entourage and all ecclesiastics from across the province at San Juan Capistrano. There to dedicate what would prove to be Spanish California's grandest monument to Christian idealism.

Teams of oxen tugging at ropes and pulleys hoisting four great bells into position within the fantastic tower of Franciscanland's largest church. Sweet smelling clouds of incense and an iridescent glow from thousands of candles temporarily banishing horrors that had snatched away even the life of chief architect Ysidro Aguilar.

Nine days of feasting, fandangos, native dances, and song not only at San Juan but in every mission community restoring for a moment some semblance of well being and normalcy.

Still the amoral ravages of Nature were not to be dissuaded.

A series of violent earthquakes subsequently shaking the fledgling civilization to its very foundations. Toppling many a splendid mission, including the paradigmatic great stone church at San Juan Capistrano.

Rendering gods the likes of Chupu and Chinigchinich empowered anew. Reviving determination on the part of emboldened shaman to eradicate Christianity together with its accomplices. Engendering renewed confrontations.

Concomitant being the continued threat of Don Carlos IV, who in his blatant move to confiscate troubled Utopia unexpectedly ordered that all Franciscans,

cease from the government
and administration
of the property of the Indians
of California.

A mandate published on March 19, 1812 that nonetheless did not reach California until 1820 and then on the eve of events that were about to sweep away not only Indian missions but a greedy and indifferent monarchy as well.

ROSSOYA

I f Governor Arrellaga seemed eternally on edge he was not without due cause. What with his first administration having been compromised even prior to arriving and by no less than Admiral George Vancouver of the British Navy. Then returning following Borica's unanticipated departure only to discover the entire province caught up in an escalating state of civil unrest.

And now the urgent knocking upon his door.

Which when opened revealed a messenger sent by sixteen-year-old Luis Antonio Arguello. Who had been left behind by his father, Commandante of the San Francisco Presidio Josef Dario Arguello (being away on a hunting expedition), only to find himself entertaining no less than an emissary from the Russian Imperial Court of Czar Alexander.

Arrellaga was well aware of a Russian presence. California's own Indios aiding Aleutians working for Slavic fur trappers in an on-going and illegal harvest of sea otter skins.

And also recognizing that not merely Russians but English and now Yankee trappers were presently engaged in the illicit harvest. Frequent sightings keeping a rumor mill along El Camino Real grinding away with revelations concerning various and sundry clandestine trapping and trading operations.

His own earlier attempts at curtailing said smuggling

but accelerating as if out of spite its proliferation.

When upon confiscating two foreign droghers reporting in at San Diego to request permission for engaging in trapping, Arrellaga found himself if not persona non grata than branded most despised man in all of California.

The fact remaining that by restricting trading options to Spanish merchants who at long last exhibited interest in developing California as a trading partner, the fledgling kingdom found itself saddled with an unintentional yet very real commercial embargo.

And where pragmatic Josef Dario Arguello, serving intermittently as governor between the aborted administration of ailing Romeu and subsequently disenchanted Sir Diego, opted ever to look the other way concerning said illegal but useful commercial exchange, Governor Arrellaga's contradictorily arbitrary if not draconian actions serving but to drive further underground chaffare that otherwise accommodated might well have alleviated what La Perouse and Vancouver had both identified as,

the country's economic stagnation.

Arrellaga's tyranny soon proving even life threatening for a Russian colony at Sitka (Alaska) who found itself staring down the throws of starvation.

Retained by Russian-American Fur Company officials as inspector for New World installations, Chamberlain of the Imperial Court under Czar Alexander and First Baron, Nikkolai Petrovitch Rezanov stumbling upon said dire circumstances unexpectedly.

Where semi-tropic coastal California enjoyed its year round growing cycles, Slavic trappers to the north facing severe climatic conditions. Rendering annual importation of provisioning essential to operations.

And when in 1805 that counted upon supply ship failed to make its usual rounds Sitka sat teetering upon the brink of disaster.

In response to Resanov's missive describing the precariousness of circumstances discovered, St. Petersburg dispatching a rescue ship loaded down with emergency rations.

Which never arrived. Disappearing somewhere in route. Rendering a desperate Chamberlain with no alternative but to abandon operations altogether.

When as fortune would have it the China-bound Yankee clipper ship Juno sailed into port and laden with tradegoods.

Regardless of the fact that Spain had forbidden California's participation in foreign commerce, Baron Resanov weighing his options and deciding to gamble.

Astounding a Baltimore supercargo with his offer to purchase outright,

Lock, stock and barrel,

the entire ship.

Then pointing her south towards taboo trading options with a mindset that Spanish law be damned an otherwise successful Russian American Fur Company need be rescued from ruin.

Traveling in company with German naturalist and trusted friend Heinrich von Langsdorff, Baron Resanov arriving at San Francisco to find its Golden Gate typically shrouded in fog. Which but facilitated slipping past San Joaquin's Castle undetected.

Steadfastly sailing into a harbor from which he faced the very real possibility of expulsion. For although aware of Vancouver's reports concerning its poorly manned and inadequate battlements, Nikkolai dared not subject an enterprise upon which so much depended to any undo risks.

So it was that only after distancing himself from the Spanish presidio did he drop anchor. And this at the small cove of Yerba Buena in which Vancouver himself had moored.

When the fog lifted on May 8, 1806, San Francisco awakening to discover a Yankee ship brazenly stationed well within her harbor.

First to greet an elegantly attired Russian chamberlain and equally resplendent German colleague being the unsuspecting Luis Antonio Arguello who clad only in black trousers and Panama hat introduced himself as son of the Royal Commandante.

Minutes before being joined by an equally caught off guard contingent of royal soldiers sent out to accompany their commandante's son on his morning ride.

Fascinated at what he'd perceived as but another ship full of benign fur trappers, young Arguello's enthusiasm turning to alarm upon finding himself being addressed rather by a powerful Russian government official.

Fear of Slavic incursion having prompted settlement of San Francisco in the first place, correspondingly Californians everafter on guard against a perceived threat of invasion.

The delicate dance with diplomacy that ensued however but jettisoning California into a heady atmosphere of self-empowerment and over the top wealth.

An anxious native son hastily recruiting Fray Francisco Uria who conversed effectively with the Russian Chamberlain in Latin.

Whilst secretly Cadet Arguello dispatched a messenger off to inform Governor Arrellaga of his predicament.

The Russians were at San Francisco. His father was off hunting. He did not know what to do.

Of course young Luis did what any self-respecting Californio would have done. He threw a grand dinner party in honor of his distinguished guests. Indeed a fiesta while spontaneous yet so astounding that it overwhelmed and enchanted even a Russian Chamberlain accustomed to life amidst the Royal court.

Who sitting before tables laden with fresh produce, meat, wine and brandy, surrounded by people as beautiful in demeanor as they were in appearance fell in love. And not merely with California.

For the stunning beauty and grace of Arguello's fourteen-year-old sister Concepcion had also caught Resanov's eye.

In aping that which he'd seen done by his father on the occasion of Vancouver's unexpected visit, Luis next invited Resanov and Langsdorff to Mission San Francisco.

Thereafter bidding time by escorting them as done previously with the British on a hunting excursion.

Never had Nikkolai experienced more wonderful camaraderie. Yet diversions aside, he would not be distracted from carrying out his objective.

So it was that tactfully each morning the Baron presented gracious hosts with marvelous gifts.

Bestowing silk mantillas and ribbons upon Arguello's sister Concha (Concepcion). Presenting fine white linen and china dishes to his mother, Dona Maria Ygnacio Moraga, (daughter of San Francisco's "San" Joaquin).

Thus eliciting from other ladies in the community a desire for the same.

With soldiers left coveting the comfortable American shoes and fine cotton handkerchiefs now owned by young Luis.

Erstwhile letting it be known at every opportunity that aboard his ship were more mantillas, ribbons, linens, dishes and shoes as well as plows, axes, saws and shears for clipping the wool from sheep.

It must have seemed curious to the Californios that Nikkolai had nowhere to go with such a fabulous cargo. Yet not once did the Baron so much as suggest trade.

Co-conspirator Langsdoff remembering:

Our constant friendly intercourse
with the Arguello family, in particular,
the music, the singing, the sports, and the dancing,
awakened in the mind of Chamberlain von Rezanov
some new and very important speculations,
giving rise to his formation of a plan very different
from his first,
for establishing a commercial intercourse between
the Russian and Spanish settlements.

The bright eyes of Dona Concepcion
had made a deep impression upon his heart;
and he conceived that a nuptial union
with the daughter of the commandante
at San Francisco
would be a vast step gained towards promoting
the political objectives he now so much desired.

He had therefore nearly come to
a resolution to sacrifice himself
by this marriage
to the welfare, as he hoped,
of the two countries of Spain and Russia.

The tone of Langsdorff's account not revealing
however, that Concepcion as Heinrich would himself
thereafter confide was,

the greatest beauty in all of California.

Conceding further the authentic affections of a 42 year
old baron,

Although there was some disparity in age,
for she was just flowering into womanhood,
and he was past his first youth and a widower,
yet Nikkolai possessed unusual personal attractions.

A tall, erect figured, fair-haired and blue-eyed man,
with a singularly handsome face,
set off by his Russian uniform of dark green
and gold brocade,
the glittering order of Saint Ann upon his breast,
in appearance he was most distinguished.

Add to this his elegant manners as a European noble,
his fine intellectual attainments,
with the prestige of courts and high station,
and surely it is not difficult to understand
that his task of winning the heart of the
unsophisticated country girl
was an easy one.

To her he must indeed have seemed
the very prince of romance.
But he would not depend solely upon
his personal attractions
to achieve a hoped for success,

By day, in the intervals of the dancing and singing
and horseback riding,
he painted in his talk lively pictures
of the splendors of life
in the capital of Russia
and the luxury of the imperial court.

As compared with the monotony and plainness
of life in California
it must have seemed like a glimpse into a fairyland
to the imaginative young girl.

In this way he soon brought her to the point when
to become the wife of the Russian chamberlain
became the dearest object of her life.

Upon arriving at San Francisco Concepcion's
godfather, Governor Jose Joaquin Arrellaga faced
immediate intercession from Franciscans to whom a
foreign diplomat had entrusted his secrets.

Father Uria arguing with a known to be arbitrary
autocrat not only on behalf of this Russian
Chamberlain's starving colonists but the Brothers' own
very authentic need for those items stashed in the
hold of his ship.

To which piously Arrellaga shunted,

After having lived sixty years above reproach,
I cannot take such a trick upon my conscience.

Desperate times called for desperate measures.

Uria suggesting Resanov appeal directly to just

installed Reverend Father President Estevan Tapis who was for all practical purposes ruling potentate of California and who happened to be at nearby Mission Santa Clara on business.

Following a harrowing night of travel, during which Langsdorff obligingly defended himself with firearms against both wild bulls and grizzly bears Resanov's emissary arriving shaken but unscathed at the gates of Santa Clara.

In the interim Commandante Josef Dario Arguello returning home from a hunting foray only to encounter the nothing less than extraordinary circumstances occasioned during his absence. Expressing pride in young Luis for the manner with which he'd handled said situation. Whilst struggling over the reality that daughter Concepcion had lost her heart to a foreign diplomat and of a different religion.

Meanwhile determined to fulfil not only his longing for Concha but a lust for California, Rezanov daring to dream both of an impossible to arrange marriage between himself of the Russian Orthodox faith and this daughter of Roman Catholicism and the establishment thereafter of a collaborative Russian enterprise on Spanish soil.

Subsequently recounting to his own Minister of Foreign Affairs,

> Seeing that my situation was not improving,
> expecting every day that some
> misunderstanding would arise,
> and having but little confidence in

my own ship's people,
I resolved to change my politeness
for a more serious tone.

Finally, I imperceptibly created in Dona Concepcion
an impatience to hear something serious from me,
which caused me to ask her hand,
to which she consented.

My proposal created consternation in her parents,
who had been reared in fanaticism.
The difference in religion
and the prospective separation from their daughter
made it a terrible blow for them.

They ran to the missionaries,
who did not know what to do;
they hustled poor Concepcion to church,
confessed her and urged her to refuse me,
but her resolution finally overcame them all.
The holy fathers appealed to the decision
of the throne of Rome,
but if I could not accomplish my nuptials
I had at least the preliminary act performed,
the marriage contract drawn up,
and forced them to betroth us.

From that day forward Resanov as all but son-in-law
of Commandante Arguello finding no more secrets
existing between himself and the Californios. Each
and every Spanish government official embracing him
openly as though their own.

Ultimately even a besieged Governor Arrellaga
capitulating to this unprecedented display of

democracy amongst an otherwise autocratic society.

The Spanish Governor's complicity even going so far as to see royal soldiers under Cadet Luis Antonio Arguello's supervision being ordered both to unload a Russian's ship and correspondingly restock it as per the Chamberlain's own directives with quantities of whatever he desired.

Setting an irreversible precedent for pragmatic trade that would ultimately precipitate fortunes upon all Californios.

Padres returning armed with precious tools, ladies at the Royal Presidio in possession of new dishes and tablecloths. Even Governor Arrellaga sporting a smart pair of Yankee shoes.

And Rezanov carrying away more than enough food with which to resuscitate his enterprise. The Juno setting sail on August 1, 1806 stocked with wheat, corn, barley, oats, dried peas and beans, and of course an ample supply of wine and cheese (this was, after all, California).

Yet that first legitimized foreign trading vessel sailing out of San Francisco Bay transporting something altogether intangible and far more precious to the Californios than tradegoods.

As poet Bret Harte subsequently immortalized with eloquent prose,

It carried with it the heart of their beloved
Concepcion.

Rezanov and the Arguellos having reached an agreement.

Following his return to St. Petersburg the Chamberlain would secure special dispensation as Ambassador Extraordinare of the Czar to Madrid. Where he planned an appeal for establishment of understandings between the two superpowers concerning trade in California.

Before returning by way of Mexico to claim his bride.

Grand plans aside, the lovely senorita never seeing her prince charming again.

If Nikkolai does not come back,

she would tell those who chided her for accepting Resanov's affectation,

it is because he is dead.

And so he was.

Thirty-six years passing before head of the Hudson's Bay Company Sir George Simpson calling personally upon Concepcion to convey both condolences and details. Nikkolai having suffered a fatal fall from his horse somewhere between Okhotsk and St. Petersburg.

Sir George then presenting her as proof the gold locket containing strands of Concha's own hair, which she had given Resanov previously. Those locks now woven with that of her betrothed.

Never had Concepcion doubted Nikkolai's love for her.

And feigning subsequent lovers, assumed rather a religious vocation, serving first the Franciscan and later Dominican orders as sister and or nun.

With Russian Sitka ever revering the beautiful Concepcion as their own angel of mercy.

Meanwhile though never condoned by the Spanish Crown, Russians arriving not only to trade but to live in California.

A bond forged during crisis between Russian Alaska and Spanish California precipitating establishment of Rossoya (Russia), or Fort Ross, north of San Francisco along the Sonoma Coast.

Where on May 12, 1812, Ivan Kuskoff honored Concepcion as special Catholic intercessory and spiritual guardian of Russian California during his dedicatory prayer.

So it was that Russia committed a second and blatantly illegal act, this time of trespass against the Spanish Crown.

Nonetheless Californios, abandoned as they seemed to have become, and sympathetic towards the Arguellos, considering the perceived banality of said arrangements as albethem unorthodox otherwise mutually beneficial.

With the fact that a Russian flag now flying over California's north coast going pragmatically unreported by Arrellaga's official successor as Governor, Concepcion's father, Josef Dario Arguello.

Who eventually acknowledged said pretense in a missive to his Viceroy while assuring the same that albehim insufficiently armed to effectively repel said incursion, he was nonetheless carefully monitoring the situation.

Unspoken being the reality that he conducted said surveillance amidst convivial dinner parties over shared glasses of Russian Cognac and Spanish brandy.

Aside from which no official discourse on trade between the Russian Czar and the King of Spain is ever known to have taken place.

FOUNTAINHEAD

alifornia's utopian experience attained full stature with Lasuen's triumph at San Luis Rey de Francia.

Where the largest mission ever established anywhere in North America evoked John Duns' vision fulfilled.

Most urbane on the frontier, this, California's nineteenth installment itself sustaining three satellite settlements.

Standing as but one of two mammoth Southern California concerns. Merging on the north as it did with over the top success achieved at San Juan Capistrano.

Whose great stone Church while larger yet stood dwarfed by the expansive compound erected around San Luis Rey's central plaza.

A brilliant light visible up and down the coast for miles shining forth each night from within the highest dome of both temples at San Juan as well as San Luis Rey. Stunning imagery in an otherwise remote backwater of Western civilization.

Lasuen's King of Missions harboring great promise from its inception in 1798.

Prompting placement of the Franciscan's own architect extraordinare Fray Antonio Peyri in charge.

Who designed and constructed said splendor amidst a beautiful and densely populated coastal valley adjacent to successfully established San Juan, where as anticipated recruits came easily. It's population quickly swelling to more than three thousand baptized novices, with twice as many gentiles residing analogously therein.

Beyond its sixty-acre campus and extensive hacienda roaming fifty-five thousand head of cattle, sheep and horses across a fifteen square league stretch of Southern California beachhead.

Elsewhere, despite opposition and engendered resentment, now flourishing some two dozen private estates all grubstaked by and each mirroring the missions in both grandeur and abundance.

Indios next finding themselves compelled not only to accommodate this newly landed gentry but under orders from Don Carlos IV provisioning every Royal Presidio as well.

Whereupon shipments from San Blas ceased altogether.

The symbiotic relationship subsequently forged between Missions, Royal Presidios and private estates becoming all-important to California's survival.

Gratefully with but a few years of drought proving the exception, Nature cooperating by providing more than sufficient harvests for not merely sustaining but additionally accommodating expansion.

With now co-dependent Indian missions and private estates understandably offsetting costs incurred maintaining both each other as well as the military through bartering excess hides, tallow, brandy, grains and etc. in an albeit illegal foreign trade conveniently overlooked by understanding Governor Josef Dario Arguello.

As no longer in receipt either of pay or supplies from the Crown a pragmatic Royalist deemed such exchange necessary if only to maintain efficient government operations.

In a kingdom of expansive grasslands and developed animal husbandry all derived the true wellspring of their budding affluence from livestock.

Mission trained Indios providing America with it's first vaqueros, or cowboys, to watch over extensive herds of half-wild cattle and horses.

Managing large-scale ranching operations the size and success of which most assuredly would have impressed even Father Kino.

Stock raising underscoring all growth.

So it was that California's lifestyle came to revolve around the cowboy and or ranchero (rancher) and his horse.

Not surprisingly then with regard to horsemanship Californians stood unrivaled. Foreign visitors suggesting they surpassed even Russian Cossacks and South American gauchos in both skill and grace.

Life on but one vast rancho (ranch) engendering the correspondingly independent mindset sustained by distance from Mexico City (let alone Madrid), otherwise fiscal abandonment and a free roaming aspect inherent with any ranching society.

Bestowing upon Californios in particular an extraordinary sense of autonomy.

As personal intervention in local affairs, even to the extent of assuming responsibility for maintaining the King's soldiers, gave rise to a not only involved but proprietary citizenry.

This coupled with the fact that most Californios were additionally related through marriage and embraced as per Franciscan mentoring inclusively together with all Indios leading to an unprecedented sense of community.

Writing one outside observer,

> Being almost all related to each other,
> they live in great intimacy.
>
> There is no rank among them.
> One who has become rich by his industry
> is neither admired nor envied by any one.
>
> Theft is extremely rare.
>
> Murder is without example.

Gente de razon, which in California consisted primarily of Spanish Soldados Distinguidos, coming to assume patriarchal responsibility both for their own families as well as those of the Presidios and Mission communities.

As long standing intimates subsequently armed through clandestine trade with tremendous wealth emerging themselves a powerful cabildo destined to assume control over the entire province.

This budding local aristocracy clearly demonstrating that they were not above breaking even the law where necessary in order to secure a sound economic future for their families.

Which most did and to the dismay of officials a way off in Mexico City. The subsequent flood of merchants anxiously cashing in on such laissez-faire bypassing all protocol and taxation to establish blatantly illegal joint ventures involving themselves and not only mission communities but gente de razon directly.

Beginning in 1809 when a lucrative exchange conducted openly between British merchant ships <u>Flora</u> and <u>Eagle</u> and the citizenry of Monterey prompted John Begg and Company to set up onsite brokerage facilities.

Such daring exhibition but encouraging others to follow suit.

Contracts drawn up between John Begg and Company and California's curious business amalgam pledging annual exchange courtesy of no less than one vessel per year.

With during the first four years of said arrangement not one but rather an astounding one hundred and thirty four trading ships calling upon a heretofore obscure and off limits provincial capitol.

Precipitating in estimated income a working capital of $4.5 to $5 million nineteenth century dollars.

All of which going cavalierly unreported, rationalized away by virtue of Spain's own default.

And bestowing a seigneurialism imported from Old Spain. Rancheros and men of business suddenly employing the well-healed titles of Lordship and Lady (Don and Dona) when referring to each other.

Complicating an already complex balance of power between Californios, Franciscan tutored novices and local gentile chieftains.

Fusing California into a different sort of society altogether. Where Lords and Ladies played an active role as godparents in mentoring Indian children otherwise refused social recognition.

On the other hand should anyone Indian or otherwise express interest in trading whatever modest items they might lay claim to, all that was required, above and beyond said barter being observance of a tithe paid directly to on-site Church officials.

So it was that Mission Plazas became crowded marketplaces particularly on Sunday's following Mass when all gathered to trade.

With provincial commercialism remaining dependent upon the foreign export of hides, tallow and sea otter skins.

Yankees hailed by the Californios as rather Baltimores,

what with so many of them sailing in from out of Baltimore, endlessly remonstrating the province for failing to develop more of its own industries,

Their rejoinder was ever
that nobody starved in California.
And that many enjoyed luxurious living.

And, in fact, as English Americans hauled away larders filled with tallow, bales of hides and magazines restocked in produce, grains and wine, they left behind more than enough by way of manufactured and processed goods with which to outfit an entirely new and hybrid civilization.

Their imports reduced the crudities of frontier living.
And gave the gentry reason
to regard themselves as enjoying
the well-earned rewards of service to king and state.

Grandees without a court, aristocrats in a virtual republic, European-born, Catholic and now (by frontier standards) wealthy in the extreme, ultimately forty-five families forging an alliance that soon prevailed even over the Franciscans.

Yet as most had commenced their ascendancy to said riches and power from stations of humility and struggle, these three thousand or so suddenly affluent Californios remaining at least for the time being devoted patrons of an altered yet decidedly Franciscan agenda.

As for one brief shining moment a truly Arcadian existence distilled upon them all:

Supremest happiness was theirs;
the happiness that knows no want,
that harbors no unattainable longing,
no desires that might not be gratified.

Everyone worked hard when necessary.
All took pride in their work.

But more in anticipation
of the fun that came right at the end of it
rather than for any anticipated distant reward.

Yankee obsession with labor, profit and savings for the
future ever mystifying such a people. Who, simply
stated, did not love money.

The degree of grace and manners expressed amongst
them ever mystifying Yanks.

The empirical law of human nature,
which asserts that youth is impetuous
and old age cautious, found in them an exception.

The young men were impetuous,
and the old men scarcely less so.

A life-long experience
failed to generate circumspection amongst them.

Everyone whether wealthy in the extreme or fiscally
impoverished remaining endowed regardless with a
decidely aristocratic grace,

The standard of manners in California
always exceeded the standard of living.

So it was that ruling in harmony with the Padre (Franciscan Father) who functioned as head of neophyte community, Californio fathers (patrons) each in charge of their own prolific families eased naturally into newfound importance with a grace and order elsewhere unobserved. For,

> In the breast of the old time Californians
> love of family was stronger than selfish
> and vile interests.

As fountainhead all lines of dependency radiating outward from the embrace of either Padre or Patron.

With the mission as example affording food and shelter to anyone requesting it, a private ranchero similarly offering not only to wife and children, but in-laws, extended families, orphans, neophytes and in many cases entire gentile villages (rancherias) every amenity available.

Replicating that of a knight's largesse. Reciprocity dictating a patriarchal authority running so deep as to permit even flogging of his lordship's married children should such disciplinary action be deemed necessary.

Still, overall, as at each mission, love ruling the day.

Every evening before filing off to bed a Patron's family solemnly knelling before and kissing his hand. Mission neophytes acknowledging their respective Padre with similar displays of love and respect.

Living thusly and surrounded by such grace it seeming

to some observers as if in California the world had
returned to its infancy,

> when religion was but a love of the beautiful
>   and childhood lasted for a hundred years.

This enigmatic marriage of selflessness and pride
wherein both grace and extravagant hospitality knew
no bounds, being the stuff from which fairy tales
are made.

A FAIRY TALE

S uch was California's Golden Age of Indian missions and Spanish ranchos. A time when one traveled the entire length of El Camino Real without coin yet never lacking for food, shelter or convivial camaraderie.

Great oaken doors swinging ever inward to welcome whomsoever might call. The bounty of rancho and hacienda alike extended openly and across the board,

Esta en su casa
(You are in your own home).

A man's house and possessions like those of knights of old imparted freely be it for a day or a year to friend and stranger alike.

The occasional visitor in want discovering a satchel of gold or silver placed bedside, from which they were,

silently bidden to ease a need
their host had too much delicacy to mention.

Horses available for all to ride. Long cords or leather straps dangling from harnesses making them readily accessible. But to snatch up a leash being to conduct the beast on until it tired. Leaving off then and acquiring a different mount upon which to continue one's journey.

Which but led to the next estate or mission from which similarly gracious hospitality would be dispensed.

Celebrating a life lived out-of-doors, most estates reflecting mission template in that they were laid out around a cloister, or interior courtyard.

Writer and Indian rights activist Helen Hunt Jackson resurrecting such imagery in her classic southern California romance, <u>Ramona</u>:

The house was of adobe,
low, with a wide veranda on the three sides
of the inner court,
and a still broader one across the entire front,
which looked to the south.

These verandas,
especially those on the inner court,
were supplementary rooms to the house.
The greater part of the family life went on in them.

Nobody stayed inside the walls,
except when it was necessary.

All the kitchen work,
except the actual cooking,
was done here,
in front of the kitchen doors and windows.

Babies slept,
were washed,
sat in the dirt and played,
on the veranda.

The women said their prayers,
took their naps, and wove their lace there.

Old Juanita shelled her beans there,
and threw the pods down on the tile floor,
til towards night they were sometimes
piled high up around her,
like cornhusks at a husking.

The herdsmen and shepherds smoked there,
lounged there,
trained their dogs there;

there the young made love,
and the old dozed;

the benches, which ran the entire length
of the walls,
were worn into hollows,
and shone like satin;
the tiled floors also were broken
and sunk in places,
making little wells,
which filled up in times of hard rains,
and was then an invaluable addition
to the children's resources
for amusement,
and also to the comfort of the dogs, cats, and fowls,
who picked about among them,
taking sips from each.

The arched veranda along the front was
a delightsome place.
It must have been eighty feet long, at least,
for the doors of five large rooms opened on it.

The westernmost rooms had been added on,
and made four steps higher than the others;

which gave to that end of the veranda
the look of a balcony, or loggia.

Here the Senora kept her flowers;
great red water-jars,
hand-made by the Indians
at San Luis Obispo Mission,
stood in close rows against the walls,
and in them were always growing
fine geraniums, carnations,
and yellow-flowered musk.

The Senora's passion for musk
she had inherited from her mother.
It was so strong that she sometimes
wondered at it;
and one day,
as she sat with Father Salvierderra in the veranda,
she picked a handful of the blossoms,
and giving them to him, said,
'I do not know why it is,
but it seems to me if I were dead
I could be brought to life by the smell of the musk.'

'It is in your blood, Senora,' the old monk replied.
'When I was last in your father's house in Seville,
your mother sent for me to her room,
and under her window was a stone balcony
full of growing musk,
which so filled the room with its odor
that I was like to faint.
But she said it cured her of diseases,
and without it she fell ill.
You were a baby then.'

'Yes,' cried the Senora,
'but I recollect the balcony.
I recollect being lifted down into a bed
of blooming yellow flowers;
but I did not know what they were.
How strange!'

'No. Not strange, daughter,'
replied Father Salvierderra.
'It would have been stranger
if you had not acquired the taste,
thus drawing it in with the mother's milk.
It would behoove mothers to remember
this far more than they do.'

Besides the geraniums and carnations
and musk in the red jars,
there were many sorts of climbing vines, -
some coming from the ground,
and twining around the pillars of the veranda;
some growing in great bowls,
swung by cords from the roof of the veranda,
or set on shelves against the walls.

These bowls were of gray stone,
hollowed and polished,
shining smooth inside and out.

They also had been made by the Indians,
nobody knew how many ages ago,
scooped and polished by the patient creatures,
with only stones for tools.

Among these vines,
singing from morning till night,

hung the Senora's canaries and finches,
half a dozen of each,
all of different generations,
raised by the Senora.

She was never without a young bird-family on hand;
and all the way from Bonaventura to Monterey,
it was thought a piece of good luck
to come into possession of a canary or finch
of Senora Moreno's raising.

Between the veranda and the river meadows,
out on which it looked,
all was garden, orange grove, and almond orchard;
the orange grove always green,
never without snowy bloom or golden fruit;
the garden never without flowers,
summer or winter;
and the almond orchard,
in early spring,
a fluttering canopy of pink and white petals, which,
seen from the hills on the opposite side of the river,
looked as if rosy sunrise clouds had fallen,
and become tangled in the treetop.

On either hand stretched away other orchards-
peach, apricot, pear, apple, pomegranate;
and beyond these,
vineyards.

Nothing was to be seen
but verdure of bloom or fruit,
at whatever time of year you sat
on the Senora's south veranda.

A wide straight walk
shaded by a trellis so knotted and
twisted with grapevines
that little was to be seen of the trellis woodwork,
led straight down from the veranda steps,
through the middle of the garden,
to a little brook at the foot of it.

Across this brook,
in the shade of a dozen gnarled old willow-trees,
were set the broad flat stone washboards
on which was done all the family washing.

No long dawdling,
and no running away from work
on the part of the maids,
thus close to the eye of the Senora
at the upper end of the garden;
and if they had known how picturesque
they looked there,
kneeling on the grass,
lifting the dripping linen out of the water,
rubbing it back and forth on the stones,
sousing it,
wringing it,
splashing the clear water in each other's faces,
they would have been content to stay at the washing
day in and day out,
for there was always somebody
to look on from above.

Hardly a day passed that the Senora had not visitors.

Visitors at Monterey were more often welcomed into an
adaptation of the aforementioned home as described.

"Baltimores" elaborating upon ranch styles to conjure two-story, balconied affairs dubbed Monterey townhomes. The popular architectural hybrid soon replicated in every settlement of any consequence.

Of course few lived in ranchhouses or townhomes. Still, grand or modest, most occupied structures built of but common adobe.

And seigneurialism aside, received with equanimity whether sleeping in a many-roomed estancia on a bed imported from France or upon a cot fashioned of leather straps and wood planks in a single room shack.

As across this Latin Arcadia the beauty and grace of California's innocence flowered.

So as to be suggested abroad that a Californio might best be considered the Rembrandt or Michelangelo amongst those having mastered the art of living well.

Exemplifying as he did a tendency towards making pleasure one's chief objective. Formalizing celebrations upon the slightest of pretexts.

Social and religious festivals as in Old Spain revolving around a birth, confirmation, wedding, visitation from dignitaries, harvest or any even flimsy excuse for celebrating life in abundance.

And typically lasting days on end to the further accompaniment of solemn Te Deums and High Masses. Providing ample opportunity for full display of couture amongst clergy, gente de razon and neophyte alike.

With presidial and private feasts prepared over open fires on courtyard kitchens hosted by gracious patrons now splendidly attired in finery dripping of imported silver and gold.

Spanish guitar, violin and rhythmic hand clapping accompanying the more gregarious engaging in fiery fandangos and comic comparsas.

Inducing both playful flirtation and serious courtship and often at feminine instigation. When by snatching a sombrero or breaking cascarones (eggshells) filled with bits of gold and silver paper or scented water upon an individual's head a woman expressed her desire to dance with or otherwise engage the object of her attentions.

Lovely senoritas as gaily attired suitors (in fabrics imported from China, accessorized with shoes of velvet and satin) employing rebozos (cotton scarves) in provocative and graceful gestures.

Insatiable machismo responding with equally bold displays of sport, horsemanship and couture. Attired to the nines (in gilt-laced pants, loose fitting linen or Muslim cotton shirts and smart black boleros) cavorting in events choreographed but to flaunt their own beauty and skill.

Part and partial with such ostentation being ownership of a finely crafted saddle often inlaid with copious amounts of silver or gold and draped in ribbons. Presaging contemporary California's obsession for extravagantly accessorized automobiles.

Accessible to all "Indian baseball" uniting participant and spectator. With teams comprised of as many as two hundred players, each engagement lasting many days.

Traditional relay races between missions bridging miles both in distance and cultural diversity. As all assembled to cheer on a favored local or one deemed most fleet of foot.

Themselves inventors of communal pageantry, California's Franciscans staging posadas or processions and passion plays with abandon. Everyone cast (at Serra's instigation) as players in productions conducted against backdrops of elaborately constructed sets.

Concerts, too, being routine. Even the occasional work of original composition performed. Novices staging their own chorales, string quartets and orchestras.

Ongoing "lectures" and workshops showcasing pride in learning Spanish and or the basics of Latin.

While to the east yet stretched a wild and untamed frontier, California's kind, gentle and loving Arcadians living out the dream of Greek philosophers as interpreted by Franciscan religious and adapted through laissez faire commerce.

Fray Fermin Lasuen's triumph standing squarely upon adroit Serra's shoulders and in full possession of what Brother Junipero would have identified as authentic soul.

Orthodox successor Reverend Father President Estevan Tapis fretting over this openly displayed and uninhibited passion both for spiritual as well as physical indulgence. Yet unable or unwilling to impose censure.

Even the Sabbath failing to forestall such enthusiastic living. Assuming as it did the grandeur of but another posada, what with every family making its way in full costume from village or estate to the nearest church.

A spectacle rendered particularly stunning at the Provincial Capitol, where on Holy Days one seemingly endless (in fact, three mile long) parade making its way en masse to Mission San Carlos:

The magnificent Governor,
in company with his wife and children,
escorted by a uniformed guard
and further accompanied by caballeros
in slashed and gilt-laced pantalones and jackets,
their somewhat staid, by comparison, senoras
shrouded in black lace mantillas,
keeping an eye on their daughters,
whose glances, decorous but eager,
roved over the rim of the carretas (ox carts)
as some hero with jingling spurs
curvetted past.

Peasants under their huge sombreros,
gray-gowned friars in sandals,
Indian muleteers, vaqueros and laborers
in their brilliantly colored serapes
and dull cotton smocks.

Scarlet, gold and blue livened the black and white
and tawny brown
of this frequent procession,
as it made its way along the shore of the sea
sapphire and amethyst
and spread with the hammered gold
of the kelp fields,
on through the green slopes,
on among the giant columns
of the Monterey pines,
to San Carlos,
on the hill above the river,
with its red-tiled roof,
and thick bluish stone walls,
as the ancient lyric from its grand belfry
rang out to call all faithful
to mass.

Marginally dignified affairs compromised by oxen drawn carts, laden with families decked out in Sunday best, lurching and tipping pell-mell as each raced past the other to arrive first at Mass.

Stakes running even higher than one might at first glance suspect, what with on-lookers wagering money or livestock against the outcome.

But it would be a need to gather in free roaming cattle that provided Arcadia with it's grandest *fete champetre*. Every autumn mission Indian alcaldes broadcasting a date for collecting through communal roundup their economic wellspring.

And in which everyone participated.

Following the strenuous work of separating and branding livestock, conducting great festive overnight picnic encampments out in the open air.

With nightlong feasting on copious amounts of barbecue and paella, again, as always, accompanied by music, song and dance.

Californios becoming adept at taking the edge from off a hard day's riding through indulgence in the bounty of their own vineyards and orchards.

Straight brandy (aguardiente), as the Spaniard's distillate of choice, ubiquitously aged in casks made of native California oak, being liberally employed to eradicate the chill of an often damp and foggy coastal night.

Rodeos always held in conjunction with the annual roundups. While correspondingly each Royal Presidio conducting a grand ball, hosted by its respective commandante as his way of thanking the local constituency for funding him.

Out of doors under the starry canopy of heaven or beneath silver chandeliers within the walls of a royal presidio, every annual roundup lending romance to California's grandest social expression.

An aura of magnificent community and familial bond distilling upon such extraordinary occasions engulfing with the same joie de vive experienced since time immemorial by California's earliest inhabitants; what with everyone fed, clothed, loved and respected.

Occasioning a powerful sense of well being and shared destiny. Precipitating unrivaled contentment.

Which coupled with California's innocence occasioned true happiness. As together they lived out the romantic dream that captures a tired world's imagination still.

With outsider witnesses quickly falling under its spell,

They ate of her fruits;
they basked in her sunshine;
they breathed her 'soft Lydian airs,'

They looked upon her fair sons and daughters;
they enjoyed the generous hospitality of her people;
they tasted of the ease and peace of the life;
and, like the lotus-eaters of old,
they forgot home and family
and determined to remain forever
in this Arcadia by the western sea.

THE TREASURE CHEST

While more than one hundred thousand "gentiles" still held sway over California's destiny, yet tens of thousands had long since thrown their fortunes together in Christian utopianism.

Which following transference of Old (Baja) California over to Dominican Custodies remained confined as late as 1820 along a narrow stretch of coastal real estate extending north from San Diego to San Francisco.

And upon which some three thousand Californios bestowed a decidedly glamorous Spanish sheen to an otherwise Indian masterpiece.

Men of commerce from the great wide world beyond engaging in trade with this California of the Golden Age describing it as a most contented and happy community.

> More free from care, anxiety, and trouble
> than any other in the world,

writing one Yank destined to remain.

> After receiving so much kindness from them,
> I arrived at the conclusion that
> there was no place in the world
> where I could enjoy more true happiness
> and truer friendship
> than amongst them.

There were no courts,
no juries, no lawyers,
nor any need of them.

Shipping firms sell their wares up and
down the coast,
returning in twelve or eighteen month's time
to receive payment in hides and tallow
and without incident.

The people are honest and hospitable,
their word as good as their bond;

Indeed, bonds and notes of hand
are entirely unknown amongst the natives.

Historian Bancroft going even further to suggest that
living life as they did, absolutely unconfined either
socially or politically,

or as nearly free as it were possible
for poor erring humanity to be,

these citizens of a Saturnitus, masters of all that their
eyes surveyed, the beautiful earth together with its fruits
as free for the taking as the sweet air and sunshine,

their lands unlimited,
and cattle on a thousand hills,

how should they be less else than happy,
than lovers of home and country,

and eternally children.

Quintessentially so being Luis Antonio Arguello, who following his posting as Commandante of the Royal Presidio at San Francisco and together with cousin Gabriel Moraga, son of presidio founder Jose Joaquin, prevailed upon Father (and Jose's Uncle) Governor Josef Dario Arguello to push further afield the boundaries of Californialand.

Together marching into what are now Tehama and Shasta Counties. Surmounting the Trinity Alps to return through present-day Humboldt and Mendocino Counties ecstatic over a primeval magnificence revealed.

And correspondingly barraging Rome with petitioning to see installed additional missions amidst the giant forests and stupendous mountains surveyed.

Moraga then pressing into and across Sacramento's Delta country, where he found himself being assaulted not by savage warriors but rather butterflies. Standing before the very granite gates of California's mighty Sierra Nevada at a site accordingly christened Mariposa (Butterfly), envisioning still more missions and royal presidios rising up before him.

The possibility of implementing such grand schemes remaining anything but unrealistic, what with successor to Estevan Tapis as Reverend Father President Mariano Payeras not only turning a blind eye towards but openly participating in the illegal coastal trading frenzy that had rapidly transformed California into a wealthy frontier outpost.

Indian missions with facilities for warehousing goods now serving as California's first distribution and shopping centers.

The Dominguez/Guiterrez Rancho at San Pedro in particular evolving into an unofficial port of entry for Southern California's grandest ranchos.

Anxious to direct business away from Los Angeles so as to facilitate further growth and expansion elsewhere, Arguello the younger as Commandante of the Royal Presidio at San Francisco issuing, yet without the authority to do so, a course altering proclamation. In which he pronounced San Francisco officially open for Government sanctioned trade.

And having lent to said enterprise an aire of legitimacy shrewdly slapping tariffs upon the same. Precipitating a windfall. Which he then used to pay public officials and soldiers with the first cold hard cash most of them had ever held in their hands.

Thusly empowering all with genuine coinage of their own. To themselves become players in an escalating commercialism.

Fealty towards such a hero, who thought always of California first, remaining entire and lasting.

And put to the test following Josef Arguello's death, when Spanish Governor Pablo Vicente de Sola arrived upon the scene from Seville as successor.

Only to witness countless foreign ships offloading and taking on merchandise up and down California's coast. And discovering that such blatantly illegal trade was being used to fund unauthorized tariffs collected and distributed at the whimsy of local commandantes.

Outraged Sola promptly arresting to deport in chains all co-conspirators. Save one.

Of the famously popular native son just returning from yet another exploratory adventure into the country's interior, a Spanish Governor, fearful of mutiny on the part of not only presidial soldiery but his entire constituency, choosing prudently to administer little more than a proverbial slap on the wrist.

Only then to discover and immediately order terminated Arguello's transactions with an illegally positioned Russian outpost.

Rescue efforts implemented by Franciscans seeing exonerated and returned all of Sola's would be exiles. A briefing by Reverend Father President Payeras concerning the reality that was California's economic situation helping a stunned Spanish official recognize his communities authentic need for trade, illegal or otherwise, if only to sustain its phenomenal growth.

Once having grasped the enormity of a Spanish King's default concerning unpaid wages and in arrears operating funds Sola responding with establishment of an official Government Customs House at Monterey.

Wherein all traders were compelled to report and pay duty upon imports before conducting chaffare anywhere in California. But to a Governor appointed comptroller rather than renegade commandantes.

Posting literate, somewhat fluent in English and aspiring Juan Bautista Alvarado as overseer of said daunting task.

The phenomenal fiscal success captured by Sola's Customs House ultimately tempting fate and intern Alvarado both.

At Mission Santa Barbara alone Indian's reportedly owning 396,000 cattle, 62,000 horses and 321,000 hogs, sheep and goats; its harvest of a single year yielding 123,000 bushels of grain.

Prior to his triumph at Mission San Luis Rey Lasuen had himself launched similarly envisioned Mission Gloriosisimo Principe Arcangel Senor San Miguel.

With Christian communities established following Lasuen's reign reflecting the expanding needs of a developing and potential laden economic titan.

Santa Ines installed under directives from Reverend Father President Estevan Tapis adjacent to the Chumash village of Alahulapu on September 17, 1804. And while begun much like any other Indian mission finding itself ultimately being pressed into service as a seminary for higher education.

In 1817 Reverend Father President Mariano Payeras launching Mission San Rafael Archangel near sunny Anaguani north of San Francisco. Not as a traditional community but rather inorder to provide California with its first hospital.

Newest and last of the Franciscan communities being

undertaken at the request of none other than Governor Luis Antonio Arguello himself. Who following news of political unrest at Mexico City pressed Payeras' successor Reverend Father President Jose Senan to install a strategic mission in Sonoma.

One that might stand guard as it were against, and otherwise effectively deter any threat of incursion from potential collusion between revolutionaries in New Spain and politically indifferent Russians.

Nevertheless, even with Arguello vowing personally to secure its funding, Fray Senan hesitating.

Luis Antonio's chaplain and frequent companion in exploration Father Blas de Ordaz then intervening. Anxious to accommodate the Californio he had himself schooled, watched grow to manhood and always deeply respected.

Father Blas dedicating Mission San Francisco Solano adjacent to Huchi (today's Sonoma) on July 4, 1823. Reverend Father President Senan subsequently capitulating and ultimately bestowing upon the enterprise his blessing.

Arguello's sister Concepcion volunteering to assist all interested Indian catechums as their teacher.

Luis Antonio's presidial mission amalgam proving to be California's last Franciscan collaboration.

Whilst beyond remained as yet untrammeled millions of acres of primeval redwood rain forest, the wild American Serengeti of California's great Central

Valley and still secret granite cathedrals of its mighty Sierra Nevada.

Overwhich as Governor, Arguello the younger now ruled. When upon receipt of news concerning establishment of a new and independent Republic Pablo Vicente de Sola rushed as delegate to Mexico City.

Visions of more missions and grander cities aside, few other than Franciscans who remained ever in direct communication both with Spain and Rome, could have foreseen the sudden and entire collapse of Spanish America.

As no longer taking dictation from either Madrid or Mexico City, rumored turmoil abroad had done little to alarm independent minded and wealthy Californians.

Their magnificent sense of autonomy ending abruptly however when French-commissioned pirate ships showed up as but the vanguard of invaders intent upon plundering a now world famous and by Spanish default vulnerable Treasure Chest.

PETER AND THE PIRATES

rrival of the mighty sailing vessel Columbia brought a decidedly "American" presence into California waters.

First Yankee ship ever to circumnavigate the globe, namesake for the <u>Columbia</u> River (which its captain and crew discovered) and now putting in regularly at Monterey to collect harvested sea otter pelts for exchange in the China Trade.

<u>Columbia's</u> navigator Peter Corney well aware of a Russian presence along the California coast. But surprised to discover extant an actual Slavic base of operations on otherwise decidedly Spanish soil.

Regardless, it would be French mercenaries and not Russian trappers that caught him completely off guard. When at Honolulu in May of 1818 he found himself being recruited to assist the same with an outright raid on Monterey.

Slatting in behind Corney being the Peruvian ship <u>Santa Rosa</u>. Not in and of itself unusual. That was until it's "owners" quickly sold her to King Kamehameha for a paltry 6,000 picals of sandalwood.

At a waterfront saloon Corney discovering the truth behind wholesale abandonment of an otherwise valuable vessel.

Patriot Jose de San Martin had expelled Spanish government officials from Argentina. And was at that very moment leading an army of five thousand freedom fighters westward across the Andes to "liberate" Chile.

Without ships of his own, having issued cash concessions for assistance from any mercenary willing to blockade the Chilean coast against anticipated Spanish intervention.

War has a curious way of turning piracy into patriotism, as both Peter Corney and California were about to discover.

For the man willing to sell his political affiliations for cash is often not above exploiting with similarly wholesale abandon any other such opportunities when presented.

So it was that San Martin's milieu of "patriots" looted and pillaged indiscriminately and but for their own personal gain.

Enter Paul Andres Bouchard. Who at age twenty-five had already become a hardened veteran of the Napoleonic Wars.

And without hesitation lined his own pockets while otherwise engaged with introducing French Enlightenment to Latin America.

That is until men commandeering his consort the Santa Rosa mutinied.

Leaving officers abandoned along Old California's coast.

Then justifiably fearful of reprisal sailing directly for Honolulu as though their lives depended upon it, there to dispose of both ship and all evidence, with the hope of disappearing incognito and in style.

Upon receipt of word concerning said treason Bouchard abandoning his post as part of the Chilean blockade. Sailing <u>L'Argentina</u> unbeknownst to the <u>Santa Rosa</u> in hot pursuit.

Corney having just been engaged at a seaside tavern with one of the mutineers now surprised to find himself being interviewed by none other than Paul Andres Bouchard.

Who had already rounded up and executed ringleaders of the heist. Extending clemency to accomplices in exchange for both the return of his ship together with its South American treasure.

And this done, now focusing attentions upon retrieval of loyal crewmembers offloaded in California. Not surprisingly hitting upon the idea of conducting extra curricular plundering and pillaging in route.

And upon being apprised of Corney's familiarity with California waters now intrusively recruiting the British expatriate's services as navigator.

Bouchard's grand proclamations regarding the inherent nobility in liberating "oppressed" Spanish subjects smacked of John Paul Jones. Which of course appealed to Corney.

So it was that Peter left his commission with the <u>Columbia</u> to commandeer an incongruous band of freedom fighting mercenaries.

Anxiously avoiding detection yet in sore need of supplies conducting all first to Russian Fort Rossoya. Where Ivan Kuskoff outfitted purposefully vague Bouchard while dutifully dispatching a messenger off to alert his friend Luis Antonio Arguello at San Francisco concerning the ominous presence of ships manned by suspicious strangers.

Apprised of Kuskhoff's betrayal, Bouchard aborting plans for attacking San Francisco. Sailing rather in haste to Monterey. Striking there before word of his presence could reach the Governor. Corney remembering:

We made sail towards the Bay of Monterey.

The Commodore (Bouchard) ordered me into the bay,
and to anchor in a good position for
covering the landing,
while he would keep his ship under weigh,
and send his boats in to assist me.

Being well acquainted with the bay
I ran in and came to at midnight,
under the fort.

A Spaniard hailed me frequently
to send a boat on shore,
which I declined.

Before morning they had the battery manned,
and seemed quite busy.

I got a spring on the cable,
and at daylight opened fire on the fort,
which was briskly returned from the two batteries.

Finding it useless to fire at the batteries,
the one being so much above us
that our shot had no visible effect,
the Commodore came in with his boats,
and we landed on Point Pinos,
about three miles to the westward of the fort;

And before the Spaniards had time
to bring their field-pieces to attack us,
we were on our march against it.

We halted at the foot of the hill
where it stood for a few minutes,
beat a charge and rushed up,
the Sandwich Islanders (Hawaiians) in front with pikes.

The Spaniards mounted their horses and fled;

A Sandwich islander was the first
to haul down their colours.

We then turned the guns on the town,
where they made a stand,
and after firing a few rounds,
the Commodore sent me with
a party to assault the place,
while he kept possession of the fort.

As we approached the town,
the Spaniards again fled,
after discharging their field-pieces,
and we entered without opposition.

It was well stocked
with provisions and goods of every description,

which we commenced sending
on board the Argentina.

The Sandwich Islanders,
who were quite naked when they landed,
were soon dressed in the Spanish fashion,
and all the sailors
were employed in searching the houses for money,
and breaking and ruining everything.

We took several Creole prisoners,
destroyed all the guns in the fort, etc.

We had three of our men killed and three taken;

Next day a party of horsemen came in sight,
to whom the Commodore sent a flag of truce,
requiring the governor to give up our people
should he wish to save the town.

Three days were granted to consider this proposal,
and on the third day,
not receiving an answer,
he (Bouchard) ordered the town to be fired,
after which we took plenty of livestock on board,
wood, water, etc.,

And on the 1st day of December
got under weigh from Monterey,
and stood along the coast to the southward.

On the 4th we made a village called the Ranch.

Unaware that a Royal Presidio stood fully manned and
armed just over the hill, Bouchard landing to plunder

what was infact the private "Rincon" Rancho of Joseph Francisco Ortega, which because of its size and extensive outbuildings had been mistaken for Santa Barbara itself.

And was quickly routed by a Spanish Royal guard. Two of his men being lassoed and carried off as prisoners. Corney's account continuing,

> This so enraged Captain Bouchard,
> that he ordered the village (Ortega's Ranch)
> to be fired instantly,
> and disembarked all the men.

> After dark we again landed a party well armed
> to try and surprise the Spaniards
> and make some prisoners,
> but the next morning embarked without success.

> We then weighed and made sail along shore
> to the southward, two miles from shore,
> a great number of Spanish troops
> riding along the beach
> at whom we fired several shots.

When the morning fog dissipated on December 14th San Juan Capistrano discovering two phantom ships lying in wait off her coast.

Corney having warned Bouchard to avoid heavily garrisoned San Diego, a pirate left with no alternative but to procure needed provisioning at San Juan before facing the expansive void that is Old (Baja) California.

This fact coupled with a widely accepted rumor that

Franciscans stashed fantastic wealth gathered in from up and down the coast at ambiguous San Juan Capistrano rendering of an otherwise innocuous township a target much too enticing for any pirate to pass up.

In the misty morning air Bouchard eyeing the proverbial city on a hill; San Juan's partially ruined yet stately and radiantly luminescent cathedral crowned, he'd been told, with a cock made of solid gold. Rays of sunlight piercing through overcast skies reflecting the alabaster façade of a regal looking and presumably wealthy establishment.

Aside from whatever treasure this mysterious jewel of the missions possessed, it most assuredly held sufficient appurtenances for sustaining Bouchard's ships through to Chile. And if the fabled bank of San Juan existed, Paul Andres determining he would take that as well.

Unaware that word concerning his approach had arrived in time for transference by heavily laden oxcarts of all valuables as a precautionary measure, on the outside chance of an invasion.

Corney's account continuing:

> The bay is well sheltered,
> with a most beautiful town and mission,
> about two leagues from the beach.
>
> The Commodore sent his boat on shore,
> to say (suggest)
> that if they would give us

an immediate supply of provisions
we would spare their town;
to which they replied,
that we might land if we pleased,
and they would give us an immediate supply of
powder and shot!

The Commodore was very much
incensed at this answer,
and assembled all the officers,
to know what was best to be done.

Bravado displayed by the citizenry of San Juan but
unleashing Bouchard's rage. Corney remembering:

It was,
therefore,
agreed to land,
and give it (the town) up to be pillaged and sacked.

Next morning,
before daylight,
the Commodore ordered me to land
and bring him a sample of the powder and shot,
which I accordingly did,
with a party of 140 men,
well armed,
and two field-pieces.

On our landing,
a party of horsemen came down and fired a few
shots at us,
and ran towards the town.

They made no stand,

and we soon occupied the place.

After breakfast
the people commenced plundering;

We found the town well stocked with everything but
money.

On site prefect Fray Jose Barona describing San Juan's
assailants as,

heretics,
excommunicated persons,
heathen,
and a few Moors,

when, dodging defending gunfire, he witnessed said
mercenaries looting and setting fire to the beautiful
Franciscan Capitol.

A shout ringing out that Bouchard's men had
discovered it's extensive wine cellars, the assault
deteriorating into a four- day long drunken brawl.

Pirates leaving San Juan in torched ruins. Themselves
"toasted" to the point that more than twenty being
transported back to their ships lashed still in a stupor
to the cannons.

Four men allegedly defecting and disappearing into
Californio lore.

Leaving the treasure of San Juan (securely hidden)
together with the honor of a sobered citizenry yet intact.

OJOS AZUELES

When Don Antonio Maria Lugo retired as Commandante of the Royal Presidio at Santa Barbara in 1817 he assumed his illustrious career begun long ago, as a recruit from Sinaloa, had come to an end.

Don Carlos IV honoring a Soldado Distinguido by providing yet another of the old guard desirous of remaining in California with land concessions.

Dona Maria Dolores (Ruiz) regardless, accustomed as she was to urbane Santa Barbara, not fancying residence on far-flung Rancho Antonio. Preferring rather life in the neighboring Pueblo de Los Angeles.

Lovingly compliant Don Antonio responding by constructing there for her a grand and commodious "Monterey" townhome off the main square (plaza). Where two lifelong sweethearts plotted many more happy days together surrounded by family and friends.

Never once as a military officer had Lugo found himself facing off with foreign invaders. That is of course aside from the occasional convivial exchanges between Russian dignitaries at social gatherings and "Baltimores" with whom he swapped cow hides for home furnishings and fashions with which to delight his spouse.

One can well imagine an old soldier's surprise then when on December 6, 1818 he found himself being rousted both out of bed as well as retirement with urgent orders from Commandante Jose de La Guerra at the Royal Presidio of Santa Barbara to return poste haste and prepared for fending off pirates!

Lugo arriving in time to witness the grand Ortega family estate of Rincon going up in flames; Santa Barbara itself having been spared by a fluke of misidentification.

Gratefully no deaths occurring during the malay that ensued. But three pirates had been captured, a fact which came to bare special significance for dependable Don Antonio.

Records concerning the number of prisoners taken varying from one account to another. Peter Corney logging the loss of two men. De La Guerra insisting he'd taken three. Others claiming to have captured four.

Such confusion due no doubt at least in part to cross pollination of events as they occurred during raids conducted upon Monterey, Santa Barbara and thereafter San Juan Capistrano.

The fact remaining that in Don Lugo's capable and compassionate hands came to reside the fate of three prisoners.

Meanwhile back at Los Angeles a relieved Dona Maria hearing her husband's voice amongst the returning makeshift cavalry raced to greet him.

Tears flowing freely as on the threshold of their home she genuflected while vocally expressing gratitude for her husband's safe return.

Only after flinging into his open arms did she notice three unlikely characters sitting mounted upon horses behind him.

One man remembered as having long, thick, black hair sprinkled with gray, tied back and partially covered by a handkerchief topped with South American vicuna cap. Sitting tall in the saddle. Attired otherwise in cavalry gear complete with loose fitting, double-quilted surtout reaching just below his knees, leaving exposed bare calves covered in hair nearly as thick as that on his head and disappearing into black leather boots.

Presenting overall the most intimidating image Maria had beheld since that day long ago when as a little girl she stood before the Quechan giant Olleyqoutequiebe.

Next to said stranger riding a Moor (black man) dressed only in light gray pantaloons. His bare chest and one arm bandaged revealing severe injuries sustained. His handsome heroically angular face and smile disarming. Dona Lugo perceiving fear revealed in his otherwise clear, bright eyes. Which instantly softened her heart.

The third individual, a boyish, flaxen-haired, blue-eyed lad, riding smartly dressed in what appeared to be the uniform of a sailor.

Who are these men, mi marido (my husband)?

she whispered into her husband's ear while stepping forward to address them with the grace mandated by her upbringing.

Each responding in his respective tongue and with equal and correspondingly unexpected gentility. Whereupon Don Antonio answered,

They are our guests, Mi Amor (My Love).

Dona Maria had always trusted her man. Whose own humanity remained legendary even amongst this arguably most gracious of all communities on earth.

Truth be told, retired Commandante Lugo should have executed all three individuals, or at the very least marched them off in chains to Monterey as prisoners. For they were pirates caught red-handed in the act of destroying both private and government property.

But as their judge and potential executioner, Don Antonio having characteristically seen circumstances in a different light.

The Moor,

Lugo explaining,

speaks English.
So does the sailor boy.
They both claim to be from the United States.

As for the big, hairy fellow;
well,
Sergeant Morales insisted I strip him naked
so as to make certain he did not have a tail!

Dona Lugo's hands flying to cover her mouth as she suppressed, as best she could, both shock and

amusement at what must have surrounded the
ridiculous spectacle occasioned by simple Morales.

He does not have a tail,
my love

offering Don Antonio slyly.

His name is either Pedro Zaldivar
or Nicolas Chavarria.

A Frenchman or a Russian.
He refuses to be clear.

As to whether or not these men
are Christians or heretics,
I do not know; nor do I care,

A rascal named Napoleon has led them astray;
and pledged to dethrone our King.

I have made them to understand
that the Spanish Crown
will take good care of them.

And as for the blonde boy, Maria,

Don Lugo continuing,

his is an honest face;
even if he has been caught amongst thieves.

They want to stay here,

Antonio offering further.

I have let them know that if they behave themselves,
they are welcome to remain amongst us;
and perhaps in time
be lucky enough
to succeed as I did
in finding and marrying a beautiful California girl.

Dona Lugo did not require such campaigning to garner support for her husband's decision. Who smiling compliantly added,

As for their religion,
well,
the padre will attend to that part of it.

The result of such compassionate humanity, reflective of Californio society in general, being reformation of all three lives. Each thereafter pressed into service as day laborers with construction of a beautiful new church on the Plaza at Los Angeles.

Ultimately Lugo's decision to reform rather than remove a perceived paria proving an even greater boon then anticipated.

As following construction of the Plaza Church, both English speaking Americans Joseph Chapman and Mateo Jose Pascual, together with ever mysterious Zaldivar each now conversing fluently in Castilian going on to serve capably as mechanics; dispensing freely of their skill and Yankee ingenuity at every mission community, presidio, pueblo and private estate throughout the length and breadth of Spanish California.

Introducing advanced windmill technologies by concocting a Spanish/English/Russian woolen mill at Santa Inez. Constructing schooners in San Diego. Planting vineyards around Los Angeles.

Eventually Don Antonio escorting his wards back to the scene of the crime at Santa Barbara, where, he explained, lived the most beautiful girls in all of California.

A moment of high comedic drama witnessing Chapman discovering himself to have fallen in love with none other than Guadalupe Ortega, daughter of the very man who had restrained him with a lasso from torching the Ortega family estate on that fateful December night in 1818.

To understand all
is to forgive all.

Don Francisco, son of Serra's champion Joseph Ortega, withholding neither forgiveness nor his blessing from young Chapman.

The subsequent marriage proving a happy one. Blessed with six children, all fair-haired and blue-eyed like their father.

So it was that blue-eyed or not, from that day forward Californios ever referred to English Americans as rather Ojos Azueles (Blue Eyes).

Mateo Pascual and Joseph Chapman remaining best of friends, until lost to each other during the ensuing chaos of California's Gold Rush.

Mysterious Zaldivar disappearing into anonymity.

Despite a handful of English speaking Americans having previously jumped ship and or otherwise finding themselves offloaded in California, West Coast historians parlaying the notion that Mateo and Joseph were first to settle. Their exemplary friendship and subsequent lives as lived making desirability of such a belief understandable if perhaps inaccurate.

Meanwhile pirate Peter Corney as patriot having long since returned to New England, where he continued fighting the good fight of birthing the nation that together with Joseph and Tom would itself soon embrace California.

YORBA

So many years had come and gone since those days when a much younger Jose Antonio Yorba carried dead and dying comrades from off their Spanish transport at San Diego.

Subsequent marriage as encouraged by Fray Junipero Serra to Maria Gracia Feliz, whom he had met and fallen in love with at Tucutnut (Carmel), blessing him with three children.

The dim but poignant memory of both her death and that of youngest son Jose Domingo haunting him still.

Left alone at twenty-six and with two motherless children.

Meanwhile Sergeant Juan Pablo Grijalva having arrived upon the scene accompanied by his wife and three children riding at the head of Anza's San Francisco bound caravan.

Where in 1785 Yorba married again, this time to Grijalva's fifteen-year-old daughter Maria Josefa. Who accepted both children from the previous marriage with characteristic grace.

Still, little Diego Maria being lost in a drowning incident.

Only Jose Antonio II surviving to accompany his father when transferred back to San Diego in 1797. Following an early retirement both working full time alongside Father-in-law and step granddad Grijalva in establishing a successful hacienda and rancho.

Their royal patent on lands adjacent to Mission San Juan Capistrano not arriving however until after Juan Pablo's death in 1819.

Whereupon Jose Antonio who had himself intended to petition for similar privileges rather sued successfully for transference of Grijalva's grant over to himself.

So that his ten children might be well provided for.

An endeavor to which the Franciscan's gave their blessing freely as both Grijalva and Yorba had themselves assumed responsibility for the education, conversion (reduccion) and employment of several otherwise remote Acjachemem villages.

Who now worked either the private rancho herding cattle and sheep or on a private hacienda planting, pruning and harvesting its fields, vineyards and orchards.

Christened Rancho Santiago, Jose Antonio conducting weekly inspections of an estancia (estate) baronial in extent astride his splendid Spanish stallion. And dressed to the nines. Cutting a regal figure as an accomplished and beloved patron (patriarch).

Spain, herself having been compelled to abandon its youngest child, leaving Yorba's children to interpret as best they could an Old World social order none of them had even seen nor would ever experience first hand.

So it was that "independent" families such as the Yorbas had made unorthodox contracts between neighboring missions and foreign merchants. Which precipitated upon them their unprecedented standard of living.

At San Juan the Grijalva/Yorba amalgam having no trouble finding ready markets for its seemingly endless supply of cowhides and tallow.

Oxcarts kept busied delivering the bounty of Rancho Santiago to warehouses at San Juan Capistrano. There brokered together with those of Indian Missions to any one of numerous Yankee clippers dropping anchor off neighboring Dana Point.

The sale of which generated additional fortunes both for Mission communities as well as devoted Californios who in turn not only provided employment but delivered back more than their full tithe to the Franciscans directly.

Additionally supplementing such income with the sale of sea otter skins and thereby securing not merely gold and silver coin but all the luxuries of China, England and the United States.

Facilitating construction of such things as the stately home erected by Jose Antonio's son Bernardo atop a bluff overlooking the Santa Ana River.

And balancing otherwise personal extravagance by funding as lay Franciscan from out of his own pocket much of the costly construction work on San Juan Capistrano's great stone church.

In recognition for which Franciscans and novices had presented the Yorba Family with a splendid statue of Jose Antonio's Patron Saint Anthony. Thereafter proudly displayed above the altar of a chapel maintained by arrangement with the Order and again at Yorba's own expense for and in behalf of novices employed by him on Rancho Santiago. The beautiful Santo yet showcased and in a setting befitting at Santa Ana's magnificent Bowers Museum.

Meanwhile San Antonio developing into California's largest private estancia. Serving as a communal showplace for high-European culture.

From within the thick adobe walls of its fifty rooms, each braced with heavy wood beams and covered in tiled floors, echoing the laughter, tears and prayers of Spanish Arcadia.

And when Jose Antonio Yorba passed away on January 16, 1825 at age seventy- five, he could never have imagined that his quantum dream had die with him.

Buried together with his vision in a Franciscan habit beneath the floor of San Juan's Great Stone Church,

> So that in this way
> I might be trod upon by everyone;
> and be nearest the baptismal font
> so that a chance drop of holy water
> might fall upon me
> and thus ease my soul into
> the celestial courts of Heaven.

Nothing aside from a family burial plot elsewhere in today's city of Yorba Linda seemingly destined to remain of his communal legacy.

Even the ruins of Mission San Juan Capistrano but a few miles distant now sitting aborted and plundered.

Yet since eradicated monuments to Christianity, capitalism and concomitantly utopian idealism had not been founded in vain. Nor was that which they represented banished altogether. The magnificent nation/state of today's California sitting squarely and solidly anchored atop those self- same cornerstones.

Still, with children of men such as Yorba struggling to interpret a Franciscan masterpiece little understood even by those installing it, something profound, indeed the very purpose for the entire exercise, having become lost in translation.

As when Jose Antonio's heirs parceled out all that which had been lavished upon them, eldest son Jose Antonio II receiving nothing. Because, well after all, he was just an Indian.

Rendering undone the Indian kingdom envisioned by a pious king, erudite missionary and equally egalitarian Catalonian Yorba.

MEXICO

Touched off by precedent setting revolts leveled against England by her North American colonies as prompted by the French, parodies of a subsequently installed United States appeared thereafter in rapid fire succession throughout the Western Hemisphere.

Freemasonry's triumph, an ensconced Republic wherein Church and State stood not only apart but completely segregated from commerce, daring others to dream of similar self-empowerment.

So it was that democratic idealism with its sibling republicanism caught hold of a collective American imagination.

While in Europe autocratic rule of the Bourbon's in particular ended abruptly with public execution of Louis XVI. Leading an emboldened French citizenry to demand nothing less than abdication of his cousin Don Carlos IV.

Following which demagogue Napoleon Bonaparte, as champion of the people, sparked a domino-like series of events that successfully toppled one monarchy after another, including the one conceived of and installed by himself.

Meanwhile back in California on September 14, 1814 Monterey having witnessed the rare spectacle of a monstrous Spanish man-of-war putting in and dropping anchor. Its admiral surrendering as ordered by

Napoleon before an incredulous Governor Arrellaga.

Whose own directive from a still loyal to the Bourbon family regime yet holding court in Mexico City demanded contrarily that all orders issued by French interlopers be ignored.

Accordingly Arrellaga refusing acceptance of said maritime forfeiture. Leaving devout Royalist captain and crew to consider lingering in California amongst a yet faithful old guard constituency long enough for the smoke of political turmoil to clear at home.

At home Napoleon placing his brother Joseph upon the Spanish throne. Only to be countered not by royalists but rather an unanticipated display of Hispanic nationalism.

Which resulted in expulsion of Joseph and Napoleon both.

Fernando VII, son of Charles IV thereafter crowned King with an understood caveat that he draft a constitutional charter by means of which to construct one grand and democratic Spanish Republic.

Curiously as Old Spain began this self-styled political metamorphosis, the belligerent aristocracy of New Spain remaining steadfast against what it rightly perceived as an unprecedented threat to their own lives of political and economic privilege.

In the ensuing malaise California playing very much a role of innocent bystander. Youngest and most isolated of Spain's dominions as but a Franciscan protectorate remaining disconnected from events otherwise rapidly transforming Western civilization.

Her sublime ignorance so complete that surrendering Spanish war ships and French freedom fighting mercenaries had each caught Californios off guard.

Not that California didn't have its own devotees of Republicanism, Liberalismo and the French Enlightenment.

Ten-year-old Mariano Guadalupe Vallejo seeing in Bouchard's sacking of Monterey but great adventure and the excitement inherent with any sudden interruption of status quo.

Catching even at his tender age a sense of world history's shifting tide when as smoke lingering low across California's capitol cleared young Vallejo sat reflecting upon otherwise heresies preached by Napoleon's pirate.

As reward for openly advocating the politics of (in Vallejo's words),

Not mere pirates
but liberators,
for whom patriotism is their only incentive
and liberty their god,

a bright if impertinent youth sustaining censorship, lashings across his bared backside and temporary excommunication.

Choosing thereafter simply to bide time,

Because my elders remained
all very much attached to king and pope,
praying for both
at the break of dawn,
at noon, at sunset
and at bedtime.

Meanwhile together with nephew (and Customs House bookkeeper) Juan Bautista Alvarado and their cousin Jose Castro, forming a secret boys club. And as such indulging innocently enough in world politics exposed courtesy of a new medium of ephemera dubbed the magazine.

Which albethem banned, Mariano as a child of California's aristocracy, managed to secure without difficulty. Contriving endless ways of not only contacting foreign sources but scaring up whatever funding might be required to secret said "lurid" material into the province undetected.

To such an extent that by his eighteenth birthday Vallejo laid claim to arguably the most extensive and controversial private library anywhere north of Mexico City.

Meanwhile New Spain together with its Interior Provinces and Kingdom of California focusing all energies upon,

maintaining the bonds
to the Spanish body politick
and the Church of Rome
that have bound us together
as a people for centuries.

Collectively searching for a spokesperson who could defend them against suddenly Republican, liberal and alien Old Spain.

And found that champion not surprisingly amongst the clergy.

Growing up in Guanajuato outside of Mexico City, Miguel de Hidalgo y Costilla having while working silver mines as a common day laborer struggled to avert abject poverty in the very shadow of grand private estates and splendid cathedrals.

Recognizing with disdain the self-evident political alliances long since forged between a well-landed aristocracy and Roman Church hierarchy.

And upon ordination to the priesthood voicing his objections concerning a local collusion that had disenfranchised nearly all of his parishioners.

Seeking not to throw off but reform said sad set of circumstances,

Because he loved God.

Father Hidalgo himself remaining ever loyal to Old Spain, Rome and the ideal both represented.

So it was that when Mexican dissidents proposed recognition of Napoleon's rule over an increasingly liberal Mother Spain while correspondingly advocating dissolution both of church and state in New Spain, Hidalgo felt an obligation to move politically against said heresies and otherwise blatant treason.

From his pulpit at Dolores preaching fiery sermons championing reform rather than dissolution. Denouncing all whom would so much as consider political betrayal while admonishing that loyal Catholics everywhere raise high the standards of both majesties.

In emphasizing loyalty by lifting above his head the image of Mary, Our Lady of Guadalupe, single most powerful icon of Latin America, inadvertently unleashing a sanguine maelstrom.

When an unexpected hush fell over his congregation. Which then erupted in a flood of pent up anguish and tears. With all falling to their knees.

The sudden outpouring of passion from those identifying with Mary and not her corrupted clergy as Mexico's true standard bearer prompting to its feet a suddenly angry mob demanding an end to oppression.

In an instant both Spain and Rome standing completely forgotten.

State controlled response from the Church ordering that Hidalgo be excommunicated for having touched off a rising tide of Mexican nationalism that had shocked even the padre himself.

New Spain's proletariat insisting rather he be reinstated.

And when those demands fell on tin ears, taking matters into their own hands by proclaiming Mexico a free and sovereign nation.

The inevitable bloodbath fueled by centuries of sustained indignities beginning at Mexico City. Spain what with its own struggles at home in Europe to rendered unable to assist.

When in 1818 Viceroy Antonio Cossios agreed to pardon Fray Hidalgo if only he petition forgiveness from the State controlled Church, Mexico hearing for it's first time a now famous Grita (shout),

Pardon,

countering Father Hidalgo,

is for criminals.

Not for defenders of the Fatherland.

Viva Mexico!

The firing squad that robbed a courageous Mexican of his life simultaneously executing New Spain. Successive governments established thereafter each attempting to install the padre's reforms.

Despised cabildos remaining yet in control of Mexico's assets.

So it was that free in principal only,

Viva Mexico!

would continue to echo through a century plagued by counter-revolutionaries focused upon securing authentic republicanism and democracy.

Fifty-two different governmental regimes assuming command over the Republic of Mexico during the course of as many years.

Aloof and far removed from such chaos, Californio's receiving news in 1822 of Mexico's proclaimed independence with consummate indifference.

Long since abandoned to their own devices, even as Spanish Governor Pablo de Sola pledged fealty to a new Mexican Republic few Californians other than perhaps members of Mariano Vallejo's boysclub sensing the implications inherent in said transition.

Officials dispatched to California from Mexico City having routinely come and gone. That they now called themselves Mexican evoking little more than the raising of an eyebrow at Monterey. Were they not Catholic still?

Governors imported both from New Spain as well as Old having ever been but guardians of Franciscan stewardship and otherwise impotent figureheads for political machines whose true interests and concerns remained distant and far removed from local affairs.

Accordingly Californians tendering each a routine and polite allegiance, while dutifully noting and occasionally even obeying their customary proclamations.

Sola having positioned Luis Antonio Arguello as Governor pro-tem before making haste for Mexico City there to participate in drafting a Republican constitution.

When upon the heals of a Spanish governor's

departure arrived disturbing mandates from Mexico's first president. Who having subverted the aspirations of his own people unexpectedly proclaimed himself not president but rather Emperor.

Emperor Augustin Iturbe in fact but a puppet for an old guard ruling class focused not upon reform but rather the plunder of natural resources and skilled Indian labor developed yet still protected under jurisdictions maintained by the Church.

Standing as impediment to Iturbe's greed in California's Utopia being the brothers of Saint Francis.

Under the strictest interpretations of either Spanish or Mexican Law there having never been a Spanish Colonial California.

Development of the country though facilitated by Spain as official guardian of Mother Church nonetheless ever paid for exclusively from an independently maintained and decidedly Roman Pious Fund.

That these same mission communities installed by Church funding had themselves carried the additional financial burden of sustaining their own police protection and civic requirements leaving Spain itself rather in debt to Franciscan Custodies.

And where the monarchy had held no right beyond exclusivity in chaffare with California, a newly founded and independent Empire of Mexico stood in possession of nothing whatsoever by way of historic precedent to suggest claims of jurisdiction over the province.

In his attempt to circumvent these obstacles, which maintained Roman sovereignty over California, Iturbe implementing expulsion of the Spanish Franciscans who served as legal custodians of the same.

Reading at Monterey of this proclamation raising more than mere eyebrows.

If the Franciscan Order were expelled surely confiscation of Indian missions would follow.

A naïve response from Governor Luis Arguello leaving Iturbe and those pulling Mexico's political strings stunned.

As defying Franciscan expulsion orders, California's favorite son prevailed upon the Least of the Brothers of Christ rather to inaugurate installation of yet another mission. Which he paid for with funds forwarded by Mexico City to otherwise administer a,

program for Secularization of Indian installations.

Arguello identifying secularization as mere euphemism for criminal confiscation of Indian ranches, farms, businesses, churches and schools.

The inevitability of Iturbe's coerced abdication by his disenchanted populace followed. By which time Franciscan Mission San Francisco de Solano as prescribed by Arguello and ultimately Reverend Father President Senan was already up and operating.

Meanwhile Mexico succeeded in countering old guard cabildos to see installed an authentic Republic.

Which promptly rescinded Iturbe's Franciscan expulsion orders.

Pablo de Sola remaining at Mexico City, there to continue work with other decidedly Catholic patriots in forging a viable working constitution.

California again compelled to pledge allegiance this time as citizens of an authentic Republic.

Only then to be surprised by the unexpected arrival of a would be governor touting an aggressive and startling agenda of his own.

THE DEVIL AND ECHEANDIA

A rriving at San Diego in the spring of 1829 was one Lieutenant Colonel Jose Maria Echeandia. Who as Surveyor General for the Imperial Mexican Army announced political separation of Baja (Lower) California from Alta (Upper) California.

Loreto as Capitol of the former having already been revitalized.

An interesting and understandable dichotomy given long since established custodies between Franciscan and Dominican Orders.

Echeandia's startling second proclamation however stunning both Californias.

By who knew what authority, as a Republic become Empire had become Republic again, the grandee then presenting himself as Governor of the latter.

And in the same breath ordering transference of operations from Monterey to San Diego, where he had arranged before hand to reside in the grand home of Andres Pico.

Knowingly disrupting both tradition and the regime currently installed. Purposefully shifting Alta (Upper) California's base of operations together with its sentiments five hundred miles closer to Mexico City.

Then directing all missionaries to transmit detailed inventories of lands and assets held in common with their respective Indian novices.

Meanwhile Mexico as Empire become Republic ascribing but Territorial status to both Californias. Suggesting that neither stood in possession of populace enough for installing otherwise. Inviting that each rather send a single representative who upon arrival might assist with yet have no voice in Congress.

At Monterey previously empowered as governor Luis Antonio Arguello already in the process of establishing as prescribed a Territorial Deputation, or council, by means of which to himself maintain control as Political Chief of the Territory.

Clandestine meetings conducted between Echeandia and equally new upon the scene from Italy via Peru Juan Bandini presaging civil war.

Franciscans describing the counter deputation assembled beforehand in San Diego as being comprised of,

> a class of politicians who in proclaiming general
> emancipation
> seek but to emancipate themselves
> from civic duties imposed by Christianity.

And who in so seeking rendered Mexican countrymen unhappy to the present day.

Wooing Southern California's gente de razon with promises of position and power as part of a new San

Diego based regime if only they would support Echeandia's posting as Governor.

Winning over a confused constituency through embracing Californio traditions of conviviality.

Staging the grandest fete anyone in San Diego or Monterey for that matter had ever attended.

A self-appointed Governor having been apprised by Pico of the double wedding about to be conducted on behalf of California's two highest-ranking military officers, seizing opportunities inherent in such an occasion for beginning his political ruse.

Insisting upon hosting the much-anticipated celebrations. Nuptials to be exchanged not in the presidial chapel or mission church but at a Pico estancia- become California's new seat of government.

His army of forged alliances under the guise of a wedding procession thereafter marching on Monterey.

Echeandia seducing in route Californio families by prevailing upon each to similarly host at their own estates week long fiestas in honor of the happy couples. Then exploiting said occasions by plying the same with gifts, alcohol and promises of position and riches if only all would aid him in ridding California of the one thing standing between themselves and true wealth—Franciscan missionaries.

A growing army of compromised citizens advancing slowly northward.

In his cache Echeandia carrying papers demanding Luis Arguello's resignation, expulsion of every Spanish Franciscan and confiscation of all Indian missions.

His ranks of supporters upon arriving at Monterey numbering nearly three hundred purchased co-conspirators.

An understandably outraged northern constituency headed up by boysclub members Mariano Vallejo, Juan Alvarado and Jose Castro countering such blatant foreign effrontery. Registering fierce objections motivated not out of righteous indignation but rather anger with Echeandia for having failed to include them as equal players.

Aware that Sola, in league with other devout and loyal Catholics, yet sat laboring at Mexico City over a constitution that would never condone exploitation of Christian Indian community, Vallejo opting rather to back legitimate Governor pro-tem Luis Arguello in ousting not Franciscans but rather Jose Maria Echeandia.

Who in a scenario that spawned the legends of Zorro, found himself being expelled at the point of a bayonet.

Meanwhile Franciscan overlords witnessing from their calm retreats the gathering of a storm.

At Mexico City a new republican Congress eyeing with lust but restraining from seizing either Pious Fund or mission properties.

Still, where Spain had herself been compelled to raise money, through divestiture of the Crown's own acreage while hinting impatience with utopian mission experiments, a fledgling Mexican republic could not help but to ultimately summon liquidation of all such "neglected" resources.

And did not wait long before so doing. Though longer than she had played at Empire.

Seeds of egregious dissension having been irretrievably sown. In California a society of innocents poisoned with dreams of conquest left fixating upon transforming self-governing Indian Missions into private ranchos and haciendas.

Forty-five Californio families standing compromised. Each now eyeing the other with suspicion. All focusing upon an unholy San Diego based Bandini/Pico alliance.

Simultaneous loss of individual integrity and lack of trust signaling an end to California's Golden Age.

That evil day being postponed, however, with the arrival of an authentic successor assigned as Governor over Alta California by the Republic of Mexico.

Manuel Victoria appearing without ceremony at Santa Barbara on January 10, 1831.

Who, underestimating the depth of Echeandia's subterfuge, placed unmerited confidence in Commandante Jose Portilla of the San Diego Presidio. Marching north to Monterey directly rather than south.

And there discovering Luis Arguello busy arming the

province militarily against possible invasionary forces from San Diego.

Echeandia having resurfaced and laying siege to Utopia's capitol at San Juan Capistrano. Leaving a heightened sense of alarm hanging heavy over Southern California.

THE CURSE OF CAPISTRANO

uch to Luis Arguello's surprise and relief Governor Victoria produced the new Republic's completed constitution. Which acknowledged Indians as equal citizens under the law while expressly forbidding interventions such as those being proposed by Echeandia while further mandating compulsory allegiance to the Church of Rome.

When, in a blatant if not shameful display of treason, Southern California unexpectedly rebelled openly against accepting either their new governor or the Mexican constitution.

From San Juan Capistrano Echeandia's rhetoric designed to undo Indian innocents admonishing rather that novices abandon both commitments to the Church and this new republic in exchange for a freedom designed but to render them vulnerable.

All the while conspiring with Northern factions through an operative (Juan Padez) in his effort to overthrow Arguello and or Victoria in favor of confiscating the entire province for himself.

A timely report from San Diego's Commandante Portilla delivered to Victoria by Padez concerning intentions aimed at countering the Governor's authority prompting his quick response.

The Victoria arriving in Los Angeles only to discover

Commandante Portilla himself leading said open rebellion as but another member of Echeandia's cartel.

Who to the chagrin of Northern Californians promptly escorted Mexico's appointed representative out of the province altogether, while reinstating previously exiled Echeandia at San Diego.

Northern and Southern California standing polarized. The Republic of Mexico expressing outrage. And deploying into a political standoff decidedly Indian (Aztec/mestizo) and highest-ranking officer ever to administer over California General Jose Figueroa.

Who while serving previously as Governor of Sonora had endeavored to reopen Anza's overland road.

And now stood determined to maintain harmony between mounting aspirations of both Californios and Indian novices alike.

To the consternation of Echeandia, Mexico's

Indian Governor

presenting himself at San Diego on May 1st of 1833, accompanied by ten brown robed Mexican Franciscans (from Zacatecas) recruited for the express purpose of securing missions compromised when previously threatened with exile of all Spanish priests.

In true Franciscan ethos performing as his first official act a granting of pardon upon every man, woman and child involved in expelling Governor Victoria.

Then announcing restoration of Monterey as California's seat of government.

Where in response Arguello hosted a grand reception against which even the fiestas and fandangos of Echeandia's contrivance paled.

And during which Figueroa met with the Californio voice of Liberalismo, Mariano Guadalupe Vallejo.

Pragmatically appointing him Military Prefect. Evoking in an instant restoration of the traditional Governor/Military Prefect arrangement with which California had itself ever been most familiar.

Discovering in Vallejo both the Spanish face and family connections necessary for effectively containing Echeandia's meddling.

Following consultations with patrons and padres Figueroa establishing a regional and democratic congress by means of which every voice Indian or otherwise might be heard with equal fairness.

And thereby knowingly placating his compromised constituency through removing courtesy of said public forum even the possibility for doubletalk.

With one fail stroke of his pen a devote Catholic Indian undoing Jose Maria Echeandia's covert machinations.

Still Figueroa never failing to recognize said nemesis as yet poising a threat while additionally acknowledging the dangers inherent with ambiguous and potentially turncoat Russians positioned along

California's northwest littoral.

And accordingly ordering that Vallejo as commander of the military bolster troops while maintaining his residence in Sonoma, from whence to closely monitor yet a second political unknown.

Vallejo's grandparents, Don Antonio and Dona Maria Lugo, residing as they did in courtesy of collusion with Echeandia what had suddenly become Pico and Bandiniland, dutifully serving as disciples and spys for their grandson's own agenda. Of whom his grandmother wrote,

> He has a puritanical strength of character,
> resolute will,
> and an ambitious spirit.
>
> And has always been a free thinker,
> like his grandfather.

The Franciscans seeing things differently. Reverend Father President of California's Indian Missions Jose Senan stating flatly,

> Vallejo is not to be trusted.

To eradicate the pallor of Echeandia's presence still hanging over Southern California, Figueroa establishing his own residence neither at Monterey nor San Diego but rather near Los Angeles.

And there drafting a new order that embraced the Age of Individualism without abandoning socialistic Indian communities.

Broadsiding Figueroa's noble endeavor being Mexico City itself.

Where in an unexpected turn of events secularization of all mission properties was suddenly ordained together with a new Governor for Monterey.

Recognizing the likelihood of Figueroa's failure and intent of a new Mexican regime to in fact implement plans not unlike those previously proposed by Echeandia, many Californios determining then and there to themselves confiscate the entire province.

Governor Jose Maria Hijar together with a large number of Mexican colonists, each holding claims to land previously set aside by Luis Arguello as Mission San Francisco Solano, arriving at San Diego on September 1, 1834.

Figueroa receiving advance orders to accommodate the same through transference of said mission properties at Sonoma over to Hijar and his entourage.

Meanwhile, back in Mexico City, General Antonio Lopez de Santa Anna moving on and seizing the government from President Gomez Farias. Firing orders off overland to Figueroa that he not transfer lands or his office to Hijar. Then seizing all assets of the Pious Fund for himself.

Santa Anna thereafter issuing his own not to be forestalled agenda,

It being a matter of the greatest necessity
that the neophytes rise from the state of abasement

to which they find themselves reduced.

You will cause to be distributed
to such as are fitted for it
such fields of the mission lands
as they are capable of cultivating,
in order that they may thus become fond of labor
and may go on acquiring property.

Figueroa left to accommodate as best he could a suddenly marginalized Governor Hijar while counteracting complete disillusionment on the part of both his Californio and Franciscan mentored Indian constituency.

From Monterey admonishing that Mexico City reconsider Santa Anna's edict as at best ill advised. While reminding Congress that Indians of his department already "owned" their respective communities all be in common.

Seeing clearly through but another thinly veiled scheme to divest neophytes of their lands, openly opposing and outright refusing implementation of the President's order.

Demanding rather a return of all Mission properties confiscated previously to be supervised by his Zacatecan (Mexican) Franciscans while threatening the prosecution of any Californio found guilty of theft with regard to Indian property.

For such obstinance Figueroa would pay with his life.

And regardless an Indian masterpiece of social

engineering would be confiscated. With not surprisingly Echeandia being first to sack it.

As unwilling to await a dropping of the proverbial other shoe, anxious Californios took quick action cloaked in secrecy.

Figueroa's posting of Vallejo as general having unwittingly given rise to a new and independent republic.

Vallejo conscripting at his own expense the finest standing army California had ever seen as but a means of securing unprecedented influence. Daring to dream of carving political self-empowerment out of impending chaos.

Openly purchasing weapons from Russians while secretly conspiring with Yanks to align Monterey not with Mexico but rather the United States. Yet not before he and his associates had taken complete and entire possession of the same.

Vallejo's brothers-in-law (Carmen's husband, Ohio born Jacob Leese and Luisa's English-become Yank John Cooper), both of whom now owned mercantile operations at Monterey, assuring him that should California establish itself as an American State both political stability as well as enhanced prosperity could not help but to follow.

Suggesting further that under the protective blanket provided by a United States Constitution together with its Bill of Rights, Californio's would continue to enjoy unprecedented autonomy.

Vallejo's political interests having grown urgent upon receipt of news concerning General Antonio Lopez de Santa Anna's appointment as president of the Mexican Republic.

Boy's Club member Jose Castro stepping into the void occasioned by Figueroa's untimely death only to discover self- reinstated Echeandia busy transforming each mission into but a holding company through replacing "emancipated" neophyte alcaldes with Californio co-conspirators as administrators.

Mexican Army lieutenant Nicolas Guiterrez arriving upon the scene to forestall all such actions and restore law and order prior to the impending arrival of Governor Mariano Chico as authentic successor. Who but three months after his arrival was himself ousted at the point of a bayonet.

Meanwhile Mexico prevailing upon Guiterrez to maintain control of the region now as Governor pro-tem. Even as illegally appointed mission administrators commenced ruination of the missions by running each into a contrived paper bankruptcy.

Splendid Mission San Juan Capistrano reduced to scribble on a balance sheet. Under Bandini's administration all properties being sold at auction for a pittance to Pio Pico's sister Isabella and her British husband John Forster.

Whose grandson, Marquitos Antonio Forster witnessed first hand sublimation of "emancipated" Indian novices to peonage. Their beautiful chapel pressed into service as a barn. Mission cloister serving as an arena for bullfights. Themselves compelled to work off contrived debts as sharecroppers in lieu of abandoning a capitol city they had themselves built with their own blood, sweat and tears.

Prompting the taking of extraordinary measures on Marquitos' part. As under cover of darkness he set about righting a rapidly mounting roster of wrongs.

This clandestine hero of the people garnering for himself the intimidating sobriquet Curse of Capistrano. And as such providing inspiration for Johnston McCulley's fictional ZORRO.

'Tis a night for evil deeds!'
declared Sergeant Pedro Gonzales,
stretching his great feet in their loose boots
toward the roaring fire
and grasping the hilt of his sword in one hand
and a mug filled with thin wine in the other.

'Devils howl in the wind,
and demons are in the raindrops!

'Tis an evil night, indeed—eh Senor?'

"It is!' agreed the landlord hastily,
as he rushed to fill the wine mug again.
For Sergeant Gonzales had a temper
that was terrible when aroused,
as it always was when wine was not forthcoming.

'An evil night,' the big sergeant repeated,
and drained the mug without stopping
to draw breath,

a feat that had attracted
considerable attention in its time
and had gained the sergeant a certain
amount of notoriety
up and down El Camino Real.

Gonzales sprawled closer to the fire and
cared not that other men thus were robbed
of some of its warmth.

Sergeant Pedro Gonzales often had expressed his
belief that a man should look out for his own
comfort before considering others;
And being of great size and strength,
and having much skill with the blade,
he found few who had the courage
to declare that they believed otherwise.

Outside the wind shrieked,
and the rain dashed against the ground
in a solid sheet.

It was a typical February storm
for southern California.

At the missions the frailes (brothers)
had cared for the stock
and had closed the buildings for the night.

At every great hacienda big fires
were burning in the houses.

The natives keeping to their little adobe huts,
glad for shelter.

And here in the little pueblo of Los Angeles,
where in years to come a great city would grow,
the tavern on one side of the plaza housed
for the time being
men who would sprawl before the fire until the dawn
rather than face the beating rain.

Sergeant Pedro Gonzales,
by virtue of his grand size,
hogged the fireplace,

And a corporal and three soldiers from the presidio
sat at table a little in rear of him,
drinking their thin wine and playing at cards.

An Indian crouched on his heels in one corner,
no neophyte who had accepted the religion
of the Franciscans,
but a gentile and renegade.

For this was in the day of the decadence
of the missions,
when there was little peace between
the robed Franciscans
who followed in the footsteps
of the sainted Junipero Serra
(who had founded the first mission
at San Diego de Alcala,
and thus made possible an empire),
and those who followed the politicians
and had high places in the army.

The men who drank wine in the tavern at Los Angeles
had no wish for a spying neophyte about them.

Just now conversation had died out,
a fact that annoyed the landlord
and caused him some fear;

For Sergeant Pedro Gonzales in an argument
was Sergeant Gonzales at peace;
and unless he could talk
the big soldier might feel moved to action
and start a brawl.

Twice before Gonzales had done so,
to the great damage of furniture and men's faces:

And the landlord had appealed
to the commandante of the presidio,
Captain Ramon, only to be informed that the captain
had an abundance of troubles of his own,
and that running an inn was not one of them.

So the landlord regarded Gonzales warily
and edged closer to the long table
and spoke in an attempt to start
a general conversation
and so avert trouble.

'They are saying in the pueblo,' he announced
'that this Senor Zorro is abroad again.'

His words had an effect that was both unexpected
and terrible to witness.

Sergeant Pedro Gonzales hurled his
half-filled wine mug
to the hard dirt floor,
straightened suddenly on the bench,

and crashed a ponderous fist down upon the table,
causing wine mugs and cards and coins
to scatter in all directions.

The corporal and the three soldiers retreated
a few feet
in sudden fright,
and the red face of the landlord blanched;
the native sitting in the corner started
to creep toward the door,
having determined that he preferred the storm
outside to the big sergeant's anger.

'Senor Zorro, eh?' Gonzales cried in a terrible voice.
'Is it my fate always to hear that name?
Senor Zorro, eh?
Mr. Fox, in other words!
He imagines, I take it, that he is as cunning as one.
By the saints, he raises as much stench!'

Gonzales gulped, turned to face them squarely,
and continued his tirade.

'He runs up and down the length of El Camino Real
like a goat of the high hills!
He wears a mask,
and he flashes a pretty blade, they tell me.

'He uses the point of it to carve his hated letter Z
on the cheek of his foe! Ha!

'The mark of Zorro they are calling it!

'A pretty blade he has, in truth!
But I cannot swear as to the blade—

I never have seen it.
He will not do me the honor of letting me see it!

'Senor Zorro's depredations never occur in the
vicinity of Sergeant Pedro Gonzales! Perhaps this
Senor Zorro can tell us the reason for that? Ha!

He glared at the men before him,
Threw up his upper lip,
and let the ends of his great black mustache bristle.

'They are calling him the Curse of Capistrano now,'
the landlord observed,
stooping to pick up the wine mug and cards
and hoping to filch a coin in the process.

'Curse of the entire highway
and the whole mission chain!'
Sergeant Gonzales roared.
'A cutthroat, he is!
A thief! Ha!

'A common fellow
presuming to get him a reputation for bravery
because he robs a hacienda or so
and frightens a few women and natives!

'Senor Zorro, eh?

'Here is one fox it gives me pleasure to hunt!
Curse of Capistrano, eh?

'I know I have led an evil life,
but I only ask of the saints one thing now—
that they forgive me my sins long enough

to grant me the boon
of standing face to face
with this pretty highwayman!'

'There is a reward—'the landlord began.

'You snatch the very words from my lips!'
Sergeant Gonzales protested.
'There is a pretty reward for the fellow's capture,
offered by his excellency the governor.

'And what good fortune has come to my blade?

'I am away on duty at San Juan Capistrano,
and the fellow makes his play at Santa Barbara.

'I am at Los Angeles,
and he takes a fat purse at San Luis Rey.

'I dine at San Gabriel,
let us say,
and he robs San Diego de Alcala!

'A pest, he is!

'Once I meet him—'
Sergeant Gonzales choked on his wrath
and reached for the wine mug,
which the landlord had filled again
and placed at his elbow.
He gulped down the contents.

'Well, he never has visited us here,' the landlord said
with a sigh of thanksgiving.

'Good reason! Ample reason!
We have a presidio here and a few soldiers.
He rides far from any presidio, does this pretty Zorro!
He is like a fleeting sunbeam.
I grant him that—
'And with about as much real courage!'

Sergeant Gonzales relaxed on the bench again,
and the landlord gave him a glance
that was full of relief,
and began to hope that there would be
no breakage of mugs
and furniture and men's faces this rainy night.

'Yet this Senor Zorro must rest at times—
he must eat and sleep,'
the landlord said.

'It is certain that he must have some place
for hiding and recuperation.

'Some fine day the soldiers will trail him to his den.'

'Ha!' Gonzales replied.
'Of course the man has to eat and sleep.
And what is it that he claims now!
He says that he is no real thief, by the saints!
He is but punishing those who mistreat
the men of the missions,
he says.

'Friend of the oppressed, eh?

'He left a placard at Santa Barbara recently
stating as much,

Did he not? Ha!
And what may be the reply to that?

The frailes of the missions are shielding him,
hiding him, giving him his meat and drink!

'Shake down a robed fray
and you'll find some trace
of this pretty highwayman's whereabouts,
else I am a lazy civilian!

'I have no doubt that you speak the truth,'
the landlord replied.
'I put it not past the frailes to do such a thing.
But may this Senor Zorro never visit us here!'

'And why not?' Sergeant Gonzales cried
in a voice of thunder.

'Am I not here?
Have I not a blade at my side?
Are you an owl, and is this daylight
that you cannot see as far as the end
of your puny, crooked nose?
By the saints—'

'I mean,' said the landlord quickly
and with some alarm,
'that I have no wish to be robbed.'

'To be—robbed of what?
Of a jug of weak wine and a meal?

'Have you riches, fool? Ha!
Let the fellow come!

Let this bold and cunning Senor Zorro
but enter that door
and step before us!

'Let him make a bow, as they say he does,
and let his eyes twinkle through his mask!

'Let me but face the fellow for an instant—
and I claim the generous reward
offered by his excellency!'

'He perhaps is afraid to venture
so near the presidio,'
the landlord said.

'More wine!' Gonzales howled.
'More wine, and place it to my account!

'When I have earned the reward,
you shall be paid in full.
I promise it on my word as a soldier! Ha!

'Were this brave and cunning Senor Zorro,
this Curse of Capistrano,
but to make entrance at that door now—'

The door suddenly was opened.

LONE STAR

" **G**overnor" Nicholas Guiterrez aside, California was being torn asunder by Echeandia's southern alliances and Vallejo's northern "boys club" constituency.

With Mariano's nephew Juan Alvarado now serving simultaneously both as head of an all-important Customs House, from whence the government's cash flow was derived, and as secretary of Figueroa's previously installed Territorial Deputation.

So that when Guiterrez ordered guards be posted at clandestine trading points up and down the California coast, a knowing Alvarado protested.

Suspicious Mexican Governor Guiterrez responding with issuance of an order for Alvarado's arrest.

Who sought asylum in the cabin of brother-in-law Isaac Graham. Tucked away as it was amidst the giant redwood forests of Santa Cruz. And there drafted presumably on the spot plans to oust both Guiterrez and Mexico altogether in favor of calling for Californio independence.

An enthusiastic Yank from Tennessee, Graham raising in but a few days fifty rifle men from amongst his compatriots. Thereafter joined by one hundred Californios. Who under the leadership of Jose Castro then marched on Monterey.

Where upon obtaining ammunitions from an

American vessel listing at anchor in the harbor entered under the cover of night to capture an unsuspecting presidio.

The firing of but a single cannonball compelling Guiterrez to surrender. Afterwhich he simply disappeared. His lifeless body discovered later in a Mexican bound brigantine.

With Alvarado stepping forward to pronounce himself "Governor of the Department of the Californias" or as he grandeloquently proclaimed it a free and independent Californio Republic.

Then shipping double-crossed Graham together with his Yankee cavalry off to Mexico City and in chains as convicted revolutionaries!

Thereafter bankrolling the new Republic with tariffs collected not only through the Customs House but courtesy of those self-same prescribed by Guiterrez armed guards up and down the coast as well as through imposition of fees for services rendered by Californios appointed as mission administrators.

The fate of San Juan Capistrano soon befalling every mission.

Foreclosure bestowing ownership upon the Californio consortium who had loaned monies to a new Republic as levied by Alvarado against Indian assets.

Bandini in collusion now with Alvarado already having seized Mission San Gabriel from Echeandia to serve as his own grand private estate.

Even before a Franciscan/Indian community in mourning had intercepted and off loaded Figueroa's body from the Mexico bound vessel <u>Avon</u>.

Which they paraded in defiant procession through streets lined with would-be inheritors of Serra's dream. Interring their fallen hero in a vault beneath the floor of Mission Santa Barbara.

Overwhich now flew a flag with a lone red star as prepared previously for the new Republic by since exiled Isaac Graham.

And against which Mexico City issued an unprecedented flurry of proclamations.

At Los Angeles Luis Arguello's confidant Carlos Carillo proclaiming California faithful to Mexico and its new constitution. Only to be arrested by his uncle Juan Alvarado. Then released and placated for desisting opposition with a granting by the Californio Republic to Carillo of a clear title to Santa Rosa Island.

Meanwhile missions and formerly royal presidios each being plundered.

Mexican appointed Governor Manuel Micheltorena arriving upon the scene in August 1842 accompanied by an army of his own to demand both Alvarado's resignation as well as restoration of illegally appropriated missions and government buildings.

An officer distinguished through service to President Santa Anna marching on Monterey as champion of the Mexican Republic.

Startling news bringing his triumphal entrada to an abrupt halt.

Well calculated intelligence precipitating the alarm that sent Micheltorena and his army racing pell-mell back to Los Angeles.

Commodore Thomas Ap Catesby Jones of the United States Navy had sailed into Monterey on October 19th aboard his slope the <u>Cyane</u> and accompanied by the frigate <u>United States</u>. And taken possession of Monterey from Alvarado.

Then proudly displayed the Stars and Stripes while claiming California for the United States. Monterey's citizenry saluting with genuine delight.

Only to next day witness lowering of the Yankee standard and delivery of a handsome apology.

It had all been a mistake, explaining the commodore.

Aware of a political agenda concerning soon to be annexed Texas, Mexico's "prescribed" rampage, Americans' anticipated outcries against Mexico and ultimate proclamations of war, all calculated to leave California fair game for an American squadron sitting poised in the Pacific, the commodore knowing so much, suggesting he'd misconstrued rumors overheard and hence pounced on Monterey.

Mexican Governor Micheltorena thereafter assuming control and without opposition.

Deposed Alvarado hesitating, as if to ascertain

America's next move. Determining thereafter to again oust Mexico so as to himself await certain annexation by the United States.

Mexico then calling upon a European curiosity previously empowered by Alvarado to aid them in subduing the Californios.

Captain John Sutter as effective king of his own New Switzerland (Sacramento Valley) agreeing to cooperate in exchange for additional tracts of coveted real estate.

Micheltorena awarding those lands. Whereupon Sutter placed his Sacramento Valley based army of one hundred men at Mexico's disposal. The Republic of Mexico surrendering regardless but one day later.

That which followed

recording Bancroft,

can only be described as unconscionable.

"Ramona's" Helen Hunt Jackson adding,

the work of fifty years undone in less than five.

Aborted Governor Hijar's stranded five hundred "colonists," each in possession of Mexican land grants clamoring for real estate not previously confiscated by colluding Californios.

Refusing to surrender, determined Franciscans and Indians as Utopia's authors themselves serving as executioners of the same.

Beginning at Mission San Gabriel. Where Reverend Father President Senan ordered that all Gabrieleno Indians and lay Franciscan Californios descend upon juggernaut Echeandia under a cloak of darkness to effectively sweep the aforementioned institution from off the face of the earth.

Instructing all to take as much of the livestock and warehoused provisions as could possibly be run off or carted away.

And slaughter animals that did not disappear so as to convert their hides into revenue from traders along the coast for and in behalf of the Gabrielenos.

Having effectively sabotaged Echeandia at Los Angeles, Father Senan them repeating similar euthanasia at nine other southern California missions.

Echeandia responding by dispatching his cholos (goons) with orders that any thieving Indian be killed. Their ears to be brought back in order that a body count might be ascertained.

Such proceedings devastating heartbroken Brother Antonio Peyri. Who fled Mission San Luis Rey, intent upon catching an outbound Baltimore at San Diego.

Luisenos setting off en mass hopeful of convincing their philosopher king to stay. Witnessing instead but a tearful mentor's arms raised in his final act of blessing them even as wind-filled sails of a ship appropriately enough named Pocahontas carried the defeated Franciscan away.

Wailing commencing amongst those abandoned kneeling and or lying prostrate dockside.

As his final act a similarly defeated Governor Micheltorena responding by placing ownership of San Luis Rey into the hands of its neophyte alcalde in order to maintain intact a model Indian community. An act perceived by Father Peyri's novices as fulfillment of their mentor's blessing. And the only such concession ever made by Mexico to Mission Indians.

Mexico's governor then sailing into voluntary exile. Divesting himself of politics and power games to himself become a Franciscan.

Meanwhile Californio's finding themselves outnumbered by would-be rancheros arriving upon the scene from Mexico. And overwhelmed not only with expulsion orders for all Spanish Franciscans but the sudden displacement of more than ten thousand Mission novices.

CA

FOR WHOM THE BELLS TOLL

Aware of ongoing chaos in California courtesy of correspondence being received from American citizens residing in or transacting business with the province, a curious Yankee nation dispatched Lieutenant Colonel John Charles Fremont off to appraise said situation and investigate possibilities for intervention.

Communiqués sent by former New Englander Thomas O. Larkin, who had long since taken up residence at Monterey, fueling White House fascination. And tendering continuing assurances to President Andrew Jackson that courtesy of not only established trading partnerships but actual nuptials between Yanks and prominent Californio families the region had already aligned itself with the United States.

Missives from Californio Mariano Vallejo corroborating such testimony. Prompting Jackson's attempt to entice a nearly bankrupt Latin Republic with an offer to purchase San Francisco Bay and environs for half a million dollars.

President Santa Anna recognizing acceptance of any such transfers as being tantamount to political suicide.

Undeterred Californio factions spearheaded by Vallejo's Boys Club through intermediary Thomas Larkin keeping the heat on as it were with negotiations of their own.

President Jackson's arrogant, awkward successor James K. Polk openly espousing belief in what Yanks were referring to as Manifest Destiny. Hardcore mysticism suggesting foreordination of the United States as a nation stretching from sea to shining sea.

So it was that following endorsement of state legislation ordering wholesale extermination of all Mormons, Polk next vowing recklessly to take California at any cost.

Meanwhile in San Diego well connected with Europe and working for the British Consulate out of Mexico City Juan Bandini together with the Picos and married into Pico Family Englishman John Forster (who now sat courtesy of collusion between Pico, Echeandia and Bandini as patron of Mission San Juan Capistrano) raced to secure political ties rather with England.

Which prompted Vallejo's leverage of his own military might against both Mexico and a pro-British Southern California syndicate.

Who after successfully banishing Echeandia struck a deal with the Bandini/Pico coalition to keep California united and poised for certain to follow U.S. annexation.

Lowering the Mexican Standard across California to a collective cry of

Down with Mexico

and

Kill the Mexicans.

Raising in its place the white banner emblazoned with a single blood red star that Santa Anna had seen before—in Texas!

Reinstated governor of a self-proclaimed free and independent Californio Republic Alvarado reviving sardonic efforts to raise funds for the new administration through mortgaging what remained of southern California mission properties not previously confiscated by Echeandia's cartel.

Anticipated eviction notices following from a purposefully dilatorious government as the Free Republic continued settling liens taken against it with foreclosure on Indian missions.

Even going so far as to impose servitude upon novices by making pernicious demands that they work off the contrived debts imposed.

Soon the heinous flag of a tainted by greed local consortium flying above every formerly Indian mission.

Knowingly biding time, a Californio constituency sitting poised like the proverbial bride awaiting her groom. With but one variable lingering. Would that groom be British or a Yank.

Mexico, upon receipt of Micheltorena, dispatching Juan Maria Flores into the fray. Who attained Monterey sixteen months later but to affirm the futility of attempting control over a now rich, well-connected and powerful Californio cartel.

Even as wealthy in the extreme and well positioned to accept political postings following either U.S. or British annexation Vallejo and Alvarado both opted for a presumably temporary retirement.

During the interim posting Californio troops in the capable hands of cousin Jose Castro at Monterey, with Pio Pico agreeing to handle clerical matters from out of his home at Los Angeles.

Who in anticipation of escalating land values following U.S. annexation and to the chagrin of Yanks already residing in the province, began divvying out extraordinarily generous grants to family and friends.

An inappropriate exercise of authority that would haunt him for the rest of his life.

A life that came to embrace the full sweep of California's own youth.

Grandfather Santiago de la Cruz having come from Africa. Grandmother Maria del Carmen born in Spain. Fernando Rivera recruiting them both at Sinaloa during Neve's illegal push for colonialization of El Norte (The North).

Following Rivera's brutal murder at the hands of the Quechan Grandfather Pico and son finding themselves being intercepted at Mission San Gabriel by no less than Governor Neve himself. Who then ordered the founding not of Santa Barbara as planned but rather what California had referred to ever after as The Pueblo (Los Angeles).

Where Pio's father Jose Maria conscripted to serve as a soldier.

It would be in 1801 and while posted as a guard at Mission San Gabriel that Jose Maria's son Pio de Jesus Pico was born.

As a boy Pio purchasing and trading goods up and down the Camino Real dressed in his father's military uniform, the magic of which eliciting special favors from potential clients.

By virtue of land concessions awarded his parents young Pico ultimately abandoning sales in favor of becoming a ranchero.

As the brother of Echeandia's co-conspirator Andres Pico, and married as he was to Juan Alvarado's sister Maria Ignacia, Pio thereafter ever finding himself in the middle of otherwise family squabbles which now had a way of escalating into power struggles between northern and southern California.

And during the wholesale confiscation of Franciscan California sitting intermittently as interim Governor both for Californio as well as Mexican factions.

Pico's final stint (as Californio appointed Governor) lasting a mere sixteen months, following which neither the United States nor England but rather Mexico in the personage of appointed Governor Juan Maria Flores arrived to demand his resignation.

Pio already having generated enough controversy to engulf both himself and the entire Californio community in decades of subsequent litigation.

The consummate second generation Californio, Pio Pico living life at full throttle.

His love for Maria Alvarado undeniable, yet numerous affairs leaving a dubious legacy.

As unable to bare children herself it had not gone unnoticed that regardless Dona Pico raised four infants-each of whom bore a striking resemblance to their father.

Equally infamous being Pico's fiduciary abandon. Perpetrating the larceny launched in part by his brother Andres at San Diego, Pio as Californio Governor reputedly dispensing hard cash in a world suddenly gone commercial to any Puebleno (resident of the Pueblo, i.e. Los Angeles) petitioner.

The fact that cash distributed was but ill gotten gain from plundered mission communities providing justification enough for rampant mendicancy amongst displaced neophytes lining up outside Pico's Los Angeles office in search of a hand out.

And then there was the real estate debacle.

In his effort to placate malcontent Uncle Carlos Carillo, who stood up on behalf of the Indian community against Californio/Mexican secularization schemes, Pico having awarded him ownership of Santa Rosa Island.

While in an act of similarly ostentatious display gifting the entire Island of Santa Catalina to Yankee amigo Thomas Robbins.

For his part Pio assuming title to confiscated mission lands so vast that he could ride for six days and still traverse his own property.

Nor was such daring confined to real estate and business affairs.

A compulsive gambler, the stories concerning Pio's high stakes horse races being to this day recounted enthusiastically by aficionados.

Pico's most astounding fait accompli involving the pitting of his favored Spanish steed Sarco against benefactor of the Dominguez Estate Jose Antonio Sepulveda's Australian import, Black Swan.

The much-anticipated competition drawing a crowd large enough to line an entire nine-mile course with spectators. Amongst whom Sepulveda's wife handily distributed copious amounts of gold pieces in her effort to artificially escalate already ridiculously high stakes.

By the start of that race half a million dollars in today's currency of hard cash together with roughly another half million dollars worth of livestock hanging in the balance.

Sepulveda's Black Swan quickly out distancing Sarco. Instigating a tradition that is replicated annually near the same site at Southern California's Los Alamitos Racetrack.

In typically grand largesse a dismissive Pio conceding

defeat. Paying off his wager with alacrity.

But then why shouldn't Governor Pico yet smile, what with a popular notion that his Los Angeles estate stood brimming with gold coin and jewelry. Little did anyone suspect said loss sustained to have proven but the beginning of Pio's fiscal ruination.

In light of which Vallejo and Thomas Larkin stepped up clandestine negotiations with Washington, D.C., whilst cautioning Pio to temperance or risk facing full wrath of the United States government. Pico but smiling cavalierly.

And living to lament such naiveté.

By the time Mexican Governor Jose Maria Flores arrived in 1846 to unseat a high living Californio, an Indian mission system stood all but completely liquidated.

One of the largest privately held pastoral societies the world would ever see having risen in its place.

Plundered utopia assuming much the aspect of feudal Europe. With Californio and Mexican lords ruling over extensive commercial ranching and farming ventures created from expropriated mission properties and livestock operated by reduced to peonage Franciscan neophytes.

Anxiously maintaining sufficient pasturage upon which to run ever-increasing herds of primarily cattle, by importing indiscriminate slash and burn techniques of range development employed elsewhere throughout Latin America.

Fire, as witnessed early on even by Juan Rodriguez Cabrilho, having since time immemorial been an important environmental factor in California's natural schematic. Slash and burn techniques themselves adopted by Spain from the Indian.

Who annually set primarily Southern California ablaze so as to improve the yield of spring's sweet grasses. Which commercialranchero's now pursued in earnest and on a previously inconceivable scale. And by so doing inadvertently altering a fantastic landscape forever.

Fires burning unabated racing across valleys and hill country into lush old-growth forests. There smoldering away for weeks (sometimes even months) on end, to be extinguished only after the advent of rain, heavy fog or in the true high country winter's snowfall.

Precipitating nothing less than environmental holocaust upon an Ice Age legacy harboring countless rich botanical communities rendered unable to recover or re-establish themselves. Never catalogued by science, one being left but to imagine the extent of that which came to be lost forever.

Trained eyes gazing today upon the splendid mountain walls of Southern California in particular recognizing unmistakable scaring invoked from nearly two decades of deliberate and systematic burning. With trees such as the tecate cypress and big-cone spruce becoming so rare as to seem foreign and out of place in their natural environment.

As the mammoth hunters before them, Californio and Mexican Rancheros erasing yet another wondrous treasure from off the face of the earth by assaulting with abandon a fragile and delicate Pleistocene landscape.

Precipitating annual floods of Biblical proportions raining down upon coastal California with mud and rock from now denuded mountainslopes. Wrecking perennial havoc upon lowlands until fortunes spent in modern times contained the devastation through installation of extensive flood control systems.

Meanwhile emerald ribbons of Riparian woodlands once meandering from ancient forests in the high-country out across coastal valleys and basins to the sea, having already been sanctimoniously reduced but to supply fuel for cooking, being, in the wake of burning and flooding, all but completely destroyed. Together with the population of wildlife they sustained.

Such environmental and political chaos notwithstanding, accelerated trade but fostering proliferation of ranching operations otherwise yielding ever-expanding fortunes upon all parties involved.

Facilitating the building of bigger houses and bigger stables and bigger barns, the missions themselves picked clean of tile, brick, furniture, fountains, artwork and even vegetation.

As Indian Utopia was swept away, privatization of mission operations altering the social, environmental and economic fabric of California forever.

Yet the devastating, privately lucrative Ranchero era would prove short-lived. With those who had been so bold as to profiteer through wanton destruction of the

Indians' world soon facing similar ruination crashing down around their own heads.

Like great Spanish ghosts, plundered missions shrouded in coastal fog but taunting these destroyers of a crusader's cause. Surviving as tangible vestiges of utopianism to bare witness and testify against their assailants.

Beyond the stillness of noble relics, coastal California's landscape now standing punctuated by more than seven hundred private estancias dripping with the trappings of a society suddenly empowered by great wealth.

Padres packing up their libraries of Greek classics and Christian theology, leaving behind a new and self-absorbed generation lost to indulgence.

Their signature rowdy abandon contrasting markedly against the staid demeanor of California's past.

Old Monterey as traditional focal point of California's social life giving way to Neve's Pueblo at Los Angeles.

Showplace for the new ranchero regime, Los Angeles regardless remaining by no means grand. Most residences but modest affairs at best, and often sporting unsightly roofs of tar rather than tile. Nor did the Pueblo lay claim to a single direct avenue bisecting what was otherwise a scattering of huts, townhomes and estates.

Still all swept the front of their dwellings too as far as the middle of the street. Hanging lanterns from every doorway, so that thoroughfares and alleyways might remain well lit. Policing or standing guard, while, like their alcalde, receiving nothing in return beyond the satisfaction of volunteering as compensation.

And what Los Angeles lacked in order and architecture being more than recompensed with natural splendor. Endless flowering fields, vast grasslands, great stands of oak, purple mountains, white sand beaches all stretching off in every direction.

As a result of immigration and political alliances established between Californios and a conflicted Republic to the south, the Pueblo standing decidedly Mexican in composition.

Still, it's assent as rival to Mexico City yet all but imperceptible.

One Yank in from the United States appraising Pueblenos thusly:

The happiest people on earth.

Their time is spent in one continual round of feasting and pleasure, gaiety and happiness.

If any person was so poor
that he had no horse to ride,
some friend, relative, or compadre would give him
a splendid charger, another a saddle,
bridle, reata, and spurs;
a third a milk cow, another a bullock for beef,
and so on,
leaving no want unsupplied.

Thus it was that no one suffered,
all had plenty to eat and drink,
were provided with ample stock and clothing,
never in want, never required to labor for a living,
they would skim across the plains
or over the mountains,
perhaps catch a grizzly bear,
bring him into the settlement
and have a bull and bear fight,
and give a fandango every night.

Mexicans bringing such extravagances as Chinese firecrackers and brightly colored paper mache piñatas filled with sweets to the party that was California's Rancho Era.

Introducing a blending of brass instruments and guitars today referred to as mariachi. Together with the very fine art of distilling tequila.

Its manufacture catalyst for many a fiesta. Commencing with selection of the bateador (batter). A raucous event centering around huge oak casks filled with fermented juice from the blue agave plant.

An elected bateador being striped naked and cast into the cask. Then compelled to dance his or herself into a drunken stupor. Tequila thusly distilled served up copiously to all in attendance.

Encouraged by acceptable alcoholic binges, California's disenfranchised neophyte community beginning a seemingly irreversible slide into melancholia and drunkenness.

As resigned to rounding up and herding their own livestock into once magnificent courtyards and churches now sanctimoniously employed as the barns and corrals of private landbarons driving disheartened utopians to extinguish disillusionment through intoxication.

Those callous in their dismissal of the Indian's phlight soon sharing his fate.

One cannot help but wonder how different history might have been written had these Renchero's themselves discovered raw gold in the rivers that watered their privatized coastal kingdom.

Would Mexico have managed a fiscally sound permanency powerful enough to ward off foreign intervention?

Might the Californio Republic have succeeded in establishing itself as an independent Latin American nation?

As it was the bacanalia of California's fiery fiesta, with its many pleasures and indulgences, imparted but a brief brilliant burst of color to that tapestry begun so long ago in Iberia. Before being swept away like the Spanish missions it had plundered, as if by some tremendous Santa Ana wind.

In retrospect even co-conspirator Mariano Vallejo himself ascertaining little less than the swift and certain

Judgment of God

subsequently leveled against all who in having
destroyed the missions had robbed Indians of
their inheritance.

Still, arriving in 1847 and fraternizing exclusively with
Californios, Protestant preacher and American
military Chaplain Walter Colton marveling:

There are no people that I have ever been among
who enjoy life so thoroughly
as the Californians.

Their habits are simple;
their wants are few;
nature rolls almost everything spontaneously
into their lap.

Their cattle, horses, and sheep roam at large-
not a blade of grass is cut, and none is required.
The harvest waves wherever the plough
and harrow have been;
and the grain which the wind scatters this year,
serves as seed for the next.

The slight labor required is more
a diversion than a toil;
and even this is shared by the Indian.
They attach no value to money,
except as it administers to their pleasures.

A fortune,
without the facilities of enjoying it,
is with them no object of emulation or envy.

Their happiness flows from a fount that has very little

connection with their outward circumstances.

There is hardly a shanty among them
which does not contain more true contentment,
more genuine gladness of the heart,
than you will meet with in the most princely palace.

Their hospitality knows no bounds;
they are always glad to see you,
come when you may;
and only regret that your business calls you away.

If you are sick,
there is nothing which sympathy
and care can devise or perform
which is not done for you.
No sister ever hung over the throbbing brain
or fluttering pulse
of a brother
with more tenderness and fidelity.
This is as true of the lady whose hand
has only figured her embroidery
or swept her guitar,
as of the cottage-girl wringing
from her laundry the foam
of the mountain stream;

And all this from the **heart**!

If I must be cast in sickness
or destitution on the care of the stranger,
let it be in California;
but let it be before American avarice
has hardened the heart and made a god of gold.

ADIOS, ADIOS AMORES

P resenting the very image of Californio youth in full flower, Esteban Pico wore white linen shirt with gold filigreed black jacket and matching pantaloons. His youthful figure accentuated by a red scarf fashioned about the waist. Smart black bolero upon his head.

Still the expression of this handsome sixteen-year-old revealing anything but self-confidence.

Step sisters Jacinta and Bernarda dancing about him teasing,

> Don't forget to shave.
> Don't forget to shave.
> Monica doesn't like men who have whiskers!

Anxiously swatting the distraction away while nervously calling out,

> Mama, where are my leggings?

Prompting Bernarda and Jacinta, to taunt,

> Ohhhh, Monica has made leggings for her lover.

Pretend kissing then in unison one who was not there. The comedic performance evoking spontaneous laughter from their anxious big brother.

Who lovingly kicking them aside did an about face only to find four-year old Emilio, son of his father's mayordomo Jose Moreno, standing in the doorway wearing nothing but a pair of intricately fashioned deer skin leggings.

His sisters squealing as they pointed at little Emilio's particulars even as Esteban swept the youngster up to prevent escape.

"I will need these back, tonight," he teased.

Deer skin leggings slipping off on their own accord as playfully Esteban swung Emilio about.

The toddler giggling hysterically in response.

Esteban turning about and again calling out "Mama," only to confront her beautifully radiant and visibly proud before him.

Respectfully placing little Emilio on terra firma before repeating in a subdued and respectful tone,

Mama, never mind about the leggings.

Then stooping to pick them up from off the floor observing,

I have found them.

"I can see that, mi amor," responding Maria Ignacia Alvarado Pico, as she cupped his youthful face in her hands.

Deflecting affection, a blushing son protesting, "Mama!"

Who ignoring him put language to her thoughts, "I can hardly believe that already you have grown to become such a fine man, mi hijo (my son)."

Prompting yet another objecting "Mama," from her son's lips.

Mother's voice then assuming an authoritative air as husband Pio Pico entered the room in reminding Esteban, "Remember, you promised your Father and I to attend the Misa (Mass) before running off with Monica."

Papa Pico looking lovingly upon his boy before handing over Esteban's guitar while suggesting,

Monica will melt in your arms tonight.

"Pio!" protesting his wife, as she slapped her husband on the shoulder.

Esteban glancing away, embarrassed at his father's suggestion.

Did you remember to shave?,

Papa queried as he looked down and smiled knowingly at Jacinta and Bernarda, each having reentered the room and now holding fast to his legs.

Giggling uncontrollably when Esteban answered,

Yes, father, I have shaved.

Stroking with one hand his own grand beard Pio

running the other across Esteban's smooth face while slipping a satchel of gold reales into the boy's pocket. "Your friends are in the sala waiting for you. Be off and have a grand time."

"Thank you, Papa," responding the lad gratefully.

Dona Pico imposing, "Do you have your courtship papers from the alcalde?"

"Si, mama," replying Esteban, as he produced them from the pocket of his jacket. "Signed and paid for,".

Papa Pico then shoving him into the sala whilst laughing as he slid Maria Ignacia under his arm.

Who temporarily lost in the moment suddenly contemplated the night ahead. Crying out,

>The Misa.
>Don't forget-
>first the Misa.

"Yes mama," Esteban assuring her, before exiting to greet his companions.

Only then to halt, inspect and condescendingly query "What's this?," smiling young Pico, to his buddies Marco and Javier; each decked out as they were in Yankee dungarees and placard shirts.

"What's what?" they countered in chorus.

"So now it seems that Marco Avila and Javier Sepulveda are a couple of Yankee Doodle Dandies," grinning Esteban.

All laughing together in taking leave of the grand estancia, guitars slung over their shoulders. Climbing atop each mount prepared for their ride into town.

When suddenly bells of the Plaza Church rang out, even as Esteban's parents appeared in the doorway of the mansion house.

"Hurry, hurry," young Pico's mother admonishing, "you'll be late for the Misa."

Already it seemed as if the days had grown shorter. A full moon having risen above the dusky purple Sierra Madre.

Slight Santa Anas racing across a vast plain to dispell the stench of rotting carcasses. Its magic causing even the Evening Star to sparkle with extra intensity.

Six American trading ships in as many days had anchored off Point Fermin (Lasuen). Removing hides as fast as they could, still rancheros having been unable to keep up with demand.

Such abundance.
Unbelievable.

"Look over there," cautioning Javier, pointing at four large grizzly bears visible in the lengthening shadows as they feasted upon slaughtered cattle.

"Caballeros," demanding Marco, "Are you armed with El Segundo (Backup)?" Borrowed vernacular from a

Spanish knight's reference to his sword. And implying the Ranchero's lasso.

"Of course," responding Esteban, lifting it reverentially from off his ornately fashioned silver saddle horn as proof.

"Its a good thing," insisting Marco. "Bears are everywhere tonight."

"Do not tell my mother," entreating Esteban. "It would only make her worry unnecessarily."

"I will not tell if you don't," offering Marco.

Now riding onto and down the Alameda, each boy preparing for dismount in front of a grand church rumored to have been constructed by pirates doing penance.

Mass already begun, when a sudden gusting Santa Ana seemingly lifted the boys up and out of their saddles, as if to hurry them along. Each genuflecting respectfully before knelling at the back of the church.

Following spontaneous prayers Marco opening his eyes, to observe,

> look at all of the Baltimores.

"They're in from Mary Land," Javier contributing.

"It seems more and more of them arrive at the Pueblo," suggesting Esteban, "but I never see any come to church."

"Mary Land is not a pagan country like the rest of the United States," instructing Marco authoritatively. "The Baltimores in Mary Land are Catholics."

"Ohhh," his two students nodding, their eyes still on several dozen Yanks each decked out in dungarees and placard shirts.

Esteban then glancing up and down at both Marco and Javier, again focused upon their attire, whilst a grin crept across his face.

"What?" protesting his comrades.

"Shhhhush,"

coming the complaint of an old woman seated in front of them.

Whereupon each boy fell silent; but for a moment.

"There she is," piping up Marco, directing their gaze across a chapel filled with parishoners to the lovely Monica.

Who sat as if a vision in white lace and black mantilla adorned with red rose brocade. And already eyeing her suitor. Monica Carillo's glance flickering with the realization that she had herself been spied. Now blushing, eyes darting towards a trip tych behind the priest before the altar.

Seated at Monica's side being her mother, father and five brothers.

All of whom were eyeing Esteban. Sending his own gaze darting towards the altar, and his stomach, for the first time, churning.

A youthful heart suddenly pounding with anticipation.

Attempting to calm those fears focusing rather upon the liturgy being offered up by just in from Mission San Jose Reverend Father President Narcisso Duran.

Following communion, the Church of Los Angeles dispelling its congregates out into the warmth and magic of those Santa Ana winds. Each holding fast his or her shawl, poncho and bolero. The occasional blast throwing everything into disarray.

Dutifully each boy stepping back as Carlos Antonio Carillo's family exited on to the Plaza. Monica and Esteban sharing a fleeting smile. Marco and Javier, taking note, smiling at each other.

The boys waiting just long enough for all to arrive at home before anxiously showing up outside their doorway to conduct a well orchestrated and time honored ritual of benign courtship.

Esteban crooning something about his unrequited love to the accompaniment of three guitars.

Monica appearing in the upstairs window of her family's two-story town home, the quintessential coquette, obviously melting, as Papa Pio had predicted, at the sight of this handsome suitor.

Downstairs amongst shadows her parents, themselves

embracing each other, watching on in silence.

The Santa Ana contributing its own warmth to an innocently romantic affair.

Unnoticed being the fact that a monstrous grizzly bear disoriented from scent tossed about in that breeze, had wandered into town.

And now lumbered down a paseo leading directly to where an unsuspecting trio stood singing. Shouts of warning going unheard, what with the play of wind and enthusiastic strumming on guitars.

When engulfed in longing and passion Esteban glancing over his shoulder to be sure of Marco and Javier, caught sight of the huge beast ambling onto Carillo's courtyard.

And in that instant observing houses up and down the street emptying of their menfolk, who, together with Monica's five brothers raced, reatas in hand, to dispel a threat and avert disaster.

"Jesus, Mary and Joseph," Esteban shouting as dropping lyric and grabbing two friends, he threw them towards their horses; which, what with the confusing winds, had themselves suddenly just caught scent of the bear to race off unmounted.

A dozen reatas cracking. The great beast turning back to flee what had in an instant become its own dangerous encounter.

Whereupon the entire street burst into laughter. Papa

Carillo sweeping shaken lads up in his arms, to calm both them and the moment.

Not unnoticed was a contingent of "Baltimores," who lured by sounds of commotion, had joined the impromptu gathering.

Smiling as he acknowledged their presence, Carillo consoling his daughter's suitors by expressing in thick Spanish accent a trendy Yank, "O-kay."

Again everyone including the Yanks laughing upon hearing such a word escape from Don Carillo's mouth.

Looking about and waving his hands to suggest a call for all to submit, he admonished again, "O-kay. O-kay."

The street grew silent.

"Senor Pico, won't you sing another tune; this one for all of us," admonishing a smiling Carlos Carillo.

Courageously the boys obliging. As reassembling, they took a collective deep breath, glanced with deliberation at each other for reassurance and then standing straight and tall to face a wind that would not be turned back, belted out, as loud as they could,

Adios, Adios Amores
(Farewell my Loves, Forever).

An old Latin ballad recounting the paign of losing all that one holds most dear.

So tender of years, amidst a land of such innocence,

these children could not possibly grasp the profound significance held for everyone assembled in the lyric they so charmingly incanted.

Yet, Don Carillo, contemplating his own conversation of earlier that very day with nephew, political nemesis and father of his daughter's young suitor Pio Pico sighed heavily; knowingly.

How dare that deceitful little man refer to him as Arguello's Sancho Panza.

Regardless Carillo could see that no matter what course of action honorable men pursued none of the Franciscan missions would ever be returned to their Indian novices. Even San Luis Rey having been stolen, and by no less than Juan Bandini's Yankee son-in-law.

Nor could he or any other Californio possibly find a way to overcome the debt each had incurred with Yankee traders.

Only yesterday Bostonian Abel Stearns forcefully evicting little Javier Sepulvida's family from off their Rancho Los Cerritos for nothing more heinous than failure to bring current long overdue accounts between themselves and Stearn's brokerage house at San Pedro.

Meanwhile it remained plain as the big nose on Pio Pico's face, thought Carillo, that his bankrupt political regime was but a ruse installed purposefully temporarily, as most assuredly California would fall.

Word from Madrid was that King Fernando had himself been taken hostage. Rumors of yet another bloodbath at Mexico City were everywhere.

Which but brought to mind that good for nothing self appointed Californio Governor Alvarado.

The world Carillo had since early manhood with his own blood, sweat and tears helped to build was on its way out.

Nothing he could do would change that.

Unbidden tears unexpectedly filling the eyes through which he gazed not at lads singing but rather those "Baltimores." Considering both the implication of their presence and inevitability of not only his own fate but that of beloved Spain and cherished California.

When suddenly Maria's arm wrapped around his waist. Who having noticed her husband's condition calmed him with a fixed glance of reassurance.

Carlos embracing and holding her tight with equal affection.

Their eyes closing as in unison each offered up a silent heartfelt prayer to Mary, Queen of Heaven. Beseeching,

Because they loved God,

that she bless and protect them all.

Maria then kissing her husband's neck, squeezing his hand and with confidence whispering into his ear:

"Do not be afraid, mi Amor…"

"...BELIEVE."

EPILOGUE

Standing in possession of a history that reads more like pages from an adventure or romance novel, California's conquest by Spain formulates but prelude to events even more fantastic if not seemingly altogether incredulous.

Nevertheless this episode concerning its foundation as an extension of Western Civilization leaving indelibly etched upon all that which followed the undeniable signature both of Spain and of Rome.

Solidly anchoring a new Europe to distinctive and hallmark social institutions, architecture, legal precedent and cultural traditions borrowed and made unique through interpretation.

Amidst the milieu of otherwise mostly English parlance still resounding a Castilian spoken by its founding fathers throughout what was for nearly three centuries the northernmost American outpost of Iberian monarchs.

And, despite subsequent waves of fortune seekers, remaining decidedly Latin in character.

Endowing a staid English American nation with the quixotic imagination and courage that constitutes arguably Spain's most enduring legacy to all civilizations.

El Cid yet riding eternally triumphant astride his noble steed Balieca at San Diego as centerpiece of magnificent Balboa Park, itself resplendent in baroque Spanish revival architecture.

Muslims and Christians convening annually at Garden Grove in a postmodern architectural wonder of the world that is the largest mission California has ever produced, since constructed on lands once pertaining to Jose Antonio Yorba's Rancho Santiago, there to pursue the ongoing quest for an elusive common ground.

Manifestations of similarly extraordinary possibilities affording open access to comfort and power once reserved but for a ruling class alone.

Even as the Spanish King's standard yet catches an offshore breeze upon which still are heard the subtle intonations of Franciscan mission bells at a since reconstructed Royal Presidio in Santa Barbara.

To this day something of Spain resounding in the tenor of all things Californian.

BENEDICTION:
LITTLE PAGAN BEGGARS

Once upon a time,
during those splendid old days
when California was still a Spanish kingdom,
there lived at Monterey
a little girl named Ysabelita,

Whose mother so named her
in remembrance of
the generous Queen
who sold rubies
and emeralds and sapphires
so that Cristobol Colon
might have ships
with which to discover America.

Ysabelita resided
in a grand whitewashed adobe house
topped with red tiles
standing on a bluff overlooking the sea.

All about the grand house stretched a wide veranda.

In the middle of her house was a patio.
In the middle of the patio splashed a Cordovan fountain
surrounded by fragrant Castillian roses.

Ysabelita did not like to play under the wide veranda
where her three uncles sat in spurs
smoking big smelly cigars.

Nor did she like to play on the patio
near the splashing fountain
where Ohlone women busied themselves all day long
preparing meals and doing laundry.

Little Ysabel preferred playing
under an old oak standing near to the grand house.

For it was there that she had spent long hours
with her mother
watching ships from Spain and Russia and Valparaiso
sailing into and out of the harbor.

Ysabelita and her mother had no way of knowing
that the leaves on the old oak under which they sat
were not leaves at all
but rather tiny green fairies.

Nor could they know that the very ground underfoot
was both hallowed and enchanted.

But I am telling you this secret,
guarded by the Ohlone people,
who have lived in this land
since long before the Spaniards
(and so they know about such things).

Before she died,
little Ysabel's mother arranged with her three brothers
to provide for the child.
Promising that they would permit her to play
in the shade of this, their sister's favorite tree.

Who never had the opportunity of sharing
with her daughter

how under its branches she had fallen in love
with Ysabel's father.

And how in its shade
she had watched him sail away
never to be seen or heard from again.

And how during her long months of failing health
she returned daily ever vigilant,

hoping to spy the ship of her true love returning,
and now more than ever,
so that he might take care of little Ysabel
once she was gone.

In her pain
Ysabel's mother sensed tremendous compassion
from the spirit of the old oak tree
who unknown to all but the Ohlone
had itself witnessed and suffered great loss.

You see,
years before Ysabel's mother was born,
a brave Spanish conquistador by the name of Sebastian
sailed into this very harbor.

With men aboard his ships
so ill
that many of them would soon die.

Hoping to keep all alive
good Sebastian had set up a hospital camp
under the leafy canopy of this very same oak.

And having brought with him

the Franciscan brothers of Jesus Christ,
next prevailed upon them
to hang bells from its strong branches,
with which to summon intercession of the Christian god
on behalf of those dead and dying.

Then, as suddenly as he had appeared,
Sebastian sailed away,
like Ysabel's father,
never to be seen or heard from again.

Now as soon as the Christian conquistador
sailed out of the harbor,
jealous Chupu,
goddess of California,
incensed by such trespass
and angry at the old oak
for having sheltered the brothers of Jesus Christ,
struck it down
with a tremendous bolt of lightening.

And so it was that
for more than two hundred years
the blackened oak,
barren and without leaves,
but not dead,
yet stood guard over the graves of Christian martyrs

To mock this shamed tree
a tribe of tiny pagan fairies,
having taken up residence in the old oak,
taunting it's nakedness
by assuming for themselves
the shape of ugly, spiny green leaves.

Ohlone people
who had lived in the land
since long before the Spaniards
knew that this old oak's leaves
were not real leaves at all,
but rather tiny pagan fairies.

And this they knew because
each looked nothing like the leaves of other oaks.
Nor did they change color in season or die.

Carefully the Ohlone had spied upon the suspect tree
so cruelly punished
but for its kind act of affording shade and protection
to men lying near death.

And discovered how every evening at twilight
contumacious little fairy leaves
assumed their true shapes.

Dropping from the tree to dance wild pagan dances
while chanting insults at both it
and the Christian god.

Ohlone witnessed how at dawn
these hurtful, hate- filled pagans
ascended back up into branches blackened by
Chupu's thunderbolt,
there to sleep the day away disguised as a maligned
oak's leaves.

It was fortunate indeed that neither Little Ysabel
nor her mother
had ever disturbed anything about this enchanted tree.
For you can well imagine what might have occurred

if either of them had done so much as pull but one leaf
from off its black branches.

With minds, hearts and souls as small
as the teensy green noses on their tiny green faces
these vengeful, unforgiving little pagans
would not have taken kindly
to being disturbed from out of deep slumber.

Now and then
one itsy-bitsy green eye would open,
to see Little Ysabel and her mother
sitting there watching the ships coming and going.

A tiny green eye that would close
after taking note of woman and child;
little concerned with anything
other than its own sleepiness.

Tiny green eyes saw
but never wondered why it was
that one day
little Ysabel came to the tree alone.

They saw
but never wondered why
the pretty little girl cried and cried for days and days.

Never did they ever trouble their tiny hearts,
minds and souls
with any concern for her.

They did notice how finally,
one glorious, sunny day
the little girl stopped crying,

and began to smile again.

This they noticed
because her infernal weeping
no longer disturbed their sleep.

Now the oak tree did not grow.
And the tiny pagan fairies did not grow.
But Ysabelita grew and grew
until she came to stand five feet tall and a little over.

Arriving at the tree one day a young woman,
with her beautiful black hair fastened high in a comb
the way her mother had worn it,
a lace mantilla draped over her shoulders
just the way her mother had once done.

Yet even all grown up
Ysabel continued to spend much time alone
sitting under the old oak tree,
where she felt close to her mother
and without knowing why
still loved watching ships
from Spain and Russia and Valparaiso
sailing into and out of the harbor.

All the while yet unaware of those tiny pagan fairies
sleeping cozily upon the branches
above her unsuspecting head.

Ysabel could not remember ever having had a father.
But she did remember always having had
her three uncles,
Don Antonio, Don Andreas and Don Ramundo,
who no matter how much she had grown

continued to think of her as their little Ysabelita.

Ysabel's uncles were very famous rancheros,
each owning enormous stretches of land
upon which ran thousands of head of cattle.

And when not sitting under the veranda
smoking big smelly cigars
spent their time astride fine horses,
inspecting vast estates.

Ysabel's uncles while taking good care of her
were not otherwise particularly generous.

And each morning at breakfast grumbled
concerning the disappearance of little bits of this and that
from out of their overstuffed pantries and barns.

Always they blamed, 'those little pagan beggars,'
for everything from the disappearance of a hat
full of corn,
layers of cream scrapped from off milk pans,
or a bottle of brandy.

Any of which might otherwise have been given away
rather than wasted
had they been more thoughtful.

Fairies sleeping nearby
often overhearing the uncle's hurtful, hate-filled oaths
sworn against those Little Pagan Beggars.

And being completely self-absorbed
assuming themselves to be the pagan beggars
in question,

and therefore falsely accused of one presumption
of petty larceny after another.

And prone to do so,
grew angrier concerning said presumptions
with each passing day.

It so happened that following an annual cattle roundup
the Commandante at every Royal Presidio
held a great ball.

Following her fifteenth birthday
the Senorita Ysabel receiving an invitation to attend.

And on that special night
now so very long ago
stood resplendent
like a vision
in the doorway of the grand hall
at the Royal Presidio
dressed in saffron and silk
imported for her from China
by Uncle Antonio,
draped with a blue Italian shawl
presented to her by Uncle Andreas
and standing in jeweled Russian slippers
given to her by Uncle Ramundo.

Her dark eyes and hair catching the light
thrown from silver chandeliers suspended overhead.

Ysabel's beauty capturing the attentions of officers
dressed in glittering uniforms,
captains from many lands
and grandly outfitted Californio caballeros.

All of whom wished to dance with her.

La Senorita Ysabel dancing the night away
to the music of violin and guitar.

Uncles Antonio, Andreas and Ramundo noticing
that she danced mostly with young
Capitan Julio Romero.

So began the great love of each of their lives.

And as is the way of love
it came to pass that one day Capitan Julio Romero
appeared at the doorway
of the grand whitewashed adobe house
topped with red tiles
that stood on a bluff overlooking the sea,

to sit with Ysabel's uncles under that wide veranda
and sue permission for her hand in marriage.

Uncles Antonio, Andreas and Ramundo
agreeing amongst themselves
that the two should indeed marry.

For was not Capitan Julio an officer
in the Spanish military.
And did he not ride upon a splendid horse
bred at Mission San Antonio no less
where the finest horses in all of California were raised.

And were his saddle trappings and bridle
not inlaid with gold.

And did he not wear heavy Spanish silver

on both his sombrero and pantaloons.

Now Ysabel had never noticed Julio's horse,
nor his saddle or his sombrero.

And the fact that he was a captain in the military
was of no consequence to her.

Ysabel had ever seen only Julio himself.
And she loved him.
And now could think of little else
whenever she sat under the old oak tree
watching ships from Spain and Russia and Valparaiso
sailing into and out of the harbor.

Of course she agreed to marry him.

But before Ysabel's wedding day arrived,
three strange ships
flying the flags of French pirates
sailed into Monterey.

Armed with three hundred fighting men
and thirty-eight cannon,
these mostly South American mercenaries
attempting to storm the Royal Presidio.

Where a Spanish garrison,
under Capitan Julio Romero's command,
fought them off bravely
in an unsuccessful attempt to prevent their attack
upon the town.

After three days of intense confrontation,
the pirates abandoning their assault

to sail away.

But it would not be until after they were gone
that Julio Romero's men discovered
how a blast from a pirate's musket
had blinded him during the attack

Their courageous Capitan saying nothing,
determined as he was to encourage them
by defending his post.

Understandably everyone in Monterey
was proud of Capitan Romero.

"Did you hear how he nearly saved our City?
Everybody said to everybody else.
"And he, poor fellow,
blinded by the blast from a pirate's gun!"

Ysabel sat with Julio for long hours
under the branches of the compassionate old oak
reading to him
from out of his favorite books,
which he loved but could no longer read for himself.

And in so doing discovered for herself
the story of good King Charlemagne and
his defeat by the Spanish,
of noble Rodrigo de Vivar who united all of Spain
against the Moor,
of determined Sebastian who so loved California
and of courageous Brother Junipero Serra
who brought education and with it Christ's example
into the new kingdom.

And as she read these things to him
Ysabel came to understand why Julio Romero was
who he was.
Realizing just how very much he had strived to be
like each of these men.

Which but deepened her love for him.

Which was all well and good.
Except that when Ysabel's uncles discovered
that she still intended to marry
a man who was now blind
and accordingly retired from the military
they bellowed their disapproval.

How was he going to support her.
And more importantly
how was he going to be able to carry on for them.

Ysabel must have a husband with keen eyes,
"So that he can watch over our cattle for us
when we are old,"
they agreed amongst themselves.

And to their Ysabelita they threatened,
"we will not let you do this foolish thing."

"But I am marrying Julio,"
Ysabel answered them resolutely.
"And on the next Feast Day as planned."

Whereupon unexpectedly, and startling even to himself,
a wicked glimmer sparkled in Don Ramundo's eye.

Who drew close his two brothers,

to propose a terrible scheme
while standing beneath Ysabelita's old Oak Tree.

"How simple it would be
to do away with this blind boy
after they have married?

"If he is found floating in the sea, people will say,
'Poor Don Julio,
poor blind boy,
he must have fallen accidentally over the cliff
and into the sea.'

"And then we can wed Ysabel to someone
more capable of watching over and increasing
our great wealth."

Again surprising even himself Don Ramundo
laughed cruelly;
his two brothers surprised at themselves,
nodding their heads in agreement.

None of them realized
not for one minute
that the little pagan fairies
had overheard every last word
of this wicked plot.

The next Holy Feast Day happened to be
that of San Carlos,
patron saint of the King.

As his day approached
Ohlone novices at Mission San Carlos
set about making special preparations

to honor the king of Spain and his patron saint
and to host the marriage of Don Julio and Ysabel.

Who assisted in gathering fennel blossoms
with which to perfume water then sprinkled
upon the sanctuary floor.

Whereupon it occurred to Ysabel how very lovely
it might be
to fill the whole Church with branches
from off of her old oak tree.

And she asked friend Juanito,
whose Ohlone name was Moyla,
to go with her on the morrow,
early in the morning,
and help with gathering them in.

Now Moyla,
like all Ohlone children,
knew the secret enchantment of that tree.

And nervously countered with,
'O but we mustn't.'

Adding,
'Through the oak's acorns Chinigchinich provides
us with sustenance.'

And knowing full well that this particular oak
hadn't yielded a single acorn in more than
two hundred years suggested,
'To repay this tree's generosity by removing its limbs
would offend the great god of all creation.'

To which Ysabel retorted cheerily, 'Why Juanito,
don't be silly.'

At that very moment the two friends spotted
Father Jose Senan,
President of all the Indian Missions
throughout the kingdom,
approaching clothed in cowled grey habit,
with knotted cord; a cross suspended about his waist.

'Father,' queried Ysabel respectfully,
'I wish to decorate Mission San Carlos for my wedding
with lovely oak branches.

But Moyla tells me that to do so might offend
the spirit of the tree.
What do you say?'

It would be a long while before the old padre spoke.
All had come to recognize the wisdom of this practice.

Knowingly Ysabel and Moyla waited, patiently.
The pagan fairies,
suspended above their heads
 in the shape of ugly, spiny green oak leaves
waited too, and with much anticipation.

At last Senan spoke.

'My dear children,
Saint Francis teaches us that all living things
are imbued with the spirit of their creator.

'He also teaches us that to give of what we have,
is to receive all that we lack.

'Now the palm tree gave up its branches
to be placed at the feet of our Lord
when he entered Jerusaleum,
there to be crucified for our sins.

'And in so doing
that palm tree received a place of honor
above all other trees.

'I should think an old oak
no less humble and giving than a palm tree.

'I should think an old oak would consider it
a great honor
to be given the opportunity of sacrificing
some of its many beautiful branches
so that beneath them two courageous and
loving young people
might pledge their hearts and souls to each other.'

Now when the Queen of the pagan fairies,
heard the old padre's words
she decided to play a great joke upon him.
Who had but spoken surely in jest
about palm trees and the like.

Just before dawn of the next day,
while lights were still burning in the houses
around Monterey Bay
and on ships in the harbor
Ysabel and Moyla set out to gather branches.

Arriving so early in fact
that pagans were still dancing and reveling in ceremony,
when unexpectedly they spied

the two young people approaching.

And quickly grabbed hold of a branch.
Transforming themselves instantly into leaves.

Then held on tight,
as many were wrested from the tree,
hauled to the mission
and hung from its rafters.

A feat completed
before the first light of dawn
shown through the high windows of the sanctuary.
Whereupon the tiny fairies fell fast asleep.

At daybreak ships in the harbor began
firing off salutations
with cannon and musketry,
to announce both the Feast Day of San Carlos
and the wedding day of Capitan Julio Romero.

As the morning progressed streets filled
with gorgeous horses,
each draped by a saddle jingling of gold and silver,
their riders attired in similar extravagance
with satins and lace,

Patrons from off the ranchos,
accompanied by their extensive families
dressed to the nines,

Ohlone in colorful costume.

Grey robed Franciscans.

And even naked gentile Indians.

Everyone it seemed
responding to the bells of Mission San Carlos,
summoning all to celebration.

Once inside
each discovered a sanctuary aglow
with hundreds of candles burning upon the high altar;
as everyone in Monterey
wanted to honor and pray for brave Don Julio Romero
and his beautiful orphaned bride.

Overhead pagan fairy boughs adorning the massive
wooden beams and adobe walls of a Christian Church.

Wherein even the little green intruders gasped
when Father Senan entered draped in rare vestments
of white and gold brocade.

Julio Romero, of course, saw none of such pageantry.
He could not even see Ysabel as she approached
to stand beside him
dressed in long folds of ivory satin.
And wearing a starry headdress.

But he could hear hundreds of Mission Indians chanting
as Father Senan pronounced upon them both
their wedding vows.

And at that instant,
even as he kissed his bride,
sensed an unexpected disturbance
throughout the sanctuary.

When suddenly it filled with a shimmering display
of green sprites.

So jubilant were the pagan fairies
over having played such a trick upon Christians,
happily disrupting the Franciscan ceremony.

Wondering voices gasping
when the Fairy Queen herself perched
atop Reverend Father President's three-cornered hat.

Don Julio whispering to his bride,
'What is going on?'

Ysabel whispering back,
'I don't know.'

Reverend Father President Senan
and all of Monterey
standing silent
as if struck dumb
while the pagan Queen
descended from her perch,
to approach Ysabel.

Bowing before the startled bride
like a blade of grass in the wind.
Then thanking Ysabel for the invitation to participate
not only in her wedding but the feast day
of a Christian King.

'Whose tradition,' she offered,
'requires that I present this wedded couple with a gift.
I shall award them three.'

Though pleased Young Ysabel leaned forward quietly
and with respect whispered to the Queen,
'I have but one wish, your Majesty.
And that is for my brave Julio to be able to see again.'

Immediately the Fairy Queen summoned two acolytes,
each with a tiny drop of ambrosia
which they placed in Don Julio's eyes.

Whereupon suddenly Julio could see his beautiful Ysabel
standing before him in her starry headdress.

He could also see what appeared to be
hundreds of tiny green people
perched upon the altar of the Church.

With tears streaming from wonder-filled eyes,
Julio kissed his bride anew,
and then,
guided by Ysabel
knelt before the little fairy Queen
to thank her
for bestowing upon him such an extraordinary gift.

'Ahhhh,' responded the minute monarch boldly,
a glint of malice beaming in her itsy-bitsy eye,
'but there is more to my gift.'

'The one who refers to my people as little pagan beggars,
will find those words being the last he ever utters!'

'Why you little pagan beggar...'
the words escaped spontaneously from out of
Don Andreas' mouth.
Whereupon, to his horror,

he discovered that he could not speak at all.

'And he who plotted to destroy Ysabel's happiness,'
continued the Queen mercilessly,
'with intent to murder her lover,
will discover that the last image he shall ever see
will be the bright,
clear eyes of Capitan Julio Romero.'

Even as she pronounced upon him her curse,
Don Ramundo found himself gazing right into
Julio's eyes. Whereupon, in an instant,
a thoughtlessly cruel ranchero
saw that he could no longer see anything at all.

'And the one who heard these oaths but did nothing,'
proceeded the Queen,
'shall no longer hear anything at all.'

In an instant Don Antonio fell deaf.

Everyone stood dumbfounded,
as Ysabel's three uncles,
their sins exposed,
pled as best they could
each on their hands and knees
for a forgiveness the pagan Queen
could neither comprehend
nor bestow.

Calmly Ysabel knelt beside her husband
before the Fairy monarch.

And addressing her
with all the wisdom of Charlemagne

equanimity of Rodrigo de Vivar
determination of Sebastian
courage of Brother Junipero Serra
and the Peace of Jesus Christ
spoke softly.

'Your Majesty,' she began,
'my husband and I are deeply grateful
for these wonderful gifts.'

'Dear Fairy Queen,
evil ever walks the earth.
How unfortunate we all are
when any one of us adds but one more step to its stride.

'Might I, at this time,
without being perceived as impertinent,
prevail upon your graciousness
to award the other two wishes offered?'

'But of course, my dear,'
responded a pagan Queen wonderingly.

'Then I shall wish,
for my second wish,
that you forgive my three uncles,
who are otherwise good men,
for the evil they permitted enter into their hearts.'

A surprised Fairy Queen stood silent.
Before responding dismissively with,
'O very well.'

'And as my third wish,'Ysabel continued,
'that you restore to each his lost faculty.'

Again the pagan monarch wavered.
Before acquiescing with,
'It shall be as you desire my dear.'

In an instant Don Andreas regained the use of his voice.
Don Ramundo saw that he could see again.
Don Antonio discovering his hearing
to have been restored.

The sight of three big men
rushing to kneel before their Ysabelita
who directed them rather to return
and thank the tiny Queen,
which they did,
expressing sincere penance and gratitude
in a flood of tears
being a sight that Monterey would not soon forget.

Nor did any one of those big men ever again
utter untoward oaths
against innocents struggling hand to mouth
and in the midst of their own opulent existence.

But rather gave freely from overstuffed larders
so that anyone suffering from want
might enjoy the essentials of life.

'Thank you, your Majesty,
for blessing this happy occasion
with manifestations of both your power
as well as your mercy,'
came a sage's wisdom from the mouth
of but a young woman.

Who taking hold of her new husband's hand

gazed lovingly into his keen eyes.
Then even as she said these things
glanced gratefully
upon the image of Jesus Christ.

To see but the face of Chinigchinich,
smiling back at her.

With Father Senan's prompting
Mission San Carlos emptying out
into the mist- laden air of Carmel at midday.

The padre inviting everyone, including all pagans
to remain and take part in a wedding fiesta,
which lasted nine days.

Afterwhich the vengeful, unforgiving
and shamed by innocent Ysabelita
Fairy Queen together with her hurtful, hate- filled
and selfish legions took leave of California altogether.
Never to be seen or heard from again.

The following spring and for the first time
in more than two hundred years
Ysabel's Oak bursting forth in luxuriant foliage.
In the fall standing laden with acorns.

During the annual autumn Roundup
Ysabel's uncles discovering
that Capitan Julio could see farther and better
than anyone else in Monterey.

Who with proceeds garnered in trade
from hides and tallow
built for his Ysabel

a grand house of white-washed adobe
topped with red tiles
but a few steps from the old oak.

And there on its wide veranda
whilst holding her husband's hand
first spied the ship uponwhich
Ysabel's prodigal father returned home.

To live together with them happily everafter
watching ships from Spain and Russia and Valparaiso,
sailing into and out of the harbor
during those splendid old days
when California was still a Spanish kingdom.

GLOSSARY OF SYMBOLS

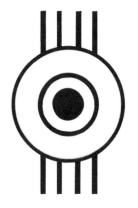

Eye of God pictograph employed
widely throughout
ancient California and thought
to represent, as aperture
of an otherwise omnipotent
creator, the sun itself.

European lion used by many an
Old World monarchy,
in this case Spain,
to suggest both presence
as well as power.

A Crusader's Cross.
Indicating one's willingness to
themselves be crucified, as
was Christ, for humanities
sake.

Often tattooed token
illustrating
a perceived kinship between
man and dolphin.

Cattle brand utilized by
Mission San Juan Capistrano.

Borrowed from the Greek
and meaning,
"I AM STILL HERE!"

✠

BOOK ONE
bibliographic notes

DON CARLOS, POR LA GRACIA de Dios, Rey de Castilla, de León, de Aragon, de las dos Sicilias, de Jerusalén, de Navarra, de Granada, de Toledo, de Valencia, de Galicia, de Mallorca, de Sevilla, de Cerdeña, de Córdova, de Córcega, de Murcia, de Jaén, de los Algarbes, de Algeciras, de Gibraltar, de las Islas de Canarias, de las Indias Orientales, y Occidentales, Islas, y Tierra-Firme del Mar Océano, Archiduque de Austria, Duque de Borgoña, de Brabante, y Milán, Conde de Abspurg, de Flandes, Tirol, y Barcelona, Señor de Vizcaya, y de Molina, &c. A los del mi Consejo, Presidente, y Oídores de mis Audiencias, Alcaldes, Alguaciles de mi Casa, Córte, y Chancillerías, y á todos los Corregidores, Asistente, Gobernadores, Alcaldes Mayores, y Ordinarios, y otros qualesquier Jueces, Justicias, Ministros, y

D. Her.do Cortes. Natural de Medellin de Valle.

Portugues descub. del estrecho de su nomb. Her. do de Magallanes.

Lagran Ciudad de Mexico en la laguna

Descubre Magallanes el estrecho

HISTORIA GENE
RAL DE LOS HECHO
DE LOS CASTELLANOS
EN LAS ISLAS I TIERRA
FIRME DEL MAR OCEANO
ESCRITA POR ANTONIO DE
HERRERA CORONISTA
MAIOR DE SV M.d DE LAS
INDIAS Y SV CORONISTA
DE CASTILLA.

DE CADA TERZERA
Al Rey Nu.tro. Senor

Aqui fue preso el Rey Quauhtimoc

Magallanes pasa a la mar del Sur

El Rey de Mechoacan visita a cortes

Muere magallanes peleando con los yndios

El ex.cito cast.no camina a las ybueras

la nao bitoria llega a Seuilla Rodeado el mundo

El Maese de Campo Xpoual de Olid de Vbeda pacifica a Mechoacan

Mexico se Redifica

Disputase en la particion del mundo

Gorito de Sandoual Capitan Valeroso Natural de Medellin

En Madrid en la emplenta Real. 1601.

BOOK ONE
BIBLIOGRAPHIC NOTES

AFFILIATIONS

MEMBER/CALIFORNIA MISSION
STUDIES ASSOCIATION

VOLUNTEER
ARCHIVIST/HISTORIAN
CATHOLIC DIOCESE OF ORANGE
MISSION SAN JUAN CAPISTRANO

MEMBER/GREAT STONE CHURCH
CONSERVATION TEAM
MISSION SAN JUAN CAPISTRANO

DOCENT/MISSION SAN JUAN
CAPISTRANO

MEMBER/CAROLWOOD
PACIFIC RAILROAD
HISTORICAL SOCIETY

DOCENT/WALT DISNEY'S BARN

MEMBER/OLD MONTEREY
PRESERVATION SOCIETY

MEMBER/HUNTINGTON
WESTERNERS

MEMBER/MORMON HISTORY
ASSOCIATION

MEMBER/FRIENDS OF THE SAN
CLEMENTE LIBRARY

MEMBER/FRIENDS OF MISSION
SANTA BARBARA
ARCHIVE/LIBRARY

MEMBER/FRIENDS
OF THE BRAUN RESEARCH
INSTITUTE/SOUTHWEST MUSEUM

MEMBER/FRIENDS OF THE
BANCROFT LIBRARY
UNIVERSITY OF
CALIFORNIA/BERKELEY

PARTICIPATING AFFILIATE/
GRAN QUIVIRA
SPANISH BORDERLANDS
STUDY GROUP

PARTICIPATING LIFE
MEMBER/YOSEMITE ASSOCIATION

VOLUNTEER/SIERRA CLUB

VOLUNTEER LAY MINISTER
OF RECEPTION
GUEST RELATIONS
CRYSTAL CATHEDRAL MINISTRIES

MEMBER/SURFRIDER
FOUNDATION

COLLECTIONS

BANCROFT LIBRARY
University of California/Berkeley

FRANCISCAN ARCHIVE/LIBRARY
Mission Santa Barbara, California

KARPELES MANUSCRIPT
LIBRARY/MUSEUM
Santa Barbara, California

BRAUN RESEARCH INSTITUTE
SOUTHWEST MUSEUM
Los Angeles, California

SHERMAN FOUNDATION
LIBRARY/ARCHIVE
Corona Del Mar, California

CATHOLIC DIOCESE OF ORANGE
ARCHIVE/LIBRARY
Mission San Juan Capistrano,
California

PRESIDIAL RESEARCH CENTER
SANTA BARBARA TRUST FOR
HISTORIC PRESERVATION
Santa Barbara, California

ELIZABETH J. SCHULTZ MEMORIAL
CALIFORNIA HISTORY ROOM/
ANAHEIM PUBLIC LIBRARY
Anaheim, California

SALA CALIFORNIANA/SAN JUAN
CAPISTRANO BRANCH
ORANGE COUNTY PUBLIC LIBRARY
San Juan Capistrano, California

CATHOLIC DIOCESE OF LOS
ANGELES ARCHIVE/LIBRARY
Mission San Fernando Rey de Espana,
California

CALIFORNIA STATE UNIVERSITY
AT FULLERTON LIBRARY

UNIVERSITY OF CALIFORNIA AT
IRVINE LIBRARY

HUNTINGTON LIBRARY
San Marino, California

CALIFORNIA HISTORICAL
SOCIETY/ARCHIVE
San Francisco, California

SAN DIEGO HISTORICAL
SOCIETY/ARCHIVE
San Diego, California

AMERICAN TITLE AND
TRUST/ARCHIVE
Santa Ana, California

LIBRARY OF CONGRESS
Washington, D.C.

PRIVATE LIBRARY OF DR. MELVIN
R. COLLINGS

PRIVATE LIBRARY/ARCHIVE OF
ADAM R. COLLINGS

ARCHIVE OF THE INDIES (AGI)
ONLINE (AND SEE CHAPMAN
AND PRESIDIAL RESEARCH
CENTER AT SANTA BARABRA)

NATIONAL ARCHIVES OF
MEXICO (AGN)
SEE PRESIDIAL RESEARCH
CENTER AT SANTA BARABRA

INTERVIEWS

THE FOLLOWING ROSTER IS
ARRANGED IN NO PARTICULAR
ORDER AND SUGGESTS NEITHER
ENDORSEMENT BY NOR
AGREEMENT WITH INDIVIDUALS
INTERVIEWED.

DAVID AND MARSHA KARPELES
KARPELES MANUSCRIPT
LIBRARY/MUSEUM
Montecito, California

LAURENCE K. GOULD JR.
REGENT/UNIVERSITY
OF CALIFORNIA
President CMSA (Californa Mission
Studies Association)

FATHER JOHN VAUGHAN, o.f.m.
MINISTER GENERAL/FRANCISCAN
ORDER/ROME
Mission Santa Barbara, California

FATHER NOEL MOHOLY, o.f.m., Ph.d
Vice Postulator for the Cause to
Canonize Fray Junipero Serra, o.f.m.
Franciscan Province of Santa Barbara

FATHER KIERAN McCARTY,
o.f.m., Ph.d
Mission San Xavier del Bac, Tucson,
Arizona
Franciscan Province of Santa Barbara

BROTHER JOSEPH SCHWAB, o.f.m.
Director/Casa de Bien y Paz,
Scottsdale, Arizona
Franciscan Province of Santa Barbara

BROTHER TIMOTHY ARTHUR, o.f.m.
Archivist/Historian
Franciscan Province of Santa Barbara

MONSIGNOR FRANCIS
LLOYD WEBER
Director of the Archive/Library for
the Catholic Diocese
of Los Angeles, located at Mission San
Fernando Rey de Espana,
San Fernando, California

DON ALFONSO DE BOURBON
La Jolla, California

DON BERNARDO YORBA
Californio descendent
Anaheim, California

DONA MARGARITA YORBA
Anaheim, California

DON EDUARDO GRIJALVA
Californio descendent
Orange, California

PETER J. MEL (BANDINI), Ph.D, MD
Californio descendent
Rancho Santa Margarita, California

SHELLY HAYES CARON
Californio descendent
Carlsbad, California

GLORIA CARILLO (FELIZ)
Acjachemem
Lake Forest, California

ELENA OROZCO
Californio descendent
Interpretive Ranger
Old Town San Diego State Historic Park
San Diego

ANTHONY PICO
Californio descendent
Santa Barbara, California

JOHN JOHNSON, Ph.D
Curator of Anthropology
Santa Barbara Museum of Natural
History
Santa Barbara, California

LINDA AGREN
Assistant Curator
Anthropology Department
Santa Barbara Museum
of Natural History

CHRISTOPHER FISCHER E.ed
Spanish American History
Brussels, Belgium

TERESA THORNE, Ph.D
Professor of History, UCI
Irvine, California

ED CASTILLO, Ph.D
Professor of History UCSD
San Diego, California

LEROY MIRANDA
Director/Cupa Cultural Center
Pala Indian Reservation, San Diego

JANET BARTELL
Mission Administrator
Mission San Diego de Alcala

MILDRED MURRAY E.ed
Daughters of the American Revolution
Newport Beach, California

DAVID & AURORA BELARDES
Acjachemem Nation/Blas Aguilar
Adobe Foundation
San Juan Capistrano, California

TONY FORSTER
Californio descendent
President/San Juan Capistrano
Historical Society

DON TRYON
Director/Archivist
San Juan Capistrano Historical Society

CHUCK BODNER
Archivist/historian
Catholic Diocese of Orange
Mission San Juan Capistrano

MARY WEYLAN
Curator/Museum Administrator
Mission San Luis Rey de Francia

BARBARA BAKER
Museum Education Coordinator
Mission San Luis Rey de Francia

BRIAN D. HALEY
Assistant Research Anthropologist
UC MEXUS
University of California Institute for
Mexico and the United States

LANCE BOWLING
Archivist/Californiana
Lomita, California

JAMES A. GRAVES
Editor/journalist for the Catholic
Diocese of Orange
and for Mission San Juan Capistrano

ILSE BYRNES
Historian/Historic preservation activist
San Juan Capistrano, California

JIM SANDOS
Professor of History
University of Redlands

KAREN FONTANETTA
Curator/Museum Administrator
Mission San Miguel

KIM WALTERS
Library Director
Braun Research Insitute/
Southwest Museum

ANTONIO SHIJE
Exhibits Curator
Southwest Museum

MAURICE BANDY
Director
San Diego Presidio Foundation

JACK WILLIAMS, Ph.D
San Diego Presidio Foundation
San Diego, California

ANITA COHEN, Pn.D
San Diego Presidio Foundation
San Diego, California

JEREMY HASS
Independent Historian
Santa Barbara, California

KRISTINA FOSS
Museum Administrator
Mission Santa Barbara

GERALD R. MILLER
Administrator
Mission San Juan Capistrano

MONSIGNOR PAUL MARTIN
Parish Priest/founder CMSA
(California Mission Studies Association)
Mission San Juan Capistrano

FATHER WILLIAM KRECKELBERG
Archivist/Historian
Diocese of Orange/Mission
San Juan Capistrano

HARRY FRANCISCO
Chief Archeologist
Mission San Juan Capistrano

NELS ROSELUND
Structural Engineer
Great Stone Church
Conservation Team
Mission San Juan Capistrano

JACK WRONKA
Contractor
Great Stone Church
Conservation Team
Mission San Juan Capistrano

LORIE GARCIA
Independent Historian
Mission Santa Clara

MICHAEL HARDWICK
Historian
Member Royal Presidio Volunteers
Santa Barbara, California

ROBERT HOOVER, Ph.D
Board Member/California Trust for
Historic Preservation
Professor of History/Archeology
California State Polytechnic University,
San Luis Obispo

JARRELL JACKMAN, Ph.D
Executive Director/
Santa Barbara Trust for Historic
Preservation

DAVID DEBS
Curator
Santa Barbara Trust for
Historic Preservation

MARY LOUISE DAYS
Research Center Director
Santa Barbara Trust for
Historic Preservation

CRESENCIA OLMSTEAD
Secretary
Provincial Archive/Library of the
Franciscan Order
Santa Barbara, California

HELEN J. NELSON
Administrator
Mission San Gabriel Archangel

CAROLINE KENYON
California Mission Art Historian
Santa Barbara, California

ROBERT M. SENKEWICZ
Professor of History
Santa Clara University

ELLEN L. SWEET
Maron Adobe Preservation Society
Rancho Guajome

NEIL MORGAN
Author/Journalist
San Diego Union Tribune

DENNIS SOMMERS
Acjachemem
San Juan Capistrano

JACKIE NUNEZ
Acjachemem/Camp Director
Mission San Juan Capistrano

BEA TORRES
Educator/Docent
Mission San Juan Capistrano

TOM CORE
President
Big Bear Valley Historical Association

OPAL KISSINGER
Commissioner
County of Orange Historical
Commission
Santa Ana, California

STEPHEN J. MEDLY
President
Yosemite Association
El Portal, California

JIM VAN METER
Curator
Bancroft Ranchhouse
Spring Valley, California

CARMEN BOONE DE AGUILAR
Board Member
CMSA (California Mission
Studies Association)
Mexico City

DORIS WALKER
Writer/Historian
Dana Point, California

ANDREW ROSALES GALVAN
Native American Indian Consultant
The Ohlone Indian Tribe,
Mission San Jose, California

ROBIN PENDEGRAFT
Publisher
The Californians
Healds burg, California

PETER AND JANE VERZIC
Mountain View California

RUDOLPH MARTINEZ
Adobe Construction Specialist
Mission San Juan Capistrano

JOSE RIVERA
Director of Education
The Marin Museum of
the American Indian
Novato, California

CHARLIE /LEE HEIZMAN
Volunteer Docents
Mission San Juan Capistrano

NELSON MENDEZ
Independent Historian
Santiago, Chile

PAUL CARLTON
Sierra Club
San Clemente, Ca

EDNA KIMBRO
The J. Paul Getty Conservation Team

HARRY KELSEY, Ph.D
The Huntington Library
San Marino, California

ROBERT RYAL MILLER
Writer/Historian
Santa Barbara, California

THE HONORABLE MAYOR OF
MONTEREY
MR. DAN ALBERT
Monterey, California

DR. DOUGLAS MONROY
Professor of History
University of Colorado

THOMAS BROWN
Landscape Historian/Architect
Monterey, California

BROTHER GUIRE CLEARY
Curator Mission San Francisco de Asis

RANDY MILLIKEN
Far Western Anthropological Resource
Group, Inc.
Monterey, California

GEORGE H. PHILLIPS
History Professor
University of Colorado

ROSE MARIE BEEBE
History Professor
Santa Clara University

CARLOS LOPEZ
History Professor
Menlo College

RICHARD J. ORSI
History Professor/Writer
California Sate University/Hayward

DANIEL K. LEWIS, Ph.D
History Professor
California State Polytechnic
University, Pomona

BABE RAMOS
San Juan Capistrano

WILLIAM HENDRICKS. Ph.D
Director
Sherman Foundation Archive/Library

IRIS ENGSTRAND, Ph.D
Department of Spanish Studies
University of San Diego

JOYCE STANFIELD PERRY
President
Payomkawichum Kaamalam/
The Westerners-first People of Earth
Mother
Irvine, California

JOHNATHAN M. HOERER
President
Foundation for Native American
Advancement
San Clemente, California

JAMES G. MILLS
President
Santa Barbara Trust for Historic
Preservation
Solvang, California

KRISTEEN PENROD
Executive Director/Biologist
South Coast
Wildlands Project
Monrovia, California

LINDSEY REED
Managing Editor/The Public Historian
University of California, Santa Barbara
Goleta, California

LISA L. WOODWARD
Research Associate/Native American
Language Center
University of California, Davis
Davis, California

GLEN DAWSON
Dealer in rare books and Californiana
Los Angeles/California

CHUCK VALVERDE
Dealer in rare books and Californiana
San Diego/California

CATHY SANDOVAL
Acjachemem
San Juan Capistrano

MARY ELLEN AND TOM YOUNG
Co-founders/President Emeritus
Old Town San Diego State Historic
Park Boosters

ROBERT DEJONG
Independent anthropologist
San Clemente, CA

CARLOS M. YTURRALDE
Hispanic Heritage Project
Escondido, California

DOYCE NUNIS, Ph.d
President
Southern California Historical Society
Los Angeles, California

PRIMARY SOURCE MATERIALS

DECREE OF POPE LUCIUS III
PROCLAIMING THE SACRED DUTY
OF THE KNIGHTS OF THE HOLY
CRUSADES.
Original document located in the
Karpeles Manuscript Library at Santa
Barbara, California. A copy located in
the Archive/Library of Adam R. Collings.

LIBRO PRIMERO, SEGUNDO,
TERCERO Y CUARTO
DEL ESFORZADO ET VIRTUOSO
CABALLERO AMADIS
INCLUYENDO EL RAMO QUE DE
LOS CUATRO LIBROS DE AMADIS
DE GAULA SALE; LLAMADO
LAS SERGAS DEL MUY ESFORZADO
CABALLERO ESPLANDIAN
HIJO DEL EXCELENTE REY AMADIS
DE GAULA
Publicado por la
Real Academia Espanola
Ediciones Atlas, Madrid 1950
Copies located in the Library/Archive
of Adam R. Collings.

ORIGINAL TEXT OF
THE RULE OF 1223
TRANSLATED INTO ENGLISH.
Original document and translation
located in the Franciscan Archives at
Vatican City/Rome.
A copy located in the Archive/Library
of Adam R. Collings.

THE BULL OF POPE HONORIUS III
CONCERNING CONFIRMATION OF
THE RULE OF ST. FRANCIS, AND
DATED NOVEMBER 29, 1223.
Original document located in the
Franciscan Archives at Vatican
City/Rome.
A copy located in the Archive/Library
of Adam R. Collings.

THE BULL OF POPE GREGORY IX
CANONIZING ST. FRANCIS OF
ASSISI.
Original document located in the
Franciscan Archives at Vatican
City/Rome.
A copy located in the Archive/Library
of Adam R. Collings.

THE COLUMBUS LETTERS.
COLUMBUS'REPORT AND
PUBLISHED TEXT OF HIS LETTER
DESCRIBING THE DISCOVERY OF
THE NEW WORLD
An original copy located in the
Karpeles Manuscript Library, Santa
Barbara, California.
A partial copy located in the
Archive/Library of Adam R. Collings.

THE COLUMBUS MAP
INCLUDING ILLUSTRATIONS TO
THE TEXT
An original copy located in the
Karpeles Manuscript Library,
Santa Barbara, California.

THE ONLY ORIGINAL WORKING
DOCUMENT OF
A LETTER FROM FERDINAND AND
ISABELLA TO THE POPE WRITTEN
FOLLOWING COLUMBUS'S
RETURN FROM HIS FIRST VOYAGE
AND ENTITLED "THE DISCOVERY
OF THE NEW WORLD IN THE
WESTERN HEMISPHERE."
IN WHICH A FINAL AGREEMENT
REGARDING POSSESSION OF THE
NEW WORLD IS ANNOUNCED.
Located in the Karpeles Manuscript
Library, Santa Barbara, California.
A partial copy located in the
Archive/Library of Adam R. Collings.

COLUMBUS' LETTER OF 1494
Translated by Dr. Heinz Kornfuehrer
Published by The Heinz Kornfuehrer
Company

Hopkins, Minnesota, 1955
Copy located in the Archive/Library of
Adam R. Collings.

LETERRA RARISSIMA
COLUMBUS' REPORT AND
PUBLISHED TEXT OF HIS LETTER
DESCRIBING HIS LAST VOYAGE OF
DISCOVERY TO THE NEW WORLD.
A handwritten contemporary copy
located in the Karpeles Manuscript
Library, Santa Barbara, California.

CORTES' ANNOUNCMENT TO THE
KING, CONCERNING HIS
CONQUEST OF MEXICO.
An original copy located in the
Karpeles Manuscript Library, Santa
Barbara, California.

HISTORIA DE NUEVA-ESPANA
ESCRITA POR SU ESCLARECIDO
CONQUISTADOR
HERNAN CORTES,
Aumentada con otros documentos, y
notas, por el ilustrissimo Senor
Don Francisco Antonio Lorenzana,
Arzobispo de Mexico,Con las licencias
necesarias en Mexico en la imprenta
del Superior Gobierno, del Br. D.
Joseph Antonio de Hogai en la Calle
de Tiburcio, ano 1770.
Containing four letters written or
dictated by Cortes.
The third of which includes his report
concerning the Discovery of California.
An original copy located in the
Archive/Library of the Braun Research
Institute/Southwest Museum at Los
Angeles, California.

RELACION DEL DESCUBRIMIENTO
QUE HIZO JUAN RODRIGUEZ
CABRILLO, NAVEGANDO POR LA
CONTRA COSTA DEL MAR DEL
SUR AL NORTE.
Juan Perez, 1542, Julio
Original manuscript located in the

Torres de Mendoza Collection, vol. XIV, pp. 165-191 and Munoz Collection, vol. XXXVI, folios 172-184, at the AGI (Archive of the Indies), Seville, Spain. Copy located in the Archive/Library of Adam R. Collings.

CALIFORNIA VOYAGES / 1539-1541
Translation of Original Documents
Edited by Henry R. Wagner
Published by John Howell
San Francisco 1925
Copy located in the Archive/Library of Adam R. Collings.

LOS NOMBRES DE CRISTO/1572
By Fray Luis de Leon
Copy of handwritten manuscript in which Fray Luis bravely exposed and condemned the excesses and injustices of the Inquisition.
Accessed courtesy of the online archive maintained by the
Universidad de Salamanca

FATHER ESCOBAR'S RELATION OF THE ONATE EXPEDITION TO CALIFORNIA (1604).
Translated and edited by Herbert Eugene Bolton
Published by the Catholic Historical Review,v.V, no. l
Washington, D.C. April 1919.
Original diary located in the AGI (Archive of the Indies), Seville, Spain.
Copy of Bolton's 'translation' located in the Archive/Library of Adam R. Collings.

PRIMERA PARTE DE LOS VEINTE UN LIBROS RITUALES I MONARCHAINDIANA, CON ELORIGEA, GUERRAS DE LOS INDIOS OCCIDENTALES, DE SUS POBLACIONES, DESCUBRIMIENTO, CONQUISTA, CONVERSION Y OTRAS COSAS MARAVILLOSAS DE LA MISMA TIERRA DISTRIBUYIDOS

EN TRES TOMOS.
Compuesto por F. Juan Torquemada, ministro provincial de la orden de nuestro Serafico Padre San Francisco en la provincia del Santo Evangelio de Mexico en la Nueba Espana.
Composed in 1612.
Second printing by Nicolas Rodriguez Franco, Madrid, 1773.
Complete works located in the Archive/Library of the Braun Research Institute/Southwest Museum at Los Angeles, California.
Copy of Chapters XLI to LX of Book Five, which includes the transcription of Sebastian Viscaino's diary for his 1603 voyage to California located in the Archive/Library of Adam R. Collings.

NOTICIA DE LA CALIFORNIA Y DE SU CONQUISTA ESPIRITUAL, Y TEMPORAL, HASTA EL TIEMPO PRESENTE, PARTE PRIMERA, DESCRIPCION DE LA CALIFORNIA, Y DE SUS HABITADORES S.L. DEL NOMBRE, SITUACION, Y EXTENSION DE LA CALIFORNIA. ESCRITO POR MIGUEL VENEGAS, S.J. 1757
Original located in the Huntington Library, San Marino, California.
Copies of various pages located in the Library/Archive of Adam R. Collings.

THE NATURAL HISTORY OF BAJA CALIFORNIA (ENGLISH TRANSLATION OF THE AFOREMENTIONED TITLE WRITTEN BY MIGUEL VENEGAS IN 1757), WITH ANNOTATIONS AND FOOTNOTES BY MIGUEL LEON PORTILLA.
Published By Dawson's Book Shop, Los Angeles, California 1980.
Copy located in the Library/Archive of Adam R. Collings.

CATALOGUE OF MATERIALS LOCATED IN THE ARCHIVO GENERAL DE INDIAS FOR THE HISTORY OF THE PACIFIC COAST AND THE AMERICAN SOUTHWEST.
By Charles E. Chapman, Ph.D
Published by the University of California Press, Berkeley 1919.
Copy located in the Archive/Library of Adam R. Collings.

HISTORIA GENERAL DE LOS HECHOS DE LOS CASTELLANOS EN LAS ISLAS Y TIERRAFIRME DEL MAR OCEANO.
Written by Antonio de Herrera.
Complete works located in the Archive /Library maintained by the Franciscan Order at Mission Santa Barbara, California.

INSTRUCTIONS FOR THE DEPARTURE OF THE INVINCIBLE ARMADA FROM KING PHILIP II TO THE DUKE OF MEDINA AND DATED 1587.
Original document located in the Karpeles Manuscript Library, Santa Barbara, California. A partial copy located in the Archive/Library of Adam R. Collings.

A ONE PAGE REQUISITION FOR SLAVES WITH WHICH TO MAN HOSPITALS IN NEW SPAIN, ISSUED BY VICEROY LUIS DE ACEVEDO, COUNT OF MONTEREY, AND DATED SEPTEMBER 12, 1649.
Original document located in the Archive/Library of the Braun Research Institute/Southwest Museum at Los Angeles, California. Copy located in the Archive/Library of Adam R. Collings.

MEMOIRES POUR SERVIR/L'HISTOIRE DU JACOBINISME.
By Abbe Barruel S.J.

Volume One and Two published in 1797
Volumes Three and Four published in 1798
Complete text located in the Library/Archive of Adam R. Collings.

PROOFS OF A CONSPIRACY AGAINST ALL THE RELIGIONS AND GOVERNMENTS OF EUROPE CARRIED ON IN THE SECRET MEETINGS OF FREEMASONS, ILLUMINATI AND READING SOCIETIES.
By John Robinson
Published by Western Islands/Boston 1797
Complete text located in the Library/Archive of Adam R. Collings.

THE BAVARIAN ILLUMINATI AND ADAM WEISHAUPT
Complete text located in the Library/Archive of Adam R. Collings.

BAPTISMAL AND CONFIRMATION CERTIFICATES, DATED CORRESPONDINGLY NOVEMBER 24, 1713 AND MAY 26, 1715, BOTH AT PETRA, MALLORCA, SPAIN OF MIGUEL JOSEPH SERRE (FRAY JUNIPERO SERRA).
Copied from the parish records of St. Peter's Church, Petra.
Certification of the same, bearing the parish seal, by Reverend Juan Coll, pastor of St. Peter's as of August, 30, 1912.
Documents located in the Archive/Library maintained by the Franciscan Order at Mission Santa Barbara, California.
Copies located in the Archive/Library of Adam R. Collings.

FIRST PAGE (INTRODUCTION)OF SERRA'S DISERTATION ENTITLED: "BREVES EN PHYSICOS ARISTOTELES…"

FROM A COPY APPEARING IN A BOOK ENTITLED "ENTREGA DE LA CASA NATAL DE FRAY JUNIPERO SERRA A DON JUAN CEBRIAN REPRESENTANTE DE LA CIUDAD Y CONDADA DE SAN FRANCISCO DE CALIFORNIA," PUBLISHED IN MADRID IN 1934.

Photo reproduction and transcription of original document located in the Archive/Library maintained by the Franciscan Order at Mission Santa Barbara, California.

FOUR PAGE ACCOUNT WRITTEN BY FRAY JOSEPH OTTES DE VELASCO AT MEXICO CONCERNING WORKS OF FRIARS OF SAN FERNANDO MISSIONARY COLLEGE IN THE SERRA GORDA MISSIONS DURING THE YEARS 1744-1746.

Photo reproduction and transcription of original located in the Archive/Library maintained by the Franciscan Order at Mission Santa Barbara California.

SIX PAGE CORRESPONDENCE FROM FRAY JUNIPERO SERRA DATED LENT, 1747, SELVA, MALLORCA, TO FRAY FRANCISCO PALOU, CONCERNING HIS EXPERIENCES IN THE MISSION FIELD OF SELVA.

Photo reproduction and transcription of original document located in the Archive/Library maintained by the Franciscan Order at Mission Santa Barbara, California.

PHOTO REPRODUCTION OF THE FIRST PAGE OF SERRA'S PERSONAL COPY OF "CONCORDANTIAE BIBLIORUM SACRORUM EMENDATAE," WHICH HE USED PRIOR TO HIS DEPARTURE FOR THE NEW WORLD.

Published in 1943 by John Davidson. Document located in the Archive/Library maintained by the Franciscan Order at Mission Santa Barbara, California.

RELIGIOUS SELF- ENRICHMENT BOOK, SIGNED BY FRAY JUNIPERO SERRA AND STATING THAT HE USED THE SAME AT THE COLLEGE OF SAN FERNANDO.

Original located in the Karpeles Manuscript Library, Santa Barbara, California.

PHOTO REPRODUCTION AND TRANSCRIPTION IN ENGLISH AND PUBLISHED ENGLISH TRANSCRIPTION OF A LETTER WRITTEN BY FRAY JUNIPERO SERRA, DATED AUGUST, 20, 1749, CADIZ, SPAIN, TO HIS FAMILY CONCERNING HIS DEPARTURE FOR THE NEW WORLD.

Original document located in the Archive/Library maintained by the Franciscan Order at Mission Santa Barbara, California.

FOUR PAGE CORRESPONDENCE FROM FRAY JUNIPERO SERRA DATED DECEMBER 14, 1749, VERA CRUZ, MEXICO, TO FRAY FRANCISCO SERRA DESCRIBING THE VOYAGE FROM CADIZ TO VERA CRUZ, INCLUDING DETAILS OF HIS STAY IN PORTO (PUERTO) RICO, TOGETHER WITH A TRANSCRIPTION OF THE SAME FROM SERRA'S MALLORQUIN INTO ENGLISH.

Photo reproduction of original document located in the Archive/Library maintained by the Franciscan Order at Mission Santa Barbara, California.

THE SILVER ENCASED WAX, MEDALLIONED ILLUMINATED GRANT OF NOBILITY AS MARQUES DE SONORA PRESENTED TO JOSEF DE GALVEZ BY DON CARLOS III AS REWARD FOR THE SUCCESSFUL FOUNDING OF CALIFORNIA.
Original document located in the Karpeles Manuscript Library, at Santa Barbara, California. Partial copy located in the Archive/Library of Adam R. Collings.

'THE PRECIOUS DIARY' OF MIGUEL CONSTANSO. TITLED BY HIM, 'DIARIO HISTORICO DE LOS VIAJES DE MAR Y TIERRA HECHOS AL NORTE DE CALIFORNIA.' AND DATED 1770, WHEREIN AS A PARTICIPANT HE REPORTS ON THE ENTRADA INTO AND FOUNDING OF CALIFORNIA.
Facsimile located in the Archive/Library of the Braun Research Institute/Southwest Museum at Los Angeles, California.
Copy of facsimile located in the Archive/Library of Adam R. Collings

THE FOUNDING MAP OF CALIFORNIA DRAWN UP BY MIGUEL CONSTANSO AND DATED 1771. UPON WHICH HE DENOTES PLANS TO SEE ESTABLISHED THROUGHOUT CALIFORNIA TOWNS OF ARTISANS SERVING AS MENTORS TO NATIVE INDIANS.
Original located in the Karpeles Manuscript Library, Santa Barbara, California.

SERRA'S DIARY, ENTITLED 'DIARIO DE LA EXPEDICION DESDE LORETO A SAN DIEGO' COMPOSED BY FRAY JUNIPERO SERRA, O.F.M. AND DATED 1769.

Facsimile located in the Archive/Library of the Braun Research Institute/Southwest Museum at Los Angeles, California.
Copy of English 'translation' located in the Archive/Library of Adam R. Collings.

RELACION HISTORICA DE LA VIDA Y APOSTOLICAS TAREAS DEL VENERABLE PADRE FRAY JUNIPERO SERRA' Y DE LAS MISIONES QUE FUNDO EN LA CALIFORNIA SEPTENTRIONAL, Y NUEVOS ESTABLECIMIENTS DE MONTEREY.
Escrita por el R.P.L. Fr. Francisco Palou Guardian actual del Colegio Apostolico de S. Fernando de Mexico, y Discipulo de Venerable Fundador: Dirigia a Su Santa Provincia de la Regular Observancia de Nr. S. P. S. Francisco de la Isla de Mallorca.
A Expensas de Don Miguel Gonzalez Calderon Sindico de Dicho Apostolico Colegio. Impresa en Mexico, en la Imprenta de Don Felipe de Zuniga y Ontiveros, calle del Espiritu Santo, ano de 1787.
A copy located in the Archive/Library at Mission San JuanCapistrano of the Catholic Diocese of Orange, California.
Copy of the original located in the Archive/Library of Adam R. Collings.

"DIARY" OF GASPAR DE PORTOLA
Written by him in 1784 while serving as Governor for the State of Puebla. And in which he describes the Entrada into and Founding of California.
A copy located in the Karpeles Manuscript Library, Santa Barbara, California.

DIARY OF FRAY JUAN CRESPI,
Participant in the sacred expedition with the overland team.

Original located in the Karpeles Manuscript Library, Santa Barbara, California.

SEVEN PAGE CORRESPONDENCE FROM JOSEPH DE GALVEZ DATED SEPTEMBER 15, 1768 TO REVEREND FATHER PRESIDENT JUNIPERO SERRA CONTAINING THE GENERAL PLAN TO BE CARRIED OUT WITH REGARD TO THE FOUNDING OF NEW CALIFORNIA.
Original document located in the Karpeles Manuscript Library. Copy located in the Archive/Library of Adam R. Collings.

FOUR PAGE CORRESPONDENCE FROM JOSEPH DE GALVEZ DATED SEPTEMBER 3, 1769 FROM LORETO TO FRAY FRANCISCO PALOU CONTAINING PERSONAL COMMENTS REGARDING HIS HEALTH, ETC AND NEWS FROM SERRA CONCERNING THE FOUNDING OF MISSION SAN FERNANDO VELICATA AND OTHERWISE BOTH PROGRESS AND SET BACKS IN THE ARENA OF NEW CALIFORNIA.
Original document located in the Karpeles Manuscript Library, Santa Barbara, California. Copy located in the Archive/Library of Adam R. Collings.

LOS INDIGENAS DE CALIFORNIA Written by Father/Brother Jeronimo Boscana, o.f.m. (1775-1831)
Original hand written document located in the Bibliotheque Nationale, Paris (Manuscript #667).
Copy of original manuscript located in the Archive/Library of Adam R. Collings.

FIVE LEATHER BOUND VOLUMES CONTAINING LISTS OF THE BIRTHS AND BAPTISMS, ASSIGNMENT OF GODPARENTS, CONFIRMATIONS, MARRIAGES AND DEATHS THAT OCCURED AT MISSION SAN JUAN CAPISTRANO BEGINNING IN 1776. Original registers located in the Archive/Library at Mission San Juan Capistrano, of the Catholic Diocese of Orange, California. Copies of various pages located in the Archive/Library of Adam R. Collings.

AN ACCOUNT CONCERNING THE FOUNDING OF MONTEREY, WRITTEN BY MARIANO CARILLO AND DATED DECEMBER 21, 1772. Original document located in the Archive/Library of California State University, Fullerton in the Don Bernardo Yorba Family Collection. Copy of English translation located in the Archive/Library of Adam R. Collings.

CORRESPONDENCE FROM JOSEPH GALVEZ DATED FEBRUARY 23, 1772, MEXICO CITY TO FATHER JUNIPERO SERRA CONCERNING DIFFICULTIES ENCOUNTERED DURING THE FOUNDING OF CALIFORNIA.
An early copy of the original located in the Archive/Library at Mission San Fernando Rey de Espana of the Catholic Diocese of Los Angeles, California. Copy of the document located in the Archive/Library of Adam R. Collings.

ONE PAGE CORRESPONDENCE FROM FRAY JUNIPERO SERRA DATED OCTOBER 13, 1772 TO SENOR CAPITAN DON PEDRO FAGES CONCERNING ALLEGATIONS MADE AGAINST

THE CONDUCT OF BOTH SERRA AND HIS FELLOW FRANCISCANS. Facsimile located in the Archive/Library of Adam R. Collings

FOUR PAGE ROYAL CEDULA (MANDATE) FROM DON CARLOS III DATED JULY 24, 1773, MADRID. Stating particulars concerning privileges and benefits extended by the Crown to non- military children and spouses of soldiers and officers serving in California. Original document located in the Presidial Research Center Archive/Library of the Santa Barbara Trust for Historic Preservation in Santa Barbara, California. Copy located in the Library/Archive of Adam R. Collings.

AN ACCOUNT CONCERNING PERSONAL CONFLICTS IMMEDIATELY FOLLOWING THE FOUNDING OF ALTA CALIFORNIA WRITTEN IN 1773 BY CORPORAL MIGUEL PERIQUEZ AS DICTATED TO PADRE JUNIPERO SERRA AT MEXICO CITY FOR THE VICEROY. Original document located in the Archive/Library of California State University, Fullerton in the Don Bernardo Yorba Family Collection. Copy of English translation located in the Archive/Library of Adam R. Collings.

A LIST OF ORDERS TO BE OBSERVED BY CORPORALS OF THE MISSION GUARDS, AS DRAFTED IN 1773 BY COMMANDANTE DON PEDRO FAGES. Original document located in the Archive/Library of California State

University, Fullerton in the Don Bernardo Yorba Family Collection. Copy of English translation located in the Archive/Library of Adam R. Collings.

FRAY FRANCISCO PALOU'S REPORT CONCERNING HIS ARRIVAL IN ALTA CALIFORNIA, STATUS OF ITS FIVE EXISTING MISSIONS, AND PERSONAL VOW TO SEE FOUNDED MISSION SAN FRANCISCO, WRITTEN TO VICEROY ANTONIO BUCARELI. Original document located in the Karpeles Manuscript Library, Santa Barbara, California.

PALOU'S REPORT CONCERNING THE ARRIVAL IN ALTA CALIFORNIA OF JUAN BAUTISTA DE ANZA AND DATED APRIL 26, 1774. Original document located in the Karpeles Manuscript Library, Santa Barbara, California.

ENGLISH TRANSLATION OF FRAY JUNIPERO SERRA'S CORRESPONDENCE DATED SEPTEMBER 9, 1774 TO VICEROY ANTONIO BUCARELI REGARDING HIS DISAPPOINTMENT WITH REGARD TO ALTERED PLANS SURROUNDING THE FOUNDING OF SAN FRANCISCO'S PRESIDIO AND ACCORDINGLY HIS DETERMINATION THEREFORE TO FOUND NOT ONLY MISSION SAN FRANCISCO BUT MISSION SANTA CLARA AS WELL (A DECISION HE DEEMED WITHIN HIS JURISDICTIONS TO MAKE). Translations prepared by James Moriarty and associates at the University of California at San Diego. Copy located in the Library/Archives of Adam R. Collings.

FOUNDING DOCUMENT OF
MISSION SAN JUAN CAPISTRANO
HANDWRITTEN BY FRAY JUNIPERO
SERRA
AND DATED 1775.
Original document located in the
Archive/Library at Mission San Juan
Capistrano of the Catholic Diocese of
Orange, California.
Copy of the original together with an
English translation located in the
Archive/Library of Adam R. Collings.

LAWS OF SPAIN AND MEXICO
CONCERNING LANDS, ALIENS,
AND THEIR RIGHTS WITH REGARD
TO COLONIZATION AND
NATURALIZATION. Located in Box 5
of the Manuel Ruiz Papers at the
Sherman Foundation Library/Archive,
Corona del Mar, California.

TWO PAGE ORDER ISSUED FROM
THE MARQUIS DE CROIX
DATED JULY 8, 1767, MEXICO
TO THE GUARDIAN OF THE
COLLEGE OF QUERETARO
PETITIONING THE FRANCISCANS
TO ASSUME CONTROL OVER THE
FORMERLY JESUIT MISSIONS OF
SONORA.
Original document located in the
Archive/Library maintained by the
Franciscan Order at Mission Santa
Barbara, California.

LETTER FROM JOSEPH GALVEZ
DATED FEBRUARY 13, 1768, MEXICO
TO FRAY FRANCISCO PALOU
CONCERNING BOTH PALOU'S
ARRIVAL AT TEPIC
AND HIS ASSISTANCE WITH THE
PREPARATION OF CALIFORNIA
BOUND SHIPS.
Original document located in the
Archive/Library maintained by the
Franciscan Order at Mission Santa
Barbara, California.

ONE PAGE ROYAL CEDULA
(MANDATE)
DATED SEPTEMBER 15, 1703,
MADRID
ORDERING THAT ALL LANDS BE
AWARDED TO THEIR RIGHTFUL
HEIRS, THE INDIANS, AND
FORBIDDING FORCED SERVITUDE
OF THE SAME.
An early copy of the original document
located in the Archive/Library
maintained by the Franciscan Order at
Mission Santa Barbara, California.

TWELVE PAGE PLAN FOR THE
INSTITUTION OF A GOVERNOR
AND COMMISSARY GENERAL TO
RULE OVER THE CALIFORNIAS,
SINALOA, SONORA AND NUEVA
VISCAYA (NEW MEXICO).
DATED JANUARY 23, 1768.
Original document located in the
Archive/Library maintained by the
Franciscan Order at Mission Santa
Barbara, California.

ONE PAGE LETTER FROM MANUEL
RIBERO
DATED MARCH 23, 1768,
TO CARLOS FRANCISCO MARQUIS
DE CROIX,
CONCERNING DEPARTURE OF THE
BRIGANTINE
SAN CARLOS (EL PRINCIPE).
Original document located in the
Archive/Library maintained by the
Franciscan Order at Mission Santa
Barbara, California.

FOUR PAGE LETTER FROM JOSEPH
GALVEZ
DATED NOVEMBER 17, 1768,
PUERTO LA PAZ,
TO FATHER FERMIN LASUEN
CONCERNING PREPARATIONS
FOR THE CALIFORNIA ENTRADA
TOGETHER WITH LASUEN'S
REMARKS

WRITTEN IN HIS OWN HAND.
Original document located in the
Archive/Library maintained by the
Franciscan Order at Mission Santa
Barbara, California.

ONE PAGE MEMORANDUM FROM
JOSEPH GALVEZ
DATED NOVEMBER 19, 1768,
PUERTO LA PAZ
CONCERNING CHARGES LEVELED
AGAINST THE JESUITS
OF LOWER CALIFORNIA.
Original document located in the
Archive/Library maintained by the
Franciscan Order at Mission Santa
Barbara, California.

FOUR PAGE MEMORANDUM FROM
JOSEPH GALVEZ
DATED NOVEMBER 21, 1768,
PUERTO LA PAZ
TO FATHER FERMIN LASUEN
CONCERNING SAINT JOSEPH,
PATRON OF THE CALIFORNIA
ENTRADA.
Original document located in the
Archive/Library maintained by the
Franciscan Order at Mission Santa
Barbara, California.

ONE PAGE LETTER FROM JOSEPH
GALVEZ
DATED JANUARY 5, 1769
TO VICENTE VICA CONCERNING
THE SIGNIFICANCE OF THE
ENTRADA INTO UPPER
CALIFORNIA.
Original document located in the
Archive/Library maintained by the
Franciscan Order at Mission Santa
Barbara, California.

ONE PAGE LETTER FROM FRAY
JUAN CRESPI
DATED JULY 5, 1769, SAN DIEGO
TO FRAY JUAN ANDRES

CONCERNING THE ENTRADA
FROM LOWER CALIFORNIA
TO SAN DIEGO AND INCLUDING A
DESCRIPTION OF
SAN DIEGO BAY.
Original document located in the
Archive/Library maintained by the
Franciscan Order at Mission Santa
Barbara, California.

INCOMPLETE SIX PAGE
TRANSCRIPTION OF A LETTER
WRITTEN BY FRAY JUAN CRESPI
AND DATED FEBRUARY 8, 1770
TO FRAY JUAN ANDRES
CONCERNING THE INDIANS OF
SAN DIEGO, THE PORT OF
MONTEREY AND THE DISCOVERY
OF SAN FRANCISCO BAY.
Document located in the
Archive/Library maintained by the
Franciscan Order at Mission Santa
Barbara, California.

THREE PAGE CORRESPONDENCE
CERTIFIED BY FRAY RAFAEL
VERGER FROM JOSEPH
FRANCISCO ORTEGA
DATED JULY 24, 1771
TO FRAY FRANCISCO PALOU
CONCERNING DISCOVERY OF
SAN FRANCISCO BAY.
A copy of the original located in the
Archive/Library maintained by the
Franciscan Order at Mission Santa
Barbara, California.

THREE PAGE MEMORANDUM
CONCERNING SUPPLIES SENT TO
THE MISSIONARIES OF MISSION
SAN DIEGO.
DATED 1771, SAN DIEGO
Original document located in the
Archive/Library maintained by the
Franciscan Order at Mission Santa
Barbara, California.

TWO PAGE MEMORANDUM
CONCERNING SUPPLIES TO BE
SENT TO THE MISSIONARIES OF
MISSION SAN ANTONIO DE LOS
ROBLES.
DATED 1771.
Original document located in the
Archive/Library maintained by the
Franciscan Order at Mission Santa
Barbara, California.

INCOMPLETE ONE PAGE
TRANSCRIPTION OF
CORRESPONDENCE FROM FRAY
RAFAEL VERGER
DATED JUNE 30, 1771
TO MANUEL LANZ CASH
CONTROLLER FOR THE SUPREME
COUNCIL OF THE INDIES
STATING THAT NO MISSIONS WILL
BE FOUNDED IN CALIFORNIA
UNLESS THEY CAN BE
ADEQUATELY FUNDED.
Document located in the
Archive/Library maintained by the
Franciscan Order at Mission Santa
Barbara, California.

NINE PAGE DESCRIPTION OF THE
MISSION FIELD OF PIMERIA ALTA,
COMPOSED BY FATHER
FRANCISCO GARCES.
DATED APRIL 30, 1772.
Document located in the
Archive/Library maintained by the
Franciscan Order at Mission Santa
Barbara, California.

TWELVE PAGE AGREEMENT
ARRIVED AT BETWEEN THE
FRANCISCANS AND THE
DOMINICANS CONCERNING THE
TRANSFER OF MISSIONS IN
LOWER CALIFORNIA.
DATED APRIL 30, 1772, MEXICO.
Document located in the
Archive/Library maintained by the

Franciscan Order at Mission Santa
Barbara, California.

ONE PAGE SELF EVALUATION OF
AND BY GOVERNOR DON PHELIPE
BARRY AND DATED DECEMBER 1773.
Document located in the Presidial
Research Center Archive/Library of the
Santa Barbara Trust for Historic
Preservation. Copy located in the
Archive/Library of Adam R. Collings.

FOUR PAGE LETTER FROM FRAY
JUAN CRESPI TO RAFAEL VERGER
CONCERNING CRESPI'S JOURNEY
FROM SAN DIEGO TO MONTEREY,
CONDITIONS IN MONTEREY AND
PROPOSALS TO LINK MONTEREY
WITH SETTLEMENTS IN NEW
MEXICO.
Document located in the
Archive/Library maintained by the
Franciscan Order at Mission Santa
Barbara, California.

ONE PAGE ROYAL CEDULA
(MANDATE)
DATED 1773.
CONCERNING THE RIGHT OF
SANCTUARY.
Original document located in the
Archive/Library maintained by the
Franciscan Order at Mission Santa
Barbara, California.

COPY OF AN EIGHTEEN PAGE
INFORME FROM MISSION SAN
CARLOS DE MONTEREY WRITTEN
IN THE HAND OF FRAY
FRANCISCO PALOU AND DATED
DECEMBER 10, 1773,
TO VICEROY ANTONIO BUCARELI
CONCERNING THE STATE OF THE
FIRST FIVE MISSIONS OF NEW
CALIFORNIA.
Document located in the Karpeles
Manuscript Library, Santa Barbara,
California.

TWO PAGE LETTER FROM FRAY
FRANCISCO PALOU, DATED
JANUARY 14, 1774, MISSION SAN
CARLOS DE MONTEREY,
FOR FRAY RAFAEL VERGER TO
PRESENT TO THE SUPREME
COUNCIL OF THE INDIES
CONCERNING PALOU'S
COMPLETION OF HIS TERM IN
OFFICE, HIS COMMITMENT TO
FORWARD A ROUGH DRAFT FOR A
BOOK CONCERNING EVENTS
TRANSPIRED IN CALIFORNIA AND
PERSONAL NEWS REGARDING
THE BAPTISM OF INDIAN CHIEFS.
Document located in the
Archive/Library maintained by the
Franciscan Order at Mission Santa
Barbara, California.

TWO PAGE ROSTER OF FAMILIES
TRAVELING ABOARD THE FRIGATE
SANTIAGO (LA NUEVA GALICIA)
TO MONTEREY UNDER JUAN
PEREZ.
DATED JANUARY 28, 1774, SAN BLAS
Document located in the
Archive/Library maintained by the
Franciscan Order at Mission Santa
Barbara, California.

TWO PAGE REPORT FROM FRAY
RAFAEL VERGER
DATED MAY 15, 1774, PACHUCA
TO THE VICEROY CONCERNING
THE STATE OF THE CALIFORNIA
MISSIONS.
Document located in the
Archive/Library maintained by the
Franciscan Order at Mission Santa
Barbara, California.

SEVEN PAGE LETTER FROM
VICEROY ANTONIO BUCARELI
DATED MAY 25, 1774, TO FRAY
FRANCISCO PALOU CONCERNING
VARIOUS MISSION AFFAIRS.

Document located in the
Archive/Library maintained by the
Franciscan Order at Mission Santa
Barbara, California.

FOUR PAGE LETTER FROM
FRAY FRANCISCO PALOU
DATED AUGUST 30, 1774, SAN
CARLOS DE MONTEREY
TO VICEROY BUCARELI
CONCERNING PROVISIONS
NEEDED IN CALIFORNIA.
Document located in the
Archive/Library maintained by the
Franciscan Order at Mission Santa
Barbara, California.

INSTRUCTIONS FROM VICEROY
BUCARELI
DATED SEPTEMBER 30, 1774,
MEXICO,
TO THE GOVERNOR OF
CALIFORNIA
FOR THE ORDERLY GOVERNMENT
OF THE TERRITORY.
Document located in the
Archive/Library maintained by the
Franciscan Order at Mission Santa
Barbara, California.

FACULTIES GRANTED TO FRAY
FERMIN LASUEN BY FRAY JOSEPH
GARCIA, COMMISSARY PREFECT
OF THE MISSIONS OF
PROPAGANDA FIDE (MISSIONARY
WORK) IN THE WEST INDIES.
DATED NOVEMBER 14, 1774,
MEXICO.
THE FOUR PAGE DOCUMENT IS
PARTIALLY PRINTED AND
PARTIALLY HAND WRITTEN.
Original located in the Archive/Library
maintained by the Franciscan Order at
Mission Santa Barbara, California.

ORDER FROM VICEROY BUCARELI
DATED DECEMBER 6, 1774, MEXICO

DIRECTING THAT ANZA'S PAPERS
BE GATHERED TOGETHER
AND ORGANIZED.
Document located in the
Archive/Library maintained by the
Franciscan Order at Mission Santa
Barbara, California.

FERNANDO RIVERA'S REQUEST
DATED JUNE 16, 1774,
FOR ITEMS TO BE TAKEN TO
CALIFORNIA.
Document located in the
Archive/Library maintained by the
Franciscan Order at Mission Santa
Barbara, California.

FERNANDO RIVERA'S LETTER
DATED OCTOBER 8, 1774,
MONTEREY
TO VICEROY BUCARELI,
CONCERNING INDIANS , THE
NEEDS OF THE PRESIDIO
AND OBJECTIONS OVER
FOUNDING MISSION SAN
FRANCISCO.
Document located in the
Archive/Library maintained by the
Franciscan Order at Mission Santa
Barbara, California.

LETTER FROM JUAN BAUTISTA
ANZA
DATED NOVEMBER 17, 1774,
MEXICO
TO VICEROY BUCARELI
CONCERNING THE UPCOMING
EXPEDITION'S MILITARY NEEDS.
Document located in the
Archive/Library maintained by the
Franciscan Order at Mission Santa
Barbara, California.

LETTER FROM JUAN
BAUTISTA ANZA
DATED DECEMBER 1, 1774, MEXICO
TO VICEROY BUCARELI
REQUESTING THE APPOINTMENT

OF A LIEUTENANT AND
SERGEANT.
Document located in the
Archive/Library maintained by the
Franciscan Order at Mission Santa
Barbara, California.

DECREE CONCERNING THE
OVERLAND ROUTE FROM
SONORA TO CALIFORNIA.
DATED DECEMBER 16, 1774,
MEXICO.
Document located in the
Archive/Library maintained by the
Franciscan Order at Mission Santa
Barbara, California.

TWENTY FIVE PAGE EXCERPT
FROM A DIARY MAINTAINED BY
FRAY JUAN DIAS OF THE SANTA
CRUZ MISSIONARY COLLEGE AT
QUERETARO WHO ACCOMPANIED
JUAN BAUTISTA DE ANSA ON HIS
1774 OVERLAND EXPEDITION
FROM TUBAC TO MONTEREY.
Original document located in the
Karpeles Manuscript Library, Santa
Barbara, California. Copy of the
original located in the Library/Archive
of Adam R. Collings.

TWENTY NINE PAGE TESTIMONY
OF JUAN BAUTISTA ANZA
DATED DECEMBER 16, 1774,
MEXICO
CONCERNING EXPEDIENCY OF
PREPARATIONS BEING MADE FOR
HIS SECOND EXPEDITION TO BE
CARRIED OUT IN 1776.
Document located in the
Archive/Library maintained by the
Franciscan Order at Mission Santa
Barbara, California.

TWO PAGE CORRESPONDENCE
FROM DON JULIAN DE ARRIAGA
DATED DECEMBER 27, 1774,
MEXICO,

TO VICEROY BUCARELI
CONCERNING EXPENDITURES
FROM THE PIOUS FUND.
Document located in the
Archive/Library maintained by the
Franciscan Order at Mission Santa
Barbara, California.

NINE PAGE DESCRIPTION OF THE
CALIFORNIA MISSIONS
FROM FRAY PABLO JOSE DE
MUGARTEGUI
DATED JULY 2, 1775, MONTEREY,
TO DON JULIAN DE ARRIAGA.
Document located in the
Archive/Library maintained by the
Franciscan Order at Mission Santa
Barbara, California.

SIX LETTERS FROM JUAN BAUTISTA
ANZA ALL DATED DECEMBER 8,
1775, CONCERNING HIS FIRST
OVERLAND MARCH TO
CALIFORNIA TOGETHER WITH A
LIST OF EFFECTS GIVEN TO FRAY
GARCES.
Docments located in the
Archive/Library maintained by the
Franciscan Order at Mission Santa
Barbara, California.

DECREE OF BUCARELI
DISPOSING MILITARY OFFICIALS
AND SOLDIERS' FATE FOLLOWING
THE EXPEDITION OF 1776.
Document located in the
Archive/Library maintained by the
Franciscan Order at Mission Santa
Barbara, California.

LETTER FROM JUAN BAUTISTA
ANZA
DATED DECEMBER 5, 1774, MEXICO
TO VICEROY BUCARELI
CONCERNING MILITARY
PERSONNEL ASSIGNED TO
PROPOSED EXPEDITION OF 1776.
Document located in the
Archive/Library maintained by the

Franciscan Order at Mission Santa
Barbara, California.

LETTER FROM FRAY JUNIPERO
SERRA TO VICEROY ANTONIO
BUCARELI AND DATED MAY 30,
1777 CONCERNING SUSPENSION
OF MISSIONS TO BE FOUNDED
ALONG THE SANTA BARBARA
CHANNEL.
Original document located in the
Karpeles Manuscript Library, Santa
Barbara, California.

LETTER FROM FRAY JUNIPERO
SERRA TO VICEROY ANTONIO
BUCARELI AND DATED JUNE 1,
1777 REGARDING HIS
RECOMMENDATIONS WITH
REGARD TO FOUNDING MISSIONS
ALONG THE SANTA BARBARA
CHANNEL.
Original document located in the
Karpeles Manuscript Library, Santa
Barbara, California.

TWO PAGE LETTER FROM
PHELIPE DE NEVE
DATED OCTOBER 7, 1778,
MONTEREY
TO FRAY FRANCISCO PALOU
CONCERNING RATIONS.
Document located in the
Archive/Library maintained by the
Franciscan Order at Mission Santa
Barbara, California.

PALOU'S OWN COPY OF THE TEN
PAGE LETTER THAT HE AND FRAY
JOSE MURGUIA SENT TO
GOVERNOR PHELIPE NEVE
CONCERNING RATIONS .
DATED OCTOBER 12, 1778, SAN
FRANCISCO.
Document located in the
Archive/Library maintained by the
Franciscan Order at Mission Santa
Barbara, California.

THREE PAGE LETTER FROM
GOVERNOR PHELIPE DE NEVE
DATED NOVEMBER 5, 1778,
MONTEREY
TO FATHERS PALOU AND
MURGUIA CONCERNING
RATIONS.
Document located in the
Archive/Library maintained by the
Franciscan Order at Mission Santa
Barbara, California.

THREE PAGE LETTER FROM
GOVERNOR PHELIPE NEVE
DATED DECEMBER 6, 1778,
MONTEREY
TO FRAY FRANCISCO PALOU
CONCERNING RATIONS.
Original document located in the
Archive/Library maintained by the
Franciscan Order at Mission Santa
Barbara, California.

FOUR PAGE LETTER FROM FRAY
MUGARTEGUI
DATED MARCH 15, 1779, SAN JUAN
CAPISTRANO
TO FRAY FRANCISCO PALOU
CONCERNING RELATIONS
BETWEEN THE MILITARY AND THE
MISSION.
Original document located in the
Archive/Library maintained by the
Franciscan Order at Mission Santa
Barbara, California.

FOUR PAGE LETTER FROM VICEROY
MARTIN DE MAYORGA
DATED MARCH 29, 1780, MEXICO,
TO TEODOCIO DE CROIX
CONCERNING RATIONS.
Document located in the
Archive/Library maintained by the
Franciscan Order at Mission Santa
Barbara, California.

ONE PAGE LETTER FROM FRAY
ANTONIO CRUZADO

DATED APRIL 4, 1780, MISSION SAN
GABRIEL,
TO JOSEPH IGNACIO OLIVERA
CONCERNING WHEAT.
OLIVERA'S RESPONSE IS WRITTEN
ON THE SAME DOCUMENT.
Document located in the
Archive/Library maintained by the
Franciscan Order at Mission Santa
Barbara, California.

SEVEN PAGE INVOICE OF GOODS
RECEIVED FROM THE MISSIONS OF
LOWER (BAJA) CALIFORNIA
WRITTEN IN THE HAND OF FRAY
FRANCISCO PALOU AND DATED
JULY 15, 1780.
Document located in the
Archive/Library maintained by the
Franciscan Order at Mission Santa
Barbara, California.

COPY DATED AUGUST 17, 1780 OF
A FOUR PAGE PETITION FOR WAR
CONTRIBUTIONS ISSUED BY THE
KING OF SPAIN DATED August 12,
1780, SAN ILDEFONSO.
Document located in the
Archive/Library maintained by the
Franciscan Order at Mission Santa
Barbara, California.

LETTER FROM VICEROY MAYORGA
DATED DECEMBER 7, 1780, MEXICO,
TO FRAY FRANCISCO PANGUA
REQUESTING INPUT REGARDING
MISSIONS PROPOSED FOR THE
(SANTA BARBARA) CHANNEL OF
ALTA CALIFORNIA AND PANGUA'S
REPLY, DATED December 18, 1780.
Documents located in the
Archive/Library maintained by the
Franciscan Order at Mission Santa
Barbara, California.

APOSTOLIC BRIEF OF PIUS VI
CONCERNING THE
ESTABLISHMENT OF CUSTODIES

IN NEW SPAIN.
DATED NOVEMBER 17, 1779, ROME.
TOGETHER WITH CERTIFICATION
OF SPANISH TRUSTS
DATED February 14, 1780, MADRID,
AND PART OF THE GENERAL
STATUTES IN REFERENCE TO THE
NEW CUSTODIES OF NEW SPAIN.
PRINTED IN MADRID.
TWENTY TWO PAGES IN ALL.
Documents located in the
Archive/Library maintained by the
Franciscan Order at Mission Santa
Barbara, California.

TWO PAGE REGLAMENTO ISSUED
BY PHELIPE DE NEVE
DATED JANUARY 1, 1781,
MONTEREY
REGARDING PRICES TO BE SET ON
COMMODITIES PRODUCED IN
CALIFORNIA.
Original document located in the
Archive/Library maintained by the
Franciscan Order at Mission Santa
Barbara, California.

SIX PAGES OF CORRESPONDENCE
COMPRISED OF A LETTER FROM
FATHER PANGUA, DISCRETORIUM
OF THE SAN FERNANDO
MISSIONARY COLLEGE
DATED APRIL 19, 1781, MEXICO
TO VICEROY MAYORGA GIVING
REASONS AGAINST NEVE'S
PROPOSED CHANGES TO THE
MISSION SYSTEM IN CALIFORNIA
AND A COPY OF A LETTER FROM
MAYORGA
DATED APRIL 15, 1781, MEXICO,
TO FATHER PANGUA ON MISSION
AFFAIRS AND FATHER PANGUA'S
RESPONSE,
DATED APRIL 17, 1781, MEXICO
AND STILL ANOTHER FROM
PANGUA,
DATED APRIL 9, 1781 MEXICO,

CONCERNING THE YET TO BE
ESTABLISHED MISSION ALONG
THE SANTA BARBARA CHANNEL.
Original documents located in the
Archive/Library maintained by the
Franciscan Order at Mission Santa
Barbara, California.

SEVEN PAGE CORRESPONDENCE
FROM NEWLY ASSIGNED CAPTAIN
GENERAL OF THE INTERIOR
PROVINCES TEODORO DE CROIX
(NEPHEW OF FORMER VICEROY
CARLOS FRANCISCO)
DATED AUGUST 12, 1781, ARISPE,
CONCERNING CONTRIBUTIONS
TO BE COLLECTED FROM EACH
MISSION SO AS TO AID WITH THE
AMERICAN REVOLUTION AGAINST
ENGLAND.
Original document located in the
Archive/Library maintained by the
Franciscan Order at Mission Santa
Barbara, California.

FOUR PAGES OF REGLAMENTOS
DRAFTED BY NEVE
FOR THE GOVERNMENT OF THE
PROVINCE OF THE CALIFORNIAS,
TITLED 15, NUMBERS TWO, THREE
AND FOUR
AND DATED OCTOBER 24, 1781.
Original documents located in the
Archive/Library maintained by the
Franciscan Order at Mission Santa
Barbara, California.

A FIFTEEN PAGE GENERAL UPDATE
WRITTEN IN 1782 BY AN
UNKNOWN HAND CONCERNING
THE STATUS OF CALIFORNIA'S
MISSIONS.
Original document located in the
Archive/Library maintained by the
Franciscan Order at Mission Santa
Barbara, California.

ONE PAGE ROYAL DECREE ISSUED
BY SECRETARY TO THE KING
ARANJUEZ
DATED MAY 20, 1782, MADRID,
ANNOUNCING THE
INAUGURATION OF CUSTODIES
(ENCOMIENDAS) ON THE
FRONTIERS OF NEW SPAIN.
Original document located in the
Archive/Library maintained by the
Franciscan Order at Mission Santa
Barbara, California.

SIX PAGE REPORT ISSUED BY
GALINDO NAVARRO
DATED AUGUST 23, 1782, ARISPE,
TO THE COMMANDANTE
GENERAL OF CALIFORNIA
INQUIRING AFTER ANNUAL
REPORTS FROM THE MISSIONS.
Original document located in the
Archive/Library maintained by the
Franciscan Order at Mission Santa
Barbara, California.

LETTER FROM VICEROY BUCARELI
DATED OCTOBER 11, 1782,
TO PHELIPE DE NEVE
REQUESTING A FULL REPORT
REGARDING THE MISSIONS OF
CALIFORNIA.
Copy of the Original located in the
Archive/Library maintained by the
Franciscan Order at Mission Santa
Barbara, California.

SIXTEEN PAGE MEMORANDUM
WRITTEN IN THE HAND OF
FRANCISCO PALOU AND DATED
1783 (?), MISSION SAN CARLOS,
CONCERNING THE CUSTODIES
PREVIOUSLY AWARDED BY FAGES
TO RETIRING SOLDADO
DISTINGUIDO DOMINGUEZ AT
MISSION SAN GABRIEL,
DESCRIBING CIRCUMSTANCES AS
THEY EXIST AT EACH OF

CALIFORNIA'S MISSIONS AND
PROTESTING THE ESTABLISHMENT
OF ANY CUSTODIES
(ENCOMIENDAS) AS BUT A
TREMENDOUS BETRAYAL TO BOTH
THE FRANCISCANS AND THE
NATIVE PEOPLE OF CALIFORNIA.
Original document located in the
Archive/Library maintained by the
Franciscan Order at Mission Santa
Barbara, California.

TWELVE PAGE MEMO ISSUED
FROM THE COLLEGE OF
QUERETARO AND DATED 1783 (?)
ON THE MATTER OF
ESTABLISHING CUSTODIES
(ENCOMIENDAS) IN CALIFORNIA.
Original document located in the
Archive/Library maintained by the
Franciscan Order at Mission Santa
Barbara, California.

ONE HUNDRED AND TWENTY ONE
PAGE INFORME GENERAL
(GENERAL INFORMANT) WRITTEN
BY PHELIPE DE NEVE, THEN
SERVING AS COMMANDANTE
GENERAL OF THE NORTHERN
PROVINCES OF NEW SPAIN TO
NOW MINISTER GENERAL OF THE
SUPREME COUNCIL OF THE
INDIES JOSEPH DE GALVEZ,
AND DATED DECEMBER 1, 1783,
FROM ARISPE,
CONCERNING NEVE'S PROPOSED
METHODOLOGY FOR
ADMINISTRATING THE
DEPARTMENT OF JUSTICIA,
HACIENDA Y GUERRA (JUSTICE,
TREASURY AND WAR)
THROUGHOUT THE INTERIOR
PROVINCES OF NEW SPAIN.
Original document located in the AGI
(Archive of the Indies), Seville, Spain.,
Seccion audiencia de Guadalajara,

legajo 520 (104-6-22). Chapman, #4912. Transcription of the same located in the Archive/Library of Adam R. Collings.

TWELVE PAGE MEMO
FROM THE COLLEGES OF SAN
FERNANDO, QUERETARO AND
ZACATECAS
DATED FEBRUARY 3, 1783, MEXICO,
TO THE VICEROY REGARDING
MATTERS OF CUSTODY.
Original document located in the Archive/Library maintained by the Franciscan Order at Mission Santa Barbara, California.

ONE PAGE CORRESPONDENCE
WRITTEN BY JUNIPERO SERRA
DATED MAY 11, 1784
TO THE MISSIONARIES AT SAN
ANTONIO, SAN LUIS OBISPO, SAN
BUENAVENTURA, SAN GABRIEL,
SAN JUAN CAPISTRANO AND SAN
DIEGO, REGARDING THE DEATH
OF FATHER JOSEPH ANTONIO
MURGEA AT MISSION SANTA
CLARA.
Original viewed at private auction held in the former Spanish Cuartel (Soldiers Barracks) at (Mission) San Juan Capistrano on September 26, 2000.

ONE PAGE CORRESPONDENCE
WRITTEN BY JUNIPERO SERRA
DATED 1784
TO (UNVIEWABLE)
Original viewed at private auction held in the former Spanish Cuartel (Soldiers Barracks) at (Mission) San Juan Capistrano on September 26, 2000.

FOUR PAGE CORRESPONDENCE
WRITTEN BY JUNIPERO SERRA
DATED 1784
DEFENDING THE WORK OF THE
SAN FERNANDO MISSIONARY
COLLEGE.

Original viewed at private auction held in the former Spanish Cuartel (Soldiers Barracks) at (Mission) San Juan Capistrano on September 26, 2000.

THE KING'S DECREE ON
CUSTODIES IN NEW SPAIN,
DATED JANUARY 14, 1784, EL
PRADO.
The original one page document located in the Archive/Library maintained by the Franciscan Order at Mission Santa Barbara, California.

A ONE PAGE LIST OF
CORRESPONDENCE SENT TO
FRANCISCO PALOU AND PEDRO
CAMBON BETWEEN JANUARY 12,
1783 AND MAY 28, 1784, AS
PREPARED BY JOSEPH MORAGA AT
SAN FRANCISCO,
Original document located in the Archive/Library maintained by the Franciscan Order at Mission Santa Barbara, California.

THREE PAGE CORRESPONDENCE
FROM JOSEPH ANTONIO RENGEL
DATED NOVEMBER 30, 1784,
CHIHUAHUA,
TO "THE PRESIDENT OF THE
CALIFORNIA MISSIONS."
CONCERNING THE DEATH OF
JOSEPH GALVEZ.
Original document located in the Archive/Library maintained at Mission Santa Barbara, California by the Franciscan Order.

ONE PAGE LETTER FROM FATHER
PRESIDENT FRANCISCO PALOU,
WRITTEN IN HIS OWN HAND AND
DATED FEBRUARY 18, 1785, SAN
FRANCISCO,
TO JOSEPH ANTONIO RENGEL
EXTENDING HIS
CONGRATULATIONS TO THE
LATTER ON HIS APPOINTMENT AS

CAPITAN/GENERAL OF THE INTERIOR PROVINCES.
Original document located in the Archive/Library maintained by the Franciscan Order at Mission Santa Barbara, California.

ONE PAGE CORRESPONDENCE FROM JOSEPH ANTONIO RENGEL DATED MARCH 13, 1785, CHIHUAHUA,
TO LIEUTENANT CORONEL PEDRO FAGES
ORDERING THAT MEASURES BE TAKEN AGAINST IMMORAL SOLDIERS.
Original document located in the Archive/Library maintained by the Franciscan Order at Mission Santa Barbara, California.

THREE PAGE CORRESPONDENCE FROM PEDRO FAGES
DATED SEPTEMBER 30, 1785, MONTEREY,
TO LASUEN CONGRATULATING THE LATTER ON HIS POSTING AS PRESIDENT OF THE CALIFORNIA MISSIONS. INCLUDES LASUEN'S ONE PAGE REPLY
DATED OCTOBER 7, 1785, SAN DIEGO.
Original document located in the Archive/Library maintained by the Franciscan Order at Mission Santa Barbara, California.

LASUEN'S COPY OF A ONE PAGE LETTER
DATED OCTOBER 11, 1785, SAN DIEGO
SENT BY HIM TO JOSEPH ANTONIO RENGEL TO INFORM THE CAPTAIN GENERAL OF THE INTERIOR PROVINCES REGARDING HIS HAVING BEEN POSTED AS PRESIDENT OF THE CALIFORNIA MISSIONS.

Original document located in the Archive/Library maintained at Mission Santa Barbara by the Franciscan Order.

THREE PAGE CORRESPONDENCE FROM FAGES
DATED FEBRUARY 7, 1786, SAN VICENTE,
TO LASUEN CONCERNING ACCOUNTABILITY FOR BOOK KEEPING AT THE MISSIONS.
LASUEN'S ONE PAGE REPLY, DATED MARCH 31, 1786, MISSION SAN CARLOS.
Original document located in the Archive/Library maintained by the Franciscan Order at Mission Santa Barbara, California.

ONE PAGE LETTER FROM FATHER LASUEN
DATED SEPTEMBER 18, 1786, SAN CARLOS (CARMEL)
TO COUNT LA PEROUSE,
OFFERING THE LATTER GIFTS AND SUPPLIES.
Document located in the Archive/Library maintained by the Franciscan Order at Mission Santa Barbara, California.

TWO PAGE OUTLINE OF FRANCISCO ANTONIO CRESPO'S PROPOSAL TO VICEROY ANTONIO BUCARELI FOR TRANSFORMING BORDERLAND MISSION COMMUNITIES.
Original document located in the AGI (Archive of the Indies), Seville, Spain. English Transcription of the same located in the Archive/Library of Adam R. Collings.

ONE PAGE LETTER FROM THE ROYAL AUDIENCIA, DATED DECEMBER 7, 1786, MEXICO,
TO DON PEDRO FAGES
CONCERNING FINANCIAL AID TO

BE AWARDED THE CALIFORNIA
MISSIONARIES FROM THE PIOUS
FUND.
Document located in the
Archive/Library maintained by the
Franciscan Order at Mission Santa
Barbara, California.

THREE PAGE FINAL TABULATION
OF THE CASH DONATIONS
COLLECTED IN SPANISH SONORA
TO REIMBURSE THE ROYAL
TREASURY FOR EXPENSES
INCURRED BY SPAIN IN AIDING
THE THIRTEEN AMERICAN
COLONIES IN THEIR WAR OF
INDEPENDENCE AGAINST GREAT
BRITAIN. DATED JULY 10, 1786,
ARISPE.
Original document located in the AGN
(Archivo General de la Nacion),
Mexico City. Copy located in the
Archive/Library of Adam R. Collings.

ONE PAGE SELF EVALUATION OF
AND BY DON PEDRO FAGES AND
DATED DECEMBER 1787.
Document located in the Presidial
Research Center Archive/Library of the
Santa Barbara Trust for Historic
Preservation. A copy located in the
Archive/Library of Adam R. Collings.

THREE PAGE LETTER FROM DON
PEDRO FAGES
DATED JANUARY 6, 1787, MEXICO,
TO FATHER FERMIN LASUEN
CONCERNING RUNAWAYS AND
PRISONERS. INCLUDES LASUEN'S
REPLY
DATED JANUARY 7, 1787, SAN
GABRIEL.
Document located in the
Archive/Library maintained by the
Franciscan Order at Mission Santa
Barbara, California.

TEN PAGE ACCOUNT SIGNED BY
COMMANDANT OF THE INTERIOR
PROVINCES, UGARTE Y LOYOLA
DATED JANUARY 12, 1787, MEXICO,
DOCUMENTING DIFFERENCES OF
OPINIONS BETWEEN DON PEDRO
FAGES AND THE FRANCISCANS.
Document located in the
Archive/Library maintained by the
Franciscan Order at Mission Santa
Barbara, California.

THREE PAGE DOCUMENT FROM
COMMANDANT OF THE INTERIOR
PROVINCES UGARTE Y LOYOLA,
DATED APRIL 22, 1787, ARISPE,
TO FATHER FERMIN LASUEN,
CONCERNING HARMONY HAVING
BEEN ESTABLISHED BETWEEN
GOVERNOR FAGES AND THE
FRANCISCANS.
INCLUDES LASUEN'S RESPONSE
DATED SEPTEMBER 25, 1787, SAN
CARLOS (CARMEL).
Original document located in the
Archive/Library maintained by the
Franciscan Order at Mission Santa
Barbara, California.

THREE PAGE CORRESPONDENCE
FROM DON PEDRO FAGES
DATED JUNE 22, 1787, MONTEREY,
TO FATHER FERMIN LASUEN
REGARDING AID FOR THE
FRANCISCANS. INCLUDES
LASUEN'S RESPONSE
DATED JUNE 29, 1787, SAN LUIS
OBISPO.
Original document located in the
Archive/Library maintained by the
Franciscan Order at Mission Santa
Barbara, California.

FIFTEEN PAGE, PRINTED ROYAL
DECREE
DATED JULY 8, 1787, MADRID,
CREATING TWO SECRETARIES OF

STATE FOR THE INDIES-
ONE TO BE IN CHARGE OF
ECCLESIASTIC AFFAIRS AND
PROVIDE FOR JUSTICE AND THE
OTHER TO HANDLE AFFAIRS OF
WAR, FINANCE, COMMERCE AND
NAVIGATION.
Original document located in the
Archive/Library maintained by the
Franciscan Order at Mission Santa
Barbara, California.

ONE PAGE NOTIFICATION
DATED JULY 14, 1787, MADRID,
DELINEATING NEW TERRITORIAL
DIVISIONS IN THE INDIES
(NEW WORLD).
Original document located in the
Archive/Library maintained by the
Franciscan Order at Mission Santa
Barbara, California.

THREE PAGE CORRESPONDENCE
FROM DON PEDRO FAGES
DATED JULY 20, 1787, MONTEREY,
TO FATHER FERMIN LASUEN
CONCERNING INDIAN LABOR.
INCLUDES LASUEN'S REPLY,
DATED JULY 23, 1787, SAN CARLOS
(CARMEL).
Original document located in the
Archive/Library maintained by the
Franciscan Order at Mission Santa
Barbara, California.

FOUR PAGE CORRESPONDENCE
FROM DON PEDRO FAGES,
DATED AUGUST 20, 1787,
MONTEREY,
TO FATHER FERMIN LASUEN
ARGUING AGAINST SUPPLYING
NEOPHYTES WITH HORSES AND
ARMS. INCLUDES LASUEN'S REPLY
DATED AUGUST 21, 1787, SAN
CARLOS (CARMEL).
Original document located in the
Archive/Library maintained by the

Franciscan Order at Mission Santa
Barbara, California.

TWO PAGE CORRESPONDENCE
FROM DON PEDRO FAGES,
DATED AUGUST 23, 1787,
MONTEREY,
TO FATHER FERMIN LASUEN ON
INDIAN EXCESSES.
NO REPLY FROM LASUEN.
Original document located in the
Archive/Library maintained by the
Franciscan Order at Mission Santa
Barbara, California.

FIVE PAGE REPORT FROM JACOBO
UGARTE Y LOYOLA, COMMANDER
GENERAL OF THE NORTHERN
PROVINCES OF NEW SPAIN TO
MANUEL ANTONIO FLORES,
VICEROY OF NEW SPAIN
DESCRIBING PAYMENTS OF THE
ROYAL STIPEND TO MISSIONARIES,
PAST AND PRESENT
DATED JANUARY 12, 1788, ARISPE.
Original document located in the AGN
(Archivo General de la Nacion),
Mexico City. Copy located in the
Archive/Library of Adam R. Collings.

THREE PAGE SELF EVALUATION OF
DON PEDRO FAGES, AND DATED
AUGUST 22, 1788, SANTA BARBARA.
Original document located in the
Presidial Research Center of the Santa
Barbara Trust for Historic Preservation.
A copy located in the Archive/Library
of Adam R. Collings.

NINE PAGE RECOMMENDATION
FROM COUNT REVILLAGIGEDO II
TO DON CARLOS IV
DATED APRIL 26, 1790
ADVOCATING RETURN OF THE
SONORAN MISSIONS TO
FERNANDINO (COLLEGE OF
PROPAGANDA FIDE/MEXICO CITY)
JURISDICTIONS.

A duplicate copy, certified in Mexico City by Vice regal Secretary Antonio Bonilla on six folios in the AGI collection, under Audiencia Guadalajara, Legajo 559 (104-7-33). Pastells Transcripts: V.43: 275-280. A copy of which is attached to an original letter on two folios (ibid) from Revillagigedo to Antonio Valdez (under same date) for submission to the Council of the Indies (pastells 43:281). Located in the Archive/Library maintained by the Franciscans at Mission Santa Barbara.

REPORT SIGNED BY JOSEF ARGUELLO AND DATED MAY 2, 1791, CONCERNING THE TWENTY YEARS OF SERVICE, SIXTEEN CAMPAIGNS AND ONE LOST EYE SUSTAINED BY DON PEDRO FAGES.
Original document located in the Karpeles Manuscript Library, Santa Barbara, California.

CORRESPONDENCE FROM ALEXANDRO MALESPINA AND JOSEPH DE BUSTAMENTE Y GUERRA DATED SEPTEMBER 23, 1791, MONTEREY, TO FATHER FERMIN LASUEN EXPRESSING APPRECIATION FOR HIS MANY COURTESIES AND HOSPITALITY. INCLUDES LASUEN'S REPLY DATED SEPTEMBER 27, 1791, SAN CARLOS (CARMEL).
Original document located in the Archive/Library maintained by the Franciscan Order at Mission Santa Barbara, California.

THREE PAGE CORRESPONDENCE FROM ACTING-GOVERNOR JOSEF DARIO ARGUELLO

DATED JULY 9, 1792, MONTEREY, TO FATHER FERMIN LASUEN REQUESTING AID FROM THE MISSIONS. INCLUDES LASUEN'S REPLY DATED THE SAME DAY.
Original document located in the Archive/Library maintained by the Franciscan Order at Mission Santa Barbara, California.

TWO PAGE CORRESPONDENCE FROM FATHER LASUEN DATED DECEMBER 15, 1792, SAN CARLOS (CARMEL),

TO GEORGE VANCOUVER, PRAISING HIS ACCOMPLISHMENTS AND EXTENDING TO HIM GOODWILL.
Original document located in the Archive/Library maintained by the Franciscan Order at Mission Santa Barbara, California.

ONE PAGE CORRESPONDENCE FROM FATHER LASUEN DATED DECEMBER 20, 1792, TO GOVERNOR JOSE JOAQUIN ARRELLAGA CONCERNING MISSION CEMETERIES.
Original document located in the Archive/Library maintained by the Franciscan Order at Mission Santa Barbara, California.

ONE PAGE PERFORMANCE EVALUATION OF LT. DON JOSEF DARIO ARGUELLO AS CONDUCTED BY DON JOSE JOAQUIN DE ARRELLAGA AND DATED DECEMBER 1793.
Document located in the Presidial Research Center Archive/Library of the Santa Barbara Trust for Historic Preservation. Copy located in the Archive/Library of Adam R. Collings.

ONE PAGE EVALUATION OF DON JUAN PABLO GRIJALVA AS CONDUCTED BY ANTONIO GRAJENA AND DATED DECEMBER 1793.
Document located in the Presidial Research Center Archive/Library of the Santa Barbara Trust for Historic Preservation and the Archive/Library of Adam R. Collings.

TWO BOUND VOLUMES CONTAINING LISTS OF THE PADRINOS (GODPARENTS) ASSIGNED AT MISSION SAN LUIS REY. SOME PAGES ARE RENDERED ILLEGIBLE, MANY NAMES ARE CROSSED OUT, OTHERS ARE DENOTED AS BEING FROM MISSION SAN JUAN CAPISTRANO OR THE ASSISTENCIAS OF LAS FLORES AND SANTA MARGARITA. ALSO INCLUDES LISTS OF EACH FAMILY, ALL WIDOWS AND THEIR CHILDREN AND ORPHANS, AND GENTILE CHILDREN, FOLLOWED BY A LIST OF ALL NEOPHYTES (BAPTIZED AND CONFIRMED MEMBERS OF THE CHURCH) THAT LIVE OUTSIDE OF MISSION SAN LUIS REY IN SURROUNDING VILLAGES. MANY OF THESE RESIDING IN TEMECULA, PAUMEGA (PAUMA?), CAGUERGA, CUPA ETC. AND THE MISSION ASISTENCIA OF PALA. SOME EVEN RESIDING IN MISSION SAN GABRIEL AND BUENAVENTURA.
Original registers located in the Archive/Library maintained by the Franciscan Order at Mission Santa Barbara, California.

THREE PAGE CORRESPONDENCE FROM ALONSO DE TORRES Y GUERRA
DATED JANUARY 25, 1793, SAN BLAS,
TO FATHER FERMIN LASUEN INQUIRING AFTER PARTICULARS SURROUNDING THE VISITS OF BOTH LA PEROUSE AND VANCOUVER.
Original document located in the Archive/Library maintained by the Franciscan Order at Mission Santa Barbara, California.

TWO PAGE CORRESPONDENCE FROM GOVERNOR JOSE JOAQUIN ARRELLAGA
DATED JUNE 12, 1793, SANTA BARBARA,
TO FATHER FERMIN LASUEN REQUESTING COPIES OF THE CALIFORNIA MISSIONS ANNUAL REPORTS. INCLUDES LASUENS REPLY, DATED JUNE 12, 1793.
Original document located in the Archive/Library maintained by the Franciscan Order at Mission Santa Barbara, California.

TWO PAGE DECREE OF REVILLA GIGEDO
DATED JUNE 21, 1793, MEXICO, CONCERNING THE FRENCH REVOLUTION.
Original document located in the Archive/Library maintained by the Franciscan Order at Mission Santa Barbara, California.

THREE PAGE CORRESPONDENCE FROM GOVERNOR JOSE JOAQUIN ARRELLAGA
DATED OCTOBER 9, 1793, MONTEREY
TO FATHER LASSUEN CONCERNING SPAIN'S DECLARATION OF WAR ON FRANCE. INCLUDES LASUEN'S RESPONSE DATED OCTOBER 28, 1793, SANTA BARBARA.
Original document located in the Archive/Library maintained by the

Franciscan Order at Mission Santa Barbara, California.

TWO PAGE CIRCULAR FROM FATHER FERMIN LASUEN WRITTEN IN THE HAND OF ESTEVAN TAPIS, DATED OCTOBER 28, 1793, SANTA BARBARA, TO ALL CALIFORNIA MISSIONARIES CONCERNING THE STATE OF WAR EXISTING BETWEEN SPAIN AND FRANCE.
Original document located in the Archive/Library maintained by the Franciscan Order at Mission Santa Barbara, California.

FOUR PAGE CORRESPONDENCE FROM TOMAS PANGUA DATED JULY 26, 1794, MEXICO, TO FATHER LASUEN CONCERNING AN INDIAN UPRISING AT MISSION SANTA CRUZ AND INQUIRING AFTER THE GENERAL STATUS OF ALL OF THE MISSIONS, WHILE COMMENTING ON THE WAR BETWEEN SPAIN AND FRANCE.
Original document located in the Archive/Library maintained by the Franciscan Order at Mission Santa Barbara, California.

FOUR PAGE CORRESPONDENCE FROM TOMAS PANGUA DATED August 13, 1794, MEXICO, TO FATHER LASUEN COMMUNICATING VICEROY BRANCIFORTE'S MESSAGE TO SAN FERNANDO MISSIONARY COLLEGE.
Original document located in the Archive/Library maintained by the Franciscan Order at Mission Santa Barbara, California.

FOUR PAGE LETTER WRITTEN BY JOSEPH FRANCISCO ORTEGA TO PHILIPE GOYCOECHEA AND DATED DECEMBER 13, 1796
Regarding a request for payment and adjustment of accounts, lists of livestock branded and/or shod and blacksmith equipment supplied.
Original document located in the Presidial Research Center Archive/Library of the Santa Barbara Trust for Historic Preservation in Santa Barbara, California. Copy located in the Library/Archive of Adam R. Collings

ONE PAGE EVALUATION OF DON JOSE MARIA DE ORTEGA AS CONDUCTED BY DON FELIPE DE GOYOECHEA AND DATED DECEMBER 1797.
Document located in the Presidial Research Center Archive/Library of the Santa Barbara Trust for Historic Preservation and the Archive/Library of Adam R. Collings.

ONE PAGE PERFORMANCE EVALUATION OF LT. COL. DON JOSE JOAQUIN ARRELLAGA CONDUCTED BY DON DIEGO BORICA AND DATED DECEMBER 1797.
Document located in the Presidial Research Center Archive/Library of the Santa Barbara Trust for Historic Preservation. Copy located in the Archive/Library of Adam R. Collings.

ONE PAGE PERFORMANCE EVALUATION OF LT. DON JOSE(F) DARIO ARGUELLO AS CONDUCTED BY DON DIEGO BORICA AND DATED DECEMBER 1797.
Document located in the Presidial Research Center Archive/Library of the Santa Barbara Trust for Historic Preservation. Copy located in the Archive/Library of Adam R. Collings.

ONE PAGE CORRESPONDENCE
FROM
GOVERNOR DIEGO BORICA
DATED May 2, 1797, MONTEREY,
CONCERNING THE FRANCISCAN
ORDER'S PROPOSAL TO FOUND A
MISSION ADJACENT TO
BRANCIFORTE (SANTA CRUZ).
Original document located in the
Archive/Library maintained by the
Franciscan Order at Mission Santa
Barbara, California.

TWO PAGE REPORT FROM
GOVERNOR DIEGO BORICA
DATED June 17, 1797, MONTEREY,
REGARDING THE FOUNDING OF
MISSION SAN JOSE.
Original document located in the
Archive/Library maintained by the
Franciscan Order at Mission Santa
Barbara, California.

ONE PAGE REPORT FROM
GOVERNOR DIEGO BORICA
DATED July 31, 1797, MONTEREY
REGARDING THE FOUNDING OF
MISSION SAN MIGUEL.
Original document located in the
Archive/Library maintained by the
Franciscan Order at Mission Santa
Barbara, California.

TWO PAGE CIRCULAR
DATED August 23, 1797, MADRID,
DISTRIBUTED BY COMMISSARY
GENERAL FRAY PABLE DE MOYA,
GUARDIAN OF THE COLLEGE OF
SAN FERNANDO,
CONCERNING THE NUMBER OF
MASSES TO BE CONDUCTED.
Original document located in the
Archive/Library maintained by the
Franciscan Order at Mission Santa
Barbara, California.

ONE PAGE COMPLAINT
FROM ISIDRO BARCENILLA
DATED October 9, 1797, MISSION
SAN JOSE,
TO VALLEJO CONCERNING
ABUSES COMMITTED BY
COLONISTS AGAINST MISSION
SAN JOSE.
Original document located in the
Archive/Library maintained by the
Franciscan Order at Mission Santa
Barbara, California.

FOUR PAGE CORRESPONDENCE
FROM THE DISCRETORY OF THE
COLLEGE OF SAN FERNANDO,
DATED October 23, 1797, MEXICO,
TO VICEROY BRANCIFORTE
CONCERNING THE PROPOSED
LAUNCHING OF YET ANOTHER
COLONY TO BE NAMED
BRANCIFORTE.
Original document located in the
Archive/Library maintained by the
Franciscan Order at Mission Santa
Barbara, California.

EIGHT PAGE CORRESPONDENCE
FROM
THE DISCRETORY OF THE
COLLEGE OF SAN FERNANDO
DATED October 23, 1797, MEXICO,
TO VICEROY BRANCIFORTE,
REQUESTING THAT THERE BE AT
LEAST TWO MISSIONARIES
POSTED TO EACH OF
CALIFORNIA'S MISSIONS.
Original document located in the
Archive/Library maintained by the
Franciscan Order at Mission Santa
Barbara, California.

FOUR PAGES OF
CORRESPONDENCE
FROM VICEROY BRANCIFORTE
DATED December 20, 1797, ORIZABA,
TO FATHER FERMIN FRANCISCO

LASUEN REGARDING THE ELECTION OF MISSION COMMUNITY ALCALDES, INCLUDING LASUEN'S REPLY, DATED April 13, 1798, MISSION SAN BUENAVENTURE.
Original document located in the Archive/Library maintained by the Franciscan Order at Mission Santa Barbara, California.

ONE PAGE EVALUATION OF JOSE MARIA ORTEGA AS CONDUCTED BY DON FELIPE DE GOYOECHEA AND DATED DECEMBER 1798.
Original document located in the Archivo General de Simancas. Copy of the document located in the Presidial Research Center Archive/Library of the Santa Barbara Trust for Historic Preservation and the Archive/Library of Adam R. Collings.

COPIES OF FIVE LETTERS FROM FATHER LASUEN
DATED FROM June 11, 1797 to June 13, 1798,
TO GOVERNOR BORICA, CONCERNING THE ESTABLISHMENT OF MISSIONS SANTA CLARA, SAN JUAN BAUTISTA, SAN MIGUEL, SAN FERNANDO AND SAN LUIS REY.
Copies located in the Archive/Library maintained by the Franciscan Order at Mission Santa Barbara, California.

ONE PAGE PERFORMANCE EVALUATION OF DON JOSE(F) DARIO ARGUELLO AS CONDUCTED BY DON DIEGO BORICA
AND DATED DECEMBER 1798.
Document located in the Presidial Research Center Archive/Library of the Santa Barbara Trust for Historic Preservation. Copy located in the

Archive/Library of Adam R. Collings.

ONE PAGE NOTICE FROM THE OFFICE OF KING DON CARLOS DECLARING ADVANCEMENT OF PABLO COTA FROM THE RANK OF SARGEANT TO THAT OF SUB LIEUTENANT.
Document located in the Presidial Research Center Archive/Library of the Santa Barbara Trust for Historic Preservation. Copy located in the Archive/Library of Adam R. Collings.

ONE PAGE SELF EVALUATION OF AND BY DON DIEGO BORICA AND DATED DECEMBER 1798.
Original document located in the Archivo General de Simancas.
Copy located in the Presidial Research Center Archive/Library of the Santa Barbara Trust for Historic Preservation and the Archive/Library of Adam R. Collings.

ONE PAGE EVALUATION OF DON JOSE MARIA ESTUDILLO AS CONDUCTED BY DON JOSE JOAQUIN ARRELLAGA AND DATED DECEMBER 1800.
Document located in the Presidial Research Center Archive/Library of the Santa Barbara Trust for Historic Preservation and the Archive/Library of Adam R. Collings.

ONE PAGE EVALUATION OF DON GABRIEL MORAGA AS CONDUCTED BY DON JOSE JOAQUIN ARRELLAGA AND DATED DECEMBER 1800.
Document located in the Presidial Research Center Archive/Library of the Santa Barbara Trust for Historic Preservation and the Archive/Library of Adam R. Collings.

ONE PAGE PERFORMANCE
EVALUATION OF DON JOSE(F)
DARIO ARGUELLO AS
CONDUCTED BY DON JOSE
JOAQUIN ARRELLAGA AND DATED
DECEMBER 1801.
Document located in the Presidial
Research Center Archive/Library
of the Santa Barbara Trust for Historic
Preservation. Copy located in the
Archive/Library of Adam R. Collings.

ONE PAGE INQUIRY FROM
PHYSICIAN ROUSET,
DATED September 26, 1805,
TO FRAY ESTEVAN TAPIS
CONCERNING THE ILLNESS OF
INDIANS THROUGHOUT
CALIFORNIA.
INCLUDES TWO ONE PAGE
REPLIES FROM FRAY TAPIS,
EACH DATED December 2, 1805,
MISSION SOLEDAD.
Original documents located in the
Archive/Library maintained by the
Franciscan Order at Mission Santa
Barbara, California.

ONE PAGE PERFORMANCE
EVALUATION OF DON JOSE(F)
DARIO ARGUELLO AS
CONDUCTED BY DON JOSE
JOAQUIN ARRELLAGA AND DATED
DECEMBER 1806.
Document located in the Presidial
Research Center Archive/Library of the
Santa Barbara Trust for Historic
Preservation. Copy located in the
Archive/Library of Adam R. Collings.

ONE PAGE PERFORMANCE
EVALUATION OF CADET DON LUIS
ANTONIO ARGUELLO AS

CONDUCTED BY HIS FATHER DON
JOSEF DARIO ARGUELLO AND
DATED DECEMBER 1806.

Document located in the Presidial
Research Center Archive/Library of the
Santa Barbara Trust for Historic
Preservation. Copy located in the
Archive/Library of Adam R. Collings.

SIX PAGE DOCUMENT COMPOSED
BY FRAY RAMON LOPEZ
DATED June, 7, 1811, LORETO,
TO FRAY ESTEVAN TAPIS
REGARDING HIS SATISFACTION
WITH THE ACTIONS EXECUTED BY
REVEREND MIGUEL HIDALGO Y
COSTILLO ON May 18, 1811.
Original document located in the
Archive/Library maintained by the
Franciscan Order at Mission Santa
Barbara, California.

TWO PAGE CORRESPONDENCE
FROM FRAY RAMON LOPEZ,
DATED September 25, 1811, LORETO,
TO FRAY ESTEVAN TAPIS
CONCERNING REVEREND MIGUEL
HIDALGO Y COSTILLO.
Original document located in the
Archive/Library maintained by the
Franciscan Order at Mission Santa
Barbara, California.

FOUR PAGE ENGLISH
TRANSLATION OF A DOCUMENT
WRITTEN BY REVEREND FATHER
PRESIDENT JOSE SENAN
DATED FEBRUARY 1813
TO HIS EXCELLENCY THE BISHOP
OF SONORA
CONCERNING CALIFORNIAN
EVENTS OF THE PAST YEAR.
Original document located in the
Presidial Research Center Archive of
the Santa Barbara Trust for Historic
Preservation. Copy located in the
Archive/Library of Adam R. Collings.

HISTORICAL MEMOIRS OF NEW
CALIFORNIA
VOLUME ONE
Written and compiled by Father
Francisco Palou, o.f.m.
Translated into English by Herbert
Eugene Bolton
Copy located in the Elizabeth J. Schultz
Memorial California History Room of
the Anaheim Public Library.

HISTORICAL MEMOIRS OF NEW
CALIFORNIA
VOLUME TWO
Written and compiled by Father
Francisco Palou, o.f.m.
Translated into English by Herbert
Eugene Bolton
Copy located in the Elizabeth J. Schultz
Memorial California History Room of
the Anaheim Public Library.

HISTORICAL MEMOIRS OF NEW
CALIFORNIA
VOLUME THREE
Written and compiled by Father
Francisco Palou, o.f.m.
Translated into English by Herbert
Eugene Bolton
Copy located in the Elizabeth J. Schultz
Memorial California History Room of
the Anaheim Public Library.

HISTORICAL MEMOIRS OF NEW
CALIFORNIA
VOLUME FOUR
Written and compiled by Father
Francisco Palou, o.f.m.
Translated into English by Herbert
Eugene Bolton.
Copy located in the Elizabeth J. Schultz
Memorial California History Room of
the Anaheim Public Library

DOCUMENTING EVERYDAY LIFE IN
EARLY SPANISH CALIFORNIA/THE
SANTA BARBARA PRESIDIO
MEMORIAS Y FACTURAS 1779-1810

Edited by Giorgio Perissinotto
Published by the Santa Barbara Trust
for Historic Preservation, 1998.
Copy located in the Library/Archive of
Adam R. Collings

ONE PAGE NOTICE
TO JOSE DE LA GUERRA
DATED OCTOBER 6, 1817, LORETO
FROM GERVASIO ARGUELLO
ACKNOWLEDGING RECEIPT OF
WARRANT TO PAY OFF THE
BALANCE OWING ON THE
ORTEGA ESTATE.
Original document located in the
Presidial Reseach Center
Archive/Library of the Santa Barbara
Trust for Historic Preservation in Santa
Barbara, California. Copy located in the
Library/Archive of Adam R. Collings.

ONE PAGE FROM 'LOST'
BAPTISMAL REGISTRY
OF MISSION SAN GABRIEL
ARCHANGEL
CARRYING ENTRIES FROM THE
YEAR 1817.
Original document located in the
Presidial Research Center
Archive/Library of the Santa Barbara
Trust for Historic Preservation in Santa
Barbara, California. Copy located in the
Library/Archive of Adam R. Collings.

TWO PAGE INSTRUCTIONS
DATED JULY 11, 1819 LORETO,
Concerning the value and
disbursement of Joseph Francisco
Ortega's estate. Original document
located in the Presidial Research
Center Archive/Library of the Santa
Barbara Trust for Historic Preservation
in Santa Barbara, California. Copy
located in the Archive/Library of Adam
R. Collings.

ONE PAGE STATEMENT OF
PAYMASTER JOSE MARIA MATA

DATED JULY 11, 1819 LORETO
Regarding the account of deceased
Joseph Francisco Ortega.
Original document located in the
Presidial Research Center
Archive/Library of the Santa Barbara
Trust for Historic Preservation in Santa
Barbara, California. Copy located in the
Archive/Library of Adam R. Collings.

ONE PAGE WARRANT FROM
PAYMASTER JOSE MARIA MATA
DATED JUNE 3, 1823, LORETO
TO GENERAL PAYMASTER OF THE
CALIFORNIAS
FOR SETTLEMENT OF DECEASED
JOSEPH FRANCISCO ORTEGA'S
ACCOUNT.
Original document located in the
Presidial Research Center
Archive/Library of the Santa Barbara
Trust for Historic Preservation in Santa
Barbara, California. Copy located in the
Archive/Library of Adam R. Collings.

TWO PAGE NOTICE FROM JOSE
MARIA MATA
DATED JUNE 3, 1823, LORETO
TO PAYMASTER GENERAL OF THE
CALIFORNIAS
DECLARING THAT WARRANT FOR
THE PAYMENT OF THE ESTATE OF
JOSEPH FRANCISCO ORTEGA HAD
BEEN SENT.
Original document located in the
Presidial Research Center
Archive/Library of the Santa Barbara
Trust for Historic Preservation in Santa
Barbara, California. Copy located in the
Library/Archive of Adam R. Collings.

ONE PAGE NOTICE FROM JOSE
RUIZ
DATED JUNE 3, 1825
TO DON ANTONIO MARIA DE
ORTEGA
STATING THAT WARRANT AGAINTS
THE ESTATE OF JOSEPH

FRANCISCO ORTEGA WAS NO
LONGER VALID.
Original document located in the
Presidial Research Center
Archive/Library of the Santa Barbara
Trust for Historic Preservation in Santa
Barbara, California. Copy located in the
Library/Archive of Adam R. Collings.

ONE PAGE NOTICE FROM JOSE
MARIA HERRERO
DATED AUGUST 10, 1827,
CERTIFYING THAT JOSE MARIA
ORTEGA HAD DRAWN A DRAFT
FOR THE BALANCE OF JOSEPH
FRANCISCO ORTEGA'S ACCOUNT.
Original document located in the
Presidial Research Center
Archive/Library of the Santa Barbara
Trust for Historic Preservation in Santa
Barbara, California. Copy located in the
Library/Archive of Adam R. Collings.

A REPORT WRITTEN BY JUAN JOSE
BANDINI IN 1828
PRESUMABLY TO THE BRITISH
CONSUL IN MEXICO CITY
CONCERNING THE GENERAL
STATUS OF CALIFORNIA.
Original manuscript located in the
Archive/Library of Jose Bandini's great,
grandson Peter J. Mel of Rancho Santa
Margarita, California.
Copy of manuscript located in the
Archive/Library of Adam R. Collings.

LAST WILL AND TESTAMENT OF
DONA GREGORIA ESPINOSA,
WIDOW OF MARIANO DE LA LUZ
VERDUGO,
DATED JUNE 1, 1830
Original document located in the
Archive/Library of California State
University, Fullerton in the Don
Bernardo Yorba Family Collection.
Copy of English translation located in
the Archive/Library of Adam R. Collings.

TWENTY ONE PAGE
SECULARIZATION DECREE AS
DRAFTED BY JOSE MARIA DE
ECHEANDIA
AND DATED DECEMBER 31, 1831.
Original document located in the
Karpeles Manuscript Library/Archive
in Santa Barbara, California.
Copy located in the Archive/Library of
Adam R. Collings

YNFORME QUE DA AL SENOR
COMANDANTE GENERAL EL
ALFERES DE LA COMPANIA
PERMANENTE DE SAN
FRANCISCO, C.M.G.V.
Report of a visit to Fort Ross and
Bodega Bay in April 1833 by Mariano
G. Vallejo.
Spanish transcription done by Dr.
Michael Mathis.
English translation of the same with
annotations by Glenn Farris.
Original text located in the Bancroft
Library. Copy located in the
Archive/Library of Adam R. Collings.

CORRESPONDENCE WRITTEN BY
GOVERNOR JOSE FIGUEROA
REGARDING INFORMATION
SUPPLIED OFFICIALS AT MEXICO
CITY PRIOR TO HIS ARRIVAL
CONCERNING THE STATE OF
FRANCISCAN AFFAIRS IN
CALIFORNIA.
Original document located in the
Bancroft Library, Berkeley, California.

PAGE DOCUMENT
FROM GOVERNOR JOSE FIGUEROA
WRITTEN IN THE HAND OF HIS
SECRETARY AGUSTIN VICENTE
ZAMORANO AND
DATED AUGUST 1, 1834
OUTLINING HIS ARRANGEMENT
WITH DON ANTONIO MARIA
ORTEGA AND DONA MAGDALENA

COTA DE ORTEGA CONCERNING
MAINTANANCE OF MISSIONS AND
ROADS IN AND AROUND BOTH
SANTA BARBARA AND SANTA
YNEZ .
Original document located in the
Presidial Research Center
Archive/Library of the Santa Barbara
Trust for Historic Preservation in Santa
Barbara, California. Copy located in the
Library/Archive of Adam R. Collings.

ARGUMENTS OF REVEREND
FATHER PRESIDENT NARCISO
DURAN AGAINST DISSOLUTION
OF THE MISSION SYSTEM.
DATED JULY 24, 1837.
Original copy located in the Karpeles
Manuscript Library, Santa Barbara,
California.

LAST WILL AND TESTAMENT OF
TOMAS ANTONIO YORBA,
TOGETHER WITH AN INVENTORY
OF HIS PERSONAL EFFECTS,
DATED JANUARY 28, 1845.
Original document located in the
Archive/Library of California State
University, Fullerton in the Don
Bernardo Yorba Family Collection.
Copy of English translation located in
the Archive/Library of Adam R. Collings.

TWO PAGE CONTRACT
DATED JULY 10, 1852
DRAFTED BY FRANCISCO DE
ORTEGA
IN WHICH HE SELLS HIS
INHERITANCE TO DONA
MAGDALENA DE COTA DE
ORTEGA.
Original document located in the
Presidial Research Center
Archive/Library of the Santa Barbara
Trust for Historic Preservation in Santa
Barbara, California. Copy located in the
Library/Archive of Adam R. Collings.

ONE PAGE CORRESPONDENCE
TO MIGUEL NORIEGA
DATED FEBRUARY 4, 1855,
FROM PIO PICO, REQUESTING
THAT A HORSE PROMISED HIM BE
SENT TO HIM.
Original document located in the
Presidial Research Center
Archive/Library of the Santa Barbara
Trust for Historic Preservation in Santa
Barbara, California. Copy located in the
Library/Archive of Adam R. Collings.

LAST WILL AND TESTAMENT OF
DON BERNARDO YORBA
TOGETHER WITH AN INVENTORY
OF HIS PERSONAL EFFECTS,

DATED NOVEMBER 14, 1858.
Original document located in the
Archive/Library of California State
University, Fullerton in the Don
Bernardo Yorba Family Collection.
Copy of English translation located in
the Archive/Library of Adam R. Collings.

THE LETTERS OF TOMAS YORBA
WRITTEN TO JOSE DE LA GUERRA Y
NORIEGA
Original documents located in the
Archive/Library of the Franciscan
Order at Mission Santa Barbara,
California.
Transcriptions of the original Spanish
text with English translations located
in the Archive/Library of Adam R.
Collings

FLAG OF THE CALIFORNIO
REPUBLIC
Located in the Archive/Library of the
Braun Research Institute of the
Southwest Museum at Los Angeles,
California.

CHASING RAINBOWS
THE UNPUBLISHED
AUTOBIOGRAPHY OF JOHN
GAFFEY

Copy located in the Archive/Library of
Peter Mel, Rancho Santa Margarita,
California.

TWO PAGE CORRESPONDENCE
FROM JOHN T. GAFFEY,
DATED MARCH 12TH, 1904, SANTA
MONICA
TO CHARLES F. LUMMIS
CONCERNING THE SPANISH
SONGS OF OLD CALIFORNIA.
Original document located in the
Archive/Library of the Braun Research
Institute at the Southwest Museum,
Los Angeles, California. Copy located
in the Archive/Library of Adam R.
Collings.

TWO PAGE LETTER FROM
CHARLES LUMMIS
TO JOHN T. GAFFEY DATED
MARCH 17, 1904
CONCERNING 'ADIOS, ADIOS
AMORES'
AND OTHER MUSIC OF OLD
CALIFORNIA.
CONTAINS GAFFEY'S THREE PAGE
RESPONSE.
Original documents located in the
Archive/Library of the Braun Research
Institute at the Southwest Museum,
Los Angeles. Copy located in the
Archive/Library of Adam R. Collings.

ONE PAGE NOTE FROM JOHN T.
GAFFEY,
DATED FEBRUARY 17TH, 1905, SAN
PEDRO,
TO CHARLES F. LUMMIS
CONCERNING HIS SUBSCRIPTION
TO OUTWEST MAGAZINE.
Original document located in the
Archive/Library of the Braun Research
Institute at the Southwest Museum in
Los Angeles, California. Copy located
in the Archive/Library of Adam R.
Collings.

TWO PAGE CORRESPONDENCE
FROM CHARLES F. LUMMIS
DATED FEBRUARY 20, 1905
TO JOHN T. GAFFEY,
EXPRESSING APPRECIATION FOR
HIS SUPPORT AND UPDATING HIM
WITH REGARD TO HIS
'SOUTHWEST SOCIETY.'
Original document located in the
Archive/Library of the Braun Research
Institute at the Southwest Museum in
Los Angeles, California. Copy located in
the Archive/Library of Adam R. Collings.

THREE PAGE LETTER FROM
CHARLES LUMMIS
TO JOHN T. GAFFEY DATED
FEBRUARY 20TH, 1905
CONCERNING 'OLD CALIFORNIA.'
Original document located in the
Archive/Library of the Braun Research
Institute at the Southwest Museum in
Los Angeles, California. Copy located
in the Archive/Library of Adam R.
Collings.

TWO PAGE LETTER FROM
CHARLES LUMMIS
TO THE BOARD OF DIRECTORS OF
THE SOUTHWEST MUSEUM,
DATED FEBRUARY 12, 1908
CONCERNING SEAL AND SPANISH
MOTTO
'TOMORROW IS THE FLOWER OF
ITS YESTERDAY.'
Original document located in the
Archive/Library of the Braun Research
Institute at the Southwest Museum in
Los Angeles, California. Copy located
in the Archive/Library of Adam R.
Collings.

ONE PAGE LETTER FROM CHARLES
LUMMIS
TO JOHN T. GAFFEY,
DATED MAY 13, 1908
CONCERNING INCORPORATION

OF THE SOUTHWEST MUSEUM.
Original document located in the
Archive/Library of the Braun Research
Institute at the Southwest Museum in
Los Angeles, California. Copy located
in the Archive/Library of Adam R.
Collings.

ONE PAGE LETTER FROM
PRESIDENT OF STANFORD
UNIVERSITY DAVID STARR JORDAN
AND DATED FEBRUARY 20, 1920
TO CHARLES FLETCHER LUMMIS
REGARDING THE PROPRIETOR
(ISADORA BANDINI) OF A
HACIENDA NEAR SAN LUIS REY.
Original document located in the
Archive/Library of the Braun Research
Institute at the Southwest Museum in
Los Angeles, California. Copy located
in the Archive/Library of Adam R.
Collings.

TWO PAGE LETTER FROM
CHARLES LUMMIS
WRITTEN AT RANCHO CAMULOS
TO M. A. NEWMARK OF LOS
ANGELES
DATED NOVEMBER 1, 1922
CONCERNING ITEMS OF HISTORIC
SIGNIFICANCE TO SPANISH ERA
CALIFORNIA GATHERED AND
BEQUEATHED BY LUMMIS TO THE
SOUTHWEST MUSEUM AND
SUBSEQUENTLY ILLEGALLY
APPROPRIATED BY THE MUSEUM
BOARD. CONTAINS NEWMARK'S
TWO PAGE RESPONSE DATED
NOVEMBER 9, 1922 TOGETHER
WITH A SECOND ONE PAGE
FOLLOWUP LETTER FROM
NEWMARK,
DATED NOVEMBER 29, 1922.
Original documents located in the
Archive/Library of the Braun Research
Institute at the Southwest Museum in

Los Angeles, California. Copies located in the Archive/Library of Adam R. Collings.

TWO PAGE LETTER FROM
CHARLES LUMMIS
TO DR. JULIAN RIBERA OF
MADRID, SPAIN
DATED NOVEMBER 17, 1924,
REGARDING 'SPANISH SONGS OF
OLD CALIFORNIA.'
Original document located in the Archive/Library of the Braun Research Institute at the Southwest Museum in Los Angeles, California. Copy located in the Archive/Library of Adam R. Collings.

THE PERSONAL DIARY OF BRUCE
ALFONSO DE BOURBON/CONDE
(aka ALFONSO YORBA)
VOLUME SEVEN, 1935
Copy located in the Library/Archive of Adam R. Collings.

THE PERSONAL NOTEBOOKS OF
BRUCE ALFONSO DE
BOURBON/CONDE (aka ALFONSO
YORBA)
Copy located in the Library/Archive of Adam R. Collings.

SECONDARY SOURCE MATERIALS

UNPUBLISHED

THE CHANGING FACE OF OLD
SPAIN
Written by Randy Collings
Dated Garden Grove, California 1967.
Original copy located in the Archive/Library of Adam R. Collings.

JUDGE GRANT JACKSON'S
SCRAPBOOKS

Containing various and sundry newsclippings, correspondence and personal notes compiled at the turn of the Nineteenth Century regarding the History of California.
Original books located in the Archive Library of the Braun Research Institute at the Southwest Museum. Copies of many items located in the Archive/Library of Adam R. Collings.

THE MISSION PAGEANT/SAN JUAN
CAPISTRANO
Written by Garnett Holme
Original script located in the Archives of the Diocese of Orange at Mission San Juan Capistrano.

MARY, A YAQUI WOMAN
By Vera Anderson
Copy located in the Archive/Library of Adam R. Collings.

SPANISH SONORA IN 1776/
FUGITIVES IN THEIR NATIVE LAND
By Father Kieran McCarty, o.f.m., Ph.d
Copy located in the Archive/Library of Adam R. Collings.

MONTEREY:
SPANISH CALIFORNIA'S ELUSIVE
CAPITAL
By Father Kieran McCarty, o.f.m., Ph.d
Copy located in the Archive/Library of Adam R. Collings.

ANTONIO COMADURAN/
DEFENDER OF THE TUCSON
FRONTIER
By Father Kieran McCarty, o.f.m., Ph.d
Copy located in the Archive/Library of Adam R, Collings.

PADRONES NOTEBOOK
Containing various and sundry copies of documents pertaining to the men who served at Santa Barbara's Royal Presidio.

Copy located in the Presidial Research Center Archive/Library
at the Santa Barbara Trust for Historic Preservation.

PRESIDIAL NEWSCLIPPINGS COLLECTION
OF THE FLORES FAMILY.
Notebook located in the Presidial Research Center Archive/Library of the Santa Barbara Trust for Historic Preservation.
Copies of some items located in the Archive/Library of Adam R. Collings.

CALIFORNIA SCRAPBOOK/RANDY COLLINGS
Copy located in the Archive/Library of Adam R. Collings.

TREES, HISTORICAL AND UNUSUAL
Researched, written and edited by unknown members of the Orange County Research Group, Santa Ana, California WPA (Works Progress Administration), 1936. And sponsored by the Santa Ana Board of Education.
Copy located in the Sherman Foundation Library.
Copy located in the Library/Archive of Adam R. Collings.

THE RISE AND FALL OF THE GRAPE INDUSTRY
Researched, written and edited by Gladyce E. Ashby and
S.B. Roberts. Santa Ana, California WPA (Works Progress Administration), 1936.
Copy located in the Sherman Foundation Library
Copy located in the Library/Archive of Adam R. Collings.

RELIGIOUS BELIEFS, PRACTICES AND CUSTOMS IN EARLY ORANGE COUNTY, CALIFORNIA.
Researched, written and edited by D.B. and C.E. Roberts, E. Standring, Mabel G. Wing and Barton O. Withall.
Santa Ana, California WPA (Works Progress Administration) 1936.
Copy located in the Sherman Foundation Library
Copy located in the Library/Archive of Adam R. Collings.

ADOBES OF ORANGE COUNTY, CALIFORNIA
By C.E. Roberts.
Funded by S.E.R.A (State Emergency Relief Association) Project.
Copy located in the Sherman Foundation Library
Copy located in the Archive/Library of Adam R. Collings.

ARCHITECTURE IN ORANGE COUNTY, CALIFORNIA
Researched, written and edited by Anna Hill and S.B. Roberts.
Funded by Santa Ana, California WPA (Works Progress Administration) 1936.
Copy located in the Sherman Foundation Library
Copy located in the Archive/Library of Adam R. Collings.

EDUCATION AND EDUCATIONAL FACILITIES IN ORANGE COUNTY.
Researched, written and edited by D.B., W. L Mayhew, C.E. Roberts, and Mabel G. Wing. Funded by Santa Ana, California WPA (Works Progress Administration) 1936.
Copy located in the Sherman Foundation Library
Copy located in the Archive/Library of Adam R. Collings.

SECONDARY SOURCE MATERIALS

PUBLISHED

HISTORIA DE ESPANA
GRAN HISTORIA GENERAL DE LOS
PUEBLOS HISPANOS
VOLUME ONE
EPOCA PRIMITIVA Y ROMANO
Publicado por El Instituto Gallach de
Libreria
y por Ediciones Barcelona.
Copy located in the Archive/ Library of
Adam R. Collings.

HISTORIA DE ESPANA
GRAN HISTORIA GENERAL DE LOS
PUEBLOS HISPANOS
VOLUME TWO
LA ALTA EDAD MEDIA
Publicado por El Instituto Gallach de
Libreria
y por Ediciones Barcelona.
Copy located in the Archive/ Library of
Adam R. Collings.

HISTORIA DE ESPANA
GRAN HISTORIA GENERAL DE LOS
PUEBLOS HISPANOS
VOLUME THREE
LA BAJA EDAD MEDIA
Publicado por El Instituto Gallach de
Libreria
y por Ediciones Barcelona.
Copy located in the Archive/ Library of
Adam R. Collings.

HISTORIA DE ESPANA
GRAN HISTORIA GENERAL DE LOS
PUEBLOS HISPANOS
VOLUME FOUR
LA CASA DE AUSTRIA
Publicado por El Instituto Gallach de
Libreria
Y por Ediciones Barcelona

Copy located in the Archive/ Library of
Adam R. Collings.

HISTORIA DE ESPANA
GRAN HISTORIA GENERAL DE LOS
PUEBLOS HISPANOS
VOLUME FIVE
LA CASA DE BORBON
Publicado por El Instituto Gallach de
Libreria
Y por Ediciones Barcelona.
Copy located in the Archive /Library of
Adam R. Collings.

BULFINCH'S MYTHOLOGY:
THE AGE OF CHIVALRY/
THE LEGENDS OF CHARLEMAGNE
A Mentor Book
Published by the New American
Library
Times Mirror Press, 1962
Copy located in the Library/Archive of
Adam R. Collings.

LA CHANSON DE ROLDAN
As presented by Henry (William)
Adams
Copy located in the Archive/Library of
Adam R. Collings.

KNIGHT ERRANT
By R. Garcia y Robertson
Published by Tom Doherty Associates
New York, N.Y. 2001
Copy located in the Anaheim Public
Library.

THE QUEEN OF CALIFORNIA/
THE ORIGIN OF THE NAME OF
CALIFORNIA
WITH TRANSLATION FROM THE
SERGAS DE ESPLANDIAN
Written by Edward Everett Hale
Published by Colt Press 1945
Copy located in the Archive/Library
maintained by the Franciscan Order at
Mission Santa Barbara, California.

ENCYCLOPEDIA OF THINGS THAT
NEVER WERE
By Michael Page and Robert Ingpen
Published by Viking Press
New York, N.Y. 1985
Copy located in the San Clemente
(Orange County) Public Library.

WHO WERE THE FIRST AMERICANS
By Sharon Begley and Andrew Murr
Published in NEWSWEEK
MAGAZINE on April 26, 1999
Copy located in the Archive/Library of
Adam R. Collings.

FRANCIS OF ASSISI/A
REVOLUTIONARY LIFE
By Adrian Clouse
Published by Hidden Spring
New Jersey 2001
Copy located in the Anaheim Public
Library.

DANTE
By R. W. B. Lewis
Published by the Penguin Group
New York, N.Y. 2001
Copy located in the Anaheim Public
Library.

FRANCISCAN PRESENCE IN THE
AMERICAS, 1492-1900
Published by the Academy of
American Franciscan History
Washington, D.C. 1984
Copy located in the Archive/Library
maintained by the Franciscan Order at
Santa Barbara, California.

THE CONQUEST OF NEW SPAIN
VOLUME ONE
Published by the Hakluyt Society
Berlin 1908
Copy located in the Archive/Library of
Adam R. Collings.

THE CONQUEST OF NEW SPAIN
VOLUME FIVE
Published by the Hakluyt Society

Berlin 1916
Copy located in the Archive/Library of
Adam R. Collings.

CONQUISTADORS
By Michael Wood
Published by the University of
California
Berkeley, California 2000
Copy located in the Orange County
Public Library System.

CRONICA DE LOS COLEGIOS DE
PROPAGANDA FIDE
DE LA NUEVA ESPANA
Written by Fray Isidro Felix de
Espinosa, o.f.m.
And published privately at Mexico City
in 1746.
Reprint published by the American
Academy of Franciscan History
Washington, D.C., at Madrid, Spain.
Copy located in the Archive/Library of
Adam R. Collings.

THE SPANISH BORDERLANDS
ALL VOLUMES
Written by Herbert Eugene Bolton.
Published by Yale University Press,
1921
Copies located in the Archive /Library
of Dr. Melvin R. Collings

THE WORKS OF HUBERT HOWE
BANCROFT
VOLUME XVIII
HISTORY OF CALIFORNIA VOLUME
ONE 1542-1800
Published by A.L. Bancroft &
Company
San Francisco, 1884
Copy located in the Library/Archive of
Adam R. Collings.

THE WORKS OF HUBERT HOWE
BANCROFT
VOLUME XXXIV
CALIFORNIA PASTORAL 1769-1848

Published by The History Company
San Francisco, 1888
Copy located in the Library/Archive of
Adam R. Collings.

THE WORKS OF HUBERT HOWE
BANCROFT
VOLUME XX
HISTORY OF CALIFORNIA VOLUME
III 1825-1840
Published by A. L. Bancroft &
Company
San Francisco, 1885
Copy located in the Library/Archive of
Adam R. Collings.

THE WORKS OF HUBERT HOWE
BANCROFT
VOLUME XXII
HISTORY OF CALIFORNIA VOLUME
V 1846-1848
Published by The History Company
San Francisco 1886
Copy located in the Library/Archive of
Adam R. Collings.

THE MISSIONS AND
MISSIONARIES OF CALIFORNIA
Written by FR. ZEPHYRIN
ENGELHARDT, O.F.M.
VOLUME ONE, LOWER
CALIFORNIA
Published by the James H. Barry
Company
San Francisco, CA 1908
Copy located in the Library/Archive of
Adam R. Collings.

THE MISSIONS AND
MISSIONARIES OF CALIFORNIA
Written by FR. ZEPHYRIN
ENGELHARDT, O.F.M.
VOLUME TWO, UPPER CALIFORNIA
Published by the James H. Barry
Company
San Francisco, CA 1912
Copy located in the Library/Archive of
Adam R. Collings.

THE MISSIONS AND
MISSIONARIES OF CALIFORNIA
Written by FR. ZEPHYRIN
ENGELHARDT, O.F.M.
VOLUME THREE, UPPER
CALIFORNIA
Published by the James H. Barry
Company
San Francisco, CA 1913
Copy located in the Library/Archive of
Adam R. Collings.

THE MISSIONS AND
MISSIONARIES OF CALIFORNIA
Written by FR. ZEPHYRIN
ENGELHARDT, O.F.M.
VOLUME FOUR, UPPER
CALIFORNIA
Published by the James H. Barry
Company
San Francisco, CA 1915
Copy located in the Library/Archive of
Adam R. Collings.

INDEX TO VOLUMES II-IV /THE
MISSIONS AND MISSIONARIES OF
CALIFORNIA/INCLUDING
SUPPLEMENT TO VOLUME ONE.
Written by Fr. Zephyrin Engelhardt,
o.f.m.
Published by the James H. Barry
Company San Francisco, CA 1916
Copy located in the Library/Archive of
Adam R. Collings

HISTORY OF CALIFORNIA
By Franklin Tuthill
Published by H.H. Bancroft
San Francisco, 1866
Copy located in the personal
Library/Archive of Adam R. Collings.

A HISTORY OF CALIFORNIA/
THE SPANISH PERIOD
By Charles E. Chapman, Ph.D.
Published by The Macmillan Company
New York, N.Y. 1939
Copy located in the Library/Archive of

Adam R. Collings.

SPANISH ARCADIA
By Nellie Sanchez
Copy located in the Archive/Library of
Adam R. Collings.

THE WORKS OF JOHN DUNS
SCOTUS/
SCOTUS ACADEMICUS SEU
THEOLOGIA SCOTI
Volumes One through Twelve
New edition of original text located in
the National Library at Paris, Edited by
Father R. P. Claudius,
Published by the Father Scotus
Academy at Rome, Italy in 1900
Copies located in the Library/Archive
of Adam R. Collings.

JOHN DUNS SCOTUS
MARY'S ARCHITECT
By Allan B. Wolter, o.f.m. and Blane
O'Neill, o.f.m.
Published by the Franciscan Press
Quincy University,
Quincy, Illinois, 1993
Copy located in the Library/Archive of
Adam R. Collings.

LA EXPULSION DE LOS JESUITAS
DE LAS PROVINCIAS DE SONORA,
OSTIMURI Y SINALOA EN 1767
Disertacion documentada y anotada por
Alberto Francisco Pradeau
Introduccion por
Gerardo Decorme, S.J.
Publicada en Mexico, 1959
Por Antigue Libreria Robredo, de Jose
Porrua e Hijos, Sucs.
Copy located in the Archive/Library at
Mission San Juan Capistrano of the
Diocese of Orange, California.

LOS INDIGENAS DE CALIFORNIA
Del P. Fr. Jeronimo Boscana, o.f.m.
Introduccion y transcripcion por
Bartolome Font Obrador

Imprenta Moderna, Lluchmayor
Mallorca 1973
Copy located in the Archive/Library
maintained by the Franciscan Order at
Santa Barbara, California.

CHINING CHINIX
Alfred Robinson's popularized version
of Father Boscana's Report LOS
INDIGENAS DE CALIFORNIA
Copy located in the Archive/Library at
Mission San Juan Capistrano of the
Diocese of Orange, California.

MUNICIPAL GOVERNMENT IN
SPANISH CALIFORNIA
By Francis F. Guest, o.f.m.
Published in the California Historical
Society Quarterly

Volume XLVI/Number 4
December 1967
Copy located in the Library/Archive of
Adam R. Collings.

EL OSO:
CALIFORNIA'S DANIEL BOONE
By Jean Sherrell
Published in THE CALIFORNIAN
July/August 1990
Copy located in the Archive/Library of
Adam R. Collings.

TOMAS YORBA'S SANTA ANA
VIEJO/1769-1847
By Wayne Dell Gibson
Published by Santa Ana College
Foundation Press 1976
Copy located in the Library/Archive of
Adam R. Collings.

THE SPANISH BOURBONS
THE HISTORY OF A TENACIOUS
DYNASTY
By John D. Bergamini
Published by G.P. Putnam's Sons
Copy located in the Library/Archive of
Adam R. Collings.

THE STORY OF JOSE ANTONIO
YORBA I (1746-1825)
By Tomas Workman Temple II
Published at San Gabriel in 1958
by the Don Bernardo Yorba Family of
Anaheim
Copy located in the Library/Archive of
Adam R. Collings.

MISSION TALES/VOLUME ONE
By Helen M. Roberts
Published by Pacific Books, Palo Alto
1948
Copy located in the San Clemente
(Orage County) Public Library.

GREAT INDIANS OF CALIFORNIA
Text by Mariano Vallejo, Francisco
Palou and Hubert Howe Bancroft

Published by Bellerophon Books, Santa
Barbara, California.
Copy located in the Library/Archive of
Adam R. Collings.

LIFE IN A CALIFORNIA MISSION/
THE JOURNALS OF JEAN
FRANCOIS DE LA PEROUSE
With an introduction by Malcolm
Mangolin
Published by Hey Day Books
Berkeley, California 1989
Copy located in the Library/Archive of
Adam R. Collings.

DIARIO Y DERROTERO (1777-1781)
By Juan Agustin de Morfi
Reprinted by Publicaciones del
Instituto Technologico y De Estudios
Superiores de Monterrey
Monterrey, Nuevo Leon, Mexico, 1967
Copy located in the Library/Archive of
Adam R. Collings.

THE DIARY OF CAPTAIN LUIS
ANTONIO ARGUELLO/1821
Translated by Vivian C. Fisher
Published by Friends of the Bancroft
Library

University of California, 1992
Copy located in the Library/Archive of
Adam R. Collings.

WESTWARD THE BELLS
By Marion Sullivan
Published by Alba House
New York, 1971
Copy located in the Provincial Archives
of the Franciscan Order at Santa
Barbara, California.

BERNARDO GALVEZ
By Father Kieran McCarty o.f.m., ph.d.
Published by the Journal of the
Southwest
Volume 36. Number 2.
Copy located in the Archive/Library of
Adam R. Collings.

A SPANISH FRONTIER IN THE
ENLIGHTENED AGE
By Father Kieran McCarty, o.f.m., ph.d.
Published by the Academy of
American Franciscan History
Washington, D.C. 1981
Copy located in the Library/Archive of
Adam R. Collings.

VIRREYES DE NUEVA ESPANA
BOOK ONE/VOLUME ONE
Direccion y estudio preliminar de Jose
Antonio Calderon Quijano
Publicado en Sevilla, 1972
Copy located in the Archive/Library
maintained by the Franciscan Order at
Mission Santa Barbara, California.

VIRREYES DE NUEVA ESPANA
BOOK ONE/VOLUME TWO
Direccion y estudio preliminar de Jose
Antonio Calderon Quijano
Publicado en Sevilla, 1972
Copy located in the Archive/Library
maintained by the Franciscan Order at
Mission Santa Barbara, California.

VIRREYES DE NUEVA ESPANA
BOOK TWO/VOLUME ONE
Direccion y estudio preliminar de Jose
Antonio Calderon Quijano
Publicado en Sevilla, 1972
Copy located in the Archive/Library
maintained by the Franciscan Order at
Mission Santa Barbara, California.

VIRREYES DE NUEVA ESPANA
BOOK TWO/VOLUME TWO
Direccion y estudio preliminar de Jose
Antonio Calderon Quijano
Publicado en Sevilla, 1972
Copy located in the Archive /Library
maintained by the Franciscan Order at
Mission Santa Barbara, California.

TEODORO DE CROIX
By Alfred Barnaby Thomas
Published by the University of
Oklahoma Press, 1941
Copy located in the Library/Archives
of Adam R. Collings.

PEDRO ANTONIO DE ALARCON'S
THE THREE CORNERED HAT/
A MODERN TRANSLATION WITH
NOTES
By Glen Willbern, Ph.D.
Published by American R.D.M.
Corporation
New York, N.Y. 1966
Copy located in the San Clemente
(Orange County) Public Library.

MEXICO/A HISTORY
By Robert Ryal Miller
Published by Oklahoma University
Press
Copy located in the Library/Archive of
Adam R. Collings.

SAN DIEGO MISSION
By Fr. Zephyrin Engelhardt, o.f.m.
Published by the James H. Barry
Company

San Francisco, CA 1920
Copy located in the Library/Archive of
Adam R. Collings.

MISSION SAN LUIS REY/THE KING
OF THE MISSIONS
By Fr. Zephryin Engelhardt, o.f.m.
Published by the James H. Barry
Company
San Francisco, 1921
Copy located in the Library/Archive of
Adam R. Collings.

MISSION SAN JUAN
CAPISTRANO/JEWEL OF THE
MISSIONS
By Fr. Zephryin Engelhardt, o.f.m.
Published for the author by The
Standard Printing Co.
Los Angeles, CA 1922
Copy located in the Library/Archive of
Adam R. Collings.

SANTA BARBARA MISSION
By Fr. Zephryin Engelhardt, o.f.m.
Published by the James H. Barry
Company
San Francisco, CA 1923
Copy located in the Library/Archive of
Adam R. Collings.

SAN FRANCISCO/
OR MISSION DOLORES
By Fr. Zephryin Engelhardt
Published by Franciscan Herald Press
Chicago, IL 1924
Copy located in the Library/Archive of
Adam R. Collings.

SAN GABRIEL MISSION/
AND THE BEGINNINGS OF LOS
ANGELES
By Fr. Zephryin Engelhardt, o.f.m.
Published by Franciscan Herald Press,
Chicago, IL 1927
Copy located in the Library/Archive of
Adam R. Collings.

SAN FERNANDO REY/
THE MISSION OF THE VALLEY
By Fr. Zephyrin Engelhardt, o.f.m.
Published by Franciscan Herald Press
Chicago, IL 1927
Copy located in the Library/Archive of
Adam R. Collings.

SAN MIGUEL, ARCANGEL/
THE MISSION ON THE HIGHWAY
By. Fr. Zephyrin Engelhardt, o.f.m.
Published for the author by The
Schauer Printing Studio, Inc.
Santa Barbara, CA 1929
Copy located in the Library/Archive of
Adam R. Collings.

MISSION SAN BUENAVENTURA/
THE MISSION BY THE SEA
By Father Zephryn Englehardt
Published for the author by the
Schauer Printing Studio, Inc.
Santa Barbara, CA 1930
Copy located in the Library/Archive of
Adam R. Collings.

MISSION SAN JUAN BAUTISTA/A
SCHOOL OF CHURCH MUSIC
By Fr. Zephyrin Engelhardt, o.f.m.
Published for the author by The
Schauer Printing Studios, Inc.
Santa Barbara, CA 1931
Copy located in the Library/Archive of
Adam R. Collings.

MISSION SANTA INES/VIRGEN Y
MARTIR
By Fr. Zephyrin Engelhardt, o.f.m.
Published for the author by The
Schauer Printing Studios, Inc.
Santa Barbara, CA 1932
Copy located in the Library/Archive of
Adam R. Collings.

MISSION SAN LUIS OBISPO/IN THE
VALLEY OF THE BEARS
By Fr. Zephryn Engelhardt, o.f.m.
Published for the author by The

Schauer Printing Studios, Inc.
Santa Barbara, CA 1933
Copy located in the Library/Archive of
Adam R. Collings.

MISSION SAN CARLOS
BORROMEO (CARMELO)
THE FATHER OF THE MISSIONS
By Fr. Zephryn Engelhardt, o.f.m.
Published for the author by The
Schauer Printing Studios, Inc.
Santa Barbara, CA 1934.
Copy located in the Library/Archive of
Adam R. Collings.

SAINT LOUIS IX/MOST CHRISTIAN
KING
Published by Mission San Luis Rey de
Francia Museum and Retreat Center.
No authorship acknowledged nor date
of publication given.
Copy located in the Archive/Library of
Adam R. Collings.

JUNIPERO SERRA, THE VATICAN,
AND ENSLAVEMENT THEOLOGY
By Daniel Fogel
Published by ISM Press,
San Francisco, CA 1988
Copy located in the Library/Archive of
Dr. Jack Williams.

EARLY CALIFORNIA REFLECTIONS/
BOOK FOR AN EXHIBIT AT
MISSION SAN JUAN CAPISTRANO
Prepared by Norman Neuerberg, H.W.
Engstrand and David Hornbeck
Published by Mission San Juan
Capistrano
Copy located in the Library/Archive of
Adam R. Collings.

FAVORITE NOVENAS TO MARY/
A SAINT JOSEPH PRAYERBOOK
CATHOLIC BOOK PUBLISHING CO.
NEW YORK.
Copy located in the Library/Archive of
Adam R. Collings.

THE HISTORY OF SAN DIEGO/THE
EXPLORERS
By Richard F. Pourade
Published by the Union Tribune
Publishing Company
San Diego, 1960-1962
Copy located in the Library/Archive of
Adam R. Collings.

THE MARCH OF PORTOLA AND
THE LOG OF THE SAN CARLOS
Translated by E. J. Molera
Published by The California Promotion
Committee
San Francisco, California 1909.
Copy located in the Archive/Library at
Mission San Juan Capistrano of the
Diocese of Orange, California.

PALOU'S LIFE OF FATHER
JUNIPERO SERRA
Translated by C. Scott Williams
Published by George Wharton James
Los Angeles, California 1913.
Copy located in the Elizabeth J. Schultz
Memorial California History Room of
the Anaheim Public Library.

ANZA AND THE NORTHWEST
FRONTIER OF NEW SPAIN
Written by J.N. Bowman and
R. F. Heizer
Published by the Southwest Museum
Los Angeles, 1967
Copy located in the Library/Archive of
Adam R. Collings.

THE EIGHTEENTH CENTURY
ENLIGHTENMENT COMES TO
SPANISH CALIFORNIA
Written by Iris. H. W. Engstrand
Published by the Santa Barbara
Mission Archive Library
Santa Barbara, California 1999
Copy located in the Archive/Library of
Adam R. Collings.

QUERETARO EN LA CONQUISTA
DE LAS CALIFORNIAS

Written by Arturo Dominguez Paulin
Self published at Mexico, D.F. in 1977
Copy located in the Archive/Library at
Mission San Juan Capistrano of the
Diocese of Orange, California.

THE FORMATIVE YEARS OF THE
MISSIONARY COLLEGE OF SANTA
CRUZ OF QUERETARO 1683-1733
Written by B. McCloskey, o.fm.
Published by the Academy of
American Franciscan History
Washington, D.C. 1955
Copy located in the Archive/Library of
Adam R. Collings

THE ECONOMIC ASPECTS OF THE
CALIFORNIA MISSIONS
Written by Robert Archibald
Published by the Academy of
American Franciscan History
Washington, D.C. 1978
Copy located in the Archive/Library of
Adam R. Collings.

WRITINGS OF JUNIPERO SERRA
Volume IV
Edited by Antonine Tibesar, o.f.m.
Published by the Academy of
American Franciscan History
Washington, D.C. 1956
Copy located in the Archive/Library of
Adam R. Collings.

UTOPIA
Sir Thomas More
Copy located in the Anaheim
Public Library.

THE BIRDS (CLOUD CITY)
By Aristophanes
Unabridged republication of
anonymous translation.
Dover Publications, Inc.
Mineola, New York
Copy located in the Library/Archive of
Adam R. Collings.

SUMMARIUM/PATRIS
JUNIPERI SERRA
Published by The Vatican
Copy located in the Library/Archive
of Adam R. Collings.

EL PADRE
BOSCANA/HISTORIADOR DE
CALIFORNIA
Written by Bartolome Font Obrador
Published by Ediciones Cort
Palma de Mallorca, Spain.
Copy located in the Archive/Library
maintained by the Franciscan Order at
Mission Santa Barbara, California.

EL PADRE FRANCISCO PALOU/
FUNDADOR DE LA MISION DE
SAN FRANCISCO, BIOGRAFO E
HISTORIADOR.
Written by Bartolome Font Obrador
Published by Ediciones Cort
Palma de Mallorca, Spain 1976.
Copy located in the Archive/Library
maintained by the Franciscan Order at
Mission Santa Barbara, California.

THE LABORS OF THE VERY BRAVE
KNIGHT ESPLANDIAN
Written by Garci Rodriguez de Montalvo
Translated by William Thomas Little
Published by Medieval Renaissance
Text Studies
Copy located in the Archive/Library
maintained by the Franciscan Order at
Mission Santa Barbara, California.

FRAY JUNIPERO SERRA/THE GREAT
WALKER
Written by McKinley Helm
Published by Stanford University Press.
Copy located in the Archive/ Library at
Mission San Juan Capistrano of the
Diocese of Orange, California.

MY BOOK HOUSE-
THE FLYING SAILS
Edited by Olive Beaupre Miller

Copy located in the Archive/Library of
Adam R. Collings.

THE FRANCISCAN FRIARS OF
MISSION SAN FERNANDO
Written by Dr. Doyce B. Nunis, Jr.
Copy located in the Archive/Library of
Adam R. Collings.

MISSION SANTA BARBARA 1782-1965
By Maynard Geiger, o.f.m.
Published for the author by Heritage
Printers, Inc.
Santa Barbara, CA 1965
Copy located in the Library/Archive of
Adam R. Collings.

CALIFORNIA UTOPIANISM/
CONTEMPLATIONS ON EDEN
Written by Robert U. Hine
Published by Boyd & Fraser Publishing
San Francisco
Copy located in the Anaheim Public
Library.

THE YALE EDITION OF THE
COMPLETE WORKS OF ST.
THOMAS MORE-KING RICHARD III
Edited by Richard S. Sylvester.
Published by Yale University.
Copy located in the Anaheim
Public Library.

THE BELLS OF CAPISTRANO
Written by S.H.M. Byers
Private Printing
Copy located in the Archive/Library at
Mission San Juan Capistrano of the
Diocese of Orange, California.

SPANISH MISSIONS OF THE
SOUTHWEST
Written by Cleve Hallenbeck
Published by Doubleday 1926
Copy located in the Archive/ Library of
Adam R. Collings.

VIRREYES DE NUEVA ESPANA
(1759-1779)
Published by the Escuela de Estudios
Hispano-Americano
Consejo Superior de Investigaciones
Cientificas de Seville.
Seville 1967
Copy located in the Archive/Library of
Adam R. Collings.

AN EXAMINATION OF THE THESIS
OF S.F. COOK ON THE FORCED
CONVERSION OF INDIANS IN
CALIFORNIA MISSIONS
Written by Francis Guest, o.f.m.
Published by the Southern California
Quarterly
Spring 1979, Volume LXI, Number One
Copy located in the Archive/ Library of
Adam R. Collings.

THE CROSS AND THE SWORD
Written by John Reed Lauritzen
Published by Doubleday
Copy located in the Archive/Library of
Adam R. Collings.

PALEO AMERICANS/
U.S. NEWS AND WORLD REPORT
October 12, 1998
Copy located in the Archive/Library of
Adam R. Collings.

HISTORY OF HERODOTUS/
GREAT BOOKS OF THE WESTERN
WORLD
Published by University of Chicago
and Encyclopedia Brittanica
Copy located in the Archive/Library of
Adam R. Collings.

OLD TOWN SAN DIEGO STATE
HISTORIC PARK
TOUR GUIDE AND BRIEF HISTORY
Published by California State Parks
Copy located in the Archive/Library of
Adam R. Collings.

JOURNEY OF LA PEROUSE
Reprinted by Heyday Books
Berkeley California
Copy located in the Archive /Library of
Adam R. Collings.

CALIFORNIA OF THE PADRES/
FOOTPRINTS OF ANCIENT
COMMUNISM
Written by Elizabeth Hughes
Published by I.N. Choynski
Corner of Second and Jessie Streets
San Francisco, 1875
Copy located in the Dr. Norman
Neuerberg Collection of the
Archive/Library maintained by the
Franciscan Order at Mission Santa
Barbara, California.

THE SELECTED POEMS OF
FEDERICO GARCIA LORCA
Copy located in the Archive /Library of
Adam R. Collings.

MIRACLE OF THE SWALLOWS
Written by Ramon Romero
Copy located in the Archive/Library at
Mission San Juan Capistrano of the
Diocese of Orange, California.

SONG OF THE SWALLOWS
Written by Leo Politit
Copy located in the Archive/Library of
Adam R. Collings.

CAPISTRANO NIGHTS
Written by Charles Francis Saunders
with Father Saint John O'Sullivan
Copy located in the Archive/Library of
Adam R. Collings.

FROM WILDERNESS TO EMPIRE/
A HISTORY OF CALIFORNIA 1542-
1900
Written by Robert Glass Cleland
Published by Alfred Knopf
New York, 1947
Copy located in the Archive/Library of
Adam R. Collings.

MISSION SAN JUAN CAPISTRANO/
DOCENT TRAINING PROGRAM
VOLUMES ONE, TWO, THREE AND
FOUR
Prepared by Mission San Juan
Capistrano Docent Association
Copies located in the Archive/Library
of Adam R. Collings.

JUNIPERO SERRA/A PICTORIAL
BIOGRAPHY
By Martin Morgado
Published by Siempre Adelante Press
Copy located in the Archive/Library of
Adam R. Collings.

THE LIFE AND TIMES OF JUNIPERO
SERRA
VOLUME ONE
Written by Father Maynard Geiger,
o.f.m.
Published by The Academy of
American Franciscan History
Washington, D.C. 1959
Copy located in the Archive/Library of
Adam R. Collings.

THE LIFE AND TIMES OF JUNIPERO
SERRA
VOLUME TWO
Written by Father Maynard Geiger,
o.f.m.
Published by The Academy of
American Franciscan History
Washington, D.C. 1959
Copy located in the Archive/Library of
Adam R. Collings.

AN ENCYCLOPEDIA OF
FAIRIES/HOBGOBLINS/BOGIES
AND OTHER SUPERNATURAL
CREATURES
By Katherine Briggs
Published by Pantheon Books, New
York 1976
Copy located in the Orange County,
California Public Library.

THE COMMON MAN THROUGH
THE CENTURIES/
A BOOK OF COSTUME DRAWINGS
By Max Barsis
Published by Frederick Ungar
Publishing Co., N.Y. 1973
Copy located in the Orange County
Public Library.

CALIFORNIA AND CALIFORNIANS
VOLUME ONE/THE SPANISH
PERIOD
By Nellie Van de Grift Sanchez
Published by The Lewis Publishing
Company
Los Angeles, CA 1930
Copy located in the Library/Archive of
Father Kieran McCarty
Mission Santa Barbara, California.

CALIFORNIA AND CALIFORNIANS
VOLUME TWO/THE AMERICAN
PERIOD
By Rockwell D. Hunt
Published by The Lewis Publishing
Company
Los Angeles, CA 1930
Copy located in the Library/Archive of
Father Kieran McCarty
Mission Santa Barbara, California.

CALIFORNIA AND CALIFORNIANS
VOLUME THREE/CALIFORNIA
BIOGRAPHY
Compiled by a Special Staff of Writers
Published by The Lewis Publishing
Company
Los Angeles, CA 1930
Copy located in the Library/Archive of
Father Kieran McCarty
Mission Santa Barbara, California.

WEST OF THE WEST
By Robert Kirsch and William S.
Murphy
Published by E.P. Dutton & Co. Inc.
New York, 1967

Copy located in the Library/Archive of Peter J. Mel.

CALIFORNIA'S MISSIONS
Edited by Ralph B. Wright
Published by California Mission Trails Assn., Ltd.
Los Angeles 1950
Copy located in the Library/Archive of Adam R. Collings.

JORGE LUIS BORGES/SELECTED NON-FICTION
Edited by Eliot Weinberger
Published by Viking Press/The Penguin Group
New York, N.Y. 1999
Copy located in the Anaheim Public Library.

SPANISH SONGS OF OLD CALIFORNIA
Collected,translated and published by Charles Fletcher Lummis
Copy located in the Library/Archive of Adam R. Collings.

MISSION MUSIC OF CALIFORNIA
A Collection of Old California Mission Hymns and Masses
Translated and edited by Reverend Owen da Silva, o.f.m.
Published by Warren F. Lewis, Los Angeles CA 1941.
Copy located in the Library/Archive of Adam R. Collings.

RAMONA
By Helen Hunt Jackson
Triangle Books Edition
New York, 1941
Copy located in the Library/Archive of Adam R. Collings.

THE CONQUEST OF DON PEDRO
By Harvey Fergusson
Published by William Morrow and Company
New York, 1954

Copy located in the Library/Archive of Adam R. Collings.

THE CALIFORNIA MISSIONS/
A COMPLETE PICTORIAL HISTORY AND VISITOR'S GUIDE
By the editors of Sunset Magazine
Published by Lane Publishing Company
Menlo Park, CA 1981
Copy located in the Library/Archive of Adam R. Collings.

BIENVENIDOS AL CANON DE SANTA ANA!
A HISTORY OF THE SANTA ANA CANYON
Produced and published by the Orange County Board of Supervisors
July 27, 1976
Copy located in the Library/Archive of Adam R. Collings.

FRANCISCO DE ULLOA/
EXPLORADOR DE CALIFORNIA Y CHILE AUSTRAL
By Luis Navarro Garcia
Published by Diputacion Provincial Badajoz
Copy located in the Library/Archive of Adam R. Collings.

THIS WAS MISSION COUNTRY/
ORANGE COUNTY, CALIFORNIA/
THE REFLECTIONS IN ORANGE OF MERLE AND MABEL RAMSEY
NARRATED BY WARREN F. MORGAN
Published by Mission Printing Company
Laguna Beach, CA 1973
Copy located in the Library/Archive of Adam R. Collings.

GOOD FAITH AND TRUTHFUL IGNORANCE/
A CASE OF TRANSATLANTIC BIGAMY

By Alexandra Parma Cook and Noble
David Cook
Published by Duke University Press 1991
Copy located in the Library/Archive of
Adam R. Collings.

THE CONQUEST OF MEXICO
AND THE CONQUEST OF PERU
By William H. Prescott,
Published by Random House
New York
Copy located in the Library/Archive of
Adam R. Collings.

JUAN RODRIGUEZ CABRILLO
By Dr. Harry Kesley
Published by the Henry E. Huntington
Library and Art Gallery
1998 San Marino, California
Copy located in the Library/Archive of
Adam R. Collings.

SOUTHERN CALIFORNIA
COUNTRY/
AN ISLAND ON THE LAND
By Carey McWilliam
Published by Duell, Sloan and Pearce
New York, N.Y. 1946
Copy located in the Library/Archive of
Adam R. Collings.

THE MANILA GALLEON
Anonymous
Published in the California History
Nugget,
Official Journal of The California
Historical Society
December 1928, Volume II, Number 3
Copy located in the Library/Archive of
Adam R. Collings.

FRANCISCANS NORTH FROM
MEXICO 1527-1580
By Father Kieran McCarty, o.f.m. Ph.D
Published in FRANCISCAN
PRESENCE IN THE AMERICAS,
1492-1900
By the American Academy of

Franciscan History, 1984
Copy located in the Library/Archive of
Adam R. Collings.

AN ACCOUNT OF JUAN
RODRIGUEZ CABRILLO
Edited by James Nauman
Published by the Cabrillo National
Monument Foundation
San Diego, CA 1999
Copy located in the Library/Archive of
Adam R. Collings.

THE FRANCISCAN MISSION
ARCHITECTURE
OF ALTA CALIFORNIA
By Rexford Newcomb
Published by Dover Books
New York, N.Y. 1973
Copy located in the Library/Archive of
Adam R. Collings.

PADRE FERMIN LASUEN/A
FORGOTTEN HERO
Anonymous
Published in The California History
Nugget
Official Journal of The California
Historical Society
December 1928, Volume II, Number 3
Copy located in the Library/Archive of
Adam R. Collings.

SIR FRANCIS DRAKE/THE QUEEN'S
PIRATE
By Harry Kelsey
Published by Yale University Press, 1998
Copy located in the Anaheim Public
Library.

FRANCIS DRAKE AND NOVA
ALBION
By Captain Adolph S. Oko
Published in the June 1964 (Volume
XLIII , Number 2) Quarterly of
The California Historical Society
Copy located in the Library/Archive of
Adam R. Collings.

JUAN ALVARADO/GOVERNOR OF
CALIFORNIA 1836-1842
By Robert Ryal Miller
Published by University of Oklahoma
Press, 1998
Copy located in the Library/Archive of
Adam R. Collings.

LUGO/A CHRONICLE OF EARLY
CALIFORNIA
By Roy E. Whitehead, M.D.
Published by the San Bernardino
County Museum Association, 1978
Copy located in the Presidial Research
Center Archive/Library of the Santa
Barbara Trust for Historic Preservation.

CALIFORNIA/A HISTORY
By Andrew F. Rolle
Published by Thomas Y. Crowell
New York, 1963
Copy located in the Archive/Library of
Adam R. Collings.

IN HIS FOOTSTEPS/
THE LIFE JOURNEY OF JUNIPERO
SERRA
Written by Gertrude Ann Sullivan
Illustrated by Gertrud Mueller Nelson
Published by California Catholic
Conference/Division of Education
Copy located in the Archive/Library of
Adam R. Collings.

ROMANCE AND LEGEND OF
CHIVALRY
By A. R. Hope Moncrieff
Published by Crown Books, New York
1985
Copy located in the Archive/Library of
Adam R. Collings.

HERNAN CORTEZ/CONQUEROR
OF MEXICO
By Salvador de Madariaga
Published by University of Miami
Press, 1942
Copy located in the Archive/Library of
Adam R. Collings.

DANGER TO ELIZABETH/
THE CATHOLICS UNDER
ELIZABETH I
By Alison Plowden
Published by Stein and Day, New York,
1973
Copy located in the Archive/Library of
Adam R. Collings.

PARADISE LOST/
By John Milton
From the FranklinLibrary Collection of
Adam R. Collings.

THE HORIZON CONCISE HISTORY
OF SPAIN
By Melveena McKendrick
Published by American Heritage
Publishing Co., Inc.
New York, N.Y. 1972
Copy located in the Library/Archive of
Adam R. Collings.

THE HOUSE IN MALLORCA
By Ernest Ingold
Published by Paul Elder & Company
San Francisco, 1950
Copy located in the Archive/Library of
the Diocese of Orange at Mission San
Juan Capistrano.

AN HISTORICAL, POLITICAL, AND
NATURAL DESCRIPTION
OF CALIFORNIA
By Don Pedro Fages
Written in1775
Edited translation into English
Published by the Catholic Historical
Review, Vol V., No. 1.
Washington, D.C., April 1919
Copy located in the Archive/Library of
Adam R. Collings.

THE MISSIONS OF CALIFORNIA/A
LEGACY OF GENOCIDE
By Rupert Costo and Jeannette Henry
Costo
Published by Indian Historian Press

San Francisco 1987
Copy located in the Archive/Library of
the Pala Band of
Mission Indians located at the Cupa
Cultural Center on the Pala Indian
Reservation, San Diego County,
California.

MISSION TO PARADISE/
THE STORY OF JUNIPERO SERRA
AND THE MISSIONS OF
CALIFORNIA
By Kenneth M. King
Published by Burns & Oates
London 1956
Copy located in the Archive/Library of
Adam R. Collings.

FAMOUS KINGS AND QUEENS FOR
YOUNG PEOPLE
By Ramon P. Coffman
Published by Dodd, Mead & Company
New York 1947
Copy located in the Archive/Library of
Adam R. Collings.

A BOOK OF FAMOUS EXPLORERS
Edited in conference with Thomas
Bailey Aldrich
Published by the Auxiliary Educational
League, Chicago 1945
Copy located in the Archive/Library of
Adam R. Collings.

HISTORIA DE CHILE
By Walterio Millar
Published by Ministerio de Educacion
Publica
Santiago de Chile, 1974
Copy located in the Archive/Library of
Adam R. Collings.

HISTORIA DE AMERICA
By Juan C. Zorrilla De San Martin. SJ
Published by Editorial Nascimento
Santiago de Chile, 1933
Copy located in the Archive/Library of
Adam R. Collings.

VIVA RANCHO
BERNARDO/REFLECTIONS OF OUR
PAST
Edited by Kathy Renner
Published by Home Federal Savings
San Diego, 1979
Copy located in the Archive/Library of
Adam R. Collings.

CHRISTMAS JOURNEY INTO THE
DESERT
By Charles Russell Quinn
Published by Elena Quinn
Downey, CA 1959
Copy located in the Archive/Library of
Adam R. Collings.

CHIVALRY
By Maurice Keen
Published by Yale University Press
New Haven 1987
Copy located in the Archive/Library of
Adam R. Collings.

THE DIVINE COMEDY OF DANTE
ALIGHIERI
Translated by Charles Eliot Norton
Published by Encyclopaedia Britannica,
Inc.
Copy located in the Archive/Library of
Adam R. Collings.

MAJORCA CULTURE AND LIFE
Edited by Ute Edda Hammer, Tonina
Oliver and Frank Schauhoff
Published by Konemann
Verlagsgesellschaft mbH
Cologne/Barcelona
Copy locate in the Archive/Library of
Adam R. Collings.

CHININGCHINIX/
AN INDIGENOUS CALIFORNIA
INDIAN RELIGION
By James Robert Moriarty
Published by the Southwest Museum
Los Angeles, 1969
Copy located in the Archive/Library of
Adam R. Collings.

CHINIGCHINICH
A revised and Annotated Version of
Alfred Robinson's Translation
of Father Geronimo Boscana's
Historical Account of the Belief,
Usages, Customs and Extravagencies
of the Indians of This Mission of San
Juan Capistrano called the
Acagchemem Tribe.
Published by Fine Arts Press,
Santa Ana, 1933
Copy located in the Archive/Library of
Adam R. Collings.

OLIVES/THE LIFE AND LORE OF A
NOBLE FRUIT
By Mort Rosenblum
Published by North Point Press,
New York, 1996
Copy located in the Archive/Library of
Adam R. Collings.

GASPAR DE PORTOLA/EXPLORER
AND FOUNDER OF CALIFORNIA.
By Fernando Boneu Companys
Published by Le Instituto de Estudios
Ilerdenses
Lerida, Spain 1983.
Copy located in the Sherman
Foundation Library/Archive.

DOCUMENTOS SECRETOS DE LA
EXPEDICION DE PORTOLA A
CALIFORNIA: JUNTAS DE GUERRA
Edited by Fernando Boneu Companys
Published by Le Instituto de Estudios
Ilerdenses
Lerida, Spain 1973

CONQUESTS AND HISTORICAL
IDENTITIES IN CALIFORNIA
1769-1936
By Lisbeth Haas
Published by the University of
California Press
Berkeley, California 1995
Copy located in the Orange Public
Library
Orange, California.

OLD CALIFORNIA/THE MISSIONS,
RANCHOS AND ROMANTIC
ADOBES
By Bret Shipman
Published by Camaro Publishing
Company
Los Angeles, 1987
Copy located in the Library/Archive of
Adam R. Collings.

EVOCATION DE JUNIPERO SERRA/
FONDATEUR DE LA CALIFORNIE
By Charles J.G. Maximin Piette, o.f.m.
Published by the Academy of
American Franciscan History
Washington, D.C. 1946
Copy located in the Library/Archive of
the Southwest Museum
Copy located in the Library/Archive of
Adam R. Collings.

JUNIPERO SERRA
By Agnes Repplier
Published by Doubleday,
Doran & Co, Inc.
Garden City, New York, 1933
Copy located in the Library/Archive of
Adam R. Collings.

UTOPIA, DYSTOPIA, MESSTOPIA!
By Cynthia Ozick
Published by Zoetrope/All-Story
Magazine
February 2002
Copy located in the Library/Archive of
Adam R. Collings.

THE ROMANCE OF THE RANCHOS
By Palmer Conner
Published by Title Insurance and Trust
Company
Los Angeles, CA 1941
Copy located in the Library/Archive of
Adam R. Collings.

EARLY CALIFORNIA
By Irmagarde Richards
Published by California State
Department of Education
Sacramento, CA 1950
Copy located in the Library/Archive of
Adam R. Collings.

THE SERRANO INDIANS OF
SOUTHERN CALIFORNIA
By Francis J. Johnston
Published by Malki Museum Press
Morongo Reservation, Banning
California 1980
Copy located in the Library/Archive of
Adam R. Collings.

THE LEGAL HERITAGE OF SPANISH
CALIFORNIA
By Iris H.W. Engtrand
Published by the Santa Barbara
Mission Archive/Library 1994
Copy located in the Library/Archive of
Adam R. Collings.

THE MARK OF ZORRO
By Johnston McCulley
Published by Buccaneer Books
Cutchogue, New York, 1996
Copy located in the Library/Archive of
Adam R. Collings.

MIXED MEDIA SOURCES

GREECE/THE INVENTION OF
POLITICS
Michael Jameson
Origins of Modern Society/
Capstone Lectures in Western
Culture/on video
Produced by the Stanford Alumni
Association
Copy located in the Orange County,
California Public Library System.

THE BARBARIAN WEST
Legacy series on video
Presented by Michael Wood

Produced by Maryland Public Television
And Central Independent Television UK
Copy located in the Orange County,
California Public Library System.

KEN BURNS PRESENTS
THE WEST
A FILM BY STEPHEN IVES
PBS Home Video
Part One: The People
Part Four: Death Runs Rampant
Copy located in the Orange County,
California Public Library System.

THE FRENCH REVOLUTION
James Shehan
Origins of Modern Society/
Capstone Lectures in Western
Culture/on video
Produced by the Stanford Alumni
Association
Copy located in the Orange County,
California Public Library System.

HANS CHRISTIAN ANDERSON/
the movie
Copy located in the Orange County,
California Public Library System.

THE AGE OF REASON AND
ENLIGHTENMENT
Carolyn Lougee
Capstone Lectures in Western
Culture/on video
Produced by the Stanford Alumni
Association
Copy located in the Orange County,
California Public Library System.

DESCARTE, BERKELEY, LOCKE,
AND THE NEW WAY OF IDEAS.
John Perry
Capstone Lectures in Western
Culture/on video
Produced by the Stanford Alumni
Association
Copy located in the Orange County,
California Public Library System.

SISTER WENDY'S GRAND TOUR/
on video
Produced by the BBC
Copy located in the Orange County,
California Public Library System.

NOVA/THE ICE AGE
Produced by PBS

CAMILA
The Movie (on video)
Produced and directed by Maria Luisa
Bemberg

1492/CONQUEST OF PARADISE
The Movie (on video)
Written by Rosyln Bush
Produced and Directed by Ridley Scott
with Alain Goldman

LA OTRA CONQUISTA
The Movie

BROTHER SON/SISTER MOON
The Movie (on video)
Written, directed and produced by
Franco Zephirelli
Copy located in the Library/Archive of
Adam R. Collings.

THE MISSION
The Movie (on video)
Copy located in the Library/Archive of
Adam R. Collings.

CIVILISATION/A Personal View
Written and presented by Kenneth
Clark
Volume Two/ THE GREAT THAW
Copy located in the Anaheim Public
Library.

CIVILISATION/A Personal View
Written and presented by Kenneth
Clark
Volume Three/GRANDEUR AND
OBEDIANCE
Copy located in the Anaheim Public
Library.

CIVILISATION/A Personal View
Written and presented by Kenneth
Clark
Volume Four/MAN, THE MEASURE
OF ALL THINGS
Copy located in the Anaheim Public
Library.

CIVILISATION/A Personal View
Written and presented by Kenneth
Clark
Volume Five/HERO AS ARTIST
Copy located in the Anaheim Public
Library.

CIVILISATION/A Personal View
Volume/WORSHIP OF NATURE
Written and presented by Kenneth
Clark
Copy located in the Anaheim Public
Library.

CIVILISATION/A Personal View
Volume/LIGHT OF EXPERIENCE
Written and presented by Kenneth
Clark
Copy located in the Anaheim Public
Library.

MEXICO
VOLUME ONE/GOLD, GOD AND
GLORY
Presented by The History Channel
Copy located in the Anaheim Public
Library.

GREAT PALACES OF THE WORLD
EL ESCORIAL
Presented by The Discovery Channel
Copy located in the Anaheim Public
Library.

FERDINAND & ISABELLA
The Hispanic and Latin American
Heritage Video Collection
Copy located in the Anaheim Public
Library.

HERNAN CORTES
The Hispanic and Latin American
Heritage Video Collection
Copy located in the Anaheim Public
Library.

THE HISPANICIZATION OF
CALIFORNIA
James J. Rawls
Lectures from The Bancroft Library
Cassette tape
University of California, Berkeley
Copy located in the Archive/Library of
Adam R. Collings.

CARLOS FUENTES
Independently produced video
Copy located in the Anaheim Public
Library.

SITES AND LANDMARKS INVESTIGATED AND STUDIED

CABRILLO NATIONAL MONUMENT
NATIONAL PARK SERVICE

MISSION BASILICA SAN DIEGO DE
ALCALA

SAN DIEGO PRESIDIO SITE
SERRA MUSEUM/ARCHIVES

OLD TOWN SAN DIEGO STATE
HISTORIC PARK
ESTUDILLO TOWNHOME
CASA BANDINI
CASA DE PICO
ROBINSON/ROSE HOUSE
WRIGHTINGTON HOUSE
SAN DIEGO HOUSE
LA CASA DE MACHADO Y SILVAS
RACINE AND LARAMIE STORE
LA CASA DE PEDRORENA
ALVARADO HOUSE

ADOBE CHAPEL/BISHOP'S HOUSE

ESTUDILLO ESTANCIA/RANCHO
EL CAJON

HUBERT HOWE BANCROFT'S
SPRING VALLEY RANCHO

RANCHO DE LOS PENASQUITOS

RANCHO BUENA VISTA

CARILLO ADOBE

RANCHO GUAJOME

MISSION SAN LUIS REY DE
FRANCIA

MISSION "ASSISTENCIA" SAN
ANTONIO DE PADUA/PALA

MISSION "ASISTENCIA" SANTA
YSABEL

SEA WORLD/SAN DIEGO

BALBOA PARK/EL PRADO/SAN
DIEGO
MUSEUM OF MAN
MUSEUM OF NATURAL HISTORY
MONUMENT TO EL CID
PALM CANYON

ANZA BORREGO DESERT STATE
PARK

CLEVELAND NATIONAL FOREST

RANCHO SANTA MARGARITA

RANCHO LAS FLORES

MISSION SAN JUAN CAPISTRANO

LOS RIOS HISTORIC DISTRICT
MONTANEZ ADOBE

BLAS AGUILAR ADOBE

MIGUEL YORBA ADOBE/EL ADOBE

VALENZUELA ADOBE

BOWERS MUSEUM

SEPULVEDA ADOBE

MISSION "ASSISTENCIA" SAN BERNARDINO

SANBERNARDINO COUNTY MUSEUM

SAN BERNARDINO NATIONAL FOREST

MISSION INN/RIVERSIDE

MISSION SAN GABRIEL ARCANGEL

LOPEZ ADOBE/SAN GABRIEL

MISSION SAN FERNANDO

EL PUEBLO DE LOS ANGELES STATE HISTORIC PARK
AVILA ADOBE
PLAZA CHURCH
PICO HOUSE HOTEL

PIO PICO MANSION STATE HISTORIC MONUMENT

THE WORKMAN/TEMPLE HOMESTEAD
LA CASA NUEVA

SOUTHWEST MUSEUM
EL ALISAL

LOS ANGELES PUBLIC LIBRARY

LOS ANGELES COUNTY MUSEUM OF NATURAL HISTORY

GEORGE C. PAGE MUSEUM

RANCHO LOS ALAMITOS

RANCHO LOS CERRITOS

DOMINIGUEZ RANCHO ADOBE

LEONIS ADOBE

OLIVAS ADOBE

MISSION SAN BUENAVENTURA

RANCHO CAMULOS

MISSION SANTA BARBARA

SANTA BARBARA PRESIDIO STATE HISTORIC PARK

CASA DE LA GUERRA

EL PASEO/SANTA BARBARA

LOS PADRES NATIONAL FOREST

RINCON

REFUGIO

MISSION SANTA YNEZ

MISSION LA PURISIMA CONCEPCION

MISSION SAN MIGUEL

BIG SUR

MISSION NUESTRO SENORA DE LA SOLEDAD

MISSION SAN CARLOS BORROMEO

ROYAL PRESIDIO OF MONTEREY SITE/
ROYAL PRESIDIAL CHAPEL OF SAN CARLOS AT MONTEREY

MONTEREY STATE HISTORIC PARK
COOPER/MOLERA STORE/ESTATE
LA MIRADA ADOBE
MADARIAGA ADOBE
CASA PACHECO
CASA MUNRAS
CASA ABREGO

"ROBERT LOUIS STEVENSON" HOUSE
GABRIELA DE LA TORRE ADOBE
FREMONT ADOBE
CASA GUTIERREZ
STOKES ADOBE
ALVARADO ADOBE (WESTSIDE)

ALVARADO ADOBE (EASTSIDE)
VASQUEZ ADOBE
COLTON HALL
CALIFORNIA'S "FIRST" THEATER
THOMAS O'LARKIN HOME
UNDERWOOD/BROWN ADOBE
LARA SOTO ADOBE

CASA SERRANO
CASA SOBERANES
OSIO/RODRIGUEZ ADOBE
SANCHEZ ADOBE
CUSTOMS HOUSE
PACIFIC HOUSE
CASA DEL ORO
WHALING STATION

MONTEREY MARITIME MUSEUM

MONTEREY STATE PARK VISITOR
CENTER

U.S. ARMY HISTORICAL
MUSEUM/MONTEREY

SLOAT MONUMENT

EL CASTILLO SITE

SERRA MONUMENT

VISCAINO/SERRA LANDING SITE

MONTEREY BAY AQUARIUM

MISSION SAN JUAN BAUTISTA

MISSION SANTA CLARA

SANTA CRUZ MOUNTAINS

BIG BASIN STATE PARK

SAN GORGONIO

MISSION SAN FRANCISCO DE ASIS
(DOLORES)

ROYAL PRESIDIO OF SAN
FRANCISCO AND CASTILLO SITE

MARIN HEADLANDS

MUIR WOODS NATIONAL
MONUMENT

MISSION SAN RAFAEL ARCANGEL

POINT REYES NATIONAL
SEASHORE
NATIONAL PARK SERVICE

ESTANCIA DE MARIANO VALLEJO/
PETALUMA ADOBE STATE
HISTORIC PARK

MISSION SAN FRANCISCO DE
SOLANO/SONOMA

SOLDIERS BARRACKS

VALLEJO TOWNHOME

HISTORIC PLAZA/SONOMA

FORT ROSS STATE HISTORIC PARK

HUMBOLDT REDWOODS STATE
PARK

REDWOOD NATIONAL PARK

MT. LASSEN NATIONAL PARK

TRINITY ALPS

MOUNT SHASTA

MUSIC

GREGORIAN CHANTS/DOMINUS-
PUER NATUS EST- RESURREXI-
ABSOLVE
The Gregorian Chorale of Eglise
Querin
Conducted by Jules Dupont
Released through World Famous
Masterpieces,
Quebec, Canada

KALENDA MAYA
Medieval and Renassance Music/Songs
and Dances from 1200 to 1530
Spain, Italy, France, Germany.
Produced by ProMusica, Norway
Relearned through Simax

HOLIDAY IN SPAIN
The Madrid Pasodobles Ensemble
Featuring Los Flamencos
Released through FANFARE, U.S.A.

VAMOS AL PORTAL
Coro Hispano de San Francisco
Juan Pedro Gafney R, - Duector
Relearned through Instituto Pro
Musica de California

759

THE ADVENTURE CONTINUES
WITH

BOOK TWO
EL DORADO

INDEX

G

H

I

N

O

P

Q

R

NOTES

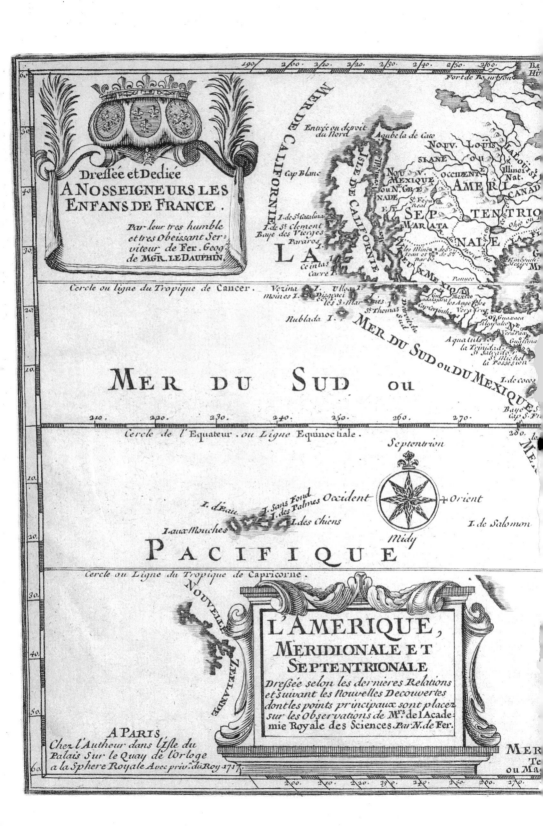